CLEP HUMANITIES

Jane Adas, Ph.D.
Rutgers, The State University of New Jersey
New Brunswick, NJ

Marguerite Barrett, M.A.
Rutgers, The State University of New Jersey
New Brunswick, NJ

Pauline Beard, Ph.D.
Pacific University
Forest Grove, OR

Jennifer Carpignano
Performing Arts Consultant
Scotch Plains, NJ

Robert Liftig, Ed.D.
Fairfield University
Fairfield, CT

Joshua Peters, M.A.
Rutgers, The State University of New Jersey
New Brunswick, NJ

G.A. Spangler, Ph.D.
California State University, Long Beach
Long Beach, CA

Gregory Suriano, M.A.
Art History Consultant
Union, NJ

Frenzella Elaine De Lancey, Ph.D.
Drexel University
Philadelphia, PA

Research & Education Association
Visit our website at: www.rea.com/studycenter

Research & Education Association
61 Ethel Road West
Piscataway, New Jersey 08854
E-mail: info@rea.com

CLEP Humanities

Printed in the United States of America

Library of Congress Control Number 2011946213

ISBN-13: 978-0-7386-1030-6
ISBN-10: 0-7386-1030-5

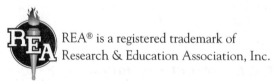

REA® is a registered trademark of
Research & Education Association, Inc.

CONTENTS

ABOUT RESEARCH & EDUCATION ASSOCIATION

Founded in 1959, Research & Education Association (REA) is dedicated to publishing the finest and most effective educational materials—including software, study guides, and test preps—for students in middle school, high school, college, graduate school, and beyond.

Today, REA's wide-ranging catalog is a leading resource for teachers, students, and professionals.

ACKNOWLEDGMENTS

We would like to thank Pam Weston, Publisher, for setting the quality standards for production integrity and managing the publication to completion; John Paul Cording, Vice President, Technology, for coordinating the design and development of the REA Study Center; Larry B. Kling, Vice President, Editorial, for his supervision of revisions and overall direction; Diane Goldschmidt and Michael Reynolds, Managing Editors, for coordinating development of this edition; Transcend Creative Services for typesetting this edition; and Weymouth Design and Christine Saul for designing our cover. We also gratefully acknowledge Miriam Perkoff, M.M., for editing our Music review.

CHAPTER 1

Passing the CLEP Humanities Exam

PASSING THE CLEP HUMANITIES EXAM

Congratulations! You're joining the millions of people who have discovered the value and educational advantage offered by the College Board's College-Level Examination Program, or CLEP. This test prep covers everything you need to know about the CLEP Humanities exam, and will help you earn the college credit you deserve while reducing your tuition costs.

GETTING STARTED

There are many different ways to prepare for a CLEP exam. What's best for you depends on how much time you have to study and how comfortable you are with the subject matter. To score your highest, you need a system that can be customized to fit you: your schedule, your learning style, and your current level of knowledge.

This book, and the online tools that come with it, allow you to create a personalized study plan through three simple steps: assessment of your knowledge, targeted review of exam content, and reinforcement in the areas where you need the most help.

Let's get started and see how this system works.

Test Yourself & Get Feedback	Score reports from your online diagnostic and practice tests give you a fast way to pinpoint what you already know and where you need to spend more time studying.
Review with the Book	Study the topics tested on the CLEP exam. Targeted review chapters cover everything you need to know.
Improve Your Score	Armed with your score reports, you can personalize your study plan. Review the parts of the book where you're weakest and study the answer explanations for the test questions you answered incorrectly.

THE REA STUDY CENTER

The best way to personalize your study plan and focus on your weaknesses is to get feedback on what you know and what you don't know. At the online REA Study Center, you can access two types of assessment: a diagnostic exam and full-length practice exams. Each of these tools provides true-to-format questions and delivers a detailed score report that follows the topics set by the College Board.

Diagnostic Exam

Before you begin your review with the book, take the online diagnostic exam. Use your score report to help evaluate your overall understanding of the subject, so you can focus your study on the topics where you need the most review.

Full-Length Practice Exams

These practice tests give you the most complete picture of your strengths and weaknesses. After you've finished reviewing with the book, test what you've learned by taking the first of the two online practice exams. Review your score report, then go back and study any topics you missed. Take the final practice test to ensure you have mastered the material and are ready for test day.

If you're studying and don't have Internet access, you can take the printed tests in the book. These are the same practice tests offered at the REA Study Center, but without the added benefits of timed testing conditions and diagnostic score reports. Because the actual exam is computer-based, we recommend you take at least one practice test online to simulate test-day conditions.

AN OVERVIEW OF THE EXAM

The CLEP Humanities exam tests general knowledge of literature, art, and music. The test covers all periods, from classical to contemporary and covers poetry, prose, philosophy, history of art, music, dance, and theater. The questions are drawn from the entire history of Western art and culture and are fairly evenly divided among the following periods: Classical, Medieval and Renaissance, seventeenth and eighteenth centuries, nineteenth century and twentieth century. Some questions could be based on African and Asian cultures.

The exam consists of 140 multiple-choice questions, each with five possible answer choices, to be answered within 90 minutes.

The approximate breakdown of topics is as follows:

50% Literature
10% Drama
10-15% Poetry
15-20% Fiction
10% Nonfiction
(including philosophy)

50% Fine Arts
20% Visual arts
(painting, sculpture, etc.)
15% Music
10% Performing arts
(film, dance, etc.)
5% Architecture

ALL ABOUT THE CLEP EXAMS

What is the CLEP?

CLEP is the most widely accepted credit-by-examination program in North America. CLEP exams test the material commonly required in an introductory-level college course. Examinees can earn from three to twelve credits at more than 2,900 colleges and universities in the U.S. and Canada. For a complete list of the CLEP subject examinations offered, visit the College Board website: *www.collegeboard.org/clep*.

Who takes CLEP exams?

CLEP exams are typically taken by people who have acquired knowledge outside the classroom and who wish to bypass certain college courses and earn college credit. The CLEP program is designed to reward examinees for learning—no matter where or how that knowledge was acquired.

Although most CLEP examinees are adults returning to college, many graduating high school seniors, enrolled college students, military personnel, veterans, and international students take CLEP exams to earn college credit or to demonstrate their ability to perform at the college level. There are no prerequisites, such as age or educational status, for taking CLEP examinations. However, because policies on granting credits vary among colleges, you should contact the particular institution from which you wish to receive CLEP credit.

Who administers the exam?

CLEP exams are developed by the College Board, administered by Educational Testing Service (ETS), and involve the assistance of educators from throughout the United States. The test development process is designed and implemented to ensure that the content and difficulty level of the test are appropriate.

When and where is the exam given?

CLEP exams are administered year-round at more than 1,200 test centers in the United States and can be arranged for candidates abroad on request. To find the test center nearest you and to register for the exam, contact the CLEP Program:

CLEP Services
P.O. Box 6600
Princeton, NJ 08541-6600
Phone: (800) 257-9558 (8 A.M. to 6 P.M. ET)
Fax: (609) 771-7088
Website: *www.collegeboard.org/clep*

OPTIONS FOR MILITARY PERSONNEL AND VETERANS

CLEP exams are available free of charge to eligible military personnel and eligible civilian employees. All the CLEP exams are available at test centers on college campuses and military bases. Contact your Educational Services Officer or Navy College Education Specialist for more information. Visit the DANTES or College Board websites for details about CLEP opportunities for military personnel.

Eligible U.S. veterans can claim reimbursement for CLEP exams and administration fees pursuant to provisions of the Veterans Benefits Improvement Act of 2004. For details on eligibility and submitting a claim for reimbursement, visit the U.S. Department of Veterans Affairs website at *www.gibill.va.gov/pamphlets/testing.htm*.

CLEP can be used in conjunction with the Post-9/11 GI Bill, which applies to veterans returning from the Iraq and Afghanistan theaters of operation. Because the GI Bill provides tuition for up to 36 months, earning college credits with CLEP exams expedites academic progress and degree completion within the funded timeframe.

SSD ACCOMMODATIONS FOR CANDIDATES WITH DISABILITIES

Many test candidates qualify for extra time to take the CLEP exams, but you must make these arrangements in advance. For information, contact:

College Board Services for Students with Disabilities
P.O. Box 6226
Princeton, NJ 08541-6226
Phone: (609) 771-7137 (Monday through Friday, 8 A.M. to 6 P.M. ET)
TTY: (609) 882-4118
Fax: (609) 771-7944
E-mail: ssd@info.collegeboard.org

6-WEEK STUDY PLAN

Although our study plan is designed to be used in the six weeks before your exam, it can be condensed to three weeks by combining each two-week period into one.

Be sure to set aside enough time—at least two hours each day—to study. The more time you spend studying, the more prepared and relaxed you will feel on the day of the exam.

Week	Activity
1	Take the Diagnostic Exam. The score report will identify topics where you need the most review.
2–4	Study the review chapters. Use your diagnostic score report to focus your study.
5	Take Practice Test 1 at the REA Study Center. Review your score report and re-study any topics you missed.
6	Take Practice Test 2 at the REA Study Center to see how much your score has improved. If you still got a few questions wrong, go back to the review and study any topics you may have missed.

TEST-TAKING TIPS

Know the format of the test. CLEP computer-based tests are fixed-length tests. This makes them similar to the paper-and-pencil type of exam because you have the flexibility to go back and review your work in each section.

Learn the test structure, the time allotted for each section of the test, and the directions for each section. By learning this, you will know what is expected of you on test day, and you'll relieve your test anxiety.

Read all the questions—completely. Make sure you understand each question before looking for the right answer. Reread the question if it doesn't make sense.

Annotate the questions. Highlighting the key words in the questions will help you find the right answer choice.

Read all of the answers to a question. Just because you think you found the correct response right away, do not assume that it's the best answer. The last answer choice might be the correct answer.

Work quickly and steadily. You will have 90 minutes to answer 140 questions, so work quickly and steadily. Taking the timed practice tests online will help you learn how to budget your time.

Use the process of elimination. Stumped by a question? Don't make a random guess. Eliminate as many of the answer choices as possible. By eliminating just two answer choices, you give yourself a better chance of getting the item correct, since there will only be three choices left from which to make your guess. Remember, your score is based only on the number of questions you answer correctly.

Don't waste time! Don't spend too much time on any one question. Remember, your time is limited and pacing yourself is very important. Work on the easier questions first. Skip the difficult questions and go back to them if you have the time.

Look for clues to answers in other questions. If you skip a question you don't know the answer to, you might find a clue to the answer elsewhere on the test.

Acquaint yourself with the computer screen. Familiarize yourself with the CLEP computer screen beforehand by logging on to the College Board website. Waiting until test day to see what it looks like in the pretest tutorial risks injecting needless anxiety into your testing experience. Also, familiarizing yourself with the directions and format of the exam will save you valuable time on the day of the actual test.

Be sure that your answer registers before you go to the next item. Look at the screen to see that your mouse-click causes the pointer to darken the proper oval. If your answer doesn't register, you won't get credit for that question.

THE DAY OF THE EXAM

On test day, you should wake up early (after a good night's rest, of course) and have breakfast. Dress comfortably, so you are not distracted by being too hot or too cold while taking the test. (Note that "hoodies" are not allowed.) Arrive at the test center early. This will allow you to collect your thoughts and relax before the test, and it will also spare you the anxiety that comes with being late. As an added incentive, keep in mind that no one will be allowed into the test session after the test has begun.

Before you leave for the test center, make sure you have your admission form and another form of identification, which must contain a recent photograph, your name, and signature (i.e., driver's license, student identification card, or current alien registration card). You will not be admitted to the test center if you do not have proper identification.

You may wear a watch to the test center. However, you may not wear one that makes noise, because it may disturb the other test-takers. No cell phones, dictionaries, textbooks, notebooks, briefcases, or packages will be permitted, and drinking, smoking, and eating are prohibited.

Good luck on the CLEP Humanities exam!

CHAPTER 2

Literature Review

CHAPTER 2

LITERATURE REVIEW

PROSE

GENERAL RULES AND IDEAS

Why do people write prose? Certainly such a question has a built-in counter: As opposed to writing what, poetry? One possible answer is that the writer is a poor poet. The requirements and restrictions of the various genres make different demands upon a writer; most writers find their niche and stay there, secure in their private "comfort zone." Shakespeare did not write essays; Hemingway did not write poetry. If either did venture outside of his literary domain, the world took little note.

Students are sometimes confused as to what exactly is prose. Basically, prose is **not** poetry. **Prose** is what we write and speak most of the time in our everyday intercourse: unmetered, unrhymed language. Which is not to say that prose does not have its own rhythms—language, whether written or spoken, has cadence and balance. And certainly prose can have instances of rhyme or assonance, alliteration or onomatopoeia. Language is, after all, **phonic**.

Fiction and Non-fiction

Furthermore, prose may be either **fiction** or **non-fiction**. A novel (like a short story) is fiction; an autobiography is non-fiction. While a novel (or short story) may have autobiographical elements, an autobiography is presumed to be entirely factual. Essays are usually described in other terms: expository, argumentative, persuasive, critical, or narrative. Essays may have elements of either fiction or non-fiction, but are generally classed as a separate subgenre.

Satire, properly speaking, is not a genre at all, but rather a **mode**, elements of which can be found in any category of literature—from poetry and

13

drama to novels and essays. Satire is a manifestation of authorial attitude (tone) and purpose. Our discussion of satire will be limited to its use in prose.

But we have not addressed the initial question: "Why do people write prose?" The answer depends, in part, on the writer's intent. If he wishes to tell a rather long story, filled with many characters and subplots, interlaced with motifs, symbols, and themes, with time and space to develop interrelationships and to present descriptive passages, the writer generally chooses the novel as his medium. If he believes he can present his story more compactly and less complexly, he may choose the novella or the short story.

These subgenres require from the reader a different kind of involvement than does the essay. The essay, rather than presenting a story from which the reader may discern meaning through the skillful analysis of character, plot, symbol, and language, presents a relatively straightforward account of the writer's opinion(s) on an endless array of topics. Depending upon the type of essay, the reader may become informed (expository), provoked (argumentative), persuaded, enlightened (critical), or, in the case of the narrative essay, better acquainted with the writer who wishes to illustrate a point with his story, whether it is autobiographical or fictitious.

Encountering satire in prose selections demands that the reader be sensitive to the nuances of language and form, that he detect the double-edged sword of irony, and that he correctly assess both the writer's tone and his purpose.

Reading Prose

Readers of prose, like readers of poetry, seek aesthetic pleasure, entertainment, and knowledge, not necessarily in that order. Fiction offers worlds—real and imagined—in which characters and ideas, events and language, interact in ways familiar and unfamiliar. As readers, we take delight in the wisdom we fancy we have acquired from a novel or short story. Non-fiction offers viewpoints which we may find comforting or horrifying, amusing or sobering, presented by the author rather than by his once-removed persona. Thus, we are tempted to believe that somehow the truths presented in non-fiction are more "real" than the truths revealed by fiction. But we must resist! **Truth** is not genre-specific.

Reading prose for the CLEP Humanities exam is really no different from reading prose for your own purposes, except for the time constraints, of course!

Becoming a competent reader is a result of practicing certain skills. Probably most important is acquiring a broad reading base. Read widely; read eclectically; read actively; read avidly. The idea is not that you might stumble onto a familiar prose selection on the CLEP and have an edge in writing about it. Instead, it's about building your familiarity with many authors and works so you have a foundation upon which to build your understanding of **whatever** prose selection you encounter on the CLEP Humanities exam. So read, read, read!

READING NOVELS

Most literary handbooks will define a novel as an extended fictional prose narrative, derived from the Italian *novella*, meaning "tale, piece of news." The term "novelle," meaning short tales, was applied to works such as Boccaccio's *The Decameron*, a collection of stories which had an impact on later works such as Chaucer's *Canterbury Tales*. In most European countries, the word for **novel** is **roman**, short for **romance**, which was applied to longer verse narratives (Malory's *Le Morte d'Arthur*), which were later written in prose. Early romances were associated with "legendary, imaginative, and poetic material"— tales "of the long ago or the far away or the imaginatively improbable"; novels, on the other hand, were felt to be "bound by the facts of the actual world and the laws of probability" (*A Handbook to Literature*, C. Hugh Holman, p. 354).

The novel has, over some 600 years, developed into many special forms which are classified by subject matter: detective novel, psychological novel, historical novel, regional novel, picaresque novel, Gothic novel, stream-of-consciousness novel, epistolary novel, and so on. These terms, of course, are not exhaustive nor mutually exclusive. Furthermore, depending on the conventions of the author's time period, his style, and his outlook on life, his *mode* may be termed **realism**, **romanticism**, **impressionism**, **expressionism**, **naturalism**, or **neo-classicism** (Holman, p. 359).

Our earlier description of a novel ("...a rather long story, filled with many characters and subplots, interlaced with motifs, symbols, and themes, with time and space to develop interrelationships and to present descriptive passages") is satisfactory for our purposes here. The works generally included on the CLEP are those which have stood the test of time in significance, literary merit, and reader popularity. New works are incorporated into the canon, which is a reflection of what works are being taught in literature classes. And teachers begin to teach those works which are included frequently among the test questions you will encounter on the CLEP. So the process is circular, but the standards remain high for inclusion on the exam.

Plots

Analyzing novels is a bit like asking the journalist's five questions: what? who? why? where? and how? The **what** is the story, the narrative, the plot and subplots. Most students are familiar with Freytag's Pyramid, originally designed to describe the structure of a five-act drama but now widely used to analyze fiction as well. The stages generally specified are **introduction** or **exposition, complication, rising action, climax, falling action**, and **denouement** or **conclusion**. As the novel's events are charted, the "change which structures the story" should emerge. There are many events in a long narrative; but generally only one set of events comprises the "real" or "significant" story.

However, subplots often parallel or serve as counterpoints to the main plot line, serving to enhance the central story. Minor characters sometimes have essentially the same conflicts and goals as the major characters, but the consequences of the outcome seem less important. Sometimes the parallels involve reversals of characters and situations, creating similar yet distinct differences in the outcomes. Nevertheless, seeing the parallels makes understanding the major plot line less difficult.

Sometimes an author divides the novel into chapters—named or unnamed, perhaps just numbered. Or he might divide the novel into "books" or "parts," with chapters as subsections. Readers should take their cue from these divisions; the author must have had some reason for them. Take note of what happens in each larger section, as well as within the smaller chapters. Whose progress is being followed? What event or occurrence is being foreshadowed or prepared for? What causal or other relationships are there between sections and events? Some writers, such as Steinbeck in *The Grapes of Wrath*, use intercalary chapters, alternating between the "real" story (the Joads) and peripheral or parallel stories (the Okies and migrants in general). Look for the pattern of such organization; try to see the interrelationships of these alternating chapters.

Characters

Of course, plots cannot happen in isolation from characters, the **who** element of a story. Not only are there major and minor characters to consider;

we need to note whether the various characters are **static** or **dynamic**. Static characters do not change in significant ways—that is, in ways which relate to the story which is structuring the novel. A character may die, i.e., change from alive to dead, and still be static, unless his death is central to the narrative. For instance, in Golding's *Lord of the Flies*, the boy with the mulberry birthmark apparently dies in a fire early in the novel. Momentous as any person's death is, this boy's death is not what the novel is about. However, when Simon is killed, and later Piggy, the narrative is directly impacted because the reason for their deaths is central to the novel's theme regarding man's innate evil. A dynamic character may change only slightly in his attitudes, but those changes may be the very ones upon which the narrative rests. For instance, Siddhartha begins as a very pure and devout Hindu but is unfulfilled spiritually. He eventually does achieve spiritual contentment, but his change is more a matter of degree than of substance. He is not an evil man who attains salvation, nor a pious man who becomes corrupt. It is the process of his search, the stages in his pilgrimage, which structure the novel *Siddhartha*.

We describe major characters or "actors" in novels as **protagonists** or **antagonists**. Built into those two terms is the Greek word **agon**, meaning "struggle." The *prot*agonist struggles **toward** or for someone or something; the *ant(i)*agonist struggles **against** someone or something. The possible conflicts are usually cited as man against himself, man against man, man against society, or man against nature. Sometimes more than one of these conflicts appears in a story, but usually one is dominant and is the structuring device.

A character can be referred to as **stock**, meaning that he exists because the plot demands it. For instance, a Western with a gunman who robs the bank will require a number of **stock** characters: the banker's lovely daughter, the tough but kindhearted barmaid, the cowardly white-shirted citizen who sells out the hero to save his own skin, and the young freckle-faced lad who shoots the bad guy from a second-story hotel window.

Or a character can be a **stereotype**, without individuating characteristics. For instance, a sheriff in a small Southern town; a football player who is all brawn; a librarian clucking over her prized books; the cruel commandant of a POW camp.

Characters often serve as **foils** for other characters, enabling us to see one or more of them better. A classic example is Tom Sawyer, the romantic foil for Huck Finn's realism. Or, in Lee's *To Kill a Mockingbird*, Scout as the naive observer of events which her brother Jem, four years older, comes to understand from the perspective of the adult world.

Sometimes characters are **allegorical**, standing for qualities or concepts rather than for actual personages. For instance, Jim Casey (initials "J. C.") in *The Grapes of Wrath* is often regarded as a Christ figure, pure and self-sacrificing in his aims for the migrant workers. Or Kamala, Siddhartha's teacher in the art of love, whose name comes from the tree whose bark is used as a purgative; she purges him of his ascetic ways on his road to self-hood and spiritual fulfillment.

Other characters are fully three-dimensional, "rounded," "mimetic" of humans in all their virtue, vice, hope, despair, strength, and weakness. This verisimilitude aids the author in creating characters who are credible and plausible, without being dully predictable and mundane.

Themes

The interplay of plot and characters determines in large part the **theme** of a work, the **why** of the story. First of all, we must distinguish between a mere topic and a genuine theme or thesis; and then between a theme and contributing *motifs*. A **topic** is a phrase, such as "man's inhumanity to man"; or "the fickle nature of fate." A **theme**, however, turns a phrase into a statement: "Man's inhumanity to man is barely concealed by 'civilization,'" or "Man is a helpless pawn, at the mercy of fickle fate." Many writers may deal with the same topic, such as the complex nature of true love; but their themes may vary widely, from "True love will always win out in the end," to "Not even true love can survive the cruel ironies of fate."

To illustrate the relationship between plot, character, and theme, let's examine two familiar fairy tales. In "The Ugly Duckling," the structuring story line is "Once upon a time there was an ugly duckling, who in turn became a beautiful swan." In this case, the duckling did nothing to merit either his ugliness nor his eventual transformation; but he did not curse fate. He only wept and waited, lonely and outcast. And when he became beautiful, he did not gloat; he eagerly joined the other members of his flock, who greatly admired him. The theme here essentially is: "Good things come to him who waits," or "Life is unfair—you don't get what you deserve, nor deserve what you get." What happens to the theme if the ugly duckling remains an ugly duckling: "Some guys just never get a break"?

Especially rewarding to examine for the interdependence of plot and theme is "Cinderella": "Once upon a time, a lovely, sweet-natured young girl was forced to labor for and serve her ugly and ungrateful stepmother and two step-sisters. But thanks to her fairy godmother, Cinderella and the Prince marry, and live happily ever after."

We could change events (plot elements) at any point, but let's take the pen-ultimate scene where the Prince's men come to the door with the single glass slipper. Cinderella has been shut away so that she is not present when the other women in the house try on the slipper. Suppose that the stepmother or either of the two stepsisters tries on the slipper—and it fits! Cinderella is in the back room doing the laundry, and her family waltzes out the door to the palace and she doesn't even get an invitation to the wedding. And imagine the Prince's dismay when the ugly, one-slippered lady lifts her wedding veil for the consum-mating kiss! Theme: "There is no justice in the world, for those of low or high station" or "Virtue is not its own reward."

Or let's say that during the slipper-test scene, the stepsisters, stepmother, and finally Cinderella all try on the shoe, but to no avail. And then in sashays the fairy godmother, who gives them all a knowing smirk, puts out her slipper-sized foot and cackles hysterically, like the mechanical witch in the penny arcade. Theme: "You can't trust anybody these days" or, a favorite statement of theme, "Appearances can be deceiving." The link between plot and theme is very strong, indeed.

Motifs

Skilled writers often employ **motifs** to help unify their works. A motif is a detail or element of the story which is repeated throughout, and which may even become symbolic. Television shows are ready examples of the use of motifs. A medical show, with many scenes alternately set in the hospital waiting room and operating room, uses elements such as the pacing, anxious parent or loved one, the gradually filling ashtray, the large wall clock whose hands melt from one hour to another. And in the operating room, the half-masked surgeon whose brow is frequently mopped by the nurse; the gloved hand open-palmed to receive scalpel, sponge, and so on; the various oscilloscopes giving read-outs of the patient's very fragile condition; the expanding and collapsing bladder mani-festing that the patient is indeed breathing; and, again, the wall clock, assuring us that this procedure is taking forever. These are all **motifs**, details which in concert help convince the reader that this story occurs in a hospital, and that the mood is pretty tense, that the medical team is doing all it can, and that Mom and Dad will be there when Junior or Sissy wakes up.

But motifs can become symbolic. The oscilloscope line quits blipping, levels out, and gives off the ominous hum. And the doctor's gloved hand sets down the scalpel and shuts off the oscilloscope. In the waiting room, Dad crushes the empty cigarette pack; Mom quits pacing and sinks into the sofa. The door to the waiting room swings shut silently behind the retreating doctor. All these elements signal "It's over, finished."

This example is very crude and mechanical, but motifs in the hands of a skillful writer are valuable devices. And in isolation, and often magnified, a single motif can become a controlling image with great significance. For instance, Emma Bovary's shoes signify her obsession with material things; and when her delicate slippers become soiled as she crosses the dewy grass to meet her lover, we sense the impurity of her act as well as its futility. Or when wise Piggy, in *Lord of the Flies,* is reduced to one lens in his specs, and finally to no specs at all, we see the loss of insight and wisdom on the island, and chaos follows.

Settings in Novels

Setting is the **where** element of the story. But setting is also the **when** element: time of day, time of year, time period or year; it is the dramatic moment, the precise intersection of time and space when this story is being told. Setting is also the atmosphere: positive or negative ambiance, calm, chaotic, Gothic, Romantic. The question for the reader to answer is whether the setting is ultimately essential to the plot/theme, or whether it is incidental; i.e., could this story/theme have been told successfully in another time and/or place? For instance, could the theme in *Lord of the Flies* be made manifest if the boys were not on an island? Could they have been isolated in some other place? Does it matter whether the "war" which they are fleeing is WWII or WWIII or some other conflict, in terms of the theme?

Hopefully, the student will see that the four elements of plot, character, theme, and setting are intertwined and largely interdependent. A work must really be read as a whole, rather than dissected and analyzed in discrete segments.

Style

The final question, **how?**, relates to an author's style. Style involves language (word choice), syntax (word order, sentence type, and length), the balance between narration and dialogue, the choice of narrative voice (first person participant, third person with limited omniscience), use of descriptive passages, and other aspects of the actual words on the page which are basically irrelevant to the first four elements (plot, character, theme, and setting). Stylistic differences are fairly easy to spot among such diverse writers as Jane Austen, whose style is—to today's reader—very formal and mannered; Mark Twain, whose style is very casual and colloquial; William Faulkner, whose prose often spins on without punctuation or paragraphs far longer than the reader can hold either the thought or his breath; and Hemingway, whose dense but spare, pared-down style has earned the epithet, "Less is more."

READING SHORT STORIES

The modern short story differs from earlier short fiction, such as the parable, fable, and tale, in its emphasis on character development through scenes rather than summary: through *showing* rather than *telling*. Gaining popularity in the nineteenth century, the short story generally was realistic, presenting detailed accounts of the lives of middle-class personages. This tendency toward realism dictates that the plot be grounded in *probability*, with causality fully in operation. Furthermore, the characters are human with recognizable human motivations, both social and psychological. Setting—time and place—is realistic rather than fantastic. And, as Poe stipulated, the elements of plot, character, setting, style, point of view, and theme all work toward a single *unified* effect.

However, some modern writers have stretched these boundaries and have mixed in elements of nonrealism—such as the supernatural and the fantastic—sometimes switching back and forth between realism and nonrealism, confusing the reader who is expecting conventional fiction. Barth's "Lost in the Funhouse" and Allen's "The Kugelmass Episode" are two stories which are not, strictly speaking, *realistic*. However, if the reader will approach and accept this type of story on its own terms, he will be better able to understand and appreciate them fully.

Unlike the novel, which has time and space to develop characters and interrelationships, the short story must rely on flashes of insight and revelation to develop plot and characters. The "slice of life" in a short story is of necessity much narrower than that in a novel; the time span is much shorter, the focus much tighter. To attempt anything like the panoramic canvas available to the novelist would be to view fireworks through a soda straw: occasionally pretty, but ultimately not very satisfying or enlightening.

Point of View

The elements of the short story are those of the novel, discussed earlier. However, because of the compression of time and concentration of effect, probably the short story writer's most important decision is **point of view**. A narrator may be *objective*, presenting information without bias or comment. Hemingway frequently uses the objective *third-person* narrator, presenting scenes almost dramatically, i.e., with a great deal of dialogue and very little narrative, none of which directly reveals the thoughts or feelings of the characters. The third-person narrator may, however, be less objective in his presentation, directly revealing the thoughts and feelings, of one or more of the characters, as Chopin does in "The Story of an Hour." We say that such a narrator is fully or partially *omniscient*, depending on how complete his knowledge is of the characters' psychological and emotional makeup. The least objective narrator is the *first-person* narrator, who presents information from the perspective of a single character who is a participant in the action. Such a narrative choice allows the author to present the discrepancies between the writer's/reader's perceptions and those of the narrator.

One reason the choice of narrator, the point of view from which to tell the story, is immensely important in a short story is that the narrator reveals character and event in ways which affect our understanding of theme. For instance, in Faulkner's "A Rose for Emily," the unnamed narrator who seems to be a townsperson recounts the story out of chronological order, juxtaposing events whose causality and significance are uncertain. The narrator withholds information which would explain events being presented, letting the reader puzzle over Emily Grierson's motivations, a device common in detective fiction. In fact, the narrator presents contradictory information, making the reader alternately pity and resent the spinster. When we examine the imagery and conclude that Miss Emily and her house represent the decay and decadence of the Old South which resisted the invasion of "progress" from the North, we see the importance of setting and symbol in relation to theme.

Similarly, in Mansfield's "Bliss," the abundant description of setting creates the controlling image of the lovely pear tree. But this symbol of fecundity becomes ironic when Bertha Young belatedly feels sincere and overwhelming desire for her husband. The third-person narrator's omniscience is limited to Bertha's thoughts and feelings; otherwise we would have seen her husband's infidelity with Miss Fulton.

In O'Connor's "Good Country People," the narrator is broadly omniscient, but the reader is still taken by surprise at the cruelty of the Bible salesman who seduces Joy-Hulga. That he steals her artificial leg is perhaps poetic justice, since she (with her numerous degrees) had fully intended to seduce him ("just good country people"). The story's title, the characters' names—Hopewell, Freeman, Joy; the salesman's professed Christianity, the Bibles hollowed out to hold whiskey and condoms, add to the irony of Mrs. Freeman's final comment on the young man: "Some can't be that simple… I know I never could."

Examples of Initiation Stories

The *initiation story* frequently employs the first-person narrator. To demonstrate the subtle differences which can occur in stories which ostensibly have the same point of view and general theme, let's look at three: "A Christmas Memory" (Capote), "Araby" (Joyce), and "A & P" (Updike).

Early in "A Christmas Memory," Capote's narrator identifies himself:

> The person to whom she is speaking is myself. I am seven; she is sixty-something. We are cousins, very distant ones, and we have lived together—well, as long as I can remember. Other people inhabit the house, relatives; and though they have power over us, and frequently make us cry, we are not, on the whole, too much aware of them. We are each other's best friend. She calls me Buddy, in memory of a boy who was formerly her best friend. The other Buddy died in the 1880s, when she was still a child. She is still a child.

Buddy and his cousin, who is called only "my friend," save their meager earnings throughout the year in order to make fruitcakes at Christmas to give mainly to "persons we've met maybe once, perhaps not at all… Like President Roosevelt…. Or Abner Packer, the driver of the six o'clock bus from Mobile, who exchanges waves with us everyday…." Their gifts to one another each year are always handmade, often duplicates of the year before, like the kites they present on what was to be their last Christmas together.

Away at boarding school, when Buddy receives word of his friend's death, it "merely confirms a piece of news some secret vein had already received, severing from me an irreplaceable part of myself, letting it loose like a kite on a broken string. That is why, walking across a school campus on this particular December morning, I keep searching the sky. As if I expected to see, rather like hearts, a lost pair of kites hurrying toward heaven."

Buddy's characterizations of his friend are also self-revelatory. He and she are peers, equals, despite their vast age difference. They are both totally unselfish, joying in the simple activities mandated by their economic circumstances. They are both "children."

The story is told in present tense, making the memories from the first paragraphs seem as "real" and immediate as those from many years later. And Buddy's responses from the early years ("Well, I'm disappointed. Who wouldn't be? With socks, a Sunday school shirt, some handkerchiefs, a hand-me-down sweater and a year's subscription to a religious magazine for children, *The Little Shepherd*. It makes me boil. It really does.") are as true to his seven-year-old's perspective, as are those when he, much older, has left home ("I have a new home too. But it doesn't count. Home is where my friend is, and there I never go.").

The youthful narrator in "A & P" also uses present tense, but not consistently, which gives his narrative a very colloquial, even unschooled flavor. Like Buddy, Sammy identifies himself in the opening paragraph: "In walks these three girls in nothing but bathing suits. I'm in the third checkout slot, with my back to the door, so I don't see them until they're over by the bread." And later, "Stokesie's married, with two babies chalked up on his fuselage already, but as far as I can tell that's the only difference. He's twenty-two, and I was nineteen this April." The girls incur the wrath of the store manager, who scolds them for their inappropriate dress. And Sammy, in his adolescent idealism, quits on the spot. Although he realizes that he does not want to "do this" to his parents, he tells us "… it seems to me that once you begin a gesture it's fatal not to go through with it." But his *beau geste* is ill-spent: "I look around for my girls, but they're gone, of course…. I could see Lengel in my place in the slot, checking the sheep through. His face was dark gray and his back stiff, as if he'd just had an injection of iron, and my stomach kind of fell as I felt how hard the world was going to be to me hereafter."

Like Buddy, Sammy tells his story from a perch not too distant from the events he recounts. Both narrators still feel the immediacy of their rites of passage very strongly. Buddy, however, reveals himself to be a more admirable character, perhaps because his story occurs mainly when he is seven—children tend not to be reckless in the way that Sammy is. Sammy was performing for an audience, doing things he knew would cause pain to himself and his family, for the sake of those three girls who never gave him the slightest encouragement and whom he would probably never even see again.

In "Araby," the unnamed narrator tells of a boyhood crush he had on the older sister of one of his chums: "I thought little of the future. I did not know whether I would ever speak to her or not or, if I spoke to her, how I could tell her of my confused adoration. But my body was like a harp and her words and gestures were like fingers running upon the wires." She asks the boy if he is going to Araby, a "splendid bazaar," and reveals that she cannot. He promises to go himself and bring her something. But his uncle's late homecoming delays the boy's excursion until the bazaar is nearly closed for the night, and he is unable to find an appropriate gift. Forlornly, "I turned away slowly and walked down the middle of the bazaar…. Gazing up into the darkness I saw myself as a creature driven and derided by vanity, and my eyes burned with anguish and anger." This narrator is recounting his story from much further away than either Buddy or Sammy tells his own. The narrator of "Araby" has the perspective of an adult, looking back at a very important event in his boyhood. His "voice" reflects wisdom born of experience. The incident was very painful then, but its memory, while poignant, is no longer devastating. Like Sammy, this narrator sees the dichotomy between his adolescent idealism and the mundane reality of "romance." However, the difference is in the narrator's ability to turn the light on himself. Sammy is still so close to the incident that he very likely would whip off his checker's apron again if the girls returned to the A & P. The "Araby" narrator has "mellowed" and can see the futility—and the necessity—of adolescent love.

READING ESSAYS

Categories of Essays

Essays fall into four rough categories: **speculative**, **argumentative**, **narrative**, and **expository**. Depending on the writer's purpose, his essay will fit more or less into one or these groupings.

The **speculative** essay is so named because, as its Latin root suggests, it *looks* at ideas; explores them rather than explains them. While the speculative essay may be said to be *meditative*, it often makes one or more points. But the thesis may not be as obvious or clear-cut as that in an expository or argumentative essay. The writer deals with ideas in an associative manner, playing with ideas in a looser structure than he would in an expository or argumentative essay. This "flow" may even produce *intercalary* paragraphs, which present alternately a narrative of sorts and thoughtful responses to the events being recounted, as in White's "The Ring of Time."

The purposes of the **argumentative** essay, on the other hand, are always clear: to present a point and provide evidence, which may be factual or anecdotal, and to support it. The structure is usually very formal, as in a debate, with counterpositions and counterarguments. Whatever the organizational pattern, the writer's intent in an argumentative essay is to persuade his reader of the validity of some claim, as Bacon does in "Of Love."

Narrative and **expository** essays have elements of both the speculative and argumentative modes. The narrative essay may recount an incident or a series of incidents and is almost always autobiographical, in order to make a point, as in Orwell's "Shooting an Elephant." The informality of the storytelling makes the narrative essay less insistent than the argumentative essay, but more directed than the speculative essay.

Students are probably most familiar with the **expository** essay, the primary purpose of which is to explain and clarify ideas. While the expository essay may have narrative elements, that aspect is minor and subservient to that of explanation. Furthermore, while nearly all essays have some element of persuasion, argumentation is incidental in the expository essay. In any event, the four categories—speculative, argumentative, narrative, and expository—are neither exhaustive nor mutually exclusive.

Elements of Essays

As non-fiction, essays have a different set of elements from novels and short stories: **voice, style, structure**, and **thought**.

Voice in non-fiction is similar to the narrator's tone in fiction, but the major difference is in who is "speaking." In fiction, the author is not the speaker—the **narrator** is the speaker. Students sometimes have difficulty with this distinction, but it is necessary if we are to preserve the integrity of the fictive "story." In an essay, however, the author speaks directly to the reader, even if he is presenting ideas which he may not actually espouse personally—as in a satire. This directness creates the writer's **tone**, his attitude toward his subject.

Style in non-fiction derives from the same elements as style in fiction: word choice, syntax, balance between dialogue and narration, voice, use of description—those things specifically related to words on the page. Generally speaking, an argumentative essay will be written in a more formal style than will a narrative essay, and a meditative essay will be less formal than an expository essay. But such generalizations are only descriptive, not prescriptive.

Structure and **thought**, the final elements of essays, are so intertwined as to be inextricable. We must be aware that to change the structure of an essay will alter its meaning. For instance, in White's "The Ring of Time," to abandon the *intercalary* paragraph organization, separating the paragraphs which narrate the scenes with the young circus rider from those which reflect on the circularity and linearity of time, would alter our understanding of the essay's thesis. Writers signal structural shifts with alterations in focus, as well as with visual clues (spacing), verbal clues (e.g., *but, therefore, however*), or shifts in the kind of information being presented (personal, scientific, etc.).

Thought is perhaps the single element which most distinguishes non-fiction from fiction. The essayist chooses his form not to tell a story but to present an idea. Whether he chooses the speculative, narrative, argumentative, or expository format, the essayist has something on his mind that he wants to convey to his readers. And it is this idea which we are after when we analyze his essay.

Example of the Structure of an Essay

Often anthologized is Orwell's "Shooting an Elephant," a narrative essay recounting the writer's (presumably) experience in Burma as an officer of the British law that ruled the poverty-ridden people of a small town. Orwell begins with two paragraphs which explain that, as a white, European authority figure, he was subjected to taunts and abuse by the natives. Ironically, he sympathized with the Burmese and harbored fairly strong anti-British feelings regarding the imperialists as the oppressors rather than the saviors. He tells us that he felt caught, trapped between his position of authority which he himself resented and the hatred of those he was required to oversee.

The body of the essay—some 11 paragraphs—relates the incident with an otherwise tame elephant gone "must" which had brought chaos and destruction to the village. Only occasionally does Orwell interrupt the narrative to reveal his reactions directly, but his descriptions of the Burmese are sympathetically drawn. The language is heavily connotative, revealing the helplessness of the villagers against both the elephant and the miserable circumstances of their lives.

Orwell recounts how, having sent for an elephant gun, he found that he was compelled to shoot the animal, even though its destruction was by now unwarranted and even ill-advised, given the value of the elephant to the village. But the people expected it, demanded it; the white man realized that he did not have dominion over these people of color after all. They were in charge, not him.

To make matters worse, Orwell bungles the "murder" of the beast, which takes half an hour to die in great agony. And in the aftermath of discussions of the rightness or wrongness of his action, Orwell wonders if anyone realizes he killed the elephant only to save face. It is the final sentence of the final paragraph which directly reveals the author's feelings, although he has made numerous indirect references to them throughout the essay. Coupled with the opening paragraphs, this conclusion presents British imperialism of the period in a very negative light: "the unable doing the unnecessary to the ungrateful."

Having discovered Orwell's main idea, we must look at the other elements (voice, style, structure) to see *how* he communicates it to the reader. The voice of the first-person narrative is fairly formal, yet remarkably candid, using connotation to color our perception of the events. Orwell's narrative has many complex sentences, with vivid descriptive phrases in series, drawing our eye along the landscape and through the crowds as he ponders his next move. Structurally, the essay first presents a premise about British imperialism, then moves to a gripping account of the officer's reluctant shooting of the elephant, and ends with an admission of his own culpability as an agent of the institution he detests. Orwell frequently signals shifts between his role as officer and his responses as a humane personage with *but*, or with dashes to set off his responses to the events he is recounting.

READING SATIRE

Satire is a *mode* which may be employed by writers of various genres: poetry, drama, fiction, non-fiction. It is more a perspective than a product.

Satire mainly exposes and ridicules, derides and denounces vice, folly, evil, stupidity, as these qualities manifest themselves in persons, groups of persons, ideas, institutions, customs, or beliefs. While the satirist has many techniques at his disposal, there are basically only two types of satire: gentle or harsh, depending on the author's intent, his audience, and his methods.

Role of Satire

The terms *romanticism*, *realism*, and *naturalism* can help us understand the role of *satire*. Romanticism sees the world idealistically, as perfectible if not perfect. Realism sees the world as it is, with healthy doses of both good and bad. Naturalism sees the world as imperfect, with evil often triumphing over good. The satirist is closer to the naturalist than he is to the romantic or realist, for both the satirist and the naturalist focus on what is wrong with the world, intending to expose the foibles of man and his society. The difference between them lies in their techniques. The naturalist is very direct and does not necessarily employ humor; the satirist is more subtle, and does.

For instance, people plagued with overpopulation and starvation is not, on first glance, material for humor. Many works have treated such conditions with sensitivity, bringing attention to the plight of the world's unfortunate. Steinbeck's *Grapes of Wrath* is such a work. However, Swift's "A Modest Proposal" takes essentially the same circumstances and holds them up for our amused examination. How does the satirist make an un-funny topic humorous? And why would he do so?

Techniques of Satire

The satirist's techniques—his weapons—include **irony**, **parody**, **reversal** or **inversion**, **hyperbole**, **understatement**, **sarcasm**, **wit**, and **invective**. By exaggerating characteristics, by saying the opposite of what he means, by using his cleverness to make cutting or even cruel remarks at the expense of his subject, the writer of satire can call the reader's attention to those things he believes are repulsive, despicable, or destructive.

Whether he uses more harsh (Juvenalian) or more gentle (Horatian) satire depends upon the writer's attitude and intent. Is he merely flaunting his clever intellect, playing with words for our amusement or to inflate his own sense of superiority? Is he probing the psychological motivations for the foolish or destructive actions of some person(s)? Is he determined to waken an unenlightened or apathetic audience, moving its members to thought or action? Are the flaws which the satirist is pointing out truly destructive or evil, or are they the faults we would all recognize in ourselves if we glanced in the mirror, not admirable but not really harmful to ourselves or society? Is the author amused, sympathetic, objective, irritated, scornful, bitter, pessimistic, mocking? The reader needs to identify the satirist's purpose and tone. Its subtlety sometimes makes satire a difficult mode to detect and to understand.

Irony

Irony is perhaps the satirist's most powerful weapon. The basis of irony is inversion or reversal, doing or saying the opposite or the unexpected. Shakespeare's famous sonnet beginning "My mistress' eyes are nothing like the sun…" is an ironic tribute to the speaker's beloved, who, he finally declares is "as rare/As any she belied with false compare." At the same time, Shakespeare is poking fun at the sonnet form as it was used by his contemporaries—himself included—to extol the virtues of their ladies. By selecting a woman who, by his own description, is physically unattractive in every way imaginable, and using the conventions of the love sonnet to present her many flaws, he has inverted the sonnet tradition. And then by asserting that she compares favorably with any of the other ladies whose poet-lovers have lied about their virtues, he presents us with the unexpected twist. Thus, he satirizes both the love sonnet form and its subject by using irony.

Poetic Satires

Other notable poetic satires include Koch's "Variations on a Theme by William Carlos Williams," in which he parodies Williams' "This Is Just to Say." Koch focuses on the simplicity and directness of Williams' imagery and makes the form and ideas seem foolish and trivial. In "Boom!," Nemerov takes issue with a pastor's assertion that modern technology has resulted in a concomitant rise in religious activities and spiritual values. Nemerov catalogues the instant, disposable, and extravagant aspects of Americans' lifestyles, which result in "pray as you go… pilgrims" for whom religion is another convenience, commercial rather than spiritual.

Satire in Drama

Satire in drama is also common. Wilde's "The Importance of Being Earnest" is wonderfully funny in its constant word play (notably on the name

Ernest) and its relentless ridiculing of the superficiality which Wilde saw as characteristic of British gentry. Barrie's "The Admirable Chrichton" has a similar theme, with the added assertion that it is the "lower" or servant class which is truly superior—again, the ironic reversal so common in satire. Both of these plays are mild in their ridicule; the authors do not expect or desire any change in society or in the viewer. The satire is gentle; the satirists are amused, or perhaps bemused at the society whose foibles they expose.

Satire in Classic Novels

Classic novels which employ satire include Swift's *Gulliver's Travels* and Voltaire's *Candide*, both of which fairly vigorously attack aspects of the religions, governments, and prevailing intellectual beliefs of their respective societies. A modern novel which uses satire is Heller's *Catch-22*, which is basically an attack on war and the government's bureaucratic bungling of men and material, specifically in World War II. But by extension, Heller is also viewing with contempt the unmotivated, illogical, capricious behavior of all institutions which operate by that basic law: "catch-22." Like Swift and Voltaire, Heller is angry. And although his work, like the other two, has humor, wit, exaggeration, and irony, his purpose is more than intellectual entertainment for his readers. Heller hopes for reform.

Heller's attack is frontal, his assault direct. Swift had to couch his tale in a fantastic setting with imaginary creatures in order to present his views with impunity. The audience, as well as the times, also affect the satirist's work. If the audience is hostile, the writer must veil his theme; if the audience is indifferent, he must jolt them with bitter and reviling language if he desires change. If he does not fear reprisals, the satirist may take any tone he pleases.

We can see satire in operation in two adaptations of the biblical story of King Solomon, who settled the dispute between two mothers regarding an infant: Cut the baby in two and divide it between you, he told them. The rightful mother protested and was promptly awarded the child. The story is meant to attest to the King's wisdom and understanding of parental love, in this case.

However, Twain's Huck Finn has some difficulty persuading runaway slave Jim that Solomon was wise. Jim insists that Solomon, having fathered "'bout five million chillen," was "waseful.... *He* as soon chop a chile in two as a cat. Dey's plenty mo'. A chile er two, mo' er less, warn't no consekens to Solermun, dad fetch him!" Twain is ridiculing not only Jim's ingenuousness, as he does throughout the novel; he is also deflating time-honored beliefs about the Bible and its traditional heroes, as he earlier does with the account of Moses and the "bulrushers." While Twain's tone is fairly mild, his intent shows through as serious. Twain was disgusted with traditional Christianity and its hypocritical followers, as we see later in *Huck Finn* when young Buck Grangerford is murdered in the feud with the Shepherdsons: "I wished I hadn't ever come ashore that night to see such things."

A second satiric variation on the Solomon theme appears in Asprin's *Myth Adventures*, in the volume *Hit or Myth*. Skeebe, the narrator, realizes that he, as king pro-tem, must render a decision regarding the ownership of a cat. Hoping to inspire them to compromise, he decrees that they divide the cat between them: "Instead they thanked me for my wisdom, shook hands, and left smiling, presumably to carve up their cat." He concludes that many of the citizens of this realm "don't have both oars in the water," a conclusion very like Huck's: "I never see such a nigger. If he got a notion in his head once, there warn't no getting it out again." The citizens' unthinking acceptance of the infallibility of authority is as laughable as Jim's out-of-hand rejection of Solomon's wisdom because no wise man would "want to live in the mids' er sich a blim-blammin' all de time" as would prevail in the harem with the King's "million wives."

POETRY

Opening a book to study for an examination is perhaps the worst occasion on which to read poetry, or about poetry, because above all, poetry should be enjoyed; it is definitely "reading for pleasure." This last phrase seems to have developed recently to describe the reading we do other than for information or for study. Perhaps you personally would not choose poetry as pleasure reading because of the bad name poetry has received over the years. Some students regard the "old" poetry such as Donne's or Shelley's as effete (for "wimps" and "nerds" only, in current language), or modern poetry as too difficult or weird. It is hard to imagine that poetry was the "current language" for students growing up in the Elizabethan or Romantic eras. Whereas in our world information can be retrieved in a nanosecond, in those worlds time was plentiful to sit down, clear the mind, and let poetry take over. Very often the meaning of a poem does not come across in a nanosecond and for the modern student this proves very frustrating. Sometimes it takes years for a poem to take on meaning—the reader simply knows that the poem sounds good and it provokes an emotional response that cannot be explained. With time, more emotional experience, more reading of similar experiences, more life, the reader comes to a meaning of that poem that satisfies for the time being. In a few more years that poem may take on a whole new meaning.

READING POETRY FOR AN EXAMINATION

This is all very well for reading for pleasure, but you are now called upon, in your present experience, to learn poetry for an important examination. Perhaps the first step in the learning process is to answer the question, "Why do people write poetry?" An easy answer is that they wish to convey an experience, an emotion, an insight, or an observation in a startling or satisfying way, one that remains in the memory for years. But why not use a straightforward sentence or paragraph? Why wrap up that valuable insight in fancy words, rhyme, para-dox, meter, allusion, symbolism, and all the other seeming mumbo-jumbo that explicators of poetry use? Why not just come right out and say it like "normal people" do? An easy answer to these questions is that poetry is not a vehicle for conveying meaning alone. Gerard Manley Hopkins, one of the great innovators of rhythm in poetry, claimed that poetry should be "heard for its own sake and interest even over and above its interest or meaning." Poetry provides intellec-tual stimulus of course. One of the best ways of studying a poem is to consider it a jigsaw puzzle presented to you whole, an integral work of art, which can be taken apart piece by piece (word by word), analyzed scientifically, labelled, and put back together again into a whole, and then the meaning is complete. But people write poetry to convey more than meaning.

MEANINGS IN POETRY

T. S. Eliot maintained that the meaning of the poem existed purely to distract us "while the poem did its work." One interpretation of a poem's "work" is that it changes us in some way. We see the world in a new way because of the way the poet has seen it and told us about it. Maybe one of the reasons people write poetry is to encourage us to *see* things in the first place. Simple things like daffodils take on a whole new aspect when we read the way Wordsworth saw them. Why did Wordsworth write that poem? His sister had written an excellent account of the scene in her journal. Wordsworth not only evokes nature as we have never seen it before, alive, joyous, exuberant, he shows nature's healing powers, its restorative quality as the scene flashes "upon that inward eye/Which is the bliss of solitude." Bent over your books studying, how many times has a similar quality of nature's power in the memory come to you? Maybe for you a summer beach scene rather than daffodils by the lake is more meaningful, but the poet captures a moment that we have all experienced. The poet's magic is to make that moment new again.

If poets enhance our power of sight they also awaken the other senses as powerfully. We can hear Emily Dickinson's snake in the repeated "s" sound of the lines:

> His notice sudden is—
> The Grass divides as with a Comb—
> A spotted shaft is seen—

and because of the very present sense of sound, we experience the indrawn gasp of breath of fear when the snake appears. We can touch the little chimneysweep's hair "that curled like a lamb's back" in William Blake's poetry, and because of that tactile sense we are even more shocked to read that the child's hair is all shaved off so that the soot will not spoil its whiteness. We can smell the poison gas as Wilfred Owen's soldiers fumble with their gas masks; we can taste the blood gurgling in the poisoned lungs.

Poets write, then, to awaken the senses. They have crucial ideas, but the words they use are often more important than the meaning. More important still than ideas and sense awakening is the poet's appeal to the emotions. And it is precisely this area that disturbs a number of students. Our modern society tends to block out emotions—we need reviews to tell us if we enjoyed a film or a critic's praise to see if a play or novel is worth our time. We hesitate to laugh at something in case it is not the "in" thing to do. We certainly do not cry—at least in front of others. Poets write to overcome that blocking (very often it is their own blocking of emotion they seek to alleviate), but that is not to say that poetry immediately sets us laughing, crying, loving, or hating. The important fact about the emotional release in poetry is that poets help us explore our own emotions, sometimes by shocking us, sometimes by drawing attention to balance and pattern, and sometimes by cautioning us to move carefully in this inner world.

Poets tell us nothing really new. They tell us old truths about human emotions that we begin to restructure anew, to reread our experiences in light of theirs, to reevaluate our world view. Whereas a car manual helps us understand the workings of a particular vehicle, a poem helps us understand the inner workings of human beings. Poets frequently write to help their emotional life—

the writing then becomes cathartic, purging or cleansing the inner life, feeding that part of us that separates us from the animal. Many poets might paraphrase Byron, who claimed that he had to write or go mad. Writer and reader of poetry enter into a collusion, each helping the other to find significance in the human world, to find safety in a seemingly alien world.

REASONS FOR READING POETRY

This last point brings any reader of poetry to ask the next question: Why read poetry? One might contend that a good drama, novel, or short story might provide the same emotional experience. But a poem is much more accessible. Apart from the fact that poems are shorter than other genres, there is a unique directness to them which hinges purely on language. Poets can say in one or two lines what may take novelists and playwrights entire works to express. For example, Keats' lines—

> Beauty is truth, truth beauty,—that is all
> Ye know on earth, and all ye need to know—

studied, pondered, and opened to each reader's interpretations, linger in the memory with more emphasis than George Eliot's *Middlemarch*, or Ibsen's *The Wild Duck*, which endeavor to make the same point.

In your reading of poems remember that poetry is perhaps the oldest art and yet surrounds us without our even realizing it. Listeners thrilled to Homer's poetry; tribes chanted invocations to their gods. Today we listen to pop-song lyrics and find ourselves, sometimes despite ourselves, repeating certain rhythmic lines. Advertisements we chuckle over or say we hate still have a way of embedding themselves in our minds with their catchy phrases or snappy repetition. Both lyricists and advertisers cleverly use language, playing on the reader's/listener's/watcher's ability to pick up on a repeated sound or engaging rhythm or inner rhyme. Think of a time as a child when you thoroughly enjoyed poetry: nursery rhymes, ball-game rhythms, jump-rope patterns. Probably you had no idea of the meaning of the words ("Little Miss Muffet sat on a tuffet..." a tuffet?!) but you responded to the sound, the pattern. As adults we read poetry for that sense of sound and pattern. With more experience at reading poetry there is an added sense of pleasure as techniques are recognized: alliteration, onomatopoeia; forms of poetry become obvious—the sonnet, the rondelle. Even greater enjoyment comes from watching a poet's development, tracing themes and ideas, analyzing maturity in growth of imagery, use of rhythm.

To the novice reader of poetry, a poem can speak to the reader at a particular time and become an experience in itself. A freshman's experience after her mother's death exemplifies this. Shortly after the death, the student found Elizabeth Jennings' poem "Happy Families." Using the familiar names of the cards, Mrs. Beef and Master Bun, the poet describes how strangers try to help the family carry on their lives normally although one of the "happy family" is "missing." The card game continues although no one wants it to. At the end the players go back to their individual rooms and give way to their individual grief. The student described the relief at knowing that someone else had obviously experienced her situation where everyone in the family was putting up a front, strangers were being very kind, and a general emptiness prevailed because of that one missing family member. The poem satisfied. The student saw death through another's eyes; the experience was almost the same, yet helped the reader to reevaluate, to view a universal human response to grief as well as encourage her to deal with her own.

On reading a poem the brain works on several different levels: it responds to the sounds; it responds to the words themselves and their connotations; it responds to the emotions; it responds to the insights or learning of the world being revealed. For such a process poetry is a very good training ground—a boot camp—for learning how to read literature in general. All the other genres have elements of poetry within them. Learn to read poetry well and you will be a more accomplished reader, even of car manuals! Perhaps the best response to reading poetry comes from a poet herself, Emily Dickinson, who claimed that reading a book of poetry made her feel "as if the top of [her] head were taken off!"

Before such a process happens to you, here are some tips for reading poetry before and during the examination.

TIPS FOR PREPARATION

1) Make a list of poets and poems you remember; analyze poems you liked, disliked, loved, hated, and were indifferent to. Find the poems. Reread them and for each one analyze your *feelings*, first of all, about the poetry itself. Have your feelings changed? Now what do you like or hate? Then paraphrase the *meaning* of each poem. Notice how the "magic" goes from the poem, i.e., "To Daffodils"—the poet sees many daffodils by the side of a lake and then thinks how the sight of them later comforts him.

2) Choose a poem at random from an anthology or one mentioned in this introduction. Read it a couple of times, preferably aloud, because the speaking voice will automatically grasp the rhythm and that will help the meaning. Do not become bogged down in individual word connotation or the meaning of the poem—let the poetry do its "work" on you; absorb the poem as a whole jigsaw puzzle.

3) Now take the puzzle apart. Look carefully at the title. Sometimes a straightforward title helps you focus. Sometimes a playful title helps you get an angle on the meaning. "Happy Families," of course, is an ironic title because the family playing the card game of that name is not happy.

4) Look carefully at the punctuation. Does the sense of a line carry from one to another? Does a particular mark of punctuation strike you as odd? Ask why that mark was used.

5) Look carefully at the words. Try to find the meaning of words with which you are not familiar within the context. Familiar words may be used differently: ask why that particular use. Having tapped into your memory bank of vocabulary and you are still at a loss, go to a dictionary. Once you have the *denotation* of the word, start wondering about the *connotation*. Put yourself in the poet's position and think why that word was used.

6) Look carefully at all the techniques being used. You will gain these as you progress through this section and through the test preparation. As soon as you come across a new idea—"caesura" perhaps—learn the word, see how it applies to poetry, where it is used. Be on the lookout for it in other poetry. Ask yourself questions such as why the poet used alliteration here; why the rhythm changes there; why the poet uses a sonnet form and which sonnet form is in use. Forcing yourself to ask the WHY questions, and answering them, will train the brain to read more perceptively. Poetry is not accidental; poets are deliberate people; they do things for specific reasons. Your task under a learning situation is to discover WHY.

7) Look carefully at the speaker. Is the poet using another persona? Who is that persona? What is revealed about the speaker? Why use that particular voice?

8) Start putting all the pieces of the puzzle together. The rhythm helps the meaning. The word choice helps the imagery. The imagery adds to the meaning. Paraphrase the meaning. Ask yourself simple questions:

What is the poet saying? How can I relate to what is being said? What does this poem mean to me? What does this poem contribute to human experience?

9) Find time to read about the great names in poetry. Locate people within time areas and analyze what those times entailed. For example, the Elizabethans saw a contest between secular love and love of God. The Romantics (Wordsworth, Coleridge, Keats, Shelley, Byron) loved nature and saw God within nature. The Victorians (Tennyson, Blake) saw nature as a threat to mankind and God, being replaced by the profit cash-nexus of the Industrial Age. The moderns (T. S. Eliot, Pound, Yeats) see God as dead and man as hollow, unwanted, and unsafe in an alien world. The Post-Moderns see life as "an accident," a comic/cosmic joke, fragmented, purposeless—often their topics will be political: apartheid, abortion, unjust imprisonment.

10) Write a poem of your own. Choose a particular style; use the sonnet form; parody a famous poem; express yourself in free verse on a crucial, personal aspect of your life. Then analyze your own poetry with the above ideas.

TIPS FOR TEST-TAKING

You will have established a routine for reading poetry, but now you are under pressure, must work quickly, and will have no access to a dictionary. You cannot read aloud but you *can* do the following:

1) Internalize the reading—hear the reading in your head. Read through the poem two or three times following the absorbing procedure.

2) If the title and poet are supplied, analyze the title as before and determine the era of the poetry. Often this pushes you toward the meaning.

3) Look carefully at the questions which should enable you to "tap into" your learning process. Answer the ones that are immediately clear to you: form, technique, language perhaps.

4) Go back for another reading for those questions that challenge you—theme or meaning perhaps—analyze the speaker or the voice at work— paraphrase the meaning—ask the simple question, "What is the poet saying?"

5) If a question asks you about a specific line, metaphor, opening, or closing lines, mentally highlight or underline them to force your awareness of each crucial word. Internalize another reading emphasizing the highlighted area—analyze again the options you have for your answers.

6) Do not waste time on an answer that eludes you. Move onto another section and let the poetry do its "work." Very often the brain will continue working on the problem on another level of consciousness. When you go back to the difficult question, it may well become clear.

7) If you still are not sure of the answer, choose the option that you *think* is the closest to correct.

VERSE AND METER

Verse

As children reading or learning poetry in school, we referred to each section of a poem as a verse. We complained we had ten verses to learn for homework. In fact the word **verse** strictly refers to a line of poetry, perhaps from the original Latin word "versus": a row or a line, and the notion of turning, "vertere," to turn or move to a new idea. In modern use we refer to poetry often as "verse" with the connotation of rhyme, rhythm, and meter; but we still recognize verse because of the positioning of lines on the page, the breaking of lines that distinguish verse from prose.

The verses we learned for homework are in fact known as **stanzas**: a grouping of lines with a metrical order and often a repeated rhyme which we know as the **rhyme scheme**. Such a scheme is shown by letters to show the repeating sounds. Byron's "Stanzas" will help you recall the word, see the use of a definite rhyme, and how to mark it:

"Stanzas"

(When a man hath no freedom to fight for at home)

When a man hath no freedom to fight for at home,	*a*
Let him combat for that of his neighbors;	*b*
Let him think of the glories of Greece and of Rome,	*a*
And get knocked on the head for his labors.	*b*

To do good to mankind is the chivalrous plan,	*c*
And is always as nobly requited;	*d*
Then battle for freedom wherever you can,	*c*
And, if not shot or hanged, you'll get knighted.	*d*

The rhyme scheme is simple: *abab* and your first question should be "Why such a simple, almost sing-song rhyme?" The simplicity reinforces the **tone** of the poem: sarcastic, cryptic, cynical. There is almost a sneer behind the words "And get knocked on the head for his labors." It is as if the poet sets out to give a lecture or at least a homily along the lines of: "Neither a lender nor a borrower be," but then undercuts the seriousness. The **irony** of the poem rests in the fact that Byron joined a freedom fighting group in Greece and died, not gloriously, but of a fever. We shall return to this poem for further discussion.

Forms of Rhymes

Certain types of rhyme are worth learning. The most common is the end rhyme, which has the rhyming word at the end of the line, bringing the line to a definite stop but setting up for a rhyming word in another line later on, as in "Stanzas": home… Rome, a perfect rhyme. **Internal rhyme** includes at least one rhyming word within the line, often for the purpose of speeding the rhythm or making it linger. Look at the effect of Byron's internal rhymes mixed with half-rhymes: "combat… for that"; "Can/And… hanged" slowing the rhythm, making the reader dwell on the harsh long "a" sound, prolonging the sneer which almost becomes a snarl of anger. **Slant rhyme**, sometimes referred to as half, off, near, or approximate rhyme, often jolts a reader who expects a perfect rhyme; poets thus use such a rhyme to express disappointment or a deliberate let-down. **Masculine rhyme** uses one-syllable words or stresses the final syllable of polysyllabic words, giving the feeling of strength and impact. **Feminine rhyme** uses a rhyme of two or more syllables, the stress not falling upon the last syllable, giving a feeling of softness and lightness; one can see that these terms for rhyme were written in a less enlightened age! The terms themselves for the rhymes are less important than realizing or at least appreciating the effects of the rhymes.

If the lines from "Stanzas" had been unrhymed and varying in metrical pattern, the verse would have been termed **free**, or to use the French term, *"Vers libre,"* not to be confused with **blank verse**, which is also unrhymed but has a strict rhythm. The Elizabethan poets Wyatt and Surrey introduced blank verse, which Shakespeare uses to such good effect in his plays, and later, Milton in the great English epic *Paradise Lost*. Free verse has become associated with "modern" poetry, often adding to its so-called obscurity because without rhyme and rhythm, poets often resort to complicated syntactical patterns, repeated phrases, awkward cadences, and parallelism. Robert Frost preferred not to use it because, as he put it, "Writing free verse is like playing tennis with the net down," suggesting that free verse is easier than rhymed and metrical. However, if you have ever tried writing such verse, you will know the problems. (Perhaps a good exercise after you learn about meter is to write some "free" verse.) T. S. Eliot, who uses the form most effectively in "The Journey of the Magi," claimed that no *"vers"* is *"libre"* for the poet who wanted to do a good job.

Meter

Such a claim for the artistry and hard work behind a poem introduces perhaps the most difficult of the skills for a poet to practice and a reader to learn: meter. This time the Greeks provide the meaning of the word from *"metron,"* meaning measure. **Meter** simply means the pattern or measure of stressed or accented words within a line of verse. When studying meter a student should note where stresses fall on syllables—that is why reading aloud is so important, because it catches the natural rhythm of the speaking voice—and if an absence of stressed syllables occurs there is always an explanation why. We "expect" stressed and unstressed syllables because that is what we use in everyday speech. We may stress one syllable over another for a certain effect, often using the definite article "THE well known author…" or the preposition "Get OUT of here!" Usually, however, we use a rising and falling rhythm, known as **iambic rhythm**. A line of poetry that alternates stressed and unstressed syllables is said to have **iambic meter**. A line of poetry with ten syllables of rising and falling stresses is known as **iambic pentameter**, best used by Shakespeare and Milton in their blank verse. The basic measuring unit in a line of poetry is called a **foot**. An **iambic foot** has one unstressed syllable followed by a stressed marked by u. Pentameter means "five-measure." Therefore, **iambic pentameter** has five groups of two syllables, or ten beats, to the line. Read aloud the second and fourth, sixth and eighth lines of "Stanzas," tapping the beat on your desk or your palm, and the ten beat becomes obvious. Read again with the stresses unstressed and stressed (or soft and loud, short or long, depending on what terminology works for you) and the iambic foot becomes clear.

Tapping out the other alternate lines in this poem you will not find ten beats but twelve. The term for this line is hexameter, or six feet, rather than five. Other line-length names worth learning are:

monometer	one foot	**dimeter**	two feet
trimeter	three feet	**tetrameter**	four feet
heptameter	seven feet	**octameter**	eight feet

Other foot names worth learning are:

the **anapest** marked u u /, the most famous anapestic line being:

u u / u u / u u / u u /

"Twas the night before Christmas, when all through the house…"

the **trochee**, marked / u, the most memorable trochaic line being:

/u /u / u /u

"Double double toil and trouble…"

and the **dactyl** marked / u u, the most often quoted dactylic line being:

/ u u / u u

"Take her up tenderly…"

Accentual Meter

Old English poetry employs a meter known as **accentual meter**, with four stresses to the line without attention to the unstressed syllables. Contemporary poets tend not to use it, but one of the greatest innovators in rhythm and meter, Gerard Manley Hopkins, used it as the "base line" for his counterpointed "Sprung Rhythm." Living in the nineteenth century, Hopkins produced poetry that even today strikes the reader as "modern," in that the rhymes and rhythms often jar the ear, providing stressed syllables where we expect unstressed and vice versa. The rhythm was measured by feet of from one to four syllables, and any number of unstressed syllables. Underneath the rhythm we hear the "regular" rhythm we are used to in speech, and an intriguing counterpoint develops. One stanza from "The Caged Skylark" will show the method at work:

As a dare-gale skylark scanted in a dull cage
Man's mounting spirit in his bone-house, mean house, dwells—
That bird beyond the remembering his free fells;
This in drudgery, day-labouring-out life's age.

The stress on "That" and "This" works particularly well to draw attention to the two captives: the skylark and Man. The accentual meter in the second line reinforces the wretchedness of the human condition. No reader could possibly read that line quickly, nor fail to put the full length of the syllable on "dwells." The dash further stresses the length and the low pitch of the last word.

If at first the terms for meter are new and strange, remember that what is most important is not that you mindlessly memorize the terminology but are able to recognize the meter and analyze why the poet has used it in the particular context of the poem. For example, Shakespeare did not want the lyrical fall and rise of the iamb for his witches around the cauldron, so he employs the much more unusual trochee to suggest the gloom and mystery of the heath in "Macbeth." Many poets will "mix and match" their meter and your task as a student of poetry is to analyze why. Perhaps the poet sets up the regular greeting card meter, rising and falling rhythm, regular end-stopped rhyme. If the poet abruptly changes that pattern, there is a reason. If the poet subtly moves from a disruptive meter into a smooth one, then analyze what is going on in the meaning. If the poet is doing "a good job" as T. S. Eliot suggested, then the rhyme, rhythm, and meter should all work together in harmony to make the poem an integral whole. Answer the test essay questions to practice the points in this section and the integrity of a poem as a single unit will become clearer.

FIGURATIVE LANGUAGE AND POETIC DEVICES

It will start becoming ever more obvious that a poem is not created from mere inspiration. No doubt the initial movement for a poem has something of divine intervention: the ancients talked of being visited by the Muse of Poetry; James Joyce coined the word "epiphany" for the clear moment of power of conception in literature, but then the poet sets to working at the expression to make it the best it can be.

Perhaps what most distinguishes poetry from any other genre is the use of figurative language—figures of speech—used through the ages to convey the poet's own particular world-view in a unique way. Words have **connotation** and

denotation, **figurative** and **literal** meanings. We can look in the dictionary for denotation and literal meaning, but figurative language works its own peculiar magic, tapping into shared experiences within the psyche. A simple example involves the word "home." If we free-associated for awhile among a group of 20 students, we would find a number of connotations for the word, depending on what the idea of "home" represented for us in our experiences: comforting, scary, lonely, dark, creepy, safety, haven, hell…. However, the denotation is quite straight-forward: a house or apartment or dwelling that provides shelter for an individual or family. Poets include in their skill various figures of speech to "plug into" the reader's experiences, to prompt the reader to say "I would have never thought of it in those terms but now I see!"

Metaphors and Similes

The most important of these skills is perhaps the **metaphor**, which com-pares two unlike things, feelings, or objects, and the **simile**. Metaphors are more difficult to find than **similes**, which also compare two dissimilar things but always use the words "as if" (for a clause) or "like" (for a word or phrase). Metaphors suggest the comparison; the meaning is implicit. An easy way to distinguish between the two is the simple example of the camel. **Metaphor**: the camel is the ship of the desert. **Simile**: a camel is like a ship in the desert. Both conjure up the camel's almost sliding across the desert, storing up its water as a ship must do for survival for its passengers, and the notion of the vastness of the desert parallels the sea. The metaphor somehow crystallizes the image. Metaphors can be *extended* so that an entire poem consists of a metaphor, or unfortunately they can be *mixed*. The latter rarely happens in poetry unless the poet is deliberately playing with his readers and provoking humor.

Start thinking of how many times you use similes in your own writing or speech. The secret is, as Isaac Babel once said, that similes must be "as precise as a slide rule and as natural as the smell of dill." The precision and naturalness coming together perfectly often set up an equation of comparison. A student once wrote "I felt torn apart by my loyalty to my mother and grandmother, like the turkey wishbone at Thanksgiving." We have all experienced divided loyal-ties. Using the graphic wishbone-tearing idea, something we have all done or have seen done at Thanksgiving lets us more easily relate to the student's expe-rience. Another student wrote of his friends waiting for the gym class to begin "like so many captive gazelles." Again, the visual point of comparison is impor-tant but also the sense of freedom in the idea of gazelle, the speed, the grace;

juxtaposing that freedom with the word "captive" is a master stroke that makes a simile striking.

The same student went on to an *extended simile* to state precisely and naturally his feelings upon going into a fistfight: "I was like the kid whose parents were killed by the crooked sheriff, waiting for high noon and the showdown that would pit a scared kid with his father's rusty old pistol against the gleaming steel of a matched pair, nestled in the black folds of the sheriff's holsters. I knew there was no way out. Surrounded by friends, I marched out into the brilliant sun, heading for the back fields of the playground, desperately trying to polish the rusty old gun." Although this student was writing in prose, his use of figurative language is poetic. He plugs into readers' movie experience with the central idea of the showdown at high noon, an **allusion** that involves the reader on the same plane as the writer. The notion of the black holster extends the allusion of the old cowboy films where the "baddies" wore black hats and rode black horses. The use of the word "nestled" provokes some interesting connotations of something soft and sweet like a kitten nestling into something. But then the gun is an implement of destruction and death; maybe "nestles" takes on the connotation of how a snake might curl in the sun at the base of a tree. The metaphor then ends with the child going out into the sun. The "rusty gun" in context of the essay was in fact the outmoded ideas and morals his father and old books had inculcated in him. All in all a very clever use of figurative language in prose. If the same concept had been pursued in poetry, the metaphor would have moved more speedily, more subtly—a poet cannot waste words—and of course would have employed line breaks, rhythm, and meter.

Personification

Personification is a much easier area than metaphor to detect in poetry. Usually the object that is being personified—referred to as a human with the personal pronoun sometimes, or possessing human attributes—is capitalized, as in this stanza from Thomas Gray's "Ode on a Distant Prospect of Eton College":

> Ambition this shall tempt to rise,
> Then whirl the wretch from high,
> o bitter Scorn a sacrifice,
> And grinning Infamy.
> The stings of Falsehood those shall try,
> And hard Unkindness' altered eye,
> That mocks the tear it forced to flow;

> And keen Remorse with blood defiled,
> And moody Madness laughing wild
> Amid severest woe.

As the poet watches the young Eton boys, he envisions what the years have to offer them, and the qualities he sees he gives human status. Thus, Ambition is not only capable of tempting, an amoral act, but also of "whirling," a physical act. Scorn is bitter, Infamy grinning, and so on. Coleridge employs a more visual personification in "Rime of the Ancient Mariner," for the sun whom he describes as:

> ...the Sun (was) flecked with bars
> (Heaven's Mother send us grace!)
> As if through a dungeon-grate he peered
> With broad and burning face.

More so than with Gray's more formal personification, Coleridge's supplies an image that is precise—we can see the prisoner behind the bars, and what's more this particular prisoner has a broad and burning face... of course because he is the sun! The personification brings us that flash of recognition when we can say "Yes, I see that!"

Image

The word **image** brings us to another important aspect of figurative language. Not a figure of speech in itself, the image plays a large role in poetry because the reader is expected to **imagine** what the poet is evoking, through the senses. The image can be **literal**, wherein the reader has little adjustment to make to see or touch or taste the image; a **figurative image** demands more from readers, almost as if they have to be inside the poet's imagination to understand the image. Very often this is where students of poetry, modern poetry particularly, find the greatest problems because the poetry of **imagism**, a term coined by Ezra Pound, is often intensely personal, delving into the mind of the poet for the comparison and connection with past memories that many readers cannot possibly share. Such an image is referred to as *free*, open to many interpretations. This concept suits the post-modern poet who feels that life is fragmented, open to multi-interpretations—there is no fixed order. Poets of the Elizabethan and Romantic eras saw the world as whole, steady, *fixed*, exactly the word used for their type of images. Readers of this poetry usually share the same response to the imagery. For example, the second stanza of Keats's "Ode to a Nightingale" sets up the taste imagery of a

> draught of vintage that hath been
> Cooled a long age in the deep-delvéd earth,
> Tasting of Flora and the country green,
> Dance, and Provençal song, and sunburnt mirth!
> O for a beaker of the warm South,
> Full of the true, the blushful Hippocrene,
> With beaded bubbles winking at the brim,
> And purple-stainéd mouth;

Even though Flora and Hippocrene are not names we are readily familiar with, the image of the cool wine, the taste, the look, the feeling evoked of the South and warmth, all come rushing into our minds as we enter the poet's imagination and find images in common.

Blake's imagery in "London" works in a similar way but as readers we have to probe a little harder, especially for the last line of the last stanza:

> But, most thro' midnight streets I hear
> How the youthful Harlot's curse
> Blasts the new-born Infant's tear,
> And blights with plagues the Marriage hearse.

Notice how the "Marriage hearse" immediately sets up a double image. Marriage we associate with happiness and joy; hearse we associate with death and sorrow. The image is troubling. We go back to the previous lines. The harlot curses her newborn—the curse of venereal disease. She also foresees that the child ultimately will wed and carry the disease into marriage. Does marriage then becomes death? The image is intriguing and open to interpretation.

Symbol

Image in figurative language inevitably leads to **symbol**. When an object, an image, or a feeling takes on a larger meaning outside of itself, then a poet is employing a symbol, something which stands for something greater. Because mankind has used symbols for so long, many have become **stock** or **conventional**: the rose standing for love; the flag standing for patriotism, love of one's country (thus the controversy over flag-burning today); the color yellow standing for corruption (hence Gatsby's Daisy Buchanan—the white-dressed virginal lady with the center core of carelessness); the bird for freedom; the sea for eternity; the cross for suffering and sacrifice. If you are not versed in the Christian tradition, it might be useful to read its symbols because the older poetry dwells on the church and the trials of loving God and loving Woman—the latter also has become a symbol deteriorating over the ages from Eve to the Madonna to Whore.

If the symbol is not conventional, then it may carry with it many interpretations, depending on the reader's insight. Some students "get carried away" with symbolism, seeing more in the words than the poets do! If the poet is "doing a good job," the poetry will steer you in the "right" direction of symbolism. Sometimes we are unable to say what "stands for" what, but simply that the symbol evokes a mood; it suggests an idea to you that is difficult to explain. The best way to approach symbolism is to understand a literal meaning first and then shift the focus, as with a different camera lens, and see if the poet is saying something even more meaningful. Blake again supplies an interesting example. In his poem "The Chimney Sweeper" he describes the young child's dream of being locked up in "coffins of black." Literally, of course, coffins are brown wood; the color of mourning is black. Shift the focus then to the young child chimney sweeper, so young he can barely lisp the street cry "Sweep" so it comes out "'weep! 'weep! 'weep! 'weep!" (a symbolic line in itself). Your reading of the Industrial Age's cruelty to children who were exploited as cheap, plentiful, and an expendable labor force will perhaps have taught you that children were used as chimney brushes—literally thrust up the thin black chimneys of Victorian houses and factories, where very often they became trapped, suffocated, sometimes burned to death if fires were set by unknowing owners. Now the black coffins stand for the black-with-soot chimneys the little children had to sweep, chimneys which sometimes became their coffins. The realization of the symbol brings a certain horror to the poem. In the dream an Angel releases the children who then run down "a green plain leaping, laughing.../And wash in a river, and shine in the sun." The action is of course symbolic in that in real life the children's movements were restricted, living in monstrous cities where green plains would be enjoyed only by the rich, and totally limited by the size of the chimneys. They were always black with soot. They rarely saw the sun, never mind shone in it! Again, the symbolism adds something to the poem. In many students there have been reactions of tears and anger when they *see* the symbolism behind such simple lines.

Allusion

The idea of reading about the Industrial Age brings us to an important part of figurative language, briefly mentioned before: **allusion**. Poets tap into previous areas of experience to relate their insights, to draw their readers into shared experiences. Remember how the student writer alluded to old cowboy movies, the classic "high noon." Poets will refer to history, myth, other older poems, plays, music, heroes, famous people. Allusion is becoming more and more difficult for the modern student because reading is becoming more and more a lost art. Core courses in schools have become hotbeds of controversy about what students should know. Fortunately, modern poets are shifting their allusions so that contemporary readers can appreciate and join in with their background of knowledge. However, be aware that for the examination in poetry it will be useful to have a working knowledge of the traditional canon of literature. Think of areas of history that were landmarks: the burning of Carthage; Hannibal's elephants; Caesar's greatness; Alexander the Great; the First World War and its carnage of young men; the Second World War and the Holocaust. Think of the great Greek and Roman myths: the giving of fire to the world; the entrance of sin into the world; the labyrinth; the names associated with certain myths (Daedalus, Hercules, the Medusa). You may never have a question on the areas you read but your background for well-rounded college study will already be formulated.

Alliteration: the repetition of consonants at the beginning of words that are next to each other or close by. The Hopkins stanza quoted earlier provides some fine examples: "skylark scanted"; "Man's mounting… mean house"; "free fells"; "drudgery, day-labouring-out life's age." Always try to understand the reason for the alliteration. Does it speed or slow the rhythm? Is it there for emphasis? What does the poet want you to focus on?

Apostrophe: the direct address of someone or something that is not present. Many odes begin this way. Consider Keats's "Ode on a Grecian Urn," for example: "Thou still unravished bride of quietness," and "Ode to Psyche": "O Goddess! hear these tuneless numbers."

Assonance: the repetition of vowel sounds usually internally rather than initially. "Her goodly eyes like sapphires shining bright." Here the poet, Spenser, wants the entire focus on the blue eyes, the crispness, and the light.

Bathos: deliberate anticlimax to make a definite point or draw attention to a falseness. The most famous example is from Pope's "Rape of the Lock": "Here thou, great Anna! whom three realms obey, /Dost sometimes counsel take—and sometimes tea."

The humor in the bathos is the fact that Anna is the Queen of England—she holds meetings in the room Pope describes but also indulges in the venerable English custom of afternoon tea. The fact that <u>tea</u> should rhyme with <u>obey</u> doubles the humor as the elongated vowel of the upper-class laconic English social group is also mocked.

Caesura: the pause, marked by punctuation (/) or not within the line. Sometimes the caesura (sometimes spelled cesura) comes at an unexpected point in the rhythm and gives the reader pause for thought.

Conceits: very elaborate comparisons between unlikely objects. The metaphysical poets such as John Donne were criticized for "yoking" together outrageous terms, describing lovers in terms of instruments, or death in terms of battle.

Consonance: similar to slant rhyme—the repetition of consonant sounds without the vowel sound repeated. Hopkins again frequently uses this as in "Pied Beauty": "All things counte<u>r</u>, o<u>r</u>iginal, spa<u>r</u>e, st<u>r</u>ange;… a<u>d</u>azzle, <u>d</u>im."

Diction: the word for word choice. Is the poet using formal or informal language? Does the poetry hinge on slang or a dialect? If so what is the purpose? Are the words "highfalutin" or low-brow? As always, the diction needs examining and questions like these answering.

Enjambment: the running-on of one line of poetry into another. Usually the end of lines are rhymed so there is an end-stop. In more modern poetry, without rhyme, poets often use run-on lines to give a speedier flow, the sound of the speaking voice or a conversational tone.

Hyperbole: is an obvious and intentional exaggeration. Donne's instruction to the woman he is trying to seduce not to kill the flea, by contrasting her reluctance with "a marriage" of blood within a flea, reinforces the hyperbole used throughout the poem:

> Oh stay, three lives in one flea spare,
> Where we almost, yea, more than married are.

This couplet is also a good example of an unexpected caesura for emphasis at the second pause.

Irony: plays an important role in voice or tone, inferring a discrepancy between what is said and what is meant. A famous example is Shelley's

"Ozymandias," which tells of the great ruler who thought that he and his name would last forever, but the traveller describes the huge statue in ruins with the inscription speaking truer than the ruler intended: "My name is Ozymandias, king of kings: /Look on my works, ye Mighty, and despair!"

Metonymy: a figure of speech in which a term is used to evoke or stand for a related idea. Example: "The pen is mightier than the sword." Pen and sword are metonymical designations for (the artful use of) words and (engagement in) physical battle.

Onomatopoeia: a device in which the word captures the sound. In many poems the words are those in general use: the whiz of fireworks; the crashing of waves on the shore; the booming of water in an underground seacave.

Oxymoron: a rhetorical device of epigrammatic form in which incongruous or contradictory terms are conjoined. Examples: "painful pleasure," "sweet sorrow."

Paradox: a situation, action, or statement that appears to be contradictory but that nevertheless holds true.

Pun: a play on words often for humorous or sarcastic effect. The Elizabethans were very fond of them; many of Shakespeare's comedies come from punning. Much of Donne's sexual taunting involves the use of the pun.

Sarcasm: when verbal irony is too harsh, it moves into the sarcastic realm. It is the "lowest form of wit" of course but can be used to good effect in the tone of a poem. Browning's dramatic monologues make excellent use of the device.

Synecdoche: when a part of an object is used to represent the entire thing or vice versa. When we ask someone to give us a hand, we would be horrified if they cut off their hand; what we want is the person's help, from all of the body!

Syntax: the ordering of words into a particular pattern. If a poet shifts words from the usual word order, you know you are dealing with an older style of poetry (Shakespeare, Milton) or a poet who wants to shift emphasis onto a particular word.

Tone: the voice or attitude of the speaker. Remember that the voice need not be that of the poet's. He or she may be adopting a particular tone for a purpose. Your task is to analyze if the tone is angry, sad, conversational, abrupt, wheedling, cynical, affected, satiric, etc. Is the poet including you in a cozy way by using "you," or is he accusing "you" of what he is criticizing? Is the poet keeping you at a distance with coldness and third person pronouns. If so, why? The most intriguing of voices is Browning's in his **dramatic monologues**: poems that address another person who remains silent. Browning brought this type of poetry to an art. Think of all the variations of voices and attitudes and be prepared to meet them in poetry.

TYPES OF POETRY

Having begun to grasp that poetry contains a great deal more than what initially meets the eye, you should now start thinking about the various types of poetry. Of course, when reading for pleasure, it is not vital to recognize that the poem in hand is a sonnet or a villanelle, but for the exam you may well be asked to determine what sort of poem is under scrutiny. Knowing the form of poem may dictate certain areas of rhyme or meter and may enhance the meaning.

Form

The pattern or design of a poem is known as **form**, and even the strangest, most experimental poetry will have some type of form to it. Allen Ginsberg's "A Supermarket in California" caused a stir because it didn't read like poetry, but on the page there is a certain form to it. Some poets even try to match the shape of the poem to the subject. Find in anthologies John Hollander's "Swan and Shadow" and Dorthi Charles' "Concrete Cat." Such visual poems are not just fun to look at and read but the form adds to the subject and helps the reader appreciate the poet's world view. **Closed form** will be immediately recognizable because lines can be counted and shape determined. The poet must keep to the recognized form, in number of lines, rhyme scheme, and/or meter. **Open form** developed from "vers libre," which name some poets objected to as it suggested that there was little skill or craft behind the poem, simply creativity, as the name suggests, gives a freedom of pattern to the poet.

Sonnets

The most easily recognized closed form of poetry is the **sonnet**, sometimes referred to as a **fixed form**. The sonnet always has 14 lines, but there are two types of sonnets, the Petrarchan (or Italian), and the Shakespearean (or English). The word sonnet in fact comes from the Italian word "sonnetto" meaning a "little song." Petrarch, the fourteenth century Italian poet, took the form to its peak with his sonnets to his loved one, Laura. This woman died before he could even declare his love, and such poignant, unrequited love became the theme for many Elizabethan sonnets. As a young man might telephone a young woman for a date in today's society, the Elizabethan would send a sonnet. The Petrarchan sonnet is organized into two groups: eight lines and six—the **octave** and the **sestet**. Usually the rhyme scheme is abbaabba-cdecde, but the sestet can vary in its pattern. The octave may set up a problem or a proposition, and then the answer or resolution follows in the sestet after a turn or a shift. The Shakespearean sonnet organizes the lines into three groups of four lines: **quatrains** and a **couplet** (two rhyming lines). The rhyming scheme is always abab cdcd efef gg, and the turn or shift can happen at one of three places or leave the resolution or a "twist in the tail" at the end.

Couplets

The couplet, mentioned earlier, leads us to a closed form of poetry that is very useful for the poet. It is a two-line stanza that usually rhymes with an end rhyme. If the couplet is firmly end-stopped and written in iambic pentameter, it is known as an **heroic couplet**, after the use was made of it in the English translations of the great classical or heroic epics such as *The Iliad* and *The Odyssey*. Alexander Pope became a master of the heroic couplet, sometimes varying to the 12-syllable line from the old French poetry on Alexander the Great. The line became known as the **Alexandrine**. Pope gained fame first as a translator of the epics and then went on to write **mock-heroic** poems like "The Rape of the Lock," written totally in heroic couplets which never become monotonous, as a succession of regularly stepped-out couplets can, because he varied the place of the caesura and masterfully employed enjambment.

Epics

Rarely in an exam will you be presented with an **epic** because part of the definition of the word is vastness of size and range. You may, however, be confronted with an excerpt and will need to recognize the structure. The translation will usually be in couplets and the meter regular with equal line lengths, because originally these poems were sung aloud or chanted to the beat of drums. Because of their oral quality, repetition plays an important part, so that if the bard, or singer, forgot the line, the audience, who had heard the stories many times before, could help him out. The subject deals with great deeds of heroes: Odysseus (Ulysses), Hector, and Aeneus, their adventures and their trials; the theme will be of human grief or pride, divided loyalties—but all "writ large." The one great English epic, *Paradise Lost*, is written by Milton and deals with the story of Adam and Eve and the Fall. Adam thus becomes the great hero. The huge battle scenes of *The Iliad* are emulated in the War of the Heavens when Satan and his crew are expelled into Hell; the divided loyalties occur when Adam must choose between obedience to God and love for his wife.

Ballads

On much simpler lines are the **ballads**, sometimes the earliest poems we learn as children. Folk or popular ballads were first sung as early as the fifteenth century and then handed down through generations until finally written down. Usually the ballads are anonymous and simple in theme, having been composed by working folk who originally could not read or write. The stories—a ballad is a story in a song—revolve around love and hate and lust and murder, often rejected lovers, knights, and the supernatural. As with the epic, and for the same reason, repetition plays a strong part in the ballad and often a repeated refrain holds the entire poem together. The form gave rise to the **ballad stanza**, four lines rhyming *abcb* with lines 1 and 3 having eight syllables and lines 2 and 4 having six. Poets who later wrote what are known as **literary ballads** kept the same pattern. Read Coleridge's "Rime of the Ancient Mariner" and all the elements of the ballad come together as he reconstructs the old folk story but writes it in a very closed form.

Lyrics

The earlier poetry dealt with narrative. The "father of English poetry," Geoffrey Chaucer, told stories within a story for the great *Canterbury Tales*. The Elizabethans turned to love and the humanistic battle between love of the world and love of God. Wordsworth and Coleridge marked a turning point by not only using "the language of men" in poetry but also by moving away from the narrative poem to the **lyric**. The word comes again from the Greek, meaning a story told with the poet playing upon a lyre. Wordsworth moves from story to emotion, often "emotion recollected in tranquillity" as we saw in "Daffodils." Although sometimes a listener is inferred, very often the poet seems to be musing aloud.

Part of the lyric "family" is the **elegy**, a lament for someone's death or the passing of a love or concept. The most famous is Thomas Gray's "Elegy Written in a Country Churchyard," which mourns not only the passing of individuals but of a past age and the wasted potential within every human being, no matter how humble. Often **ode** and elegy become synonymous, but an ode, also part of the lyric family, is usually longer, dealing with more profound areas of human life than simply death. Keats's odes are perhaps the most famous and most beloved in English poetry.

Specialized Types of Poetry

More specialized types of poetry need mentioning so that you may recognize and be able to explicate how the structure of the poem enhances the meaning or theme. For example the **villanelle**: a courtly love poem structure from medieval times, built on five three-line stanzas known as **tercets**, with the rhyme scheme aba, followed by a four-line stanza, and a **quatrain** which ends the poem abaa. As if this were not pattern and order enough, the poem's first line appears again as the last line of the 2nd and 4th tercets; *and* the third line appears again in the last line of the 3rd and 5th tercets; *and* these two lines appear again as rhyming lines at the end of the poem! The most famous and arguably the best villanelle, as some of the older ones can be so stiff in their pattern that the meaning is inconsequential, is Dylan Thomas's "Do not go gentle into that good night." The poem stands on its own with a magisterial meaning of mankind raging against death, but when one appreciates the structure also, the rage is even more emphatic because it is so controlled. A poem well worth finding for "reading for pleasure." In James Joyce's *A Portrait of the Artist as a Young Man*, writing a villanelle on an empty cigarette packet turns the young boy, Stephen Dedalus, dreaming of being an artist, into a poet, a "real" artist.

Said to be the most difficult of all closed forms is the **sestina**, also French, sung by medieval troubadours, a "song of sixes." The poet presents six six-line stanzas, with six end-words in a certain order, then repeats those six repeated words in any order in a closing tercet. Find Elizabeth Bishop's "Sestina" or W.H. Auden's "Hearing of Harvests Rotting in the Valleys" and the idea of six images running through the poet's head and being skillfully repeated comes across very clearly. You might even try working out a sestina for yourself.

Perhaps at this stage an **epigram** might be more to your liking and time scale because it is short, even abrupt, a little cynical and always to the point.

The cynical Alexander Pope mastered the epigram, as did Oscar Wilde centuries later. Perhaps at some stage we have all written **doggerel**, rhyming poetry that becomes horribly distorted to fit the rhymes, not through skill but the opposite. In contrast, **limericks** are very skilled: five lines using the anapest meter with the rhyme scheme: aabba. Unfortunately, they can deteriorate into types such as "There was a young lady from....," but in artful hands such as Shakespeare's (see Ophelia's mad song in *Hamlet*: "And will he not come again?") and Edward Lear's, limericks display fine poetry. Finally, if you are trying to learn all the different types of closed-form poetry, you might try an **aubade**—originally a song or piece of music sung or played at dawn—a poem written to the dawn or about lovers at dawn—the very time when poetic creation is extremely high!

Although the name might suggest open-form, **blank verse** is in fact closed-form poetry. As we saw earlier, lines written in blank verse are unrhymed and in iambic pentameter. Open-form poets can arrange words on the page in any order, not confined by any rhyme pattern or meter. Often it seems as if words have spilled onto the page at random with a direct address to the readers, as if the poets are cornering them in their room, or simply chatting over the kitchen table. The lines break at any point—the dash darts in and out—the poets are talking to the audience with all the "natural" breaks that the speaking voice will demonstrate. Open-form poets can employ rhyme, but sometimes it seems as if the rhyme has slipped into the poem quite easily—there is no wrenching of the word "to make it rhyme." Very often there is more internal rhyme as poets play with words, often giving the sensation they are thinking aloud. Open-form poetry is usually thought of as "modern," at least post-World War I, but the use of space on the page, the direct address of the voice, and the use of the dash clearly marks Emily Dickinson as an open-form poet, but she lived from 1830–1886.

DRAMA AND THEATER

The Glass Menagerie by Tennessee Williams begins when one of its four characters, Tom, steps into the downstage light and addresses the audience directly as though he were the chorus from a much earlier play. "I have tricks in my pocket, I have things up my sleeve," says Tom. "But I am the opposite of a stage magician. He gives you illusion that has the appearance of truth. I give you truth in the pleasant disguise of illusion."

To sit among the audience and watch a skillful production of *The Glass Menagerie* is to visit Tom's paradoxical world of theater, a magic place in which known imposters and stagecraft trickery create a spectacle which we know is illusion but somehow recognize as truth. Theater, as a performed event, combines the talents and skills of numerous artists and craftspersons, but before the spectacle must come the playwright's work, the pages of words designating what the audience sees and hears. These words, the written script separate from the theatrical performance of them, is what we call *drama*, and the words give the spectacle its significance because without them the illusion has neither frame nor content. Truth requires boundaries and substance. When Shakespeare's Hamlet advises actors just before their performance, he places careful emphasis on the importance of the words, cautioning the players to speak them "trippingly on the tongue." If all actions are not suited to the words, Hamlet adds, the performance will fail because the collaborative purpose combining the dramatist's literary art and the actors' performing art "is to hold as 'twere the mirror up to Nature."

COMPARISON OF DRAMA TO PROSE AND POETRY

Although drama is literature written to be performed, it closely resembles the other genres. In fact, both poetry and prose also can be performed, but as captivating as these public readings sometimes are, only performed drama best creates the immediate living "illusion as truth" Tom promises. Like fiction and narrative poetry, drama tells a tale—that is, it has plot, characters, and setting—but the author's voice is distant, heard only through the stage directions and perhaps some supplementary notes. With rare exceptions, dialogue dominates the script. Some drama is poetry, such as the works of Shakespeare and Molière, and all plays resemble poems as abstractions because both forms are highly condensed, figurative expressions. Even in Henrik Ibsen's social realism, the dramatic action is metaphorical.

A scene set inside a house, for instance, requires a room with only three walls. No audience complains, just as no movie audience feels betrayed by film characters' appearing ridiculously large. Without a thought, audiences employ what Samuel Taylor Coleridge called "a willing suspension of disbelief"; in other words, they know that the images before them are not real but rather representations, reflections in the mirror of which Hamlet speaks, not the real world ("Nature").

A play contains conflict which can be enacted immediately on the stage without any alterations in the written word. **Enacted** means performed by an actor or actors free to use the entire stage and such theatrical devices as sets, costumes, makeup, special lighting, and props for support. This differs from the oral interpretation of prose or poetry. No matter how animated, the public reader is not acting. This is the primary distinction between drama and other literary forms. Their most obvious similarity is that any form of literature is a linguistic expression. There is, however, one other feature shared by all kinds of narratives: the pulsating energy which pushes the action along is generated by human imperfection. We speak of tragic characters as having "flaws," but the same is true about comic characters as well. Indeed, nothing is more boring either on a stage or in a written text than a consistently flawless personality, because such characters can never be congruent with the real people of our everyday experiences. The most fundamental human truth is human frailty.

Although it can be argued that a play, like a musical composition, must be performed to be realized, the script's linguistic foundation always gives the work potential as a literary experience. Moreover, there is never a "definitive" interpretation. The script, in a sense, remains unfinished because it never stops inviting new variations, and among those invited to participate are individual readers whose imaginations should not be discounted. For example, when *Death of a Salesman* was originally produced, Lee J. Cobb played Willy Loman. Aside from the character's age, Dustin Hoffman's Willy in a revival 40 years later bore hardly any physical resemblance to Cobb's. Yet both portrayals "worked." The same could be said about the Willys created by the minds of the play's countless readers. Quite capable of composing its own visions and sounds, the human imagination is the original mirror, the place where all human truths evolve from perceived data.

Mimesis

Hamlet's mirror and Tom's truthful illusions are figures of speech echoing drama's earliest great critic, Aristotle, who believed art should create a **mimesis**, the Greek word for "imitation." For centuries this "mimetic theory" has asserted that a successful imitation is one which reproduces natural objects and actions in as realistic portrayal as possible. Later, this notion of imitation adopted what has been called the "expressive theory," a variation allowing the artist a freer, more individual stylized approach. A drama by Ibsen, for example, attempts to capture experience as unadorned raw sense, the way it normally appears to be. This is realistic imitation. As twentieth century drama moved toward examinations of people's inner consciousness as universal representations of some greater human predicament, new expressive styles emerged. The diversity in the works of Eugene O'Neill, Samuel Beckett, and Harold Pinter illustrate how dramatists' imitations can disrupt our sense of the familiar as their plays become more personally expressive. But the theater of Aristotle's time was hardly "realistic" in today's objective sense. Instead, it was highly stylized and full of conventions derived from theater's ritualistic origins. The same is true of medieval morality plays and the rigid formality of Japanese Kabuki theater, yet these differ greatly from each other and from ancient Greek and Roman dramas. In other words, imitating "what's out there" requires only that the form be consistent with itself, and any form is permissible.

PLOT STRUCTURE

Exposition

As with other narrative types, a play's **plot** is its sequence of events, its organized collection of incidents. At one time it was thought that all the actions within a play should be contained within a single 24-hour period. Few lengthy plays have plots which cover only the period of time enacted on the stage. Most plays condense and edit time much as novels do. Decades can be reduced to two hours. Included in the plot is the **exposition,** the revealing of whatever information we need in order to understand the impending conflict. This exposed material should provide us with a sense of place and time (**setting**), the central participants, important prior incidents, and the play's overall mood. In some plays such as Shakespeare's, the exposition comes quickly. Notice, for instance, the opening scenes in *Macbeth, Hamlet*, and *Romeo and Juliet*: not one presents us with a central character, yet each—with its witches or king's ghost or street brawl—clearly establishes an essential tension heralding the main conflict to come. These initial expositions attack the audience immediately and are followed by subsequent events in chronological order. Sophocles' *Oedipus Rex* works somewhat differently, presenting the central character late in the myth from which the play is taken. The exposition must establish what has come previously, even for an audience familiar with the story, before the plot can advance. Like Shakespeare, Sophocles must start his exposition at the beginning, but he takes a longer (though not tedious) time revealing the essential facts. Arthur Miller, in his *Death of a Salesman*, continuously interrupts the central action with dislocated expositions from earlier times as though the past were always in the present. He carefully establishes character, place, mood, and conflict throughout the earliest scenes; however, whatever present he places on stage is always caught in a tension between the audience's anticipation of the future and its suspicions of the past. The plots in plays like *Oedipus Rex* and *Death of a Salesman* tend not to attack us head-on but rather to surround us and gradually close in, the circle made tighter by each deliberately released clue to a mysterious past.

Complication and Crisis

Conflict requires two opposing forces. We see, for instance, how King Lear's irresponsible abdication and conceited anger are countered by Goneril and Regan's duplicity and lusts for power. We also see how Creon's excessive means for restoring order in Thebes is met by Antigone's allegiance to personal conscience. Fairly soon in a play we must experience some incident that incites the fundamental conflict when placed against some previously presented incident or situation. In most plays the conflict's abrasive conditions continuously chafe and even lacerate each other. The play's tempo might provide some interruptions or variations in the pace; nevertheless, conflicts generate the actions which make the characters' worlds worse before they can get better. Any plot featuring only repetitious altercations, however, would soon become tiresome. Potentially, anything can happen in a conflict. The **complication** is whatever presents an element capable of altering the action's direction. Perhaps some new information is discovered or a previously conceived scheme fails, creating a reversal of what had been expected. The plot is not a series of similar events but rather a compilation of related events leading to a culmination, a **crisis**.

Resolution

In retrospect we should be able to accept a drama's progression of actions leading to the crisis as inevitable. After the crisis comes the **resolution** (or **denouement**), which gives the play its concluding boundary. This does not mean that the play should offer us solutions for whatever human issues it raises. Rather, the playwright's obligation is to make the experience he presents to us seem filled within its own perimeters. George Bernard Shaw felt he had met this obligation when he ended *Pygmalion* with his two principal characters, Higgins and Eliza, utterly incapable of voicing any romantic affection for each other; and the resolution in Ibsen's *A Doll's House* outraged audiences a hundred years ago and still disturbs some people today, even though it concludes the play with believable consequences.

Terms such as **exposition, complication, crisis,** and **resolution,** though helpful in identifying the conflict's currents and directions, at best only artificially define how a plot is molded. If the play provides unity in its revelations, these seams are barely noticeable. Moreover, any successful creative composition clearly shows that the artist accomplished much more than merely plugging components together to create a finished work. There are no rules which all playwrights must follow, except the central precept that the play's unified assortment of actions be complete and contained within itself. *Antigone,* for instance, depicts the third phase of Sophocles' *Oedipus* trilogy, although it was actually written and performed before *Oedipus Rex* and *Oedipus at Colonus.* And although a modern reader might require some background information before starting, *Antigone* gives a cohesive dramatic impact independent from the other two plays.

CHARACTER

Examples of Characters from Hamlet

Essential to the plot's success are the characters who participate in it. Midpoint in *Hamlet* when Elsinore Castle is visited by the traveling theater company, the prince joyously welcomes the players, but his mood quickly returns to bitter depression shortly after he asks one actor to recite a dramatic passage in which the speaker recalls the fall of Troy and particularly Queen Hecuba's response to her husband's brutal murder. The player, caught by the speech's emotional power, becomes distraught and cannot finish. Left alone on stage, Hamlet compares the theatrical world created by the player with Hamlet's "real" world and asks: "What's Hecuba to him, or he to Hecuba,/That he should weep for her!" Under ordinary circumstances Hamlet's anxiety would not overshadow his Renaissance sensibilities, because he knows well that fictional characters always possess the potential to move us. As though by instinct, we know the same. We read narratives and go to the theater precisely because we want to be shocked, delighted, thrilled, saddened, titillated, or invigorated by "a dream of passion." Even though some characters are more complex and interesting than others, they come in countless types as the playwright's delegates to our imaginations and as the imitations of reality seeking our response.

Examples of Characters from Antigone

Antigone begins with two characters, Antigone and Ismene, on stage. They initiate the exposition through their individual reactions to a previous event, King Creon's edict following the battle in which Thebes defeated an invading army. Creon has proclaimed Eteocles and the others who recently died defending Thebes as heroes worthy of the highest burial honors; in addition, Creon has forbidden anyone, on penalty of death, from burying Polyneices and the others who fell attacking the city. Since Antigone, Ismene, Polyneices, and Eteocles are the children of Oedipus and Iocaste, the late king and queen, conflict over Creon's law seems imminent. These first two characters establish this inevitability. They also reveal much about themselves as individuals.

> ANTIGONE:... now you must prove what you are:
> A true sister, or a traitor to your family.
>
> ISMENE: Antigone, are you mad! What could I possibly do?
>
> ANTIGONE: You must decide whether you will help me or not.
>
> ISMENE: I do not understand you. Help you in what?
>
> ANTIGONE: Ismene, I am going to bury him. Will you come?
>
> ISMENE: Bury him! You have just said the new law forbids it.
>
> ANTIGONE: He is my brother. And he is your brother, too.
>
> ISMENE: But think of the danger! Think what Creon will do!
>
> ANTIGONE: Creon is not strong enough to stand in my way.
>
> ISMENE: Ah sister!
> Oedipus died, everyone hating him
> For what his own search brought to light, his eyes
> Ripped out by his own hand; and Iocaste died,
> His mother and wife at once: she twisted the cords
> That strangled her life; and our two brothers died,
> Each killed by the other's sword. And we are left:
> But oh, Antigone,
> Think how much more terrible than these
> Our own death would be if we should go against Creon

And do what he has forbidden! We are only women,
We cannot fight with men, Antigone!
The law is strong, we must give in to the law
In this thing, and in worse. I beg the Dead
To forgive me, but I am helpless: I must yield
To those in authority. And I think it is dangerous business
To be always meddling.

ANTIGONE: If that is what you think,
I should not want you, even if you asked to come.
You have made your choice, you can be what you want to be.
But I will bury him; and if I must die,
I say that this crime is holy: I shall lie down
With him in death, and I shall be as dear
To him as he to me.
It is the dead,
Not the living, who make the longest demands:
We die for ever...
You may do as you like,
Since apparently, the laws of the gods mean nothing to you.

ISMENE: They mean a great deal to me; but I have no strength
To break laws that were made for the public good.

ANTIGONE: That must be your excuse, I suppose. But as for me,
I will bury the brother I love.

ISMENE: Antigone, I am so afraid for you!

ANTIGONE: You need not be:
You have yourself to consider, after all.

ISMENE: But no one must hear of this, you must tell no one!
I will keep it a secret, I promise!

ANTIGONE: Oh tell it! Tell everyone!
Think how they'll hate you when it all comes out
If they learn that you knew about it all the time!

ISMENE: So fiery! You should be cold with fear.

ANTIGONE: Perhaps. But I am doing only what I must.

ISMENE: But can you do it? I say that you cannot.

ANTIGONE: Very well: when my strength gives out, I shall do no more.

ISMENE: Impossible things should not be tried at all.

ANTIGONE: Go away, Ismene:
I shall be hating you soon, and the dead will too,
For your words are hateful. Leave me my foolish plan:
I am not afraid of the danger; if it means death,
It will not be the worst of deaths—death without honor.

ISMENE: Go then, if you feel that you must.
You are unwise,
But a loyal friend to those who love you.

[Exit into the palace. ANTIGONE goes off…]

READING THE PLAY

All we know about Antigone and Ismene in this scene comes from what they say; therefore, we read their spoken words carefully. However, we must also remain attentive to dramatic characters, propensity for not revealing all they know and feel about a given issue, and often characters do not recognize all the implications in what they say. We might be helped by what one says about the other, yet these observations are not necessarily accurate or sincere. Even though the previous scene contains fewer ambiguities than some others in dramatic literature, we would be oversimplifying to say the conflict here is between one character who is "right" and another who is "wrong." Antigone comes out challenging, determined and unafraid, whereas Ismene immediately reacts fearfully. Antigone brims with the self-assured power of righteousness while Ismene expresses vulnerability. Yet Antigone's boast that "Creon is not strong enough to stand in my way" suggests a rash temperament. We might admire her courage, but we question her judgment. Meanwhile, Ismene can evoke our sympathies with her burden of family woes, at least until she confesses her helplessness and begs the Dead to forgive her, at which point we realize her objections stem from cowardice and not conscience.

Although we might remain unsettled by Antigone's single-mindedness, we soon find ourselves sharing her disdain for Ismene's trepidation, particularly when Ismene rationalizes her position as the more responsible and labels unauthorized intervention in royal decisions as "meddling" against the "public good." Soon, as we realize the issue here demands moral conscience, we measure Ismene far short of what is required. Quickly, though, Ismene is partly redeemed by her obvious concern for Antigone's well-being: "I am so afraid for you." Unaffected, Antigone retorts with sarcasm and threats, but her demeanor never becomes so impetuously caustic that we dismiss her as a conceited adolescent. In fact, we are touched by her integrity and devotion, seeing no pretensions when she says: "I am not afraid of the danger: if it means death,/It will not be the worst of deaths—death without honor." Ismene's intimation that loyalty and love are unwise counters Antigone's idealism enough to make us suspect that the stark, cruel world of human imperfection will not tolerate Antigone's solitary rebellion, no matter how selfless her motivation. At the same time we wonder how long Ismene could remain neutral if Antigone were to clash with Creon.

What immediately strikes us about Antigone and Ismene is that each possesses a sense of self, a conscious awareness about her existence and her connection with forces greater than herself. This is why we can identify with them. It may not always feel reassuring, yet we too can define our existence by saying "I am, and I am not alone." As social creatures, a condition about which they have had no choice, both Antigone and Ismene have senses of self which are touched by their identification with others: each belongs to a family, and each belongs to a civil state. Indeed, much of the play's conflict focuses on which identification should be stronger. Another connection influences them as well—the unbreakable tie to truth. This truth, or ultimate reality, will vary from play to play, and not all characters ever realize it is there, and few will define it the same way. Still, the universe which characters inhabit has definition, even if the resolution suggests a great human absurdity in our insufficient capacity to grasp this definition or, worse, asserts the only definition is the absence of an ultimate reality. With Antigone, we see how her sense of self cannot be severed from its bonds to family obligations and certain moral principles.

Theme

Characters with a sense of self and an identity framed by social connections and unmitigated truths dwell in all good narratives. As readers we wander within these connecting perimeters, following the plot and sensing a commentary about life in general. This commentary, the **theme,** places us within the mirror's image along with the characters and their actions. We look and see ourselves. The characters' universe is ours, the playwright would have us believe, for a while at least. If his art succeeds, we do believe him. But reading literary art is no passive experience; it requires active work. And since playwrights seldom help us decide *how* characters say what they do or interrupt to explain *why* they say what they do, what personal voice he gives through stage directions deserves special attention, because playwrights never tell as much as novelists; instead they show. Our reading should focus on the tone of the dialogue as much as on the information in what is said. Prior to the nineteenth century, dramatists relied heavily on poetic diction to define their characters. Later playwrights provided stage directions which detail stage activities and modify dialogue. Modern writers usually give precise descriptions for the set and costume design and even prescribe particular background music. But no matter when a play was written or what its expressive style is, our role as readers and audience is to make judgments about characters in action, just as we make judgments about Antigone and Ismene the first time we see them. We should strive to be "fooled" by the truthful illusion by activating our sensitivities to human imperfections and the potential conflicts such flaws can generate. And, finally, as we peer into the playwright's mirror, we seek among the populated reflections shadows of ourselves.

Types of Plays

When Polonius presents the traveling players to Hamlet, he reads from the theater company's license, which identifies them as

> The best actors in the world, either for tragedy, comedy, history, pastoral, pastoral-comical, historical-pastoral, tragical-historical, tragical-comical-historical-pastoral, scene individable or poem unlimited…

Shakespeare's sense of humor runs through this speech which sounds like a parody of the license granted Shakespeare's own company by James I, authorizing "the Arte and faculty of playing Comedies, Tragedies, histories, Enterludes, moralls, pastoralls, Stageplaies and Such others…" for the king's subjects and himself. The joke is on those who think all plays somehow can be categorized according to preconceived definitions, as though playwrights follow literary recipes. The notion is not entirely ridiculous, to be sure, since audiences and readers can easily tell a serious play from a humorous one, and a play labeled "tragedy" or "comedy" will generate certain valid expectations from us all, regardless of whether we have read a word by Aristotle or any other literary critic. Still, if beginning playwrights had to choose between writing according to some rigid strictures designating the likes of a "tragical-comical-historical-pastoral" or writing a play unrestricted by such rules (a "poem unlimited"), they would probably choose the latter.

Thought

All plays contain thought—its accumulated themes, arguments, and overall meaning of the action—together with a mood or tone, and we tend to categorize dramatic thought into three clusters: the serious, the comic, and the seriocomic. These distinctions echo the primitive rites from which theater evolved, religious observances usually tied to seasonal cycles. In the course of a year numerous situations could arise which would initiate dramatic, communal prayers of supplication or thanksgiving. Indeed, for humanity to see its fate held by the will of a god is to see the intricate unity of flesh and spirit, a paradox ripe for representation as dramatic conflict. And if winter's chill brings the pangs of tragedy and summer's warmth the delight of comedy, the year becomes a metaphor for the overall human condition, which contains both. Thus, in our attempts to interpret life's complexities, it is tempting to place the art forms representing it in precise, fixed designations. From this can come critical practices which ascertain how well a work imitates life by how well it adheres to its designated form. Of course, such a critical system's rigidity would limit the range of possible human experiences expressed on stage to a narrow few, but then the range could be made elastic enough to provide for possible variations and combinations. Like the old Ptolemaic theories which held that the Earth was the center of the Solar System, these precepts could work for a while. After a few centuries, though, it would become clear that there is a better way of explaining what a play's form should be—not so much fixed as organic. In other words, we should think of a play as similar to a plant's growing and taking shape according to its own design. This analogy works well because the plant is not a mechanical device constructed from a predetermined plan, yet every plant is a species and as such contains qualities which identify it with others. So just as Shakespeare could ridicule overly precise definitions for dramatic art, he could still write dramas which he clearly identified as tragedies, comedies, or histories, even though he would freely mix two or more of these together in the same play. For the purpose of understanding some of the different perspectives available to the playwright's examining eye, we will look at plays from different periods which follow the three main designations Shakespeare used, followed by a fourth which is indicative of modern American drama. A knowledge of *The Importance of Being Earnest*, *Othello*, *A Man for All Seasons*, and *Death of a Salesman* will be helpful.

COMEDY

Forms of Comedy

The primary aim of comedy is to amuse us with a happy ending, although comedies can vary according to the attitudes they project, which can be broadly identified as either **high** or **low**, terms having nothing to do with an evaluation of the play's merit. Generally, the amusement found in comedy comes from an eventual victory over threats or ill fortune. Much of the dialogue and plot development might be laughable, yet a play need not be funny to be comic. **Farce** is low comedy intended to make us laugh by means of a series of exaggerated, unlikely situations that depend less on plot and character than on gross absurdities, sight gags, and coarse dialogue. The "higher" a comedy goes, the more natural the characters seem and the less boisterous their behavior. The plots become more sustained, and the dialogue shows more weighty thought. As with all dramas, comedies are about things that go wrong. Accordingly, comedies create deviations from accepted normalcy, presenting incongruities which we might or might not see as harmless. If these incongruities make us judgmental about the involved characters and events, the play takes on the features of **satire**, a rather high comic form implying that humanity and human institutions are in need of reform. If the action triggers our sympathy for the characters, we feel even less protected from the incongruities as the play tilts more in the direction of **tragi-comedy**. In other words, the action determines a figurative distance between the audience and the play. Such factors as characters' personalities and the plot's predictability influence this distance. The farther away we sit, the more protected we feel and usually the funnier the play becomes. Closer proximity to believability in the script draws us nearer to the conflict, making us feel more involved in the action and less safe in its presence. It is a rare play that can freely manipulate its audience back and forth along this plane and still maintain its unity. Shakespeare's *The Merchant of Venice* is one example.

Example of a Comedy

A more consistent play is Oscar Wilde's *The Importance of Being Earnest*, which opened in 1895. In the following scene, Lady Bracknell questions Jack Worthing, who has just announced that Lady Bracknell's daughter, Gwendolyn, has agreed to marry him. Being satisfied with Jack's answers concerning his income and finding his upper-class idleness and careless ignorance about world affairs an asset, she queries him about his family background. In grave tones, the embarrassed Jack reveals his mysterious lineage. His late guardian, Thomas Cardew—"an old gentleman of a very charitable and kindly disposition"—had found the baby Jack in an abandoned handbag.

LADY BRACKNELL: A hand-bag?

JACK (very seriously): Yes, Lady Bracknell. I was in a hand-bag—a some-what large, black leather hand-bag, with handles to it—an ordinary hand-bag in fact.

LADY BRACKNELL: In what locality did this Mr. James, or Thomas, Cardew come across this ordinary hand-bag?

JACK: In the cloak-room at Victoria Station. It was given him in mistake for his own.

LADY BRACKNELL: The cloak-room at Victoria Station?

JACK: Yes. The Brighton line.

LADY BRACKNELL: The line is immaterial, Mr. Worthing. I confess I feel somewhat bewildered by what you have just told me. To be born, or at any rate bred, in a hand-bag, whether it had handles or not, seems to me to display a contempt for the ordinary decencies of family life that reminds one of the worst excesses of the French Revolution. And I presume you know what that unfortunate movement led to? As for the particular locality in which the hand-bag was found, a cloak-room at a railway station might serve to conceal a social indiscretion—has probably, indeed, been used for that purpose before now—but it could hardly be regarded as an assured basis for recognized position in good society.

JACK: May I ask you then what would you advise me to do? I need hardly say I would do anything in the world to ensure Gwendolyn's happiness.

LADY BRACKNELL: I would strongly advise you, Mr. Worthing, to try and acquire some relations as soon as possible, and to make a definite effort to produce at any rate one parent, of either sex, before the season is over.

JACK: Well, I don't see how I could possibly manage to do that. I can produce the hand-bag at any moment. It is in my dressing-room at home. I really think that should satisfy you, Lady Bracknell.

LADY BRACKNELL: Me, sir! What has it to do with me? You can hardly imagine that I and Lord Bracknell would dream of allowing our only daughter—a girl brought up with the utmost care—to marry into a cloak-room, and form an alliance with a parcel. Good morning, Mr. Worthing!

(LADY BRACKNELL sweeps out in majestic indignation.)

This dialogue between Lady Bracknell and Jack is typical of what runs throughout the entire play. It is full of exaggerations, in both the situation being discussed and the manner in which the characters, particularly Lady Bracknell, express their reactions to the situation. Under other circumstances a foundling would not be the focus of a comedy, but we are relieved from any concern for the child since the adult Jack is obviously secure, healthy, and, with one exception, carefree. Moreover, we laugh when Lady Bracknell exaggerates Jack's heritage by comparing it with the excesses of the French Revolution. On the other hand, at the core of their discussion is the deeply ingrained and oppressive notion of English class consciousness, a mentality so flawed it almost begs to be satirized. Could there be more there than light, witty entertainment?

TRAGEDY

Terms

The term "tragedy" when used to define a play has historically meant something very precise, not simply a drama which ends with unfortunate consequences. This definition originated with Aristotle, who insisted that the play be an imitation of complex actions which should arouse an emotional response combining fear and pity. Aristotle believed that only a certain kind of plot could generate such a powerful reaction. Comedy, as we have seen, shows us a progression from adversity to prosperity. Tragedy must show the reverse; moreover, this progression must be experienced by a certain kind of character, says Aristotle, someone whom we can designate as the **tragic hero**. This central figure must be basically good and noble: "good" because we will not be aroused to fear and pity over the misfortunes of a villain, and "noble" both by social position and moral stature because the fall to misfortune would not otherwise be great enough for tragic impact. These virtues do not make the tragic hero perfect, however, for he must also possess **hamartia**—a tragic flaw—the frailty which leads him to make an error in judgment which initiates the reversal in his fortunes, causing his death or the death of others or both. These dire consequences become the hero's **catastrophe**. The most common tragic flaw is **hubris**, an excessive pride that adversely influences the protagonist's judgment.

Often the catastrophic consequences involve an entire nation because the tragic hero's social rank carries great responsibilities. Witnessing these events produces the emotional reaction Aristotle believed the audience should experience, the **catharsis**. Although tragedy must arouse our pity for the tragic hero as he endures his catastrophe and must frighten us as we witness the consequences of a flawed behavior which anyone could exhibit, there must also be a purgation, "a cleansing," of these emotions which should leave the audience feeling not depressed but relieved and almost elated. The assumption is that while the tragic hero endures a crushing reversal somehow he is not thoroughly defeated as he gains new stature though suffering and the knowledge that comes with suffering. Classical tragedy insists that the universe is ordered. If truth or universal law is ignored, the results are devastating, causing the audience to react emotionally; simultaneously, the tragic results prove the existence of truth, thereby reassuring our faith that existence is sensible.

Example of a Tragedy

Sophocles' plays give us some of the clearest examples of Aristotle's definition of tragedy. Shakespeare's tragedies are more varied and more modern in their complexities. *Othello* is one of Shakespeare's most innovative and troublesome extensions of tragedy's boundaries. The title character commands the Venetian army and soon becomes acting governor of Cypress. He is also a Moor, a dark-skinned African whose secret marriage to the beautiful Desdemona has infuriated her father, a wealthy and influential Venetian, whose anger reveals a racist element in Venice which Othello tries to ignore. Iago hates Othello for granting a promotion to Cassio which Iago believes should rightfully be his. With unrelenting determination and malicious deception, Iago attempts to persuade

Othello that Desdemona has committed adultery with Cassio. The following excerpt catches Iago in the early stages of his successful manipulation:

IAGO: In Venice they [wives] do let heaven see pranks
They dare not show their husbands; their best conscience
Is not to leave 't undone, but keep 't unknown.

OTHELLO: Dost thou say so?

IAGO: She did deceive her father, marrying you;
And when she seem'd to shake and fear your looks,
She lov'd them most.

OTHELLO: And so she did.

IAGO: Why, go to, then;
She that so young could give out such a seeming,
To see her father's eyes up close as oak,
He thought 'twas witchcraft; but I am much to blame;
I humbly do beseech you of your pardon
For too much loving you.

OTHELLO: I am bound to thee forever.

IAGO: I see, this hath a little dash'd your spirits.

OTHELLO: Not a jot, not a jot.

IAGO: I' faith, I fear it has.
I hope you will consider what is spoke
Comes from my love. But I do see you're mov'd;
I am to pray you not to strain my speech
To grosser issues nor to larger reach
Than to suspicion.

OTHELLO: I will not.

IAGO: Should you do so, my lord,
My speech should fall into such vile success
As my thoughts aim not at. Cassio's my worthy friend—
My lord, I see you're mov'd.

OTHELLO: No, not much mov'd:
I do not think but Desdemona's honest.

IAGO: Long live she so! and long live you to think so!

OTHELLO: And yet, how nature erring from itself,—

IAGO: Ay, there's the point: as, to be bold with you,
Not to affect many proposed matches
Of her own clime, complexion, and degree,
Whereto, we see, in all things nature tends;
Foh! one may smell in such, a will most rank,
Foul disproportion, thoughts unnatural.
But pardon me; I do not in position
Distinctly speak of her, though I may fear
Her will, recoiling to her better judgment,
May fall to match you with her country forms
And happily repent.

OTHELLO: Farewell, farewell:
If more thou dost perceive, let me know more;
Set on thy wife to observe. Leave me, Iago.

IAGO: My lord, I take my leave. (Going)

OTHELLO: Why did I marry? This honest creature, doubtless,
Sees and knows more, much more, than he unfolds.

Notice that Iago speaks much more than Othello. This is typical of their conversations, as though Iago were the superior of the two. Dramatically, for Iago's machinations to compel our interests we must perceive in Othello tragic proportions, both in his strengths and weaknesses; otherwise, *Othello* would slip into a malevolent tale about a rogue and his dupe. Much of the tension in this scene emanates from Othello's reluctance either to accept Iago's innuendos immediately or to dismiss them. This confusion places him on the rack of doubt, a torture made more severe because he questions his own desirability as a husband. Consequently, since Iago is not the "honest creature" he appears to be and Othello is unwilling to confront openly his own self-doubts, Iago becomes the dominant personality—a situation which a flawless Othello would never tolerate.

HISTORY

The playwright's raw data can spring from any source. A passion play, for instance, is a dramatic adaptation of the Crucifixion as told in the gospels. A history play is a dramatic perspective of some event or series of events identified with recognized historical figures. Television docudramas are the most recent examples. Among the earliest histories were the chronicle plays which flourished during Shakespeare's time and often relied on *Chronicles* by Raphael Holinshed, first published in 1577. Holinshed's volumes and similar books by others glorified English history and were very popular throughout the Tudor period, especially following the defeat of the Spanish Armada. Similarly, Shakespeare's *Henry V* and *Henry VIII* emphasize national and religious chauvinism in their treatments of kings who, from a more objective historical perspective, appear less than nobly motivated. These plays resemble romantic comedies with each one's protagonist defeating some adversary and establishing national harmony through royal marriage. *King Lear* and *Macbeth*, on the other hand, movingly demonstrate Shakespeare's skill at turning historical figures into tragic heroes.

Example of a History Play

Ever since the sixteenth century history plays have seldom risen above the level of patriotic whitewash and political propaganda. Of course there are notable exceptions to this trend: Robert Bolt's *A Man for All Seasons* is one. The title character, Sir Thomas More, is beheaded at the play's conclusion, following his refusal to condone Henry VIII's break from the Roman Catholic Church and the king's establishment of the Church of England with the monarch as its head. Henry wants More to condone these actions because the Pope will not grant Henry a divorce from Queen Catherine so that he can marry Anne Boleyn, who the king believes will bear him the male heir he desperately wants. The central issue for us is not whether More's theology is valid but whether any person of conscience can act freely in a world dominated by others far less principled. In Henry's only scene he arrives at Sir Thomas's house hoping his Lord Chancellor will not disappoint him:

[music in background]

HENRY: Son after son she's borne me, Thomas, all dead at birth, or dead within a month; I never saw the hand of God so clear in anything... I have a daughter, she's a good child, a well-set child—But I have no son. (He flares up). It is my bounden duty to put away the Queen, and all the Popes back to St. Peter shall not come between me and my duty! How is it that you cannot see? Everybody else does.

MORE: (Eagerly) Then why does Your Grace need my poor support?

HENRY: Because you are honest. What's more to the purpose, you're known to be honest... There are those like Norfolk who follow me because I wear the crown, and there are those like Master Cromwell who follow me because they are jackals with sharp teeth and I am their lion, and there is a mass that follow me because it follows anything that moves—and there is you.

MORE: I am sick to think how much I must displease Your Grace.

HENRY: No, Thomas, I respect your sincerity. Respect? Oh, man, it's water in the desert... How did you like our music? That air they played, it had a certain—well, tell me what you thought of it.

MORE: (Relieved at this turn; smiling) Could it have been Your Grace's own?

HENRY: (Smiles back) Discovered! Now I'll never know your true opinion. And that's irksome, Thomas, for we artists, though we love praise, yet we love truth better.

MORE: (Mildly) Then I will tell Your Grace truly what I thought of it.

HENRY: (A little disconcerted) Speak then.

MORE: To me it seemed—delightful.

HENRY: Thomas—I chose the right man for Chancellor.

MORE: I must in fairness add that my taste in music is reputably deplorable.

(From *A Man for All Seasons* by Robert Bolt. Copyright © 1960, 1962 by Robert Bolt. Reprinted by permission of Random House, Inc.)

To what extent Henry and More discussed the king's divorce and its subsequent events nobody knows, let alone what was actually said, although we can be certain they spoke an English distinctively different from the language in the play. Bolt's imagination, funneled through the dramatist's obligation to tell an interesting story, presides over the historical data and dictates the play's projections of More, Henry, and the other participants. Thus, we do not have "history"; instead, we have a dramatic perception of history shaped, altered, and adorned by Robert Bolt, writing about sixteenth century figures from a 1960 vantage point. But as the scene above shows, the characters' personalities are not simple reductions of what historical giants should be. Henry struts a royal self-assurance noticeably colored by vanity and frustration; yet although he lacks More's wit and intelligence, the king clearly is no fool. Likewise, as troubled as More is by the controversy before him, he projects a formidable power of his own. *A Man for All Seasons* succeeds dramatically because Bolt provides only enough historical verisimilitude to present a context for the characters' development while he allows the resultant thematic implications to touch all times, all seasons. When we read any history play, we should search for similar implications; otherwise, the work can never become more than a theatrical précis with a narrow, didactic focus.

MODERN DRAMA

Forms of Modern Drama

From the 1870s to the present, the theater has participated in the artistic movements reflecting accumulated theories of science, social science, and philosophy which attempt to define reality and the means we use to discern it. First caught in a pendulum of opposing views, modern drama eventually synthesized these perspectives into new forms, familiar in some ways and boldly original in others. Henrik Ibsen's plays began the modern era with their emphasis on **realism**, a seeking of truth through direct observation using the five senses. As objectively depicted, contemporary life received a closer scrutiny than ever before, showing everyday people in everyday situations. Before Ibsen, theatrical sets were limited, with rare exceptions, to castles and country estates. After Ibsen the farmhouse and city tenement were suitable for the stage. Ibsen's work influenced many others, and from realism came two main variations. The first, **naturalism**, strove to push realism towards a direct transformation of life on stage, a "slice of life" showing how the scientific principles of heredity and environment have shaped society, especially in depicting the plights of the lower classes. The second variation, **expressionism**, moved in a different direction and actually denied realism's premise that the real world could be objectively perceived; instead—influenced by Sigmund Freud's theories about human behavior's hidden, subconscious motivations and by other modernist trends in the arts, such as James Joyce's fiction and Picasso's paintings—expressionism imitated a disconnected dream-like world filled with psychological images at odds with the tangible world surrounding it. While naturalism attempts to imitate life directly, expressionism is abstract and often relies on symbols.

A modern play can employ any number of elements found in the spectrum between these extremes as well as suggest divergent philosophical views about whether humanity has the power to change its condition or whether any of its ideas about the universe are verifiable. Moreover, no work of art is necessarily confined within a particular school of thought. It is quite possible that seemingly incongruent forms can appear in the same play and work well. *The Glass Menagerie, A Man for All Seasons,* and *Death of a Salesman* feature characters and dialogue indicative of realistic drama, but the sets described in the stage directions are expressionistic, offering either framed outlines of places or distorted representations. Conventions from classical drama are also available to the playwright. As previously noted, Tom acts as a Greek chorus as well as an important character in his play; the same is true of the Common Man, whose identity changes from scene to scene. Playwrights Eugene Ionesco and Harold Pinter have created characters speaking and behaving in extraordinary ways while occupying sets which are typically realistic. In short, anything is possible in modern drama, a quality which is wholly compatible with the diversity and unpredictability of twentieth century human experiences.

Example of a Modern Drama

In a sense all good drama is modern. No label about a play's origin or form can adequately describe its content. Establishing the people, places, and thought within the play is crucial to our understanding. For the characters to interest us, we must perceive the issues that affect their lives, and eventually we will discover why the characters' personalities and backgrounds, together with their social situations, inevitably converge with these issues and create conflicts. We must also stay aware of drama's kinship with lyric poetry's subjective mood and tone, a quality dominating all plays regardless of the form. *Death of a Salesman* challenges the classical definitions of tragedy by giving us a modern American, Willy Loman, who is indeed a "low man," a person of little social importance and limited moral fiber. His delusionary values have brought him at age 64 to failure and despair, yet more than ever he clings to his dreams and painted memories for solace and hope. Late one night, after Willy has returned from an aborted sales trip, his rambling conversation with his wife Linda returns to the topic which haunts him the most, his son Biff.

WILLY: Biff is a lazy bum!

LINDA: They're sleeping. Get something to eat. Go on down.

WILLY: Why did he come home? I would like to know what brought him home.

LINDA: I don't know. I think he's still lost, Willy. I think he's very lost.

WILLY: Biff Loman is lost. In the greatest country in the world a young man with such—personal attractiveness, gets lost. And such a hard worker. There's one thing about Biff—he's not lazy.

LINDA: Never.

WILLY (with pity and resolve): I'll see him in the morning; I'll have a nice talk with him. I'll get him a job selling. He could be big in no time. My God! Remember how they used to follow him around in high school? When he smiled at one of them their faces lit up. When he walked down the street… (He loses himself in reminiscences.)

LINDA (trying to bring him out of it): Willy, dear, I got a new kind of American-type cheese today. It's whipped.

WILLY: Why do you get American cheese when you know I like Swiss?

LINDA: I just thought you'd like a change—

WILLY: I don't want change! I want Swiss cheese. Why am I always being contradicted?

LINDA (with a covering laugh): I just thought it would be a surprise.

WILLY: Why don't you open a window in here, for God's sake?

LINDA (with infinite patience): They're all open dear.

WILLY: The way they boxed us in here. Bricks and windows, windows and bricks.

LINDA: We should have bought the land next door.

WILLY: The street is lined with cars. There's not a breath of fresh air in the neighborhood. The grass don't grow any more, you can't raise a carrot in the backyard. They should've had a law against apartment houses. Remember those two beautiful elms out there? When I and Biff hung the swing between them?

LINDA: Yeah, like a million miles from the city.

WILLY: They should've arrested the builder for cutting those down. They massacred the neighborhood. (Lost) More and more I think of those days, Linda. This time of year it was lilac and wisteria. And then the peonies would come out, and the daffodils. What fragrance in this room!

LINDA: Well, after all, people had to move somewhere.

WILLY: No, there's more people now.

LINDA: I don't think there's more people. I think—

WILLY: There's more people! That's what's ruining this country! Population is getting out of control. The competition is maddening! Smell the stink from that apartment house! And another on the other side... How can they whip cheese?

In Arthur Miller's stage directions for *Death of a Salesman*, the Loman house is outlined by simple framing with various floors represented by short, elevated platforms. Outside the house the towering shapes of the city angle inward presenting the crowded oppressiveness Willy complains about. First performed in 1949, the play continues to make a powerful commentary on modern American life. We see Willy as more desperate than angry about his condition, which he defines in ways as contradictory as his assessments of Biff. In his suffocating world so nebulously delineated, Willy gropes for peace while hiding from truth; and although his woes are uniquely American in some ways, they touch broader, more universal human problems as well.

Drill: Literature

1. Though often considered a work for children, this nineteenth century classic continues to amuse and amaze adults interested in puzzles, poems, and hidden meanings.

   (A) *The Cat in the Hat Comes Back*
   (B) *Lord of the Rings*
   (C) *Alice in Wonderland*
   (D) *Gulliver's Travels*

2. Which of the following presents a series of entertaining monologues and bawdy tales told by individuals with a common purpose?

   (A) *The Canterbury Tales*
   (B) *The Martian Chronicles*
   (C) *Tales from the Twilight Zone*
   (D) *The Complete Works of Edgar Allan Poe*

3. Which of the following is generally recognized as the most accurate literary representation of American soldiers in battle?

   (A) Heller's *Catch-22*
   (B) Remarque's *All's Quiet on the Western Front*
   (C) Mailer's *The Naked and the Dead*
   (D) Crane's *Red Badge of Courage*

4. In which of the following works does the author deal with his or her blindness?

   (A) Dickinson's "My Life Closed Twice Before Its Close"
   (B) Malory's *Le Morte d'Arthur*
   (C) Milton's "When I Consider How My Light Is Spent"
   (D) Asimov's *Nightfall*

5. Which of the following can be seen as a fable in which the main characters represent political personages engaged in the conflict of political systems?

    (A) *Gulliver's Travels*
    (B) *The Time Machine*
    (C) *1984*
    (D) *Animal Farm*

6. Which of the following presents a fascinating survey of English life at the time of William the Conqueror?

    (A) *Edwin Drood*
    (B) *The Battle of Malden*
    (C) *Twickenham Garden*
    (D) *The Domesday Book*

7. Many of Shakespeare's works are based on which of the following philosophical and literary constructs?

    (A) The Platonic Ideal
    (B) The Great Chain of Being
    (C) The Duality of Man
    (D) Man's Inhumanity to Man

8. Which of the following was written by Charles Dodgson under a pen name?

    (A) *Tom Sawyer*
    (B) *The Heart of Darkness*
    (C) *Alice in Wonderland*
    (D) *Locksley Hall*

9. Which of the following poets is known for dramatic monologues such as "Andrea del Sarto"?

    (A) Alfred Tennyson
    (B) Robert Browning
    (C) S. T. Coleridge
    (D) P. B. Shelley

10. Which of the following American novelists was known for his love of deep sea fishing and bullfighting?

    (A) Norman Mailer
    (B) Theodore Dreiser
    (C) John Steinbeck
    (D) Ernest Hemingway

11. Which of the following novels revolved around the bureaucratic aspects of the pursuit of war?

    (A) Steinbeck's *Grapes of Wrath*
    (B) Heller's *Catch-22*
    (C) Remarque's *All Quiet on the Western Front*
    (D) Mailer's *The Naked and the Dead*

12. John Donne is considered one of the

    (A) decadents.
    (B) Beat poets.
    (C) metaphysicals.
    (D) restoration poets.

13. Considered one of the greatest expressions of Existentialism, this play by Beckett chiefly involves only two characters.

    (A) *The American Dream*
    (B) *The Zoo Story*
    (C) *The Fantasticks*
    (D) *Waiting for Godot*

14. Which of the following modern novels portrays a New England prep school as America is about to go to war?

    (A) *The Catcher in the Rye*
    (B) *A Separate Peace*
    (C) *Being There*
    (D) *Goodbye, Mr. Chips*

15. Which famous ship is the subject of a novel about World War II mutiny?

    (A) HMS *Bounty*
    (B) USS *Nautilus*
    (C) USS *Caine*
    (D) *Golden Hinde*

16. Which nineteenth century novel ends with a hanging at sea?

    (A) Melville's *Billy Budd*
    (B) Capote's *In Cold Blood*
    (C) Clark's *The Oxbow Incident*
    (D) Bierce's *An Occurrence at Owl Creek Bridge*

17. Some of Shakespeare's sonnets are presumed to be written to someone critics call

    (A) Lady Ruffles.
    (B) Dark Lady.
    (C) Lady Jane.
    (D) Lady Juliet.

Question 18 refers to the following verse:

The Silkworm and the Spider Houses make,

All their materials from their Bowels take...

Yet they are Curious, built with Art and Care,

Like Lovers, who build Castles in the Air,

Which ev'ry puff of Wind is apt to break,

As imaginations, when Reason's weak.

18. The poem is written in

    (A) iambic pentameter.
    (B) iambic pentameter and rhyming couplets.
    (C) iambic pentameter and concrete language.
    (D) feminine rhyme.

19. What are the rules for a villanelle?

    (A) A fixed form of 14 lines with a concluding couplet
    (B) Six stanzas of six lines each
    (C) A free-form poem of five tercets
    (D) A fixed form with five tercets and a quatrain

20. An aubade is a poem that greets

    (A) the moon.
    (B) the sun.
    (C) nightfall.
    (D) the dawn.

Literature Review

Answer Key

1.	(C)	6.	(D)	11.	(B)	16.	(A)
2.	(A)	7.	(B)	12.	(C)	17.	(B)
3.	(D)	8.	(C)	13.	(D)	18.	(A)
4.	(C)	9.	(B)	14.	(B)	19.	(D)
5.	(D)	10.	(D)	15.	(C)	20.	(D)

Detailed Explanations of Answers

Drill: Literature

1. **(C)** Lewis Carroll's *Alice in Wonderland*, written in the 1870s, has long been considered a children's book—though critics have spoken about it for years as a work of intricate imagination and always in need of revised analysis (as in the new work *The Annotated Alice*). Some have considered it a compendium of playful games—reversed poems, anagrams, riddles, and gibberish rhymes. Others see in the book drug references, psychological allegories, and a fantastic map of the unconscious.

   Each possible answer has been considered at some time a children's book, although *Gulliver's Travels* (D) is a political satire. Seuss's *The Cat in the Hat* (A) is of course very popular with adults, but only insofar as it provides fun tongue-twisters and the like. The storyline clearly is aimed at the younger set. Tolkien's work (B) may have been interpreted well by animators, but is certainly too difficult to be considered children's material.

2. **(A)** The key to this answer is the word "bawdy." Many students who have only a cursory knowledge of Chaucer's "Canterbury Tales" (A), do not realize that many of his stories ("The Wife of Bath's Tale," for example) are risqué, and, if written in modern English instead of Middle, and if composed by a writer of less importance, would probably be avoided by many high schools, and even some colleges. Chaucer's unifying premise is that the monologues and stories within stories are being told by travelers on a pilgrimage to the church of Canterbury. Poe (D) is certainly horrifying, but not bawdy. The same may be said about Rod Serling's wonderful stories (C). Bradbury's *Martian Chronicles* (B) is certainly a collection in which the stories have a singular purpose (describing the colonization of Mars by Earthmen), but, again, "bawdy" does not apply.

3. **(D)** This question may pose some difficulties, as all the choices are well-known war novels. The operative phrase here is "generally recognized," and for this, the student must be aware of the particular strength of Crane's *Red Badge of Courage* (D) as well as the recognized critical viewpoint that perhaps no other war story so accurately portrays the heat of battle. This point

is always emphasized when *Red Badge* is taught, for two reasons. Crane was a Realist writer who believed that his works should record sound, sight, and sensation as much as any painter would. Secondly, Crane was a newspaper reporter who was born after the Civil War (the subject of *Red Badge)*, and who never witnessed battle until after the book was published! Even so, veterans of the Civil War and other wars since regularly cite *Red Badge* for its accuracy.

Catch-22 (A) discusses the dizzying aspects of bureaucratized war; *All Quiet* (B) is certainly vivid in its portrayal of German soldiers during World War I. Mailer's *The Naked and the Dead* (C) has enjoyed great popularity by veterans of World War II, but is not recognized for the attention to the universality of emotions that suffuse all soldiers in battle.

4. **(C)** Though all of the choices here deal with different ways to experience darkness, this question requires specific biographical knowledge of John Milton (C). His famous short poem which speaks of "this dark world" and his desire in remaining years to serve "my Maker" contains the famous line: "They also serve who only stand and wait." While the title of Asimov's science fiction classic work (D) is tantalizing, *Nightfall* deals with darkness of a different kind: an eclipse. Malory's work (B), as its title indicates, deals with the death of the legendary King Arthur. The American poet Dickinson (A) is generally considered to be speaking about a lost love.

5. **(D)** Orwell's *Animal Farm* is perhaps the most artful of his works, because it combines fable with political commentary. Swift's *Travels* (A) does the same, but without a consistent representation of political systems in conflict, as in *Animal Farm,* in which Marxist-Leninism, Monarchy, and Western Democracy play out their conflict according to Orwell's interpretation of history from the Russian Revolution to World War II. Orwell's other great work, *1984* (C), is a more straightforward explication of the dangers of totalitarianism. H. G. Wells's work (B) offers intriguing possibilities: there are animal-like characters, and political systems in conflict, but one would be hard put to construe this novel as a fable.

6. **(D)** *The Domesday Book*, commissioned by William the Conqueror, which surveyed manor farms throughout England around the year 1086 C.E., presents the most accurate picture we have today of the early feudal society that William governed. Population estimates, lists of individuals and their trades, and a general mapping of the main cities, marketplaces,

and monasteries create a vivid picture. Donne's poem (C) was written in the 1600s. *Edwin Drood* (A) was Dickens' unfinished novel. *The Battle of Malden* (B) would be an interesting choice, but that it speaks of a specific Viking invasion of Britain in 991 C.E.

7. **(B)** Shakespeare respected a fundamental Elizabethan world construct: The Great Chain of Being. The Chain conjectured a world in which all the creatures of the Earth—including man—were set forth in increasing importance and decreasing distance to the angels and to God. Mankind was closest to the angels, but within our species was further ordering: kings, for example, were of a higher order than regular workmen, with lesser royalty somewhere in-between. Shakespeare's writings have regularly been seen to respect this order. Revolution is punished. Rash and irrational acts result in equally brutal retribution.

Platonism (A) holds that the real world is but a shadow of the ideal. Duality (C)—the existence of good and evil in the same individual—is not a key-note Shakespearean characterization, and Man's Inhumanity to Man (D) is a rather modern concept—far different in perspective from Shakespearean justice where those who disrupt the proper order of things get all the bad things they deserve.

8. **(C)** Lewis Carroll was the pen name of Charles Dodgson, the Oxford Don who wrote *Alice in Wonderland* for Alice Liddle ("Little Alice"), the daughter of a friend. It has been suggested that a pen name was a must for an Oxford mathematician with an academic reputation to uphold. The novel *Tom Sawyer* (A) was written by an author under the pen name Mark Twain. Tennyson's poetic work (D) was authored without the use of a pseudonym. Joseph Conrad (author of *Heart of Darkness*) is an anglicization of Jozef Konrad Korzeniowski.

9. **(B)** Robert Browning is known for his dramatic monologues, in which the poem takes the form of a speech by the subject—and in so doing, elucidates the personality of the individual. "Andrea del Sarto" is perhaps one of Browning's most famous poems in this form—a form which Browning is credited with developing. Tennyson (A), Shelley (D), and Coleridge (C) did not employ this technique.

10. **(D)** Ernest Hemingway was a very active sportsman, and was considered to personify "machismo" in both his personal and literary life. *The Old*

Man and the Sea, for example, was based on his experience deep-sea fishing off the coast of Cuba. Later research has tended to contradict this once popular conception of the author. Mailer (A) has also pursued sports like boxing, but not deep sea fishing or bullfighting. Dreiser (B) and Steinbeck (C) are not known as sportsmen, nor do they concentrate upon sport in their writing.

11. **(B)**   Heller's famous novel about American bomber pilots flying out of Sicily during World War II is based on a fundamental but changing principle of the battle group Catch-22. Briefly put, in order to be pulled off combat duty, a soldier would have to be crazy, but, of course, anyone who wanted to be removed could surely not be crazy, because the business of war is crazy. Remarque's novel (C) is about trench warfare during World War I; Mailer's (D) is about jungle warfare during World War II. Steinbeck's novel (A) has nothing to do with war, though its title might indicate that it does.

12. **(C)**   John Donne is considered the leader of the Metaphysical poets of the seventeenth century, which include Crashaw and Crowley. The Decadents (A) were writers at the end of the last century; the Beats (B) were Greenwich Village poets of the 1950s; Restoration poets (D), like Dryden, are of the period after 1660.

13. **(D)**   Beckett's play uses the conversation of two "bums" as they wait for Godot. Beckett's own beliefs (he and Sartre are considered fraternal Existentialists) and the content and interpretation of the play indicate Existentialist influence. Albee's plays—(A) and (B)—do not involve only two characters. *The Fantasticks* (C) is not Existentialist.

14. **(B)**   John Knowles' autobiographical work depicts the Devon School (actually St. Paul's in New Hampshire) just before and during the early stages of World War II. The impending war came to profoundly affect life "inside" the prep school, as teachers were called up, and then students began to help the war effort by volunteering in town. Salinger's work (A) took place at a Pennsylvania prep school in the late 1940s, and there are no references to war. (D) *Goodbye, Mr. Chips* is a famous story about an English prep school. Kosinski's work (C) is not relevant here.

15. **(C)**   *The Caine Mutiny* is based on a real incident that took place on an American minesweeper in the South Pacific during World War II. The

tyrannical Captain Queeg is replaced by his first officers for incompetence during battle. One of the most famous mutinies in the British navy occurred on the *Bounty* (A). Drake's ship (D) of the 1500s and the first atomic submarine (B) were never objects of mutiny.

16. **(A)**   All of the novels but one presented here involve a hanging, but only *Billy Budd* involves a hanging at sea. Billy, a foretopman aboard the HMS *Indomitable*, is sentenced to death for inadvertently killing John Claggart, the evil master at arms. (B) Capote's work involves the hanging of a murderer in the 1950s, Clark's (C) deals with a hanging in the Wild West, and Bierce's (D) an impromptu execution during the Civil War.

17. **(B)**   About one-third of Shakespeare's 108 known sonnets are written to someone who has come to be known as the "Dark Lady of the Sonnets." The themes of these poems are many, but consistent: love that endures through time; love of an older man for a younger woman; testimonials to beauty that endures even after death. There has been some discussion as to whether these poems are simply formulaic: that Shakespeare had no specific person in mind. Many of Shakespeare's sonnets are addressed to a young boy. The other possibilities here are simply incorrect, although Lady Juliet (D) is clearly meant to trip up the reader with a specific reference. (C) is a reference to a Yeats poem, and (A) is an invention.

18. **(A)**   Through your review you will now be familiar with all the various terms for meter and rhyme; note that iambic pentameter is the form favored by Shakespeare and Milton, easily recognized by the ten beat, stressed/unstressed syllabic line. (B) is incorrect because the poem is not entirely composed of rhyming couplets. Concrete language (C) is present early in the poem, but it moves to abstract language after line 3 for the contrast. Although some of the rhymes are feminine, the opening couplet is masculine, so (D) is incorrect.

19. **(D)**   You may not be familiar with this term so work your way through what you do know—pull in other works you have read: Stephen Dedalus in *Portrait of the Artist as a Young Man* demonstrates his skill as a young budding poet by writing a villanelle in a few minutes on the back of a cigarette packet! Choices (A), (B), and (C) do not meet the requirements of a villanelle, so they are incorrect choices.

20. **(D)**   Learn the various poetry forms from glossaries in anthologies—they may not cover all the terms but then you can distinguish and eliminate all those you do know that do not fit the definition. If the poem had greeted (A) the moon, (B) the sun, or (C) nightfall, then it would not be an aubade. Thus, all of these choices are incorrect.

CHAPTER 3

Visual Arts and Architecture Review

VISUAL ARTS AND ARCHITECTURE REVIEW

CLASSICAL PERIOD

More than 20,000 years before the start of recorded history, humans were creating art. In an effort to master their environment, Paleolithic artists painted graceful and realistic animals on the walls of caves (Paleolithic sites of Lascaux in France and Altimira in Spain) and carved stone statuettes of females, symbols of fecundity (the "Venus" figures of Willendorf, Lespugue, and Lausell, named for their European discovery sites). Neolithic people erected megalithic structures (Stonehenge in England) of huge stones to create an environment for religious ritual and the sophisticated measurement and tracking of celestial bodies.

With the rise of the great cities, stable agricultural communities, trade, political systems, and organized religion, art and architecture became the powerful tools of kings, priests, and commerce. An obsession with the afterlife caused the ancient Egyptians to build lavish tombs, especially for their pharaohs, or god-kings. These tombs appeared first in the form of pyramids, like the Great Pyramid of Khufu at Giza (c. 2500 B.C.E.), and later as mortuary temples built into the sides of cliffs, like that for Queen Hatshepsut at Deir El-Bahri (c. 1500 B.C.E.). The Egyptians also constructed magnificent temples at Karnak and Luxor, which are characterized by massive stone columns and heavy walls organized along a central axis. The monuments and carvings of the Mesopotamian kingdom of the Assyrians (about 1500–612 B.C.E.) recorded in powerful visual terms the warrior-kings' victories over rival nations and in the hunt. An extraordinary example of these stylized and meticulously decorative relief carvings (sculptural images only slightly raised from their stone surfaces) and the nearly naturalistic depiction of animals are the Lion-Hunting Reliefs of the palace of King Assurbanipal (Nineveh, c. 645–640 B.C.E.). Their exciting energy provides a striking contrast to the stately repose of most Egyptian art.

The classical period of architecture and art begins with, and is best represented by the civilization of the ancient Greeks, the city-state of Athens being the most dominant. The accomplishments of Athenian architecture, drama, philosophy, government, science, and sculpture laid the foundation for all of western European culture. The Greeks of the classical period were fascinated by physical beauty: their Olympian gods were fashioned in the human image, and a universe of perfection, guided by a master plan, was re-created in their idealized and gracefully proportioned sculptures, architecture, and paintings.

The amazing innovations of classical Greek art had their origins in earlier "Greek" civilizations—the Minoans of Crete and the people of mainland Mycenae. The Minoans flourished about 2500–1400 B.C.E. Their palace at Knossos is known for the lively, sinuous forms of their characteristic wall paintings, revealing a people enamored of acrobatics, leisure, and the beauty of the sea. The Minoans produced increasingly sophisticated terracotta and bronze figurines and painted vases. Both Crete and Mycenae were sources for many of the heroic tales of the ancient Greeks. For example, in the mazelike complex of the palace at Knossos, frescoes of bull-leaping games can be found, suggesting a basis for the Greek legend of the battle of Theseus with the Minotaur in the labyrinth. The Mycenaeans on mainland Greece were more warlike, but they traded with the Minoans, whose culture they adapted after the destruction of Crete by a natural disaster about 1450 B.C.E. The Mycenaeans produced beautiful work in gold, such as face masks, and artistically adopted the Minoans' ritual animal, the bull, but with a more aggressive character. Much of their best ornamentation was reserved for weapons. The culture of the Mycenaeans was destroyed about 1100 B.C.E. Only after three more centuries was a revitalized mainland-Greek culture able to spread trade (and settle colonies) throughout the Mediterranean, and organize into a system of city-states.

The earliest period of Greek city-state civilization, the Archaic, boasted exemplary art in the form of vase paintings, whose simple, precise, linear decoration evolved from the earlier, geometric style of the ninth and eighth centuries B.C.E.—zigzag, meandering, and triangular designs—to include, by the end of the eighth century, lively animals and humans. By the sixth century the dominant method of painting black figures as silhouettes on vases gave way to red figures with drawn-in details on a black background; pictured were heroes, athletes, feasts, weddings, and genre scenes. Contact with Egyptian culture in the mid-seventh century encouraged development of marble statuary in Greece: *The Lady of Auxerre* prefigures the standard forms of Greek *korai* and *kouroi* (life-sized draped female and nude male figures), and in its stylized pose resembles Egyptian statues. The emphasis on nakedness in the *kouros* led quickly to the virtuosic treatment of naturalistic representation. The *Kouros of Anavysos* (Attica, 540–515 B.C.E.) retains the static Egyptian pose but already displays great subtlety in muscular modeling. The famous *Kritios Boy* (c. 490- 480 B.C.E.) marks the apogee of Archaic sculpture, with an elegance and naturalism of form and relatively relaxed pose that befitted a culture increasingly dedicated to exalting beauty. It epitomizes the elements that were to characterize the spirit of ancient Greek art: respect for and re-creation of visual reality; a love of beauty in itself; and the application of rules and formulas to achieve representations of ideal beauty. The philosopher Plato's emphasis on the existence, in the spiritual realm or mind of God, of ideal forms for everything on earth was the basis of much artistic creativity in both art and architecture.

The Greek temple developed as a columnar structure, with sculptures on the pediments (triangular space just below the roof) and relief sculpture (usually of narrative action) on the rectangular panels of the friezes (metopes) that banded the buildings above the columns. The most perfect example of classical proportions is found in the great Greek temples on the Athenian Acropolis. In the Parthenon (fifth century B.C.E.), the architect Ictinus created a structure that represented the striving for perfection and ideal beauty in Athenian culture; refinement and perfect proportions are achieved by subtle curvatures in the relation of vertical elements and the tapering of the Doric columns. The style and elements of the Parthenon and other Greek buildings (such as the Erechtheion and the Temple of Athene Nike, also on the Acropolis) provided the forms—from the three major classical orders of columns (Doric, Ionic, and Corinthian) to pediments and sculptural friezes (relief sculptures in realistic narratives)—for two millennia of Western architecture.

The turning point for Greek sculpture came with the preeminence of Athens, after that city's victory over the Persians in the early fifth century. The classical period of the next hundred years boasted the great tragic playwrights Euripides, Aeschylus, and Sophocles, the historians Thucydides and Herodotus, and the moral philosophers Plato and Aristotle. Pericles established Athenian democracy and built a massive complex on the Acropolis, including the Parthenon (447–432 B.C.E.). Under the direction of the sculptor Phydias (d. 432 B.C.E.) there were created ninety-two figures in high relief on the metopes, in mythological combat scenes; sculptural figures on the pediments are characterized by fluid movement and dynamic drapery. Many Greek sculptures are known through Roman marble copies, notably Myron's *Discobolos* (c. 400 B.C.E.), a masterpiece of ideal grace and potential action.

In the fourth century the Greek city-states warred upon one another, and Macedonia prevailed, first under Philip II, then under his son Alexander, who by 323 B.C.E. had expanded the Greek empire to include Persia. The art of this period is characterized by greater naturalism, a wider variety of poses and of emotional display, and the intricate play of drapery. Praxiteles (*Hermes and the Infant Dionysus,* c. 350–330 B.C.E.) was skilled in portraying the human body in a rhythmic curve; he produced the first free-standing lifesize female nude, *The Cnidian Aphrodite* (known from a marble copy; originally c. 350–330 B.C.E.). Scopus was known for his naturalistic portraiture, notably the statues on the tomb of Mausolos at Halicarnassus (c. 353 B.C.E.).

During the Hellenistic period (323–31 B.C.E.), Greek culture spread throughout the Mediterranean. Art was characterized by new freedoms, insistent naturalism, more genre subjects (not merely heroic figures, but old women, sportsmen, etc.), less symmetry, and emphasis on technical virtuosity and the depiction of movement. Examples are the Altar of Zeus at Pergamum (180–150 B.C.E.), especially the *Battle of the Gods and Giants* frieze—a tour-de-force of light and shade, whirling movement, and expressive musculature and gestures. One of the most famous of Hellenistic sculptures is also from Pergamum: *The Dying Gaul* (c. 200 B.C.E.), an ultranaturalistic genre piece, with its shaggy hair and palpable agony. Few examples of Greek painting survive, but notable painters were Apelles and Nikias in the fourth century B.C.E. Many works, however, survive in later mosaic copies, such as the Alexander painting by Philoxenos (about 300 B.C.E.), found at Pompeii in a mosaic copy (90 B.C.E.): it depicts Alexander the Great's dramatic meeting with the Persian king Darius in battle—and brilliantly conveys depth, light, and shade.

The Romans adopted much of the art and architectural forms of ancient Greece. The culture of Rome excelled in engineering and building, whose purpose it was to efficiently organize a vast empire and to provide an aesthetic environment for private and public use. The Romans built temples, roads, bath complexes, civic buildings, palaces, and aqueducts.

The cult of individual prestige and power was of major significance in Roman culture, and thus many of the statues were personalized and realistic. Greek ideal beauty was replaced by monuments and portraiture exalting specific personalities. The decoration of homes and public places by paintings and mosaics reflects the importance of a leisure-oriented "consumer" lifestyle. The paintings of Pompeii and Herculaneum (both towns victims of the Mt. Vesuvius eruption in 79 C.E.) reveal the Roman mastery of realistic form and modeling, of inspired decorative elements, and attempts at convincing spatial relationships. Roman architecture's strides emanated from the value placed on engineering and include innovations important for later centuries. The first-century development of the dome—a major engineering and artistic contribution to world architecture—for public buildings was important for the Renaissance and later periods, when the writings of the great Roman architect Vitruvius (first century B.C.E.) were widely studied. The Roman basilica (an oblong building ending in a semicircular apse) was the basis for church architecture during the early Christian and medieval periods (300–1300).

Roman culture dates from the time of the mythical founding of Rome by Romulus and Remus in 753 B.C.E. Roman territory gradually expanded to include the Etruscan, or native Italian, culture in the fourth century, the Greek colonies in southern Italy in the third, and continuous expansion throughout the Mediterranean world until the height of Roman power in 100 C.E. under the emperor Trajan. Roman art was heavily influenced by the Greeks, especially after the sack of Syracuse in 212 B.C.E., when Greek artistic treasures—including the artists themselves—began pouring into Rome. While Greek forms were adopted, Greek ideas of beauty and perfection were not: Roman art served to provide luxury, as status symbols, and to enhance social position. Portraiture became very important, and the Romans eagerly adopted the innovation of the portrait bust from the Etruscans. Significant early busts are the *Capitoline Brutus* (third century B.C.E.) and *Pompey* (c. 50 B.C.E.), the earliest realistic likeness of a major Roman historical figure. In the Augustan age (first century C.E.), Greek prototypes were readopted to portray an idealized emperor. One of the most famous sculptures of the Roman empire is the *Laocoon* (first century C.E.), usually attributed to three Greek artists from Rhodes (Agesander, Athenodorus, and Polydorus): in this masterful, energetic, and dynamic composition (in the Hellenistic style of Pergamum), serpents sent by Apollo slay Laocoon and his sons. Examples of Roman painting fortunately still exist, due to their preservation by the hardened volcanic ashes of the destroyed southern towns of Pompeii and Herculaneum. The decorative paintings at Pompeii, such as those at the House of the Vettii (before 79 C.E.), depict realistically modeled humans in convincing landscapes, portraits of real characters, and the Roman fondness for trompe l'oeil —painting intended to fool the eye into believing one is seeing real three-dimensional objects, architectural details, or natural vistas.

The major Roman artistic statements were related to monumental architecture and sculpture. The Arch of Titus (c. 81 C.E.) describes the emperor's triumph and the spoils of Jerusalem in deep relief sculpture, a narrative of real events with lively poses. Trajan's Column (98–117 C.E.) is unlike any previous carved record: its story of Trajan's campaigns against the Dacians winds unbroken for more than 650 feet up the shaft of the 125-foot-high marble column; in low relief, like most ancient sculpture it was originally heightened with color. In the golden age of the empire, the emperor Hadrian (reigned 117–138 C.E.), an admirer of Greek culture, built extensively. His villa at Tivoli is a magnificent complex of baths, temples, gardens, and pavilions, and he commissioned the rebuilding of the greatest achievement of Roman architecture, the Pantheon in Rome. The relatively plain exterior of this temple "of all the gods" belies the astonishing technical accomplishment and interior decorative details. Inside, the wall of the main circular section of the building is characterized by rectangular niches and apses, small tabernacles, and a wealth of variously colored marble panels. A massive concrete dome is broken by a central oculus, or hole, that lets in an ever-moving shaft of light. Another imperial monument, to the emperor Marcus Aurelius, is the best surviving equestrian statue from antiquity, and the inspiration for the revival of the form in Renaissance Italy by Donatello.

The late classical era overlaps the early Christian period. Beginning with the monuments in the age of Constantine—the first Roman emperor to embrace Christianity—a new emphasis can be seen, more on spiritual meaning and symbolism, less on the realistic depiction of the world and personal accomplishments. The commanding bust of Constantine (c. 313 C.E.) is a large (eight feet high) head expressive of personality and majesty, but its huge eyes already represent the medieval Christian concept of "windows of the soul" to express inner being. In the Arch of Constantine, celebrating the emperor's victory over Maxentius in 312, there is little attempt at a cohesive style or realism, with many sculptural elements from other architecture physically incorporated. Already the familiar medieval large heads and squat figures are apparent. Similar de-emphasis of the real world and a burgeoning Christian iconography (salvation of souls, divine intervention, miracles) can be found in the art of the Catacombs, underground burial chambers outside Rome (200-400 C.E.); the image of Apollo was adopted to represent Christ in a small wall painting, *The Good Shepherd,* in the Catacomb of Priscilla.

MEDIEVAL AND RENAISSANCE PERIODS

During the Middle Ages, the Romans' cultural and artistic legacy lived on in the Byzantine empire, whose capital was the magnificent city of Constantinople (modern Istanbul, in Turkey). This empire lasted for a thousand years after the fall of the western Roman empire. Perhaps the greatest of the Byzantine emperors was Justinian (527–565 C.E.), who reaffirmed the empire and made Ravenna, a northeast Italian city on the Adriatic coast, the government center of the West. In Ravenna the important surviving art in the Byzantine style is at its finest. There, the seventh-century church of San Vitale echoes the mosaic mastery of the eastern Roman, or Byzantine, empire in Constantinople: its grandiose apse mosaics of glittering gold and sparkling color include walls depicting Emperor Justinian and Empress Theodora. The Byzantine style was meant to convey a supernatural, otherworldly effect. The most important church in Constantinople was Hagia Sophia, designed by the architects Isidorus and Anthemius—a magical, soaring structure with a beautiful dome, commissioned along with many other buildings by the Emperor Justinian in the mid-sixth century.

During the Dark Ages (about fifth to eighth centuries), Celtic artists of Ireland, Scotland, and northern Britain, especially in the monasteries, kept Western art alive in stone carvings and crosses with interlace patterns, and in magnificent illuminated manuscripts, whose design was influenced by Celtic metalwork. Among these manuscripts are the Book of Durrow (680), the Lindisfarne Gospels (c. 690), and the Book of Kells (c. 800—the most sophisticated and flamboyant, with four hundred decorative initial letters). The end of the Dark Ages was officially marked by the coronation of the Frankish king Charlemagne as Holy Roman Emperor by the pope on Christmas Day 800. Charlemagne, whose capital was at Achen (Aix-la-Chapelle), aspired to create an empire that rivaled the Roman empire as well as reviving classical culture and learning. He acquired ancient Roman sculptures, established schools, gathered around him the scholars Alcuin and Theodulf, and commissioned illuminated manuscripts. Some of the finest of the early ninth-century manuscripts are the Utrecht Psalter, the Ebbo Gospels, and the Lorsch Gospels. The empire lapsed after Charlemagne but was revived by Otto the Great (after his 955 victory over the Hungarians). This period is marked by a revival of early Christian, Carolingian, and Byzantine art (Echternach Gospels, bronze doors at Hildesheim).

The Romanesque style of art and architecture was preeminent in the eleventh and twelfth centuries. A great expansion of building and sculpture occurred. It was the era of the First Crusade. Europe was more secure and settled, and there were more professional artisans, who traveled all over Europe. By then many local styles, including the decorative arts of the Byzantines, the Near East, and the German and Celtic tribes, were contributing to European culture. Common features of Romanesque churches are round arches, vaulted ceilings, and heavy walls that are profusely decorated—primarily with symbolic figures of Christianity, the realism of which for its creators had become less and less important and was, instead, subordinate to the message. Examples of the style are the abbey church in Cluny, France; Worms Cathedral (St. Peter's) in Germany; and Durham Cathedral in England. Sculpture, usually relief in stone, was an integral part of church architecture on portals (doorways) and capitals (column crowns). In France, prominent sculptural areas were around the door jambs and the semicircular area above the door, the tympanum. Romanesque sculpture grew out of the church almost organically, and was decoratively sophisticated. Examples are the tympanums at Sainte Foy in Conques and the Abbey of Moissac near Toulouse (the *Apocalypse*). The Great Tympanum depicting *Christ in Majesty* and the *Last Judgment* at St. Lazare (Autun Cathedral) is the work of Gislebertus, who signed his name. It is marked by an overall unity of design and an inventive use of narrative detail; it contains biblical scenes, allegories, and imagery from the mystery plays. One of the finest free-standing Romanesque sculptural works is the brass baptismal font of Renier de Huy, a work whose figures display realistic proportions and classical influence, thus pointing the way to the innovations of the Gothic and early Renaissance styles.

Gothic art flourished in Europe from the twelfth through the fifteenth centuries and was primarily a French and northern European style. The cathedrals in this style are some of the purest expressions of an age: they combine a continued search for engineering and structural improvement with features that convey a relentless verticality, a reach toward heaven, and the unbridled adoration of God. Soaring and airy, these cathedrals were constructed using such elements as flying buttresses and pointed arches and vaults, and are decorated by a profusion of sculptures and stained-glass windows that were, for the worshippers, visual encyclopedias of Christian teachings and stories. The first major Gothic church was Abbot Suger's Church of St. Denis, outside Paris (begun 1137–1144). The finest example of the Gothic use of stained glass is the decoration of Sainte Chapelle (c. 1245) in Paris, whose walls of stained glass create a jewel-like flood of heavenly light. Gothic art emphasized greater spirituality, as well as greater humanity and tenderness, than previous Christian art; its most important religious figure is the Virgin Mary. The style in sculpture displays grace and realism, and figures are often elongated to match the skyward-stretching form of the architecture. Rheims Cathedral, one of the masterpieces of the northern Gothic style, boasts some two thousand sculptures (c. 1230-1240). Other important Gothic cathedrals are Chartres, Beauvais, Bourges, and Amiens in France, and in England, Salisbury and Wells.

The work of Nicholas of Verdun at the end of the twelfth century reveals a classical style; the awakening of the spirit of humanism in Gothic art led to a new interest in the natural world and a revival of the classical tradition. The thirteenth and fourteenth centuries were a vital and exciting period that came to be considered both Gothic and proto-Renaissance. In northern Europe, life itself became more festive, the artisan and merchant classes achieved some status—among richer courts, tales of knights, and the great romances—all of which inspired the colorful and realistic paintings of the sumptuous books of hours (the Limbourg Brothers: *Les Très Riches Heures du Duc de Berry,* 1413–1416).

The Italian school of this period—from 1250 onward—provides the first glimmers of the Renaissance—in a new naturalism, plus an emphasis on wall decoration in fresco and the painting of altarpieces (panels—the forerunners of the easel paintings). The Florentine painter Cimabue (active 1272–1302) produced tempera paintings that signaled a clear movement toward the naturalistic treatment of human figures (*San Trinita Madonna*). Duccio (active 1278–1318) of Sienna painted the *Rucellai Madonna,* in which Mary is portrayed as a real human in real space, shown from the side. And Duccio's *Virgin in Majesty* (from the *Maesta* altarpiece, 1308–1311, for Siena Cathedral) has figures of even greater solidity, clearly inhabiting realistic space. Giotto (c. 1267–1337) was famed and successful in his lifetime; his work is often regarded as the beginning of Renaissance art in Florence. He is known for his ability to depict physical beings, dramatic and realistic details and gestures, human reactions, and real spatial arrangements. His *Ognissanti Madonna* shows real people beneath the drapery, as well as delicacy and grace and convincing spatial relationships. His Arena Chapel paintings in Padua depict the life story of the Virgin and Christ in a series of independent but continuous-narrative pictures, full of drama and psychological nuance. Giotto's other works include *The Life of St. Francis* paintings in the Bardi Chapel, Santa Croce, Florence (1316–1320) and *The Life of St. John the Baptist* in the Peruzzi Chapel. In the fourteenth century, Sienese painters were among the leaders in innovation in the new realism: Simone Martini (1285–1344; *The Annunciation*) and Ambrogio Lorenzetti (active first half of the fourteenth century; *The Presentation in the Temple* and *The Allegory of Good Government* and other frescoes in the Palazzo Publico in Sienna).

Lines were often blurred between the Gothic and the early Renaissance in sculpture. In Pisa, innovations were made in the thirteenth and fourteenth centuries by Nicola Pisano (active 1258–1284) and his son Giovanni. Nicola created the marble pulpit for the Baptistery at Pisa (he signed and dated it); based on

classical models, it has crowded figures, multiple poses, and realistic movement. His pulpit for Sienna Cathedral is marked by even more animated movement. Giovanni's Pisa Cathedral pulpit (1302–1310) contains a naked female
figure and merges Gothic and classical influences.

In fifteenth-century Florence, first among all the newly rich and independent Italian cities, wealthy patrons, merchants, and nobles consciously revived
classical art and philosophy, set humankind at the center of life, and made cel-
ebrations of civic pride of the highest importance. The technical discovery of
proportion was used in architecture and art, and the great artists of the Renaissance often combined talents in all fields. Architecture, in the hands of Filippo
Brunelleschi and Leon Battista Alberti, revived the Greco-Roman elements and
took a scientific, ordered approach, one similarly expressed in painting with the
emphasis on the calculated composition of figures in space known as perspective. Brunelleschi (1377–1440) invented single-vanishing-point perspective,
and the dome he designed for Florence Cathedral (added 1420–36) was a symbol of both technical and classical rebirth. Alberti (1404–1472) was an important early Renaissance architect (Palazzo Rucellai, Florence, 1446–55) and
wrote on the mathematics of perspective in *On Painting* (1435). Michelozzo
(1396–1472) designed the first great Renaissance palace, the Palazzo Medici
in Florence. In Rome, Donato Bramante (1444–1514) designed—in addition
to ambitious plans for rebuilding St. Peter's—a structure for the spot where St.
Peter was crucified, the Tempietto (San Pietro in Montorio, 1502). It is the first
Renaissance building created in imitation of a circular Roman temple and is
vaulted by a hemispherical dome and encircled by classical columns. Andrea
Palladio (1508–1580), the writer of the most influential treatise on architecture
for centuries *(The Four Books of Architecture)*, created in the Villa Rotonda
in Vincenza (begun 1567–69) a perfect unity of geometric forms: four temple
fronts face the four compass points and surround an inner cube of rooms; the
central dome provides a symbol of unity.

The sculptor Lorenzo Ghiberti won the 1401 competition for the bronze
doors of the Florence Baptistery—his relief-sculpted panels boast graceful,
realistic, classical figures. Other important sculptors were Nanni di Banco and
Jacopo della Quercia. The greatest of the early Renaissance sculptors, however,
was Ghiberti's pupil Donatello (1386–1466), whose work was not only classically inspired and realistic, but highly theatrical and full of psychological
undertones. *St. George* is a lifesize marble statue of a handsome hero, full of
earthly life and potential power. His *David,* one of the most famous Renaissance bronze sculptures, marks the revival of the classical free-standing nude

male—sinuous in form, in an elegant, almost impish pose. His *Gattamelata* (1443–48) revived the free-standing equestrian statue, based on the ancient Marcus Aurelius statue in Rome.

The first great painter of the Renaissance was Masaccio (1401–c.1428). In the *Holy Trinity* fresco for the Church of Santa Maria Novella in Florence, he used perspective based on Brunelleschi's ideas; there is a clear light source that unifies the whole, plus classical details, such as the Corinthian pilasters framing Ionic columns. In the *Tribute Money* (fresco for the Brancacci Chapel in Santa Maria Carmine in Florence) real characters in expressive poses inhabit a realistic landscape (based on the hills east of Florence), all united by Brunelleschian perspective. Other important early Renaissance painters were Paolo Uccello, who was obsessed by perspective (*The Battle of San Romano,* c. 1455); Fra Angelico (c. 1395–1455), whose work was colorful and calmly sweet (*The Deposition; The Annunciation*); Fra Filippo Lippi (1406–1469; *The Madonna and Child with Two Angels);* and Piero della Francesca (c. 1416–1492; *The Flagellation of Christ; The Resurrection* [with its foreshortened sleeping soldiers]). More than any other painter, Botticelli (c.1445–1510) epitomized the spirit of the early Renaissance. A favorite of the Medicis, his work is intensely religious and allegorical and insistent on recalling the images of classical antiquity. He painted many Madonnas (which since the nineteenth century have been admired for their sweet countenances), as well as humanist allegories of classical inspiration: *The Birth of Venus* (the ultimate symbolic depiction of the period's rebirth) and *Primavera* (a visual celebration of spring). Other notable artists of this period were Andrea Mantegna (known for his bold experiments in perspective), who worked in Mantua (Ducal Palace paintings), and Giovanni Bellini of Venice (*St. Francis in Ecstasy*).

The three pillars of the High Renaissance of the early sixteenth century are Leonardo da Vinci, Michelangelo, and Raphael. Leonardo's intellectual curiosity led him to make scientific deductions (and sketch out inventions such as flying machines) based on observed reality; these he recorded in his famous Notebooks. In addition to *The Last Supper* (1495–98) and the *Mona Lisa* (1503), he painted *The Virgin of the Rocks* (1483–85), which epitomizes his artistic approach: strange and metaphysical, suffused with mysterious light, the picture uses the technique of sfumato, a smoky-shadowy way of modeling form.

Michelangelo, too, excelled in many fields: he was a poet, painter, sculptor, and architect. In addition to his architectural designs of the Medici Chapel in San Lorenzo and the Laurentian Library, he redesigned St. Peter's in Rome, adding an enormous dome and completing the work previously planned by Bramante and Raphael. His sculptures (*David; Moses;* the Tomb of Giuliano de' Medici), which are powerful and heroic, seek to portray bodily perfection, and convey a perfect synthesis of the human and the divine—the epitome of the Neoplatonic philosophy of the Renaissance (that is, the body expresses the spirit). The Sistine Chapel frescoes in the Vatican in Rome are his masterpieces: in painting a complex system of dynamic figures full of raw human power and divine spirit, Michelangelo created some of the world's most unforgettable artistic images (*The Creation of Adam; The Creation of Eve;* the Sybils; the Prophets; *The Creation of the World,* all on the ceiling [1508–12], as well as *The Last Judgment,* on the wall [1534–41]). For centuries the paintings of Raphael (1483–1520) have been the measure of artistic perfection. Raphael's Madonnas are both spiritual ideals and clear personalities, set against a serene landscape, and represent perfect compositional balance (*The Madonna and Child with St. John* [c.1506] and *The Sistine Madonna* [1512]). In *The School of Athens* at the Stanza della Segnatura in the Vatican (1509–11), Raphael combines, in a massive composition of figures and architecture, elements of major Renaissance paintings—obvious perspective, classically inspired architecture, portraits of ancient philosophers, and even likenesses of Leonardo, Michelangelo, and himself. His *Transfiguration,* with its dramatic lighting, mixture of heavenly and earthly spheres, and floating figures in clouds, crowns the Renaissance ideal of art and is a blueprint for the pictorial elements used in Baroque art.

Venetian and northern Italian painters worked in highly personal styles, leading toward the style called Baroque. The Mannerists of the first half of the sixteenth century produced work full of exaggerations: floating angels, the confusion of illusion and reality, contorted and elongated figures, awkward spatial relationships, and strange lighting effects. The great Mannerists were Parmagianino (*The Madonna with the Long Neck*), Pontormo (*The Deposition*), and Bronzino (*Venus, Cupid, Folly, and Time*). Giulio Romano painted the fantastic Sala dei Giganti in Mantua's Palazzo del Te, a structure he designed with typical Mannerist wildness: amidst classical perfection in form, massive stones jut out like monstrous ruins. In Parma, Correggio created pre-Baroque art full of drama and mysterious light, and incorporated floating angels (*The Adoration of the Shepherds*). Among the great Venetians were Bellini (the San Zaccaria Altarpiece) and Giorgione (an innovator in "mood painting": of pastoral classical worlds, a favorite subject of the Baroque and later Rococo artists; *The Tempest; Venus*). The giant among the Venetians is Titian (active c. 1500–1576), whose brilliant color and dynamic brushwork made him one of the most admired artists of his time and made his name synonymous with great art through the succeeding centuries. There are plenty of floating clouds and cherubs in Titian's paintings, and the importance of the female nude is evident in *The Rape of Europa, Sacred and Profane Love,* and *The Venus of Urbino* (significant because this female nude is not associated with a classical/mythological theme). Among his religious masterpieces are *The Assumption of the Virgin* and the *Pesary Madonna.* Drawing ever closer to the Baroque spirit were two other Venetians: Veronese, who specialized in vast pageants unfolding in a single, grand painting (*The Feast in the House of Levi*), and Tintoretto, whose unique canvases team with vibrant life and dramatic incident, from the intimate *Susanna and the Elders* (c. 1557) to the astonishing, turbulent, glowing scene of *The Last Supper* (1592–94).

The northern European Renaissance also displayed a renewed interest in the visible world, and works by Albrecht Dürer, Lucas Cranach, Matthias Grünewald, and Albrecht Altdorfer reveal an emphasis on the symbolism of minutely observed details and an accurate realism based on observation of reality rather than on prescribed rules. This unique northern emphasis can be seen as far back as the fifteenth century. Northern art, particularly in the Netherlands (later Flanders and Holland) and Germany, pursued a parallel course to that in Italy from the Gothic period to the Baroque era—but with a clear difference: the reawakening to the material world was less intellectual and less based on classical models than in the south. Rather, it was a realism based on the tastes of a rising wealthy merchant and middle class, delighting in their everyday lives. This joyous visual naturalism was marked by jewel-like color in painting. In sculpture, Claus Sluter (d. 1406) carved the Well of Moses, an innovative masterpiece of realism and human characterization. Jan van Eyck (c. 1385–1441) exemplified the continuous northern insistence on the symbolism of objects, on a naturalism so precious in its details and observation of reality that all paintings, whether portraits or religious scenes, seem to have real-life bourgeois persons and their possessions as subjects. Among van Eyck's vibrantly colored masterpieces are the *Madonna with Chancellor Rolin* (c. 1435) and *The Arnolfini Marriage* (1434). Other important Flemish painters of the fifteenth century were Rogier van der Weyden (*The Last Judgment* [c. 1450] and *Portrait of a Young Woman* [c. 1440]); Hugo van der Goes (the Portinari Altarpiece) and Hans Memling (c. 1430–1494). In the work of Hieronymus Bosch (active 1470–1516), the symbolism of the north is taken to its most extreme in his bizarre and highly personal mystical masterwork, *The Garden of Earthly Delights* (c. 1505–10).

In Germany the Renaissance produced many outstanding painters: Dürer, Grünewald, and Altdorfer, as well as Lucas Cranach, Hans Holbein, and Pieter Bruegel. By far the greatest of these was Albrecht Dürer (1471–1528), in many ways equal to Michelangelo in stature and innovation. Dürer traveled extensively and was influenced by the art of the Venetians; his scientific curiosity about the natural world was nearly equal to Leonardo's. Dürer lavished the same meticulous attention on lowly subjects (*The Piece of Turf; Hare*) that he did on major paintings (*The Four Apostles; The Adoration of the Trinity*). Dürer's fame spread throughout Europe because of his prolific and groundbreaking work in the area of printmaking (*The Great Passion* and *The Apocalypse* series; *Adam and Eve; Melancolia I*); as a virtuoso in the art of the woodcut (multiple copies printed from a raised surface) and metal engraving (multiple copies printed from an incised surface), Dürer has never been surpassed. The masterpiece of Grünewald (c. 1475–1528) is the Isenheim Altarpiece of 1515; Lucas Cranach the Elder (1472–1553) painted several portraits of Martin Luther, as well as *Adam and Eve* (1526); Albrecht Altdorfer depicted majestic landscapes, full of power and mystery, that dwarf the people in them (*St. George and the Dragon; The Battle of Alexander and Darius on the Issus*). One of the finest painters of the sixteenth century was Hans Holbein the Younger (1497–1543), who continued the northern emphasis on symbolic detail and highly finished realism, particularly in the area of portraiture. When he moved to London he became court painter to Henry VIII (*The Ambassadors* of 1553; *Sir Thomas More;* portraits of the king), and he is also known for his woodcut series *The Dance of Death.* The Flemish artist Pieter Bruegel specialized in robust depictions of peasants and ordinary people at work and play (*The Hunters in the Snow; The Peasant Wedding; The Corn Harvest*), often in landscape vistas viewed from a height.

THE SEVENTEENTH AND EIGHTEENTH CENTURIES

Presaged by the works of the Venetian artist Tintoretto (the radiating *Last Supper*) and El Greco in Spain (the visionary *Toledo; The Immaculate Conception*), the Baroque period of the seventeenth century produced artists who added heightened drama to the forms of Renaissance art. Bernini (1598–1680) was the giant of the style in Italy and enjoyed papal patronage, working in sculpture and architecture to create some of the most dynamic and personal statements of art. His architectural triumph was the design for the Piazza of St. Peter's in Rome, which united the various buildings of two centuries in two colonnaded galleries resembling outstretched arms. Bernini's sculpture is equally innovative and startling: his *David* is not an elegant, noble youth, but a powerful, angry warrior in motion; *St. Peter's Chair* is a complex sculpture of bronze, marble, stained glass, and stucco that grows out of the architecture of the church, incorporates the light of the oval stained glass, and overlaps the surrounding pilasters and walls with protruding shafts of bronze light-rays, clouds, and cherubs. *The Vision of the Ecstasy of St. Teresa* (Cornaro Chapel, Santa Maria della Vittoria in Rome) is a mesmerizing portrayal of mystical ecstasy, from the bronze shafts of heavenly light to the agitated and quirky folds of the saint's garment. Bernini's rival was Francesco Borromini, the other great Italian architect of the Baroque; his masterpieces in Rome include the Oratorio di San Filippo Neri, with its marriage of curved and triangular pediments, and Sant'Ivo della Sapienza, with its plan based on two interlocking equilateral triangles forming a six-pointed star with a single domed center.

In France, Baroque splendor was carried to its grandest at Versailles, a complex supervised by Charles Le Brun. Vast terraces, water gardens, fountains, and the gallery of mirrors were all calculated to equate Louis XIV, the Sun King, with the god Apollo. In England, however, the seventeenth century marked the beginning of a new classicism, particularly through the influential writings of Palladio. The designs of Inigo Jones (1573–1652) were sober, grand, classical (the Banqueting House and Queen's Chapel in London). Christopher Wren (1632–1723) rebuilt much of London after the fire of 1666 in a new style of Baroque energy, classical elements, and even a touch of Gothic. The Palladian/classical "revival" in architecture—neoclassicism—continued throughout the eighteenth and early nineteenth centuries. Examples in England are William Kent's Mereworth Castle (1723); Lord Burlington's Chiswick House (1720–25); and Robert Adam's Syon House in Isleworth (1762–69), with its interior of green marble and gilt copies of famous ancient classical statues. In America, the author of the Declaration of Independence and third U.S. president, Thomas Jefferson, designed his Monticello estate in Virginia according to Palladian principles.

In painting, the most significant proponent of the Italian Baroque was Caravaggio (1571–1610), whose models were ordinary people, and whose use of contrasting shadow and light was revolutionary and made for works of bold drama (*The Calling of Saint Matthew; The Conversion of Saint Paul*). The Flemish masters Peter Paul Rubens (1577–1640; *Marie de Medici Lands at*

Marseilles; The Raising of the Cross; The Descent from the Cross) and Jacob Jordaens portrayed figures in constant motion, draperies of agitated angles, and effects of lighting and shadow that amplified emotional impact and mystery. In this spirit followed such painters of court life and middle-class portraiture as Velazquez (1599–1660; *The Infanta Margarita; The Maids of Honor)* in Spain; Anthony Van Dyck *(Charles I Hunting)* in England; and in Holland, Frans Hals (1581–1666; *The Laughing Cavalier)* and Rembrandt van Rijn. Rembrandt (1601–1669), one of the greatest artists of all time, used expressive brushwork and mysterious light contrasts to enliven religious and genre painting and por-traiture, particularly of groups. Rembrandt's influence has remained consis-tently potent throughout the centuries, since his art appears to impart universal truths, and sections of his compositions glow with a mysterious inner light (*The Night Watch; The Descent from the Cross; The Anatomy Lesson of Dr. Tulp;* many self-portraits). Rembrandt also set the standard for perfection in the art of etching (printing from a metal plate with incised lines that have been etched away by acid; *Christ Healing the Sick*).

The art of the early eighteenth century is often called Rococo. Painters like Jean Antoine Watteau (*Embarkation for Cythera*, 1717), Giambattista Tiepolo (frescoes of the Wurzberg Residenz), François Boucher (*Diana Bathing,* 1742), and Jean Honoré Fragonard (*Women Bathing,* 1777), often creating decora-tive wall and ceiling schemes, turned the agitated drama of the Baroque into light, pastel-toned, swirling compositions that seem placed in an idyllic land of a golden age. Rococo style in architecture is marked by a profusion of elegant and fantastic decorative elements, often employing representations of shells, scrolls, and leaves. The influence of Versailles, with its mirrors radiating light and theatricality, is seen in the stucco fantasies covering Rococo interiors like living organisms, the relentless vegetation often supported by floating cherubs (the Zimmermann brothers, Church of Die Wies, Bavaria). The major Rococo palaces are the Residenz at Wurzburg by Balthasar Neumann, and the Munich Residenz, Amalienburg Pavilon, and Residenz Theater, all designed by François Cuvillies in the 1730s.

In the seventeenth and eighteenth centuries, European artists also responded to middle-class life and everyday objects to create genre paintings: Jan Ver-meer (1632–1675; *The Artist's Studio; The Head of a Girl)*; Adriaen van Ost-ade; Jean Baptiste Chardin (1699–1779; *The House of Cards; Saying Grace*). Jean Baptiste Greuze in France (*The Broken Pitcher)* and William Hogarth (*The Rake's Progress* and *Marriage ala Mode* series) in England endowed their everyday subjects with a wealth of narrative detail that aimed to impart a specific moral message. Such narrative art combined in the late eighteenth and early nineteenth centuries with romantic literature—Goethe, Byron, Shelley, Scott, Wordsworth, and others—and political events to produce works with a political point of view or a story to tell, in a variety of styles. Jacques Louis David (1748–1825) used a severe classical sculptural style (Neoclassicism) in his paintings to revive antique art and ennoble images of the French Revolution and Napoleon's empire (*The Death of Marat; The Oath of the Horatii; Napoleon in His Study*). The spiritual godfather of Neoclassicism is Nicholas Poussin (1593–1665), whose paintings of the seventeenth century are perfectly balanced, severe, idealized, and sculptural models of pristine classicism (*The Holy Family on the Steps; The Poet's Inspiration*). Neoclassical sculpture in the late eighteenth century revived the aloof severity and perfection of form of ancient art. Leading sculptors were Jean Antoine Houdon (*Voltaire; George Washington*), Antonio Canova (*Pauline Borghese as Venus Victrix*), and Bertal Thorvaldsen (*Hebe*). In England, the draughtsman and engraver John Flaxman produced engraved outline illustrations reminiscent of Greek vase paintings for illustrations to the *Illiad;* his work was the basis for the enduring style of Wedgwood pottery.

THE NINETEENTH CENTURY

In the late eighteenth century, with the rise of democracy and republics, the revolutions in France and America, and the discovery of the preserved Roman city of Pompeii, there occurred a full-blown revival of Greek and Roman design. Important architectural examples are the Bank of England by John Soane, Canova's Temple of Possagno—which combines elements of both the Parthenon and the Pantheon—and the Virginia State Capitol in Richmond, designed by Thomas Jefferson to resemble a Roman temple. Another revival stressed the Gothic style, championed by architect Augustus Pugin and writer John Ruskin—inspiring numerous Victorian Gothic buildings in England (Charles Barry's Houses of Parliament in London, 1840–65) and America (Richard Upjohn's Trinity Church in New York).

Political and other national events were important subjects for the romantic-realist painters of the early nineteenth century. The Spanish painter Francisco de Goya commented powerfully on political events in his painting *May 3, 1808*. In France, Eugene Delacroix (1798–1863; *The Death of Sardanapalus; Liberty Leading the People*) and Theodore Gericault (1791–1824; *The*

Raft of the Medusa) imbued subjects from literature, the Bible, exotic lands, and current events with dramatic, heroic intensity. The grandeur and transcendence of nature, the emotional reaction to inner dreams, and metaphysical truths of romanticism are seen in the work of such mystical artists as England's William Blake (a master of innovative printmaking), Henry Fuseli, and John Martin, and America's Thomas Cole. Caspar David Friedrich in Germany and the English Pre-Raphaelites (William Holman Hunt, John Everett Millais, Dante Gabriel Rossetti, Ford Madox Brown, Arthur Hughes, and others) endowed their keenly observed, minutely detailed works with a romantic spirit of poetic yearning and literary references, and accurately re-created the natural world in brilliantly colored landscapes.

In the first half of the nineteenth century, landscape painting in England reached a zenith with the works of John Constable (1776–1837; *The White Horse; The Haywain*) and Joseph Mallord William Turner (1775–1851; *The Slave Ship; Snowstorm: Hannibal Crossing the Alps*). Turner's awe-inspiring landscapes, revolutionary in their lighting effects achieved through bold, expressive brushwork, form a bridge between the spirit of romanticism and the expressionistic brushwork and realism of the Barbizon School in France, whose chief painters were Charles Daubigny and Jean Baptiste Camille Corot. Beginning with Barbizon, the French painters of the nineteenth century concentrated more and more on the reporter-like depiction of everyday life and the natural environment in a free, painterly (gestural brushwork) style. The realist pioneers Gustave Courbet (*The Stone Breakers; A Burial at Ormans*), Jean Francois Millet (*The Sower; The Angelus*), and Honoré Daumier (*The Third-Class Carriage*)—renowned as a political caricaturist, Daumier's chief medium was the lithograph—paved the way for the stylistic and subject innovations of the Impressionists.

In Impressionism, traditional means of composing a picture—academic methods of figure modeling, of color relations, and accurate and exact rendering of people and objects—were rejected in favor of an art that emphasized quickly observed and sketched moments from life, the relation of shapes and forms and colors, the effects of light, and the act of painting itself. Beginning with Edouard Manet (*Le Déjeuner sur l'Herbe; Olympia*) in the 1860s, French artists continually blurred the boundaries of realism and abstraction. The great Impressionist painters concentrated on landscapes and scenes of everyday life. Claude Monet (1840–1926) painted *Ladies in the Garden, Gare St. Lazare* (a steam-drenched train station), and multiple views of haystacks and Rouen Cathedral in varying daylight conditions. Auguste Renoir (1841–1919) painted people from contemporary life as well as robust female nudes (*Umbrellas; The Luncheon Party; The Bathers*). Like Manet and many other French artists, Edgar Degas (1834–1917) was influenced by the compositional techniques of Japanese prints; he delighted in achieving spontaneity by depicting his subjects from unusual angles and with figures seemingly arbitrarily cut off at the edge. Degas specialized in scenes of Parisian life and horses, nudes, and dancers (*The Glass of Absinthe; Ballet Rehearsal*). Other important Impressionist painters are Camille Pissarro, Alfred Sisley, Frederic Bazille, and Mary Cassatt—an American whose domestic interiors were greatly influenced by the flatness and coloring of Japanese prints. Auguste Rodin (1840–1917; *The Burghers of Calais; The Thinker; Honoré de Balzac)* produced powerful sculptures with the freedom of Impressionist style, and Degas also depicted his favored ballet dancers in bronze.

By the 1880s pure Impressionism gave way to the more experimental arrangements of form and color of the Postimpressionists—Japanese prints held much allure for Paul Gauguin (1848–1903), who arbitrarily placed almost garish colors in compositions where design and shape took precedence over any sense of perspective or proportion (*Vision After the Sermon,* which shows Jacob wrestling with the angel); and two works inspired by his stay in Tahiti: *Nevermore* and the woodcut *Noa Noa*. Vincent van Gogh (1853–1890) was the exception that seems to have become a rule: the misunderstood, struggling, emotionally disturbed genius whose art was only recognized after his death. Van Gogh adopted Gauguin's harsh and unusual color schemes that were unrelated to the reality of a scene, and painted with an innovative, personal, expressive brushwork of thick swirling lines—which paved the way for twentieth-century expressionism (*The Night Café; Sunflowers; Starry Night*). Georges Seurat (1859–1891) produced noble and serene compositions in a style called pointillism, which allowed the viewer to visually mix the colors of a painting that had been applied in minute individual dots (*La Grande Jatte; The Circus*). Henri de Toulouse-Lautrec, more than any other French artist, concentrated on themes of night life and entertainment and employed thick outlines and the flatness of shapes and color of Japanese prints, especially in his many color lithographic posters. Paul Cézanne, considered by many to be the father of modern art, used the lessons of Impressionism to make the subjectivity of the artist paramount. He bent his subjects' shapes and contours away from realistic proportions and relationships, and assigned colors based on harmonious balance in the picture. Cézanne (1839–1906; numerous self-portraits; *The Great Bathers; Still Life with Onions*) was able to break apart and re-form reality, and make the act of painting itself significant, and in so doing he was able to usher in the achievements of twentieth-century Cubism and abstract art.

Other important groups in the last two decades of the nineteenth century that distorted reality and pursued sinewy forms or abstract patterning were the Nabis (Pierre Bonnard and Edouard Vuillard); the art nouveau artists (Toulouse-Lautrec, Aubrey Beardsley [illustrations for *Le Morte d'Arthur* and *Salome*], and Gustav Klimt [*The Kiss*]), the early expressionists (James Ensor [*The Entry of Christ into Brussels*] and Edvard Munch [*The Scream*]), and the Symbolists (Gustave Moreau, Odilon Redon, Puvis de Chavannes, and Edward Burne-Jones).

The most significant innovations in nineteenth-century architecture were related to technical accomplishment; the possibility of construction on a large scale in metal, iron, and glass allowed for revolutionary skeletal structures. The Crystal Palace, built for London's Great Exhibition in 1851 by Joseph Paxton, was 1600 feet long, and basically a glass building. A famous metal monument of no apparent purpose other than to symbolize another world's fair (in Paris in 1889) was Gustave Eiffel's tower. English railway stations had similar designs, using metal and glass vaulted roofs (John Dobson's Central Railway Station, Newcastle-upon-Tyne). And in America, the steel-skeleton structure dictated no-nonsense, stripped-down, functional city buildings by Daniel H. Burnham and John W. Root (Reliance Building, Chicago, 1890-1894) and Louis Sullivan (Wainwright Building, St. Louis, 1890-1891). The curves and vegetal ornamentation of the art nouveau style were employed in the buildings of Hector Guimard, Victor Horta, and Antonio Gaudi.

THE TWENTIETH CENTURY

Architecture in the twentieth century announced a clean break with the past, building upon the technical and structural innovations of such nineteenth-century masters as Joseph Paxton and Louis Sullivan. Frank Lloyd Wright (1867–1959) was perhaps the new century's greatest innovator, who transformed both commercial and residential architecture into structures that perfectly matched their surroundings, broke with the decorative language of the past, and offered functionalism in working and living spaces. Such private residences as the Robie house (1909) in Illinois and Fallingwater (the Kaufman house) in Pennsylvania brilliantly and innovatively mingle interior and exterior space. In the

1920s, the Bauhaus school of design in Dessau, Germany, championed abstract art, geometric design, machine-age elements, and restricted ornament. The director was the important architect Walter Gropius, whose design for the Bauhaus school building featured glass facades—pure line and geometric shapes. In Berlin in the 1920s Miës van der Rohe abandoned the ornamental vocabulary of the past for glass and steel skyscrapers and concrete office blocks. In America, Miës van der Rohe's apartment buildings on Chicago's Lake Shore Drive are rectangular blocks (1948–51), and his Seagram building in New York (1954–58) is perhaps the most famous example of the trend of skyscraper glass rectangles. This American glass-box aesthetic is also seen in Wright's Johnson Wax building (1936–39) in Racine, Wisconsin; the Lever Brothers and Pepsi-Cola buildings in New York by the firm of Skidmore, Owings, and Merrill; the presidential Palace of the Alvorada in Brasilia (1958) by Oscar Neimeyer; and Le Corbusier's United Nations design. This style of technology-driven, unadorned, stripped-to-essentials architecture in the industrialized nations since the 1930s has been called International Style or simply modernism. In the last twenty years, the austerity of modernism has been redirected into a more decorative and humanistic style, often termed postmodernism, which incorporates cultural influences, imaginative decorative touches, and historical architectural elements into designs appropriate to modern technology and uses. Among the architects working in the style are Robert Venturi and Michael Graves.

Sculpture and painting, from the beginning of the twentieth century, built upon the rejection of realistic proportions and naturalistic depiction, substituting a breakup of forms and a play of shape and color such as employed by Gauguin, Van Gogh, Cezanne, the Nabis, and others. The new freer form of art centered around the personality of the artist and celebrated personal style and the manipulation of two-dimensional pictorial elements. In the late nineteenth and early twentieth centuries this evolved in a number of directions. Some artists turned inward to explore mystical, symbolic, and psychological truths: Symbolists, expressionists, and exponents of art nouveau, such as Odilon Redon, Jan Toorop, Edvard Munch, James Ensor, and Gustav Klimt. The German Expressionists portrayed disturbing psychological truths through highly personal styles and disjointed compositions, and they frequently worked in woodcut. These German artists banded together from 1905 to 1913 in a group called Die Brucke; their aims were unabashedly revolutionary, and their work was often meant to shock. Die Brucke's members were Ernst Kirchner, Karl Schmidt-Ruttluff, Erich Heckel, Otto Mueller, Max Pechstein, and Emil Nolde—all of whose compositions emphasized distortion, angular and contorted figures, sometimes screaming color, and outrageous themes. In the face of the horrors of World War I, shock value and humor were the artistic weapons of choice for the Dada artists (Francis Picabia, Man Ray, Hans Arp, Kurt Schwitters, Marcel Duchamp, Max Ernst), whose "antiart" or "nonart" works often assembled any materials available ("found objects"), from newspaper clippings and photographs to bicycle wheels (Marcel Duchamp's *Ready-made,* 1913, a wooden stool with a bicycle wheel attached).

Among the artists who pursued formal innovations were Henri Matisse, Pablo Picasso, Georges Braque, and Juan Gris. Matisse (1869–1954) was the leading figure of the Fauves (dubbed "wild beasts" because of their relentlessly unreal use of color). Matisse's most important works reduced a picture to its essentials—flat color and line (*The Dance; Le Luxe II*). Other Fauves were Andre Derain, Georges Braque, Maurice Vlaminck, and peripherally, Georges Rouault, whose art was distinctly religious. The most revolutionary and far-reaching art movement of the twentieth century was Cubism—which, by its blatant visual decomposition and reassemblage of observed reality, seemed the most direct call for the total destruction of realistic depiction and for abstraction. The greatest Cubist artist and one of the most important figures in the history of art was Pablo Picasso (1881–1973; *Les Demoiselles d'Avignon; Three Musicians; Ma Jolie*). His use of African and Oceanic tribal art, and his emphasis on taking objects apart and reassembling them—thus showing a subject's multiplicity of aspects and dissolving time and space—led to similar experiments by Georges Braque, Juan Gris, Fernand Léger, Marcel Duchamp (*Nude Descending a Staircase,* 1912), the sculptors Alexander Archipenko and Jacques Lipchitz, and the Italian Futurist Umberto Boccioni (*Unique Forms of Continuity in Space,* sculpture, 1913, and *The City Rises,* painting, 1911).

In the first decades of the twentieth century, pure abstraction, with little or no relation to the outside world, was approached in the more emotional, expressionistic, and color-oriented paintings of Wassily Kandinsky (with Franz Marc, a proponent of the Blue Rider school), Robert Delaunay, and Paul Klee. More cerebral arrangements of abstract geometrical shapes and colors were the mark of Kasimir Malevich (his Suprematist compositions), Piet Mondrian, and the Bauhaus School of Design in Germany (Klee, Kandinsky, Joseph Albers, Walter Gropius, Laszlo Moholy-Nagy; where Marcel Breuer originated the first tubular steel chair, a standard of mid-century "modern" furniture design). The Bauhaus's simplified and usually geometric-oriented aesthetic influenced architecture, industrial and commercial design, sculpture, and the graphic arts for half a century. In architecture can be seen the most obvious results of this new tradition, the simplified, sleek structures of Mies van der Rohe, Walter Gropius, Le Corbusier, and Frank Lloyd Wright.

Inspired by the psychoanalytic writings of Sigmund Freud and Carl Jung, the subconscious and the metaphysical became another important element in art, especially in the work of the Surrealist artists Salvador Dali (*The Persistence of Memory*), Giorgio de Chirico, Max Ernst, René Magritte, Joan Miró, and Yves Tanguy. Important sculptors who manipulated abstract shapes and/or were influenced by tribal arts in the twentieth century include Constantin Brancusi (*The Kiss,* 1910), Henry Moore (influenced by American Pre-Columbian art; *Mother and Child,* 1924; *Reclining Figure,* 1929), Hans Arp, and Alberto Giacometti. Alexander Calder created floating assemblies called mobiles, and Louise Nevelson made constructions and wall sculptures from scraps of everyday objects.

Obsession with self and with abstraction also led to the major American art movement after World War II, Abstract Expressionism, whose chief exponents were Clyfford Still, Jackson Pollock ("drip" paintings), Willem de Kooning, Franz Kline, and Robert Motherwell. Other Americans took this movement into the area of color-field painting, a cooler, more reserved formalism of simple shapes and experimental color relationships: Mark Rothko, Barnett Newman, Joseph Albers, and Ad Reinhardt.

Other important trends in American art in the twentieth century were reflective of a democratic and consumer society. The muralists and social realists during the first half of the century created art that was dynamically realistic—representative of a youthful and vigorous America—and whose subjects were accessible to the average person. John Sloan, George Bellows (*Stag at Sharkey's,* 1909), Edward Hopper (the new life in the lonely city, noble, quiet, stark: *The Automat,* 1927; *Nighthawks,* 1942), Thomas Hart Benton, Grant Wood, and John Stuart Curry were among those who celebrated the American scene in paintings, and frequently in murals for public buildings and through widely available fine prints. The great Mexican muralists, who usually concentrated on political themes—Diego Rivera, José Clemente Orozco, and David Siqueiros—brought their work to the public both in Mexico and in the United States.

The icons of American popular culture found their way, in the movement known as Pop art, into canvases by Andy Warhol (the multiplied silk-screened images of Campbell Soup cans and Marilyn Monroe), Robert Indiana, Larry Rivers, Jasper Johns (use of the American flag), Roy Lichtenstein (enlarged comic book panels), and Robert Rauschenberg. Other developments during the last thirty years include: Kinetic art (works that move or produce an illusion of movement) and Op art (manipulation of abstract color and repetitive patterns to play tricks on the eye [Victor Vasarely; Bridget Riley]); Minimal art (the work reduced to essentials) and Conceptual art (the idea itself, rather than the technical accomplishment); and the actual movement of, or covering of, land and monuments on a massive scale (Christo: *The Arco della Pace Wrapped,* 1970; *Running Fence,* 1972–76, a 24.5-mile-long nylon fence along the hills of Sonoma and Marin counties in northern California). Super- or Photorealism is the style of the sculptor Duane Hanson and the painters Chuck Close, Richard Estes, and Philip Pearlstein.

Visual Arts and Architecture

1. Pop artists used recognizable imagery from the mass media such as commercial products, comics, and celebrities because

   (A) they wanted to criticize the superficiality and consumerism of American culture.
   (B) they wanted to celebrate the images of their time.
   (C) they wanted to take advantage of new techniques and materials to present new products.
   (D) None of the above.

2. The Minimalists sought to

   (A) reduce shape and form to its simplest, purest state.
   (B) remove all evidence of the human hand's part in the construction of their work.
   (C) imitate industrial production in the slickness and coldness of their work.
   (D) All of the above.

3. Andy Warhol, the first artist to truly make use of the mass media, worked in which of the following media?

   (A) television.
   (B) film.
   (C) sculpture.
   (D) All of the above.

4. Warhol often repeated the same image many times within a single painting because

   (A) he was imitating the way the media saturates us with an image.
   (B) he wanted to show how we become numb to an image after seeing it so many times.
   (C) it was easy.
   (D) All of the above.

5. Which of the following is NOT considered by artists to be a technique of forming clay "by hand"?

   (A) Throwing
   (B) Coiling
   (C) Slab building
   (D) Modeling

6. "Form Follows Function" is an expression coined by

   (A) Frank Lloyd Wright.
   (B) Louis Sullivan.
   (C) Le Corbusier.
   (D) Mies van der Rohe.

7. Which of the following architects were founding members of the Bauhaus School of architecture?

   (A) Walter Gropius and Ludwig Mies van der Rohe
   (B) I.M. Pei and Robert Venturi
   (C) Theo van Doesburg and Le Corbusier
   (D) Benjamin Latrobe and Louis Sullivan

8. The Ionic Order of Greek architecture is characterized primarily by

   (A) cushion-shaped capitals.
   (B) volute-shaped capitals.
   (C) bell-shaped capitals.
   (D) fluted columns.

9. Giacomo della Porta's design for the facade of the Church of II Gesu in Rome dates from which of the following periods of art history?

   (A) Early Christian
   (B) Romanesque
   (C) Northern Renaissance
   (D) Baroque

10. The central vertical supporting pillar of Romanesque and Gothic portals is called a

   (A) lintel.
   (B) jamb.
   (C) column.
   (D) trumeau.

11. The twentieth-century movement in architecture which immediately succeeded the International Style, and which was defined largely by the writings of Robert Venturi, is

   (A) Modernismo.
   (B) Post-Modernism.
   (C) Constructivism.
   (D) Romanticism.

12. The staircase in the Hotel van Eetvelde, designed by Victor Horta in 1895, illustrates which one of the following art historical styles?

   (A) Art Nouveau
   (B) Post-Modernism
   (C) Neo-Classicism
   (D) Post-Impressionism

13. The earliest known example of town planning in the history of architecture is

   (A) Forum of Caesar, Rome.
   (B) Stonehenge, England.
   (C) Acropolis, Athens.
   (D) Catal Huyuk, Turkey.

14. The dome of Florence Cathedral was built in the fifteenth century according to which of the following architect's designs?

   (A) Leonardo da Vinci
   (B) Filippo Brunelleschi
   (C) Leon Battista Alberti
   (D) Giuliano da Sangallo

15. Supports used in post-and-lintel architecture that are carved in imitation of female figures are called

    (A) sirens.
    (B) caryatids.
    (C) atlantes.
    (D) Corinthian columns.

16. The central dome of St. Mark's in Venice rests on curved triangular supports called

    (A) squinches.
    (B) pendentives.
    (C) corbelled arches.
    (D) fan vaults.

17. Reinforced concrete, also known as ferroconcrete, is defined as concrete that is

    (A) covered with brick facing.
    (B) combined with stone masonry blocks.
    (C) embedded with iron rods or mesh.
    (D) mixed with a water repellant.

18. The plan of Charlemagne's Palace Chapel at Aachen is often compared to that of which of the following buildings?

    (A) Hagia Sophia, Istanbul
    (B) The Pantheon, Rome
    (C) Sant'Apollinare in Classe, Ravenna
    (D) San Vitale, Ravenna

Visual Arts and Architecture Review

Answer Key

1.	(D)	6.	(B)	11.	(B)	16.	(B)
2.	(D)	7.	(A)	12.	(A)	17.	(C)
3.	(D)	8.	(B)	13.	(D)	18.	(D)
4.	(D)	9.	(D)	14.	(B)		
5.	(A)	10.	(D)	15.	(B)		

Detailed Explanations of Answers

Drill: Visual Arts and Architecture

1. **(D)** Pop artists wanted neither to criticize nor celebrate American culture, but simply to take pieces of it, hold up a mirror and reflect it back to the society which produced it. (A) is incorrect. This is too simplistic a reading of Pop art and there is no evidence to show this intent. (B) is incorrect. This is also too simplistic a reading of Pop art. There is no evidence to show this intent over any other. (C) is incorrect because the pop artists employed already-established techniques such as silk screening and lithograph for their works.

2. **(D)** Choices (A), (B), and (C) are all goals of minimalism.

3. **(D)** The correct answer is (D), all of the above. (A) is incorrect because Warhol had a short-lived TV show on MTV called *Andy Warhol's Fifteen Minutes*. (B) is incorrect because Warhol made many films including the experimental *Sleep*, an eight-hour-long shot of a man sleeping. (C) is incorrect because Warhol worked in sculpture from the 1960s onward. His most famous pieces are the *Brillo Boxes* from the early part of that decade.

4. **(D)** Choices (A), (B), and (C) are all true, according to statements which Warhol himself made.

5. **(A)** Coiling, slab building, and modeling are all methods of forming clay strictly by hand. "Throwing" clay involves the use of a potter's wheel, and thus is not technically considered a method of hand-forming clay.

6. **(B)** Louis Sullivan, an architect best known for his late nineteenth century skyscrapers, promoted the idea that a building's form should follow its function. His slogan "form follows function" became one of the Great Truths for modern architects of the twentieth century, among them Gropius and Mies van der Rohe.

7. **(A)** Walter Gropius and Ludwig Mies van der Rohe helped found the Bauhaus School in Germany in the 1920s but later moved to the United

States, where they exerted profound influence on twentieth-century American architecture. I.M. Pei and Robert Venturi (B) were active as architects in the later twentieth century (especially in the 1970s), well after the founding of the Bauhaus. Theo van Doesburg and Le Corbusier (C) were architectural contemporaries of the Bauhaus founders, but were not themselves involved in the school. Benjamin Latrobe and Louis Sullivan (D) were architects working in the nineteenth century, thus pre-dating the founding of the Bauhaus. Inigo Jones, the first of the great English architects, precedes the Bauhaus, having lived and worked in the seventeenth century.

8. **(B)** Volute-shaped capitals, whose circular spiral motifs, or volutes, are carved on the corners of the capitals at the tops of each column, are the distinguishing characteristic of the Ionic order. Cushion-shaped capitals (A) characterize the Doric order of Greek architecture; and bell-shaped capitals (C), usually adorned with acanthus tendrils, identify the Corinthian order. Fluted columns (D) appear in all Greek architectural orders and are not used as criteria to identify the individual order.

9. **(D)** The two-storied facade, the levels of which are unified by the large flanking scrolls; the paired columns; and the pedimented windows and niches were widely imitated in the Baroque period to varying degrees on other buildings. The dramatic effect of the building's overtly anti-classical design was typical of Baroque-era architecture. Early Christian (A) and Romanesque (B) churches were designed with much simpler, more austere facades; and there are no comparable facades in the architecture of the (C) Northern Renaissance.

10. **(D)** Trumeau, which is often in imitation of human or animal forms. A lintel (A) is the horizontal beam that rests upon the (B) jambs (frames) of a doorway. A column (C) refers to any simple cylindrical support; however, simple columns were not used as central supports in such doorways.

11. **(B)** Post-Modernism was the period of architectural history that was formulated in the 1970s. The definition of Post-Modern architecture is complex, and the phrase is rejected by many modern architectural historians; loosely defined, it refers to contemporary architecture that seeks to challenge and re-examine traditional methods of architectural expression. Modernismo (A) refers to the Spanish version of Art Nouveau. (C) Constructivism is a term used to define the works (both sculptural and architectural) of a group of early twentieth century Russian artists. Romanticism

(D) is a nineteenth-century movement in architecture, in which architects sought to imitate architectural styles of past eras, including those of classical Greece and Rome and medieval Europe.

12. **(A)** Art Nouveau is distinguished by the use of such curvilinear, decorative details of interior design. Post-Modernism (B) is a later period in the history of architecture, and is not defined by such decorative elements. Neo-Classicism (C), a nineteenth-century era of architecture, is characterized by the use of classical Greek and Roman architectural details, which are more austere in nature Post Impressionism (D) is a movement in painting, which has no equivalent in the history of architectural design.

13. **(D)** Catal Huyuk, Turkey, which dates from ca. 6000 B.C.E., revealed upon excavation multiple dwelling units and structures apparently designed for worship, indicating that the complex was designed for the dwelling of a large number of persons. The Forum of Caesar, Rome (A) dates from the first century B.C.E. Stonehenge, England (B) dates from c. 2000 B.C.E. and is not believed to have served as living space. The Periclean Acropolis, Athens (C) dates from the fifth century B.C.E.

14. **(B)** Filippo Brunelleschi, whose dome (built 1420–1436) was unprecedented in design. To span the 140-foot space, Brunelleschi designed his dome with an avoid profile (to reduce the thrust at the dome's base), and with a double shell and 24 ribs to lighten the weight yet provide the dome with sufficient stability. Leonardo da Vinci (A) is not known to have designed a comparable dome, nor has any such construction been attributed to him. Leone Battista Alberti (C) was much influenced by Brunelleschi, but had no part in the design of the dome of Florence Cathedral, nor did Giuliano da Sangallo (D), who succeeded Brunelleschi as an architect.

15. **(B)** The correct choice is (B) Caryatids. Sirens (A) are female *characters* from Greek mythology, not an architectural form. Atlantes (C) are supports in post-and-lintel architecture which are carved in imitation of *male* figures; they are the counterparts of caryatids. Corinthian columns (D) are an order of Greek architecture, and are distinguished by bell-shaped capitals carved with acanthus tendrils.

16. **(B)** The correct choice is (B) pendentives. Squinches (A) are also utilized to support domes, but these are block-like members laid across the corners of a structural unit to support a dome of similar structure. Corbelled arches

(C) are arches formed by stepping stones outward from a base until the stones meet at midpoint. Fan vaults (D) are elaborate groin vaults, with tracery defining their wedge-shaped forms.

17. **(C)** Embedded with iron rods or mesh, as indicated by the term *"fer-ro*concrete." Concrete that is (A) covered with brick facing or (B) used with stone masonry blocks, is simply concrete that is combined with other building materials. Concrete mixed with a water repellant (D) is referred to as an *ad*mixture.

18. **(D)** San Vitale, Ravenna, which is also a centrally-planned building with central nave and encircling ambulatory. It is commonly believed that Charlemagne either visited Ravenna and viewed the plan of San Vitale, or that he was made familiar with its plan through architects at his court. Hagia Sophia in Istanbul (A), the Pantheon in Rome (B), and the Orthodox Baptistery in Ravenna are all centrally-planned buildings, but in size, interior elevation, and division of interior space, they are not comparable to Charlemagne's Palace Chapel. The church of Sant'Apollinare in Classe in Ravenna is not centrally-planned, but designed along a longitudinal axis.

CHAPTER 4

Philosophy Review

PHILOSOPHY REVIEW

ANCIENT PHILOSOPHERS

All of the Greek philosophers before Socrates are known as the pre-Socratics. Pythagoras was a sixth century B.C.E. pre-Socratic philosopher and mathematician. Pythagoras, who made many scientific and mathematical discoveries, believed in the transmigration of souls.

Thales, a sixth and fifth century B.C.E. pre-Socratic philosopher, is sometimes called "the father of Western philosophy." Thales held that the first principle, or substance, that everything in the universe is made out of is water.

Parmenides was a pre-Socratic philosopher in the fifth and fourth century B.C.E. He denied the existence of time, plurality, and motion. He is considered the founder of metaphysics.

Heraclitus, in the fourth century B.C.E., was a pre-Socratic philosopher. Heraclitus was said to have believed that everything is in a continuous state of flux. He was opposed to the idea of a single ultimate reality.

Zeno was a pre-Socratic philosopher in the fourth century B.C.E. and a disciple of Parmenides. He was famous for a set of paradoxes, which are intended to show that plurality and motion do not really exist.

Socrates was an Athenian fourth century B.C.E. philosopher. He supposedly wrote down none of his views, because he believed writing distorted ideas. His ideas have survived only through the writings of his followers, most notably Plato. It is unclear to what extent the views attributed to Socrates' character in Plato's dialogues were the views of the actual historical Socrates.

Atomism is the belief that matter consists of atoms. Both Leucippus, a fourth century B.C.E. Greek philosopher, and Democritus, a fourth and third century B.C.E. Greek philosopher, were atomists. They both concluded atoms are different-shaped bits of matter.

Plato, who lived from 427 to 347 B.C.E., was a Greek philosopher. Plato wrote dialogues, many of which contain Socrates as the main character. These dialogues provided the starting point for many later developments in various areas, for example: ethics, the study of morals; epistemology, the study of knowledge; and metaphysics, the study of reality. Plato's best known theory is the theory of Forms (or Ideas). According to this theory, the objects of knowledge are universals, such as The Good and The Just. Because specific things in this world, such as a just person, are mere reflections of the Forms, they can only be the objects of opinion.

Aristotle, who lived in the third century B.C.E., was an extremely influential Greek philosopher. Aristotle, who criticized Plato's theory of Forms, was the first to systematize logic. The medieval study and development of Aristotle's philosophy is known as Aristotelianism.

PHILOSOPHERS OF THE FIRST MILLENNIUM

Neoplatonism was the dominant philosophy in Europe from 250 through 1250 C.E. Begun by Plotinus, a third century C.E. philosopher, Neoplatonism is a combination of Plato's ideas with those of other philosophers, such as Aristotle and Pythagoras. Another Neoplatonist was Augustine, a fourth and fifth century bishop and philosopher. Augustine had a profound effect on medieval religious thought.

St. Anselm, an eleventh century philosopher, was an Italian monk who became archibishop of Canterbury. He founded Scholasticism. Anselm was best known for his ontological argument for the existence of God.

St. Thomas Aquinas, a thirteenth century philosopher, was best known for his "Five Ways," five proofs of the existence of God. The philosophy of Aquinas and his followers is called Thomism. He is considered the greatest thinker of the Scholastic School. His ideas were made the official Catholic philosophy in 1879.

Ockham was a fourteenth century English philosopher and cleric. He was famous for the dictum "Do not multiply entities beyond necessity."

Hobbes (1588–1679) was a British materialist. One of his famous works is *Leviathan*, in which he argues that men are selfish by nature. Because of this belief, Hobbes felt that a powerful absolute ruler is necessary.

Rationalism is the view that knowledge of the external world can be derived from reason alone, without recourse to experience. Notable rationalists include Descartes, Leibniz, and Spinoza. Descartes (1596–1650) was an extremely influential French philosopher and mathematician. He held a view of the relation between the mind and body which has come to be known as Cartesian dualism. In this view, the mind and body are two distinct, though interactive, entities. Descartes is famous for the statement "*cogito ergo sum*," or "I think therefore I am."

Two other well known Rationalists were Gottfried Wilhelm von Leibniz and Benedict Spinoza. Leibniz (1646–1716) was a German philosopher who argued, in his *Theodicy*, that this is the best of all possible worlds. He is considered one of the greatest minds of all times. Spinoza (1632–1677), a Dutch-born philosopher, is best known for his *Tractacus Theologico-Politicus*. He felt mind and body are aspects of a single substance, which he called God or Nature.

Blaise Pascal (1623–1662) was a French philosopher, mathematician, and theologian. He is most famous for an argument called "Pascal's Wager," which provides prudent reasons for believing in God. His work, *Pensées* (Thoughts), published after his death, argues that reason is by itself insufficient for man's spiritual needs and cannot bring man to God.

Empiricism is the view that all knowledge is derived from experience. Three well-known empiricists are Locke, Berkeley, and Hume. John Locke (1632–1704) was an English philosopher. In his *Essay Concerning Human Understanding*, Locke attempted to present an empiricist account of the origins, nature, and limits of human reason. Berkeley (1685–1753), another empiricist, was an Irish philosopher and an idealist. Idealism is the view that the so-called "external world" is actually a creation of the mind (another well-known idealist is Hegel). Finally, David Hume (1711–1776) was a Scots philosopher. An empiricist, Hume drew attention to the problem of induction.

Jean-Jacques Rousseau (1712–1778) was a German-born political philosopher and a philosopher of education. His major work was *The Social Contract* (1762). Rousseau emphasized man's natural goodness.

Adam Smith (1723–1790) was a Scots philosopher and political economist. He wrote *The Wealth of Nations*. Smith has had an enormous impact on economics into the present day.

Immanuel Kant (1724–1804) was a German idealist philosopher. He was most famous for the categorical imperative—"Act only on that maxim which you can at the same time will to become a universal law"—as a test of moral principles. Kant is also well known for his epistemological work, including his ideas of the Noumenon and Phenomenon.

Jeremy Bentham (1748–1832) was a British philosopher and a lawyer. He was one of the founders of utilitarianism. He was a powerful reformer of the British legal, judicial, and prison system.

Georg Wilhelm Friedrich Hegel (1770–1831), a German idealist philosopher, is famous for his theory of the dialectic. According to the theory, a dialectic is a process of argument which proceeds from a thesis and its antithesis to a synthesis of the two. His idealistic system of metaphysics was highly influential.

James Mill (1773–1836) was a Scots philosopher and economist. Mill was also the father of the better-known philosopher J.S. Mill (1806–1873), who was an English empiricist philosopher. J.S. Mill is best known both for his *System of Logic* and for his ethical writings, including *Utilitarianism* and *On Liberty*.

Arthur Schopenhauer (1788–1860), a German philosopher, was a Kantian best known for *The World as Will and Idea*. Schopenhauer believed that only art and contemplation could offer escape from determinism and pessimism. Schopenhauer had a strong influence on Freud, Nietzsche, Proust, Tolstoy, and Thomas Mann.

Søren Kierkegaard (1813–1855), a Danish philosopher, was probably the first existentialist. Existentialism is the view that the subject of philosophy is *being*, which cannot be made the subject of objective inquiry but can only be investigated by reflection on one's own existence. Sartre is another notable existentialist.

Karl Marx (1818–1883), author of *Das Kapital*, was a German social theorist. Engels (1820–1895), Marx's collaborator, was a dialectical materialist.

Dialectical materialism is the metaphysical doctrine originally propounded by Engels. According to the doctrine, matter, rather than the mind, is primary. Matter, also, is governed by dialectical laws in this view. Dialectical materialism is included in Marxism, the body of doctrines originally held by Marx and Engels.

Brentano (1838–1917) was a German philosopher and psychologist who is remembered for his "doctrine of intentionality."

Charles Peirce (1839–1914), an American philosopher, was the founder of pragmatism. As used by Peirce, pragmatism was originally a theory of meaning. Later, William James (1842–1910), an American (empiricist) philosopher and psychologist, used pragmatism as a theory of truth according to which "ideas become true just so far as they help us get into satisfactory relations with other parts of our experience."

Friedrich Wilhelm Nietzsche (1844–1900), a German philosopher, is best known for introducing the concept of the *Übermensch,* or the Overman. As a moralist, he rejected Christian values.

Bradley (1846–1924) was an English philosopher. An idealist, Bradley wrote *Appearance and Reality.*

Frege (1848–1925) was a German philosopher and mathematician. Frege is considered the founding father of modern logic, philosophy of mathematics, and philosophy of language.

Edmund Husserl (1859–1938), a German philosopher, developed phenomenology. Phenomenology is a method of inquiry which begins with the scrupulous inspection of one's own conscious thought processes. Husserl's goal was to create a completely accurate description of consciousness and conscious experience.

John Dewey (1859–1952) was an American pragmatist philosopher and educational theorist. Dewey developed the views of William James and Charles Peirce into his own version of pragmatism. He emphasized the importance of inquiry into acquiring knowledge. George Santayana (1863–1952) was an American Platonist philosopher, novelist, and poet. Santayana was a student of James. He attempted to reconcile Platonism and materialism.

Bertrand Russell (1872–1970) was a British philosopher. Along with Whitehead, he was the author of the extremely influential *Principia Mathematica.*

Russell, in such seminal papers as "On Denoting" and "The Principles of Logical Atomism," argued that the structure of the world can be revealed by the proper analysis of language.

G.E. Moore (1873–1958), a British philosopher, is best known for his *Principia Ethica*. Moore emphasized the common sense view of the reality of material objects.

Logical positivism, a radical empiricist position, is the doctrine that the meaning of a proposition consists in the method of its verification. Logical positivism is also known as "logical empiricism." A group of logical positivists, known as the Vienna Circle, centered around the University of Vienna in the 1920s and 1930s. Founded by Schlick (1882–1936), a logical positivist philosopher, the Vienna Circle also included Neurath (1882–1945), an Austrian logical positivist philosopher, and Carnap (1891–1970), a German logical positivist philosopher.

Ludwig Wittgenstein (1889–1951), a Viennese-born philosopher, has had an enormous influence on the later philosophy of language. *Tractatus Logico-Philosophicus*, his first and most famous work, was a defense of a picture theory of meaning. This work contains such often quoted aphorisms as "The world is everything that is the case."

Martin Heidegger (1889–1976), a German philosopher, is commonly regarded, despite his objections, as an existentialist. Heidegger studied with Husserl and was influenced by Kierkegaard. Heidegger's own philosophy emphasized the need to understand "being."

Alfred Tarski (1902–1993) was a logician and mathematician. He is famous for his definition of the concept of truth for formal logical languages, which has been used extensively by philosophers of language as a basis for theories of meaning for natural language.

Sir Karl Popper (1902–1994), a philosopher of science, wrote *The Logic of Scientific Discovery*. He is best known for his claim that falsifiability is the hallmark of science.

Jean-Paul Sartre (1905–1980) was a French philosopher. Sartre was a founder of Marxism and existentialism. Sartre believed man is condemned to be free and to bear the responsibility of making free choices.

Hempel (1905–1997) was a German empiricist philosopher of science. His theories of confirmation and explanation have been extremely influential. Goodman (1906–1998), an American philosopher, was a nominalist. Goodman wrote, most notably, *Fact Fiction and Forecast* and *Languages of Art*.

Merleau-Ponty (1908–1961) was a French philosopher who worked on ethics and problems of consciousness. Willard Van Orman Quine (1908–2000) was an American empiricist philosopher of language and a logician. Sir Alfred Jules Ayer (1910–1989), an English philosopher, is a logical positivist and member of the Vienna Circle. He wrote *Language, Truth and Logic*. Austin (1911–1960) was a British philosopher of language. He developed the speech act theory. P. F. Strawson (1919–2006), a British philosopher of language and a metaphysician, is best known for arguing, in "On Referring," that some meaningful sentences have no truth value. John Rawls (1921–2002), an American political philosopher, is best known for *A Theory of Justice*. Noam Chomsky (1928–   ) is an influential American linguist and philosopher. Chomsky argues that there is an innate universal grammar. Donald Davidson (1917–2003) is an American philosopher of language and the mind. He holds a theory of the mind called anomalous monism. Saul Kripke (1941–   ) is an American philosopher of language, philosopher of the mind, and logician. His most influential work, "Naming and Necessity," launched the causal theory of reference. His theory, in part, deals with the distinction between a statement's sense and its reference.

Drill: Philosophy

1. It is not surprising that Rationalists like Leibniz, Spinoza, and Hegel all accepted some version of the Coherence theory of truth because the main alternative, the Correspondence theory, places too much weight on

    (A) innate ideas.
    (B) experience.
    (C) the relations among ideas.
    (D) knowledge.

2. Benjamin Franklin, Thomas Jefferson, and George Washington all rejected theism, but were not atheists. This is because they were

    (A) deists.
    (B) skeptics.
    (C) Christians.
    (D) immoralists.

3. Sextus Empiricus was the codifier of Greek skepticism, a view that held we cannot give our firm assent to any

    (A) creed.
    (B) dogma.
    (C) belief.
    (D) moral code.

4. Jealousy and envy are often conflated or confused, but cases of jealousy and envy differ in at least one important respect:

    (A) Jealousy involves more than two people.
    (B) Envy can be expressed.
    (C) Jealousy involves a belief.
    (D) Jealousy is sexual.

Philosophy Review

Answer Key

1. (B)   2. (A)   3. (C)   4. (A)

Detailed Explanations of Answers

Drill: Philosophy

1. **(B)** Choice (B) identifies the Correspondence theory with experience. Hence, the Correspondence theory is mainly identified with Empiricism, the main rival to Rationalism. Choice (A) cannot be correct because Empiricists do not accept a doctrine of innate ideas, nor do they think truth is a function of the relations among ideas (C). Both Empiricists and Rationalists are concerned with (D) knowledge. However, they approach these matters differently.

2. **(A)** The early Americans rejected theism but were not atheists because they believed in a God, but not the God of theism. Their God was a Creator but otherwise an "absentee God" of the sort proclaimed by Voltaire and other deists. Choice (B) is too vague, for it does not specify what the skepticism concerned. Choice (C) is incorrect because some Christians were theists while others were deists. None of the three was (D) an immoralist.

3. **(C)** The Skeptics differed from the dogmatists who believed that certain knowledge was possible but also differed from those who dogmatically asserted that knowledge is impossible. Sextus recommended suspending judgment about all beliefs, preferring to remain an open-minded inquirer. The correct answer is (C), since his skepticism was sweeping. All the other terms are too narrow to capture the scope of his view. One might suspend judgment about a (B) dogma, or (A) creed, or (D) moral code without suspending judgment about all beliefs. Sextus does not claim these are all false, but only that we are not in a position to know that they are true. He thus thinks other skeptics went too far in claiming falsehood.

4. **(A)** A person can envy his neighbor's good fortune, but jealousy involves more than two people since it typically involves a response to the belief that another person is paying too much attention to a third person. Thus, Tom may be jealous of Jane's attention to Fred, but not envious of Jane's attention to Fred. The other answers all mention a feature that is common to jealousy and envy, as various philosophies of emotion have shown. Both jealousy and envy involve belief (C), and envy could be sexual (D), since, for example, one might envy someone's sexual prowess.

CHAPTER 5

Music Review

CHAPTER 5

MUSIC REVIEW

Music is the organization of sound in time. Because it exists only in time, what some people call the fourth dimension, rather than in three-dimensional space, music is one of the more elusive art forms. Given this abstract quality and the enormous variety of music that exists in the world, it is surprising to realize that there are only four ways that one sound can differ from another. Each individual tone has four properties that give it a particular character: duration, frequency, intensity, and timbre. Musicians make choices within each of these categories to create the effect they hope their music will have on its listeners.

Duration refers to how long a sound or a silence lasts and the rate at which one sound succeeds another. **Rhythm** is based on this fundamental property of sound and is essential to our perception of time. Rhythm is built into the natural world. There is rhythm in the movement of the stars, in the cycle of seasons, in the alternation of day and night, in our very heartbeats and breathing. If there were no rhythm, we would not be aware that time was happening.

Most of the music that we hear and all music to which we dance or march has a steady beat, a regular **pulse** that underlies the melody. Whereas the pulse is steady with an unchanging note value, melodic rhythm involves a variety of note values. If you sing any song and clap the pulse, you will notice that some of the beats have more than one melodic note to them and some melodic notes extend over several beats. For instance, in "Happy Birthday to You," both of the notes of "happy" occur on a single beat while "you" extends over two beats.

Tempo refers to the speed of the pulse. The designation for different tempi are in Italian. Thus, if the beats are in the range of our heartbeats, around 72 pulses a minute, the tempo is *moderato* (moderate). If the beats are faster than our heartbeats, the tempo is *vivace*, or if very much faster, it is *presto*. If the beats are slower than our heartbeats, the tempo is *lento* or *largo*. A fast tempo conveys a mood of energy and excitement; a slow tempo produces a more somber or thoughtful feeling.

As rhythm in nature involves repeated patterns, such as the tide moving in and out twice a day, so the beat in music is most often organized into patterns. Patterns are formed when some beats are regularly stronger than others. Music organized in this fashion is said to be **metric**. In order to have meter, there must be both a steady pulse and a pattern of accented and unaccented beats. Music that does not have a steady pulse (such as recitative in operas or some atonal music), or music that has a steady pulse but no accents at all (such as Gregorian chant) or has unpredictable accents that do not form a recognizable pattern (such as Stravinsky's *Rite of Spring*) is said to be **ametric**. Most of the music in the world, however, is metric.

In Western music, we have only two basic patterns. A strong beat followed by a weak beat (ONE two, ONE two) or a strong beat followed by three weak beats (ONE two three four) is said to be **duple meter.** This is a meter you can walk and march to; it has a left - right, left - right straight-ahead sort of feeling. Almost all popular music is duple. The other pattern is **triple**, with a strong beat followed by two weak ones (ONE two three, ONE two three). Triple meter has a more swaying, side-to-side feeling and is used for waltzing, skating, or skipping. Some triple-meter songs are "Happy Birthday to You," "The Star-Spangled Banner," and "My Country 'Tis of Thee."

In notated music, each occurrence of the pattern constitutes a **measure** or **bar** and is set off by vertical bar lines. The meter itself is denoted by a **time signature** placed at the beginning of the music. This consists of two numbers positioned vertically. The upper number indicates how many beats are in a measure and the lower number identifies which kind of note gets the beat. For example, if the time signature is $\frac{3}{4}$, there are three beats per bar and each bar will have the equivalent of three quarter notes.

Duple and triple refer to how beats are joined together. Beats can also be subdivided, that is, a single beat may carry several melodic notes. If the beat is subdivided into two or multiples of two, the meter is said to be **simple**. Duple simple meter is counted 1 & 2 & / 1 & 2 &, and triple simple meter is counted 1 & 2 & 3 & / 1 & 2 & 3 &. Sometimes, however, there are three melodic notes evenly spread over a single beat. In this case, the meter is said to be **compound**. "Row, row, row your boat" is in duple compound meter, counted 1 & a 2 & a / 1 & a 2 & a. This is evident in the words "merrily, merrily, merrily, merrily." Compound triple meter, counted 1 & a 2 & a 3 & a, also exists, but is less common. A beautiful example is J. S. Bach's "Jesu, Joy of Man's Desiring."

Sometimes there is a strong underlying meter, but the melodic accents come where you don't expect them — between the beats or on weak rather than strong beats, as in 1 & 2 **&**. This is called **syncopation** and is the means by which jazz conveys a feeling of swing.

Meter in much of the rest of the world is more complex than it is in even the most sophisticated Western music. In the music of India and the Arab world, for instance, the patterns might extend for over 20 beats, in contrast to our simple two- or three-beat patterns. In the music of Africa, many different patterns are heard simultaneously, creating a layering of patterns that produces a dense, highly complex meter.

Sound happens when something that is capable of vibrating, such as a taut string or a vocal chord, is set in motion by the movement of air. If the vibrations are irregular, the result is noise, such as the sound of wind in the trees, a car engine, or a cough. If the vibrations are regular, the result is a tone that has the property of pitch. Pitch refers to how high or low the ear perceives the tone to be. Frequency determines pitch and measures the number of regular vibrations per second. These are too fast to see; 440 vibrations per second produces the pitch to which instrumentalists tune, which is the note "A." The higher the frequency, the more vibrations per second and the higher the pitch; fewer vibrations per second produce a lower pitch.

When the number of vibrations is doubled or halved, the pitch that is produced is the same, but in a different register. That is to say, as pitches rise or descend, they repeat at a regular distance. Since 440 vibrations per second produce a note called "A," 220 will also produce an "A" but in a lower register; 880 will produce an "A" but in a higher register, and so on. An **interval** is the distance between two pitches. The interval from one pitch to its next repetition, for example from A220 to A440, is called an **octave.**

There are several ways of dividing up the octave into smaller intervals. In music of the Arab world and India, for example, the octave is divided into two dozen different pitches producing quarter-steps. In Western music, the octave is divided into only twelve intervals of equal size. These are called **half steps** and are the smallest intervals possible in Western music.

We name the pitches according to the alphabet, from A to G, at which point the pitches repeat. On a piano keyboard, pitch ascends as we move from left to right. Only the white keys are given alphabet names:

C D E F G A B C D E F G A B

Notice that the black keys are arranged in a pattern of alternating twos and threes. This asymmetrical arrangement helps in identifying the pitches. The white key between the pair of black keys is always D. The black keys are named according to their relationship to the white keys. When the black key is named in relationship to the white key on its left, it raises the pitch of that key a half step and is called a **sharp.** The symbol for a sharp is ♯. When the same black key is considered in relationship to the white key on its right, its pitch is a half step lower and is called a **flat.** The symbol for a flat is ♭. Thus the same pitch may have two different names, depending on the context. For example, C♯ is the same pitch as D♭.

On a keyboard, a half step is between adjacent keys, such as between a black key and its neighboring white key. There are also two places on the keyboard where half steps exist between two white keys that have no intervening black key: between E and F, and between B and C. A whole step consists of two half steps, for instance the distance from C to D, and from C♯ to D♯, and so on.

The arrangement of pitches within an octave is called a **scale,** which comes from the Italian *scala,* meaning ladder. Pitches are like the rungs of a ladder going from one level to the next. There are many different kinds of scales. A scale which contains all twelve half steps, that is, one that uses every key on the piano, is called a **chromatic** scale. A scale consisting only of whole steps is called a whole tone scale. Most scales, however, are a mixture of whole and half steps, and some have augmented 2nds, which is an interval of three half steps.

Almost all Western music is based on **diatonic** scales, that is, scales that use each letter name only once, and thus have seven different pitches. Not all scales are diatonic. A **pentatonic** scale has, as its name suggests, only five different pitches and therefore skips some letter names. Using only the black keys on the piano, you can produce a pentatonic scale. Much Japanese, Indonesian, Scottish, and folk music is based on pentatonic scales, as is the well-known hymn "Amazing Grace." A **blues scale** has six different pitches, but one letter name is repeated and two are skipped: G B♭ C C♯ D F G.

There are two forms of diatonic scales: **major** and **minor**. If you play a scale from one C to the next using only white notes, you will produce a major scale. It consists of half steps between the 3rd and 4th notes and between the 7th and 8th notes. All other steps are whole steps. As long as this arrangement is kept intact: 1 - 2 - 3 4 - 5 - 6 - 7 8, a major scale can be built from any note. A scale built on D would be spelled: D - E - F♯ G - A - B - C♯ D. One on F would be: F - G - A B♭- C - D - E F. Notice that each letter name is used only once. In the scale on F, although A♯ would produce the same pitch as B♭, we have already used an A and may not skip the letter B.

The scale that a piece of music is built on is indicated in notated music by a **key signature** at the beginning of the music, just after the time signature. For example, in the scale built on D, the key signature would have two sharps, one on F and one on C. For the scale on F, the key signature would have one flat on B.

A diatonic scale in the **minor** mode is found on the white keys beginning on A. Here the half steps are between 2 and 3 and between 5 and 6 to produce the arrangement:

1 - 2 3 - 4 - 5 6 - 7 - 8. It may seem like a small detail, whether the third note of the scale is two whole steps or a whole step and a half step above the starting pitch, but the difference in effect is big. To most people, music using a major scale sounds bright and happy compared to music in a minor key, which sounds darker and sadder. Perhaps that is why most popular music is in a major mode.

The note on which a diatonic scale is built is called the **tonic**. Music that uses a diatonic scale is said to be **in the key of** the tonic note upon which the scale is built. Thus, music that uses the white notes beginning on C is said to be **in the key of** C major. Music that uses the scale beginning on C but with half-steps between 2 & 3 and 5 & 6 (C - D E♭ - F - G A♭ - B♭ - C) is said to be **in the key of** C minor. In both cases, C is the tonic, the home note, the goal of the music. Music that is in C major or C minor will not sound finished until it arrives on its tonic note of C. All the other notes of the diatonic scale are named in relation to this most important note. The note an interval of a 5th above the tonic (G in C major) is called the **dominant**. The one a 5th below the tonic (F in C major) is called the **subdominant**. The note between the tonic and the domi-nant (E in C major) is the **mediant**; that between the subdominant and the tonic is the **submediant**. The second step of the scale is the **supertonic**. And the note a half-step below the tonic in a major scale is called the **leading tone.** The notes can also be identified by solfege syllables:

Tonic	Supertonic	Mediant	Subdominant	Dominant	Mediant	Leading Tone	Tonic
Do	Re	Mi	Fa	Sol	La	Ti	Do

When three or more notes are sounded simultaneously, the result is a **chord**. The most prevalent chord is a **triad**. As the name suggests, a triad is a three-note chord comprised of alternating scale degrees. Examples are C - E - G; D - F - A; E - G - B, and so on. The tonic triad in C major is spelled C - E - G. C is the root of the triad; E is the third and G the fifth of the triad. From C to E are two whole steps, which is called the interval of a **major 3rd (M3rd)**. From E to G are a whole step and a half step, an interval of a **minor 3rd (m3rd)**. The distance from the root to the fifth is three and a half steps, the interval of a **perfect 5th (P5th)**. This is the definition of a major triad: M3rd on bottom; m3rd on top; P5th from root to fifth. There are four possible kinds of triads, depending on the arrangement of major and minor thirds:

Quality of triad	MAJOR	MINOR	DIMINISHED	AUGMENTED
Root to Third	Major	Minor	Minor	Major
Third to Fifth	Minor	Major	Minor	Major
Root to Fifth	Perfect	Perfect	Diminished	Augmented

Triads may be built on each step of the scale. Their position and quality are identified by roman numerals: upper case for major, lower case for minor, a small circle for diminished, and a plus sign (+) for augmented. For example, a tonic triad is indicated by the roman numeral I. In a major scale, the triads built on the first, fourth, and fifth steps of the scale are major, hence the upper-case roman numerals. The triads built on the second, third, and sixth steps of the scale are minor, hence the lower-case roman numerals. And that built on the seventh step is diminished:

	Tonic	Supertonic	Mediant	Subdominant	Dominant	Mediant	Leading Tone	Tonic
Major scale:	I	ii	iii	IV	V	vi	vii°	I
Minor scale:	i	ii°	III	iv	v	VI	VII	i

The most common triads are I, IV, and V. With only these three chords, many songs can be accompanied.

Chords are pitches that happen simultaneously, or vertically. Pitches that occur horizontally, that is, in succession over time, create melody. **Melody** is a succession of pitches in a particular rhythmic pattern. Melody is a broad term that includes music that we may not consider very melodic. Melodies we can remember easily are "tunes." Each of us has hundreds of tunes stored in our memories.

Melodic direction refers to the shape of the arrangement of pitches. A melody may be mostly ascending, mostly descending, may seem to curl around itself, or, as is most often the case, use a mixture of all three. **Range** refers to how far the highest note is from the lowest note in a given melody. The wider the range, the more energy the music seems to have.

Melodic motion is how a tune gets from one pitch to the next. If the melody moves by small steps, it is said to be using conjunct motion. If it moves by leaps, it is using disjunct motion. All of these factors together produce the mood of a melody. If a composer wants to portray happy excitement, she will probably use much disjunct motion that mostly ascends over a wide range. Gloomy disappointment would be portrayed by conjunct motion, limping downward within a very narrow range.

Melodies are organized according to the principle of repetition and contrast. If a melody has too much repetition, it is dull; too much contrast sounds chaotic and unmemorable. So a good melody has the right balance between the two. As an example, "Twinkle, twinkle, little star" is in four musical phrases. The second and fourth phrases are exactly like the first —repetition. The third is different—contrast. So the phrases of this simple tune could be diagrammed as: a a b a. Large symphonic movements are more complex and happen over a larger space of time, but are in musical forms organized according to this same principle.

Texture refers to how melodies are presented. If there is only a single melody with no accompaniment at all, the texture is monophonic. This is true even if many performers and singers are playing the same melody. For instance, the famous opening notes of Beethoven's fifth symphony, "ta ta ta dum," are monophonic. If two or more melodies are happening at the same time and seem to be of equal interest and to be competing for the listener's attention, as happens when people sing a round beginning at different times, the texture is polyphonic. If there is a single melody in the foreground with subsidiary melodies or chords accompanying it in the background, the texture is homophonic. The use of harmony to accompany melody is what sets Western music apart from other kinds of music. Most of the music in much of the non-Western world is monophonic, but in the West the most prevalent texture is homophony.

Intensity refers to how loud or soft a tone is. The musical term for this is **dynamics**. As with tempo markings, the names for dynamics are in Italian. Ranging from softest to loudest they are:

pianissimo	*piano*	*mezzopiano*	*mezzoforte*	*forte*	*fortissimo*
pp	**p**	**mp**	**mf**	**f**	**ff**

Dynamics are a big factor in contributing to the effect of a piece of music. The louder the music, the more extroverted and energetic; softer music is more intimate and tender. Music can also gradually go from loud to soft (*decrescendo*) or from soft to loud (*crescendo*). It can be in a *piano* dynamic and suddenly become loud (*subito forte*), or in a *forte* dynamic and suddenly get soft (*subito piano*).

Timbre refers to the source of the musical sound, which instrument or what kind of voice is producing the music. Timbre has to do with the physics of sound, specifically what overtones are present and in what proportions. The concept is difficult to explain, but easy to hear. It's why we can tell the difference between a trumpet and a flute or a piano and how we can recognize our friends' voices.

The earliest musical instrument was undoubtedly the human voice. Using our voices in a musical manner seems to be universal in the human community. Voices are classified partly according to their range and partly according to their tone color. The lowest male voice is a bass, the highest a tenor, and in between the two is the baritone. The comparable female voices are alto, soprano, and mezzosoprano.

Instruments are categorized according to two different systems. One method is based on how the sound is produced and is useful for many different kinds of music. Chordophones produce sound when a taut string or chord is set in motion, by either bowing, hammering, or plucking. Violins, pianos, harpsichords, and guitars are chordophones. Aerophones are instruments that confine a column of air that is set in motion by breath. They include flutes, trumpets, and whistles. Membranophones produce sound when a membrane that is stretched across a hollow cavity is struck. These are drums of all kinds.

Idiophones are instruments that themselves vibrate when struck, such as bells, cymbals, and rattles.

The second method classifies instruments according to families in a symphony orchestra and is appropriate only for Western music. The string family includes violins, violas, cellos, and double basses. The wind family includes flutes, single-reed instruments like the clarinet, and double-reed instruments like the oboe and bassoon. The brass family comprises trumpets, French horns, trombones, and tubas. The percussion section includes all drums and anything that is struck, such as the xylophone.

Timbre is particularly important in the music of China. The Chinese have a large assortment of instruments that are classified according to the material of which they are made, such as silk, bamboo, brass, clay, wood, and so forth. Each timbre and each musical tone carries an extra-musical significance that is more important than any purely musical considerations. For example, a single tone may carry the connotation of autumn, water, and the north.

We have seen, in passing, that in different cultures, certain aspects of music are emphasized more than others. In Western music, harmony is treated in a sophisticated manner, while rhythm and melody remain relatively simple. In the music of Africa, rhythm is given a highly complex treatment, while harmony and melody are less developed. In the music of the Arab world and India, both melody and rhythm are more intricate, but there is little, if any, harmony. And in China, the emphasis is placed on subtleties of timbre.

WESTERN MUSIC

The history of Western music is divided into six periods, each with recognizably distinct characteristics: Medieval, Renaissance, Baroque, Classical, Romantic, and Twentieth Century. The pattern seemed to be that a musical style emerged, and, over a period of time, grew more and more intricate. There is then a reaction against that complexity, resulting in a new stylistic period.

The **MEDIEVAL** period begins with the earliest music in Europe for which any notated music survives and ends around the year 1450. Gradually during this period, musical notation was developed. It came about because monks in monasteries were required to learn an enormous body of chants that required some sort of *aide memoire*. At first only the direction of the melodic motion was indicated. Then, over time, a more precise method was devised for fixing pitches: noteheads were placed on ledger lines, which numbered anywhere from two to ten before finally settling into today's five-line staff. These fixed a relative, but not absolute, pitch. For that, a clef sign was needed to identify a single pitch from which the others could be derived. Clef signs therefore are designed to resemble letter names: the G-clef is our soprano clef; the F-clef our bass clef. There are also C-clefs, which are used by voices and violas. Finally, late in the period, a method was devised for indicating durations of notes, thus allowing rhythmic variety.

Paper was precious and expensive, and very few people could write words, let alone music. The only music that was notated was liturgical chant—that is, music that was performed as part of a religious service. Although this is the only music from the early part of this period that has come down to us, we can be sure that secular, popular music did, in fact, exist, but because it was not written down, we don't really know what it was like. We do know that there were nomadic poet-musicians known as troubadours and trouvères who sang songs of chivalric devotion and crusader feats as well as pilgrim songs, and that these were monophonic.

The liturgical music was called plainchant, or more commonly, albeit misleadingly, Gregorian chant. It was performed *a capella*—that is, voices only with no instrumental accompaniment or doubling, and was monophonic. Beginning around the tenth century, a stunning innovation took place. Perhaps emerging because boys and men sing at different octaves, or because some monks sang "out of tune," medieval polyphony gradually came about. At first the accompanying lines were mere drones, but little by little a second independent melodic line was achieved, and this eventually laid the foundation for the development of harmony.

By the twelfth century, Paris was the most important cultural center in Europe, and it is there that we have the first named composers. The cathedral of Notre Dame, then in the process of being built, had attached to it musicians who constituted the School of Notre Dame. **Leonin** (c. 1135–1201) composed the first complete annual cycle of chants for the mass in two parts. His successor **Perotin** (fl. 1190–c. 1225) did the same in four parts.

The fourteenth century was a turbulent period that saw the Hundred Years War, the Black Death, and great corruption in the church. Because of advances in musical notation, especially in the area of rhythm, music got enormously complex. Musicians of the time, as **Guillaume Machaut**, self-consciously called themselves *Ars Nova*, to set themselves apart from what they considered old-fashioned, conservative musical practices. In some secular music, as in the *Roman de Fauvel*, which was a cynical critique of both church and government, the voices simultaneously have different texts, often in different languages, and different melodic lines. Two or more of the voices would be quite active and independent of one another while one or more other voices would hold long drone notes. The inevitable reaction against an excess of complexity led to the next stylistic musical period.

The **RENAISSANCE** period in music begins around 1450 and extends to 1600. The word literally means "rebirth." It was a time of renewed confidence and a flowering of the arts influenced in part by the discovery of classical Greek philosophy. Renaissance musicians, inspired by the Greeks' belief in the power of music to shape one's soul and of words to express emotions and influence actions, had a great reverence for the importance of text when combined with music. In what was a new urge toward cohesion, all the voices have the same text set to the same music, although not sung at the same time, as the voices enter one after the other. Unlike *Ars Nova* polyphony, all the voices are of equal value; none is relegated to drone status. This new kind of texture, called **imitative polyphony**, is the most characteristic feature of Renaissance music.

As the church had reformed itself, there was a renewed emphasis on sacred compositions. Whereas Medieval composers had set mainly the Propers of the mass, those sections which change from day to day such as the Gradual and the Introit, Renaissance composers concentrated on the Ordinary of the mass, the Kyrie, Gloria, Credo, Sanctus and Benedictus, and Agnus Dei, that never vary from day to day. These, being sacred and for liturgical use, were in Latin, and were sung *a capella* in imitative polyphony. Free standing religious compositions, called **motets**, have the same characteristics as mass settings. Renaissance composers also wrote secular (non-religious) compositions called **madrigals.** They are similar to mass movements and motets, except they are in the vernacular—such as Italian or English—rather than Latin and tend to be in a livelier style.

Renaissance musical instruments were of two kinds: softer "indoor" instruments like the viol and lute, and louder "outdoor" ones like shawms, crumhorns, and sackbuts. The indoor instruments tended to be used for instrumental music that was modeled on vocal forms to create a textless imitative polyphony. Outdoor instruments were used for movement, such as procession-als and dances, and were therefore more obviously metrical.

The most outstanding composer of the Renaissance period was **Josquin Desprez** (1440–1521). Martin Luther, the moving spirit behind the Reforma-tion, said of Josquin that he was master of the notes, whereas the reverse was true for other composers. During the period of the Counter-Reformation, when the Catholic church was again trying to reform itself from within, the deci-sion was taken at the Council of Trent to ban polyphony from church services. Legend has it that **Giovanni Palestrina** (c. 1525–1594) saved Catholic church music by demonstrating to the cardinals at the Council of Trent that music could be polyphonic and yet be clearly understood with his Pope Marcellus Mass. Music written for the Roman Catholic church has been conservative ever since.

Experimentation was, however, taking place in the area of secular vocal music. Composers like **Carlo Gesualdo** (c. 1561–1613) wrote madrigals that displayed daring harmonic dissonances, but had a precious, mannered approach to the text. Each separate word was given its own illustrative treatment, making nonsense of the text as a whole. The reaction to this practice not only ushered in a new stylistic period, but led to the creation of an entirely new musical genre.

The **BAROQUE** period begins around 1600 with the invention of **opera** and ends around 1750 with the death of Johann Sebastian Bach. In the last decade of the sixteenth century, a group of intellectuals in Italy called the "Florentine Camerata" once again looked back to classical Greece for inspiration to reform music. Whereas at the beginning of the Renaissance, it was Greek philosophy that influenced music, for the Florentine Camerata it was Greek drama. They conceived of the idea that drama could be sung throughout with the simplest of accompaniments, and thus **opera** was created.

This produced far-reaching changes in musical style. The Renaissance ideal sound was three to six equal voices with no instrumental accompaniment. Each vocal line was conceived of horizontally, as a melodic line. In early opera, the ideal was a solo voice with a light instrumental accompaniment. The latter consisted of a bass line with a system of numbers over certain bass notes to indicate vertical harmony. A sustaining instrument such as a cello played the bass line while the harmony was improvised by a harpsichord or lute player. This was called **basso continuo** and is characteristic of almost all Baroque music. The Baroque ideal sound was a solo melodic line supported by a strong bass line with the space between the two filled in by harmony—in other words, a more vertical approach to musical organization. It was during this period that **functional tonal harmony** using major and minor diatonic scales was established.

Another difference in style between the Renaissance and Baroque has to do with rhythm. Except for instrumental music expressly written for the dance, Renaissance music is free-flowing and almost without accents, hence not quite metric. Baroque music, on the other hand, is strongly metrical. Baroque music, of all kinds and for whatever purpose, dances. Very often in Baroque music, once a rhythmical pattern is established, it persists throughout the entire piece or movement, reflecting an urge toward cohesion and unity.

The first great opera composer was **Claudio Monteverdi** (1567–1643), whose *Orfeo* is still performed today. But the most famous composer of Italian *opera seria* was a German who spent most of his creative life in London: **George Frideric Handel** (1685–1759). As the name suggests, *opera seria* deals with serious topics borrowed from Roman mythology or from ancient history. The elements of Italian opera are an instrumental overture, then alternating vocal recitative and arias. **Recitative** is like heightened speech and occurs in that part of the drama where action is carried forward. It is in prose with only basso continuo accompaniment. An **aria** is more akin to poetry and has a fuller orchestral accompaniment. When London audiences turned against Italian opera as an "irrational and exotic entertainment," Handel gave them unstaged opera in English using biblical stories as his subject matter and adding the new ingredient of the chorus: the **oratorio.** His *Messiah* is one of the most beloved musical works of all time.

An exact contemporary of Handel's whose music is the epitome of the High Baroque style is **Johann Sebastian Bach** (1685–1750). Bach never wrote an opera, but he wrote **cantatas** and The St. John and St. Matthew **passions** for the Lutheran church that, like Handel's oratorios, have all the characteristics of opera. Bach included in them the Lutheran chorale, a form of congregational hymn-singing introduced by Martin Luther.

During the Baroque period, instrumental music for the first time came to be as important as vocal music. This was the beginning of **absolute music**—that is, abstract instrumental music that is not dependent on words or movement for its form. Composers therefore had to look within the music itself, to the principles of repetition and contrast, to create musical forms. The rapidly developing tonal system also contributed to the creation of form, which essentially consists of establishing the tonic, moving away from the tonic, and returning to the tonic.

The most important of the new instruments was the violin, made popular by, among others, **Arcangelo Corelli** (1653–1713), who wrote exclusively for the violin in the genres of solo sonatas (one solo instrument plus continuo), and trio sonatas (two solo instruments plus continuo), and **Antonio Vivaldi** (1678–1741), who established the three-movement instrumental concerto (one or more solo instruments plus orchestra), as in his famous *The Four Seasons*, a set of four concerti with each one representing a season of the year.

Keyboard music was also important. The harpsichord was essential to almost all Baroque music as part of the *basso continuo*, but was also used extensively as a solo instrument. Bach, who was the greatest organist of his day, wrote **fugues** for organ and harpsichord as well as for vocal chorus. "Fugue" comes from the Italian *"fuga,"* meaning to chase. As in imitative polyphony, different voices sing the same melody at different times. In Renaissance imitative polyphony, however, each phrase is given its own music. In the Baroque fugue, a single musical idea, called the fugue subject, appears throughout, first in the tonic, then in other key areas, and finally in the tonic again. The repetition of the fugue subject provides unity; its appearance in different keys provides contrast.

The **CLASSICAL** period, dating from the death of J. S. Bach in 1750 until the 1820s, came about because of great changes taking place in society. The traditional sources of musical patronage, the aristocracy and the church, were losing ground to the emerging middle classes. Quality music was no longer limited to the privileged few. This period saw the proliferation of public concerts, which anybody could attend for the price of a ticket. Music publishing flourished, meaning the latest compositions were quickly available for the amateur music market. Composers therefore had to find ways of appealing to a broader public. They imbued their music with clarity, naturalness, and a pleasing variety, all hallmarks of the newly emerging Classical style.

The beginnings of the new style are found in what happened to opera late in the Baroque period. Italian *opera seria* comprised three acts. In the first half of the eighteenth century, a two-act *opera buffa* (comic opera) was often inserted between the acts to entertain the audience. In *opera seria*, the drama was less important than beautiful and bravura singing, and the characters were lofty historical figures. *Opera buffa* was about real people in everyday situations, such as problems between servants and their bourgeois masters. The emphasis was on fast-moving dramatic action, clever dialogue, and lightly accompanied and appealing arias. In time, *opera buffa* became so popular that it was detached from *opera seria* and became a genre in its own right, eventually eclipsing *opera seria* entirely. The best known examples are Mozart's *Marriage of Figaro, Don Giovanni,* and *Cosi fan tutte.*

Franz Josef Haydn (1732–1809) did much to develop two new classical instrumental genres, and **Wolfgang Amadeus Mozart** (1756–1791) further perfected them. The **symphony**, a work for full orchestra, and the **string quartet** (two violins, viola, and cello) are generally in four movements. The first movement is usually in **sonata** form, which is more of a dynamic process than a form. It comprises three sections that correspond to three acts of a drama. In the **exposition,** a musical idea is presented in the tonic key. There is then a transition to a new key area and, usually, contrasting thematic ideas. There is thus tension between the two key areas. In the **development** section, the plot thickens as material presented in the exposition is broken apart, combined in new ways, and taken to more distant key areas. The denouement in the **recapitulation** is brought about by repeating the exposition, but this time keeping everything in the tonic—the home key—to provide a resolution. Sonata form was so fundamental to the classical approach that it influenced other forms as well.

The second movement of symphonies and quartets is often a slow movement. It might be in sonata form, or theme and variations, or ternary form. The latter has three parts diagrammed as A B A: the first is in the tonic, the middle section presents contrasting material in a different key, and the third is a repetition of the first. The third movement, paired dances that hark back to the Baroque suite, is also in ternary form, with the A sections being a minuet or scherzo and the contrasting B section a trio. The fourth movement is usually fast and may be in sonata form, theme and variations, or rondo-sonata. Rondo form, inherited from the Baroque period, is an extension of the ternary idea with several contrasting sections, each in a different key, alternating with the A section, which is always in the tonic, for example A B A C A D A. In rondo-sonata form, the D section is replaced by the B section, which is now resolved in the tonic.

The classical **concerto** for soloist and orchestra omits the fourth movement, but is otherwise organized in the same manner, as is the classical **piano sonata,** for which the number of movements is more variable. The *fortepiano* was invented around the middle of the eighteenth century. Because it was capable of producing a wide range of dynamics, the piano rapidly replaced the softer-voiced harpsichord as the keyboard instrument of choice for solos, concerti, and chamber music that was performed in ever larger public concert halls.

Unlike Haydn and Mozart, **Ludwig van Beethoven** (1770–1827) was born late enough to have been influenced by the French Revolution. His music is considered revolutionary, not because he overthrew existing practices, but because he expanded all the elements of the classical style and enlarged the range of expression. His nine symphonies, for example, are longer and for larger performing forces than Haydn's or Mozart's. His dynamic range is wider, his rhythm more propulsive, and his harmonic resources greatly extended.

Rather than reacting against the Classical style, composers of the **ROMANTIC** period, which extends through the end of the nineteenth century, carried Beethoven's innovations even further to new levels of expressiveness. Where Classical composers aimed at clarity, Romantic composers sought ambiguity. Rhythm became more complex through the use of shifting meters and *rubato*, a surging forward or holding back of the pulse. Tonal harmony was obscured through the increasing use of *chromaticism*, which is the inclusion of notes that are foreign to the key, and through a tendency to defer a sense of resolution by seeming to evade arrival at the tonic. Phrases became longer and less clearly articulated. The symphony orchestra was enlarged and included a greater variety of wind and brass instruments.

Music during the Romantic period tended toward the grandiose, and audiences prized showy virtuosity. The pianist and composer **Franz Liszt** (1811–1886) and the violinist **Niccolo Paganini** (1782–1840) enjoyed the kind of adulation we associate with today's rock stars. **Program** music grew in importance during this period. Program music, in contrast to absolute music, is instrumental music that depends for its inspiration and its understanding on something external to music—a landscape, as in the *Hebrides Overture* by **Felix Mendelssohn** (1809–1847); drama, as in the symphonic overture *Romeo and Juliet* by the Russian composer **Peter Ilyich Tchaikovsky** (1840–1893); nature, as in the piano character piece *Papillons* (butterflies) by **Robert Schumann** (1810–1856); or even the composer's autobiography, as in the *Symphonie Fantastique* by the French composer **Hector Berlioz** (1803–1869). One composer who resisted the trend was **Johannes Brahms** (1833–1897). His symphonies, concerti, and chamber music adhere to abstract musical principles.

In an age when bigger seemed to be better, it is surprising to find two new intimate genres. *Lieder*, which is German for art songs, is poetry set to music for a solo singer with piano accompaniment. **Franz Schubert** (1797–1828) wrote hundreds of *lieder,* including one written when he was only eighteen, his well-known setting of Goethe's ballad-poem *Der Erlkönig*. Like *lieder*, piano character pieces are one-movement miniatures that aim to set a mood in a brief space of time. Most Romantic composers wrote in many genres, but one, **Frederic Chopin** (1810–1849), wrote exclusively for the piano. His solo piano works include polonaises, études, and impromptus.

Opera during the nineteenth century was dominated by two composers. The Italian **Giuseppe Verdi** (1813–1901) wrote 28 operas, including some of the most beloved in the repertoire: *Rigoletto, La Traviata, Aida,* and *Otello*. His exact German contemporary, **Richard Wagner** (1813–1883), wrote his own *libretti* drawing on German mythic legends. His masterpiece, *Der Ring des Nibelungen*, is a cycle of four operas.

By the end of the nineteenth century, the romantics had stretched the elements of Western music so far that there was a reaction against what was viewed as emotional excess. Composers experimented with new techniques of composition and explored new directions for their music. Music of the **twentieth century** is therefore not distinguished by a single style. Instead we find several different approaches, none of which seem to have firmly caught hold. Most have in common an abandonment of tonality.

In the period preceding the first world war, contemporary movements in painting inspired three distinct musical styles. Impressionist painters, such as Monet, fragmented the visual into its elements of color and shape. **Impressionism** in music tried to do the same thing by careful attention to tone color and the manipulation of melodic fragments. An example is the three-movement orchestral work, *La Mer*, by the French composer **Claude Debussy** (1862–1918). **Expressionist** painters and composers were influenced by the work of Sigmund Freud on the irrational subconscious. They depict the outer world through a sort of deranged subjectivity. *Pierrot Lunaire* is a song cycle for soprano and five instrumentalists by the German composer **Arnold Schönberg** (1874–1951) that depicts the increasing lunacy of "Pierrot." The soprano uses *sprechstimme*, a style of performing characterized by wide, angular, unpredictable intervals where the exact pitches of the notes are not indicated. **Primitivism** was influenced by the Spanish painter Pablo Picasso, who painted the sets for the ballet *Sacre du Printemps* depicting the fertility rites of early Slavic tribes with music by the Russian composer **Igor Stravinsky** (1882–1971). This music is characterized by powerful dissonances; *ostinatos* in which Stravinsky obsessively repeats fragments taken from Russian folk songs; and an enlarged percussion section that was given unprecedented prominence.

In the 1920s, Arnold **Schönberg** devised a new method for organizing atonal music. He called it the *twelve-tone* method or *serialism*, whereby the composer makes a pre-compositional decision about the order in which the twelve notes of the chromatic scale will be heard. This was called the *tone row*. Once the composer sets the tone row, the pitches may only come in that order, although the row may be inverted (turned upside down) or played retrograde (back-wards). Other composers, such as the American **Milton Babbitt** (b. 1916), took this even further and "serialized" duration and dynamic level as well as pitch.

Diametrically opposed to such total control was **chance music**, which also had parallels in the other arts such as participatory theater and art events known as "happenings." The ultimate example of this is *4'33"* by the American com-poser **John Cage** (1912–1992), wherein the performers sit in silence for the entire piece, drawing attention to ambient sounds in the environment. With advances in technology, some composers experimented with computer-gener-ated music, such as *poème électronique* of the French composer **Edgard Varèse** (1883–1965). **Minimalism**, a more recent movement, represents a return to tonality and meter, but with a minimum of musical ideas obsessively repeated, for example *Glassworks* by the American composer **Philip Glass** (b. 1937). Composers today find inspiration from music of the distant past, from other cul-tural traditions, and from other fields, such as jazz.

Many people consider **JAZZ** to be America's only original contribution to music. It originated in American black culture around the beginning of the twentieth century. Some of its roots are found in the **call and response** of "field hollers," work songs where a leader sings a line and the others respond sym-pathetically, a technique that is still heard in African folk songs; **blues** songs; **gospel** singing; and the **ragtime** piano style of black artists like **Scott Joplin** (1868–1917).

Jazz is more of a performer's than a composer's art since the music is impro-vised rather than read from a score or memorized. This means that the per-formers agree on a tune, key, tempo, and form, then, based on that, make up what they play as they go along in a spontaneous way. Syncopation—putting an accent where one doesn't expect it—is an important element in jazz. This happens at two levels: the rhythm section provides a steady "back-beat" (one TWO one TWO) over which the melody instruments move a fraction of a beat ahead or behind the pulse. When this happens, the music is said to swing.

In its brief history, jazz has gone through several styles. The earliest is **New Orleans** style, also called Dixieland. Small ensembles consisted of a rhythm section of drums, piano, and/or bass and two or more soloists on trumpet, saxophone, clarinet, trombone, or voice. **Louis Armstrong** (1900–1971) played trumpet and sang in a style called "scat," where the voice, singing syllables rather than words, is used as another instrument. During the Depression years of the early 1930s, solo piano came to the fore with **stride** and **boogie woogie**. In the late 1930s and early 1940s during World War II, **swing** or **big-band** jazz "crossed over" and became widely popular. Swing bands were large ensembles of ten to twenty performers playing under the direction of a leader from written-out arrangements called "charts," which left less room for improvisation. One of the greatest of the swing band leaders was the pianist and composer **Duke Ellington** (1899–1974).

After the war years, when the popularity of the big bands collapsed as the mass market turned to rock and roll, jazz performers returned to the emphasis on improvisation afforded by smaller ensembles. But they did so with a new virtuosity and more sophisticated, complex harmonies in a style called **bebop**. Some of the outstanding performers of bebop were the alto saxophonist **Charlie Parker** (1920–1955) and the trumpeter **Miles Davis** (1926–1991). Bebop has been succeeded by many different jazz styles, such as the more laid back cool jazz and free jazz (total improvisation), as well as a nostalgic return to the "classical" New Orleans style. As in art music, jazz musicians are currently looking to other fields, such as rap, Afro-Cuban music, and the music of other cultures, to produce a blended style called **fusion.**

Drill: Music

1. Which of the following are examples of musical scales?

   I.   Chromatic
   II. Octatonic
   III. Blues
   IV. Raga

   (A) I only
   (B) I and III
   (C) I and II
   (D) All of the above.

2. Which of the following is an example of ametric music?

   (A) African drumming
   (B) Gregorian chant
   (C) Jazz
   (D) Rap music

3. A major diatonic scale has half-steps between

   (A) 1-2 and 5-6.
   (B) 2-3 and 5-6.
   (C) 3-4 and 7-8.
   (D) 4-5 and 7-8.

4. A major triad has

   (A) two major thirds.
   (B) a minor third below a major third.
   (C) two minor thirds.
   (D) a minor third above a major third.

5. An important innovation during the Medieval period was

    I.   notation.
    II. serialism.
    III. opera.
    IV. polyphony.

    (A) I and IV
    (B) I only
    (C) I and II
    (D) I and III

6. An important characteristic of Renaissance music is

    (A) compound meter.
    (B) *sprechstimme*.
    (C) imitative polyphony.
    (D) recitative.

7. Which of the following is an example of absolute music?

    (A) Bach's *St. John Passion*
    (B) Beethoven's Symphony
    (C) Brahms' Piano Concerto No. 1
    (D) Tchaikovsky's *Swan Lake* No. 6

8. Swing, in jazz, has to do with

    (A) stop time.
    (B) improvisation.
    (C) 32-bar chorus.
    (D) rhythm.

9. J.S. Bach never wrote for which of the following instruments?

    I.   Viola da gamba
    II. Clarinet
    III. Fortepiano
    IV. Oboe de caccia

    (A) I and III
    (B) III and IV
    (C) II and III
    (D) I and II

10. Which of the following does not belong with the others?

    (A) Mozart's *The Magic Flute*
    (B) Stravinsky's *Firebird*
    (C) Tchaikovsky's *The Nutcracker Suite*
    (D) Prokofiev's *Romeo and Juliet*

11. Which of the following contributed to the development of Rock and Roll in the 1950s?

    I.   Economic prosperity
    II. Country and Western
    III. Tin Pan Alley
    IV. Rhythm and Blues

    (A) II and IV
    (B) II, III, and IV
    (C) I and II
    (D) All of the above.

12. Which of the following is not a genre typical of the Romantic period?

    (A) Tone poem
    (B) Concerto grosso
    (C) Symphonic overture
    (D) Song cycle

Music Review

Answer Key

1.	(D)	4.	(D)	7.	(C)	10.	(A)
2.	(B)	5.	(A)	8.	(D)	11.	(D)
3.	(C)	6.	(C)	9.	(C)	12.	(B)

Detailed Explanations of Answers

Drill: Music

1. **(D)** All are examples of scales. The chromatic scale is one that uses every note in the Western octave and consists only of half-steps. The octatonic scale is one devised by Igor Stravinsky and consists of alternating half and whole steps. The blues scale is a particular arrangement of pitches (it has two augmented 2nds, two half steps, and two whole steps) that gives the blues its distinctive sound. Raga refers to both the arrangement of pitches within the octave and to the musical form of classical Indian music.

2. **(B)** Metric music has both a steady pulse and a pattern of regular accents. Gregorian chant is ametric because, although it has a steady pulse, it has no accents. Rap music, which is essentially poetic, is strongly metric. In African drumming, several meters occur simultaneously, producing polymeters. Jazz exhibits rhythmic complexity in having a great deal of syncopation, but this occurs over and within a strong, underlying meter.

3. **(C)** A major scale has half-steps between the third and fourth notes and the seventh and eighth notes. (B) is where the half-steps occur in a diatonic minor scale. The other two arrangements are of medieval modes; (A) is the phrygian mode, beginning on the pitch E, and (D) is the lydian mode, beginning on F. The other medieval modes are dorian (half-steps between 2-3 and 6-7, beginning on D) and mixolydian (half-steps between 3-4 and 6-7, beginning on G).

4. **(D)** A major triad consists of a major third between the root and middle note and a minor third between the middle note and the upper note, producing a perfect fifth between the outer notes. If their position is reversed, with the minor third on the bottom, the result is a minor triad. If both thirds are major, the resulting fifth is augmented, and the triad is an augmented triad. If both thirds are minor, the fifth is diminished, and the triad is a diminished triad.

5. **(A)**   Both the notation of music and the development of medieval polyphony had their beginnings before 1000 C.E. Opera was invented around 1600 and serialism, also called the twelve-tone method, in the 1920s.

6. **(C)**   The Renaissance sound ideal was *a capella* voices singing the same text to the same melody but entering at different times—imitative polyphony. The rhythm was flexible, without strong accents and therefore not strongly metric. Recitative refers to those sections of baroque and classical operas that were written in heightened speech style with a minimum of instrumental accompaniment. *Sprechstimme* was a singing style developed by Arnold Schoenberg, wherein the direction of the melodic motion, but not exact pitches, is indicated.

7. **(C)**   Absolute music is abstract instrumental music that is not based on extra-musical references, such as Brahms's two piano concertos. Most of Beethoven's symphonies are examples of absolute music, but the sixth is not. Beethoven entitled it *Symphonie Pastorale* and gave each of its five movements a descriptive heading. This particular symphony is thus an example of program music. Bach's two Passions are for voices as well as instruments. Tchaikovsky's *Swan Lake* is ballet music.

8. **(D)**   Swing is the essential rhythmic component of jazz. Trumpeter Wynton Marsalis says jazz swings when the bass player is walking his instrument and the drummer is riding the cymbals. The rhythm section is then providing a steady beat over which the lead instruments are free to syncopate around the beat. Improvisation is equally essential to jazz. The performers embellish a given tune, adding notes and continuously varying the melody as they go along, making it up on the spot. The 32-bar chorus is one of several jazz forms. It consists of four phrases of which is each eight bars long: A A B A. The first phrase is repeated, probably in a varied style; the third phrase is a contrasting one called the bridge; the fourth phrase is again a repetition of the first. In the last two bars of the second and fourth phrases, the rhythm section falls silent to allow the lead performer to improvise freely. This is called stop-time.

9. **(C)**   Bach wrote for both the viola da gamba and the oboe da caccia. The viola da gamba is a bowed, fretted, six-string instrument tuned like a guitar that was widely used during the Renaissance. Little is known of the oboe da caccia. The conjecture is that it was an alto oboe that had a curved shape like a hunting horn. The fortepiano, a keyboard instrument with a hammer

action, was invented in 1709. Bach had the opportunity to try one out in the 1730s, but was unimpressed with it. In the following decades, rapid technological improvements gained the fortepiano broad favor. The clarinet, a single-reed woodwind instrument, was not invented until the mid-eighteenth century.

10. **(A)** Mozart's *The Magic Flute* is an opera, or more appropriately a *singspiel*, meaning it is in the German language with sung arias interspersed with spoken dialogue. The other three are all ballets.

11. **(D)** The postwar prosperity of the 1950s in America meant that, for the first time ever, enough young people had sufficient disposable income to constitute a separate, lucrative market for music. Tin Pan Alley, shorthand for the popular music consumer industry and so called because it was centered in a noisy street full of shops with player pianos in New York City, aimed for as broad an appeal as possible, including cross-generational. Tin Pan Alley composers ranged from hacks to George Gershwin. Rhythm and Blues came about with the southern migration of blacks to the cities. It is an urbanized version of the country blues, often more energetic and with an electric guitar. Muddy Waters, John Lee Hooker and Howlin' Wolf were some of the great rhythm and blues singers. Country and Western was, in the beginning, southern, white, and rural. When Sam Phillips signed Elvis Presley because he was a white man who sounded like a black man, Phillips brought together the two strains of black and white popular music to create rock and roll.

12. **(B)** The concerto grosso is a baroque genre. It is a multi-movement work for two or more soloists. The passages for the soloists alternate with *tutti* sections where all the performers participate. The *tutti* passages are called *ritornelli* because they generally "return" to the opening theme while the *soli* passages usually contain contrasting material. Both the Tone Poem and the Symphonic Overture are one-movement orchestral works and are almost always examples of program music. Liszt was particularly associated with the former. His *Les Préludes* was inspired by the French Romantic poet Lamartine. An overture was historically used to introduce something—a drama, opera, or ballet. But the Romantic symphonic overture lost that function and is heard in concert as a free-standing work. An example is Brahms's *Academic Festival Overture*.

CHAPTER 6

Performing Arts Review

PERFORMING ARTS REVIEW

THEATER REVIEW

ORIGINS OF THEATER

As long as humans have been capable of communication, they have probably employed some form of drama and performance. Cave paintings supply evidence for the early use of costumes and masks to bolster mimetic performances, which, either as magic or prayer, functioned to encourage the productivity of nature.

THEATER IN GREECE

In keeping with this tradition, the earliest Greek plays were probably ritualistic performances that might involve, for instance, a conflict between winter and summer, and that would include a combat, a death, and a resurrection. These simple plays may have evolved into the dithyramb, a frenzied and impassioned hymn performed by a chorus of 50 men costumed in goatskins. The purposes and concerns of the earliest plays were reflected in the first **dithyrambs**, which celebrated Dionysus, the god of the abundance of nature. Aristotle described the dithyramb as the forerunner of tragedy, and the gradual development from dithyramb to tragic drama began as spoken lines were inserted into the lyrics, causing the leader of the chorus to become a solo performer.

According to legend, the fundamental changes that brought these early performances to the level of drama were made by Thespis, a poet and actor from whose name we derive the word *thespian*. He is known as the founder of classical **tragedy**. He is credited with inventing a new breed of performer, the actor, who would engage the audience by impersonating one or more characters between the dances of a chorus. Thespis also came up with the notion of a

171

prologue to the choral narrative. With the creation of the actor to tell the story, the reaction of the chorus assumed greater importance, for it served to offer commentatary on the struggles of the narrative's hero. Thespis is also credited with directing the emotional scope of Classical drama to concentrate on the hero's faults, on the obstacles facing the hero, and ultimately on the hero's death—i.e., the elements of tragedy.

Aeschylus, another actor and author of a trilogy of plays entitled the *Oresteia*, further refined the form and content of the Greek tragedy. Among the many improvements attributed to him is the addition of a second and third actor, which allowed for conflict between the characters. Conflict, requiring resolution, provoked a more developed sense of plot, and Aeschylus heightened this by providing a structure with which to organize the narrative episodes. He also introduced the concept of choice, providing the hero with a decision he or she must make, which frequently leads to his or her downfall.

By the fifth century B.C.E., the form of Greek tragedy had taken on a recurring structure. Most plays began with a prologue, spoken by a single actor in iambic verse, which described the events leading up to the action of the play. This was usually followed by the entrance of the chorus, a body of 15 people who chanted in anapestic meter to introduce the action and to create the desired mood in the audience. This was followed by a series of alternating **episodes** (scenes of action) and **stasima** (lyric songs sung by the chorus). The play was concluded by the **exodos**, during which the chorus continued to chant as the characters departed.

Aside from Aeschylus, there are only two other playwrights of this period from whom we have a substantial amount of work extant. Sophocles (496?–406 B.C.E.) is thought to have written nearly 125 plays, among them *Oedipus Tyrannus, Antigone*, and *Electra*. His plays deal with men and women whose flaws lead to suffering and destruction, but ultimately result in increased wisdom and divine retribution. Euripides (480?–406 B.C.E.) is the author of nineteen extant plays, including: *The Trojan Women, Medea*, and *The Bacchae*. Euripides is known for the dramatic realism of his plays, achieved by complex plots, increasingly natural speech, and the combination of good and evil found in all of his characters, be they human or divine.

Greek drama was a seasonal event, performed only at certain times of year during specific festivals. The plays were performed in competition with each other, as part of the festival. All dramatists were required, along with mastering the art of creating tragic trilogies, to perfect at least one comic form. Very few comedies survived, so little is known about the form of Classical Greek Comedy. It is thought that there were three forms of comedy—Old, Middle, and New. The Old Comic form probably employed three actors, contained burlesque, parody, and farce, and was wild and bawdy. Old Comedies always featured music, and frequently made use of fantastical subjects and settings. Old Comedy had a rigid structure similar to that of Classical Tragedy, combining lyrical, prosaic, and choral passages. Aristophanes (450–385 B.C.E.), as the only Old Comedian whose work survived intact, is considered the father of Greek comedy. His plays include *The Clouds* and *The Birds*.

Middle Comedy, the primary dramatic form between 400 and 338 B.C.E., was far less obscene than Old Comedy, and led to the much more refined and sophisticated New Comedy. New Comedies were usually comedies of manners designed for an educated leisure class. They involved a number of stock scenes and stock characters and followed a five-act structure. The only New Comedies that survive are those of Menander of Athens (c. 342–c. 292 B.C.E.), including *The Grouch*.

Greek tragic actors wore large masks that covered their whole faces and made them appear much taller than they actually were. Actors would wear several masks during a performance, to allow them to play a variety of roles. Characters might require a number of different masks to represent the changes that they undergo over the course of the play. The weight and size of the masks contributed to an emphasis on the study of movement, which tended to be slow, graceful, and stately, and to emphasize a number of standard gestures. The costumes for comedy were more colorful and fantastic than those for tragedy, and tended to exaggerate certain parts of the actors' bodies. Comedians, too, wore masks; however, comedic masks portrayed a larger variety of characters than the tragic masks.

THEATER IN CHINA

The first performances in China were recorded about 1500 B.C.E., during the Shang Dynasty. Dance, music, and ritual were important elements in Chinese life. Temples were associated with performers and records of a raised stage were found by archaeologists.

The Han Dynasty (206 B.C.E.–C.E. 221) actively encouraged the arts and founded the Imperial Office of Music in 104 B.C.E., which functioned to organize entertainment and to promote dance and music.

Chinese Shadow Puppets (c. 121 B.C.E.) were first used to materialize departed gods or souls, but later evolved into a source of entertainment.

Marionettes, puppets moved by string or hand, were created between C.E. 265 and C.E. 420. Many festivals and plays continued to spread through China around C.E. 610.

Emperor Hsuan Tsung established "The Pear Garden," a school for dancers, singers, and various court entertainers that stressed current forms of performance. Storytelling using puppets became a popular dramatic form from C.E. 960–C.E. 1279.

Historians in the 1920s uncovered the oldest surviving Chinese plays, *Chang Hsieh* and *The Doctor of Letters*, which consisted of a prologue and a main story.

Stage direction was practiced in Chinese theaters by the fourteenth century. The stage was usually stripped bare, with a door on either side for exits and entrances and an embroidered decorative wall hanging between the two doors as a backdrop. Both men and women performed in productions, and swords and fans were used as props during performances.

Drama began to emerge from the south. The southern plays tended to be long and formal, usually consisting of 50 or more acts, each of which had its own title. Theater in China was influenced by Western drama early in the twentieth century and gradually became less formal.

MEDIEVAL PERIOD

Medieval theater originally began as a springtime religious observance. It was a communal and public event that drew large audiences to celebrate the teachings of the Old and New Testaments of the Bible. Religious theater was restricted by such elements as the liturgy, church calendar, and ecclesiastical dress.

In England during the Middle Ages, pageant plays known as **cycles** were created using biblical and religious literature. The cycles were performed by a troupe of actors who traveled from town to town in wagons that also served as stages for performances. The double-decker wagon was narrow with two vertical levels that were utilized to demonstrate scenes of heaven and hell. Curtains concealed the wagon's undercarriage and served as the dressing area for the actors.

Morality plays were also performed during this time. They represented the conscience of the Middle Ages. After approximately 200 years, drama moved out of the church because the troupes were too restricted by the church's ruling.

Medieval producers made use of special effects such as trap doors in stages that were movable or fixed. The stages were set against buildings at outdoor festivals, and a stage wagon transported background scenery. This type of stage made special effects easy to perform.

The playwrights in the Medieval period wrote anonymously. Historians document that women never performed in medieval plays for two reasons. First, male-dominated, rigidly hierarchical groups like clergy, craftsmen, and merchants predominated. Secondly, it was believed that boys with trained voices could produce more volume than women.

Medieval audiences consisted of local and neighboring citizens. There was no fee charged to spectators of English cycle plays.

ELIZABETHAN THEATER IN ENGLAND

During the Elizabethan era in England, theater was used for the first time as a commercial enterprise. Philip Henslowe of London was the best-known theatrical manager. The stage became lavish with detailed scenery and colorful costumes. There were two basic types of costumes, contemporary and symbolic. Symbolic costumes were worn to distinguish the important characters from the ordinary people.

Theater companies acquired new plays by request from freelancers and from actor/playwrights. Notable playwrights of the Elizabethan era include Christopher Marlowe (1564–1593), author of a number of plays including *The Jew of Malta* and *Edward II,* and Ben Jonson (1573–1637), satirist, critic, and author of plays ranging from comedy and satire to court masques and tragedy, including *Every Man in His Humour* and *The Devil Is an Ass.* Ben Jonson said of his contemporary William Shakespeare that "He was not of an age but for all time!" It is certainly true that in his more than thirty tragedies, histories, and comedies, Shakespeare created enduring characters and addressed timeless questions that still resonate for us today. It would be impossible in a short space to describe Shakespeare's contribution to poetry, drama, and language.

THEATER IN ITALY

The Romans, borrowing architectural design from the Greeks, built amphitheaters of permanent stone. These theaters were built for a variety of entertainment, such as dancing, acrobatics, and gladiatorial events.

Italy's professional theater evolved from *commedia dell'arte* in the mid-1500s. *Commedia dell'arte* was a popular form of entertainment akin to street theater, designed to appeal to a mass audience. The plays, performed by a number of traveling troupes, were largely improvisational, though their plots were usually limited to the misadventures of a set of stock characters whose actions were commented on by a chorus of clowns or *zannis*. Many of the characters' names, personalities, and costumes are still familiar today—among them Harlequin, Pulcinella, Pantalone, Dottore, and Scaramuccia.

Throughout Europe in the late fifteenth century, audiences were entertained between the acts of larger comedies by short dramatic and musical works. In Italy, these became known as Intermezzi, and became more and more centered around spectacle. Eventually, dialogue was almost entirely phased out in favor of elaborate presentation. These works usually involved music, and as the entr'acte spectacles became longer and more important than the acts themselves, opera was born.

THEATER IN SEVENTEENTH-CENTURY FRANCE

French playwright/actor/director, Jean Baptiste Poquelin (1622–1673), also known as Molière, wrote and acted in *Tartuffe*, *The Misanthrope*, *The Doctor in Spite of Himself*, *The Miser*, and *The Imaginary Invalid*. Molière's comedies weigh follies of humanity against common good sense. Two other famous playwrights at this time were Pierre Corneille (1606–1684) and Jean Racine (1639–1699). Corneille's most successful play was entitled *The Cid*. Racine's most widely performed plays were *Phaedra* and *Iphigenie en Aulide*.

Costumes, hairstyles, and makeup on the French stage mirrored popular fashions on the street or at court. The audience in Parisian theaters varied from valets, soldiers, and pickpockets to nobility, gentlemen, and merchants. Respectable women usually did not attend the theater in the early 1600s. Women who did attend wore masks and sat in loges.

The first proscenium arch stage, which resembled a picture frame, was built in France in 1618 by Teatro Farnese. The proscenium was a wall with one large center opening that divided the theater-goers from the raised stage.

RESTORATION PERIOD

During the Interregnum period in England (1649–1660), theater and acting were banned due to political upheavals at the command of Oliver Cromwell. Once theaters were reopened, Charles II (1630–1685) marked the start of the modern proscenium playhouse, and repertory companies flourished. Two official theatrical companies, the King's Company and the Duke's Company, were started at this time.

Popular playwrights of the Restoration period were John Dryden, Richard Steele, William Wycherley, William Congreve, George Farquhar, George Etherege, and Richard Brinsley Sheridan. The term "comedy of manners" describes the majority of the Restoration prose plays. They were witty in dialogue and revolved around sexual intrigue.

CONTEMPORARY THEATER

Many successful playwrights emerged from nineteenth-century Europe. Henrik Ibsen, Johann Wolfgang Goethe, and August Strindberg are a few among many popular writers. These playwrights introduced stage realism and naturalism. English naturalist Charles Darwin and French philosopher Auguste Comte were two major influences on the theater of realism. Contemporary theater emerged from this emphasis on naturalism and realism.

In Russia, Konstantin Stanislavsky (1863–1938) developed an acting technique that came to be called "The Method" on account of its broad impact on the schooling of Western actors. Stanislavsky's approach to actor-training was essentially psychological. Cheryl Crawford, Harold Clurman, Lee Strasberg, and Stella Adler taught acting technique using "**The Method**." In 1931 they formed the Group Theater in America, which consisted of actors and directors who provided actor-training workshops in New York City.

Playwright Eugene O'Neill brought to American drama a powerful insight into human passion and suffering. Other accomplished American playwrights of the twentieth century include Arthur Miller, Tennessee Williams, and Lillian Hellman. Their plays are produced on and off-Broadway. Experimental shows are generally produced in off-off Broadway theaters.

In Britain, the **Fringe theater** was considered equivalent to America's off-off Broadway theater. **Mobile theater** (the Fun Bus) and **avant-garde theater** brought the arts into urban communities and bridged the gap between nations and classes.

There were a number of significant off-off Broadway companies. La Mama theater, for example, provided a showcase for new playwrights. The Circle Repertory Company stressed the development of new plays by its own performing group. The Manhattan Theatre Club opened three theaters to assist playwrights through readings and productions. The New York Shakespeare Festival Public Theatre was founded by Joseph Papp in 1954. Papp's goal was to make theater more accessible. Papp established free summer performances at the Delacorte Theatre in Central Park, New York City.

In 1968, censorship of British theater was abolished. The rock musical *Hair*, which contained nudity and obscenity, was produced in London. Plays with homosexual themes, such as John Osborne's *A Patriot for Me*, were performed. Meanwhile, in the United States during the late 1960s, musicals like *Oh, Calcutta*, which included various scenes involving nudity, and *Che!*, which displayed explicit sexual acts, challenged theater audiences.

DANCE REVIEW

ORIGINS OF DANCE

Archaeologists have studied ancient drawings depicting dancing hunters costumed as animals wearing make-up and masks. Egyptian dance paintings were found that depict religious dancing in funeral processions. War dances, hunting dances, medicine dances, dances for health, and fertility dances were performed as a form of sympathetic magic or medicine. There were dances for death, birth, peace, and courtship.

The emergence of dance was evident in early Greek culture. Plato believed that dance was not solely an exercise for the body, but an art form given to us by the gods so we could please them. The Greeks themselves used dance accompanied by music in the intermezza of a performance event. Dance was a communal activity, enjoyed as entertainment and religious ritual.

For the Romans, dance was a vehicle for spectacle rather than for a classic dramatic presentation, and commonly included acrobatics. As Christian emperors became more powerful, the church became more controlling, and pagan rituals, spectacles, and gladiatorial combats were forbidden.

Dancing was incorporated in Christian services until the twelfth century at which time theologians decided that dancing was distracting and impious. In 1207, the Pope banned the clergy from wearing masks and dancing because theologians felt that these practices might cause the mind to wander from God. Later, music and acting were banned by the church.

FORMS OF DANCE

The first major ballet, entitled *The Ballet Comique de la Reine,* was choreographed by an Italian named Balthasar de Beaujoyeux (formerly Baldassari de Belgiojoso) in 1581. This event was commissioned by Catherine de' Medici in France, who was the daughter of one of the greatest families.

In France, Louis XIV, who was an accomplished dancer himself, and a great champion of ballet in particular, was known as a patron of the arts. His passion for dance favored court ballets. In 1661, he established a school which produced the best and most experienced dance masters. This school was called the Academie Royale de Danse.

The establishment of the five positions of the feet became the foundation of ballet technique. In the first position, legs are turned out away from the hips and heels and knees touch each other. The feet are to be out so as to form a straight line. Similar to first position, the legs remain turned out away from the hips during the second position, but the heels must be approximately 10 to 12 inches apart. During the third position, the heel of each foot is touching the middle of the other foot while one foot is placed directly in front of the other. The legs must be turned out away from the hips. In the fourth position, one foot is in front of the other with about eight inches separating the two feet. In the fifth position, the legs are turned out from the hips, and one foot is directly in front of the other. The heel of the front foot should also be placed at the joint to the toe of the rear foot. Correct weight and body balance, arm control, and attitude are essential in ballet.

Marius Petipa (1822–1910), often referred to as the father of classic ballet, transplanted the glory of the Romantic ballet from France to Russia. This was a turning point at the birth of a new era. Petipa reached success with one five-act ballet entitled *La Fille du Pharaon*. Petipa made Russia the leading country of ballet, and he raised the standard of dance technique with assistance from Swedish dancer Christian Johansson, Italian dancer Enrico Cecchetti, and Russian dancer Lev Ivanov. His other works include *La Bayadère* and *Sleeping Beauty*.

Isadora Duncan (1878–1927) contributed greatly to the creation of Modern Dance. She believed dancing was an expression of one's whole self, including body, mind, and soul. She wanted to be free of the control of ballet and desired to let the body rather than the mind dictate movement. She took off her ballet slippers and danced barefoot, wearing loose-fitting clothing so her body was not restricted. Her works were based on Greek art. Duncan founded schools in Berlin, Paris, and Moscow. In modern dance, there are no established patterns or steps. It requires the dancer to create his or her own, emanating from the natural movement of the body. Other contributors to modern dance were Agnes de Milles, Martha Graham, Ruth St. Denis, and Ted Shawn.

American dancer and choreographer Martha Graham's technique begins with the center of the body and follows contractions and releases of muscles when movement occurs. Ultimately, her technique is based on breath rhythms and is recognized for sharpness and preciseness.

Choreographer Doris Humphrey's movement technique was softer and more lyrical than Graham's. Humphrey's technique was created from natural observations of human movement. She examined rhythms of breath, weight shifts, motion, and successional flow.

The bridge between classical ballet and modern dance was connected under Agnes de Mille's direction. She stressed the understanding that dance is movement, and the body is its instrument. Choreographers worked with time, force, and space. De Mille believed that a personal exploration must be completed to understand and use the body.

Jazz dancing is a controlled style of dancing, though it is creative and allows free body movements. It is characterized by parallel feet, flat-footed steps, undulating torso, body isolation, and syncopated rhythms. Jazz became a popular form of dance in American musicals.

Ballet troupes and opera houses were established in America, among them the New York City Ballet, the Metropolitan Opera, Lincoln Center for the Performing Arts, and the American Ballet Theater. Edward Villella, Jacques d'Amboise, Arthur Mitchell, Diana Adams, Tanaquil Le Clerq, and Maria Tallchief became well-known dancers in New York City. In the 1950s, 18-year-old Darci Kistler became the youngest principal dancer in the City Ballet's history.

In the 1960s, Americans flocked to clubs and dance halls. Ballroom dancing, the foxtrot, the samba, and the salsa became popular. In the 1970s, choreographers added jazz to the most successful American musicals, such as *West Side Story, Fiddler on the Roof, 42nd Street, Chicago, A Chorus Line,* and *Evita.* A few famous choreographers and directors were Jerome Robbins, Gower Champion, Bob Fosse, Michael Bennett, and Harold Prince.

A form of dance known as body art became popular in the 1970s, which emerged from the general mood of most Americans, which at the time was irritated and angry. This form of dance was used to demonstrate at political rallies. The artists were costumed or appeared nude and performed in galleries and small performance spaces.

American dancing has gone through many styles. Popular dances of the 1930s were the Peabody and the foxtrot. In the 1940s, they danced the jitterbug. The 1950s brought about the stroll, the mashed potato, and the cha-cha. The salsa, the monkey, and the pony were created in the 1960s. In the 1970s, two new types of dances were born—the hustle and the boogie, which became American favorites. In the 1980s, head banging to heavy metal rock and roll music emerged and faded away. With each new decade, dance styles change and vibrant new forms emerge.

FILM REVIEW

ORIGIN OF FILM

The creation of film was the result of a centuries-old fascination with the control and capture of movement. There is no one moment of history and no one inventor who can be credited with the creation of cinema as we know it today. A series of inventions and ideas, from Plato's shadows on the cave wall to magic lanterns and zoetropes, by means of curiosity, ingenuity, and accident, by the turn of the twentieth century we could reproduce movement. This new invention, which hung somewhere between a science and an art, was to capture the international imagination as a means to entertain, to shock, and increasingly, to earn money.

Around 1889, Thomas Alva Edison and his assistant, W.K.L. Dickinson, combined a number of existing inventions to create the **kinetoscope**, the original motion picture machine. This machine was designed as a cabinet that held revolving spools of film. When a coin was inserted, an electric light was projected on the rear of the cabinet. To view the movie, one would look through a small peephole. The average film ran for one minute and was 50 feet in length. Edison usually filmed action or movement, such as an animal eating or a person dancing.

Edison believed that films were simply a passing fad. Consequently, he did not develop a way to project films on screen. This task was performed by the Lumière brothers, Louis and Auguste. The Lumière brothers developed their own camera, which also served as a developing machine and projector. The Lumières held the first public showing of motion pictures projected on a screen at the Grand Café in Paris. The Lumière brothers helped to develop the form cinema would take.

Edison soon abandoned kinetoscopes to form his own production company to make films for theaters. Edison founded the first motion picture studio, "The Black Maria," in West Orange, New Jersey. In the studio, **vaudeville** entertainers and celebrities performed for the camera. There were several actors who later gained fame in the early days of motion picture, among them Mme. Bertholdi, a contortionist; Annie Oakley; and Colonel William Cody, the original Buffalo Bill.

In 1895, the Lumière brothers produced their first experimental film entitled *L'Arroseur Arrosé*. Previously, the cinema had consisted of mainly newsreel footage, but narrative form quickly entered. The brothers understood the profit to be made from narrative films, so they perfected their experiment. The first two French production houses were established by Charles Pathé and Léon Gaumont. Their competitor was Georges Méliès. The Lumière brothers wanted to catch nature in the act, but Méliès, who was fascinated with the art of illusion, was considered "the creator of cinematic spectacle." Méliès constructed the first cinema set building that was completely made of glass for daylight shooting purposes.

The first American motion picture theater, established on April 16, 1902, was called "The Electric." Because each show cost a nickel, movie theaters were nicknamed "**nickelodeons**." Meanwhile, in France, Méliès created a film entitled *Trip to the Moon*. In America, Edwin Porter made *The Great Train Robbery*, an early prototype for the classic American Western. As motion pictures prospered, American and French companies regularly employed actors, and more theaters and nickelodeons were built.

Vitagraph, Edison's motion picture company, began producing one-reel films of Shakespearean plays like *Richard III*, *Antony and Cleopatra*, *The Merchant of Venice*, and *Romeo and Juliet*. Edison's determination to exploit the cinema for residuals led to his attempt to force competing filmmakers out of business by bringing lawsuits against them for violation of patents. Several companies, particularly Biograph, managed to survive by inventing cameras that differed from those Edison had patented. In 1908, Edison brought these companies under control by forming the Motion Pictures Patents Company (MPPC), a group of ten firms based primarily in Chicago, New York, and New Jersey. The MPPC never succeeded in eliminating its competition. Many independent companies were formed throughout this period. D.W. Griffith, considered to be Biograph's most important director, formed his own company in 1913. The U.S. government brought a lawsuit against the MPPC in 1912, and in 1915 it was declared a monopoly.

In France, the first Theatre Pathé was built in 1901. It was later rebuilt to hold larger audiences. The progress of French cinema was becoming paralyzed at the time of World War I. France, Germany, and Russia became influenced by realism used in theater. Most Soviet silent films dealt with themes of conflict and revolution.

In the 1920s, America, which did not experience the post–World War I depression as strongly as European countries, became dominant in film production. Particularly in Hollywood, the star system controlled the medium, causing it to become superficial and commercial. After 1912, old nickelodeons were outdated and new theaters were rapidly being built.

German actor/director/writer/set and costume designer Erich von Stroheim brought eroticism, brutality, and cynicism to American cinema after 1920. Stroheim's first films were entitled *Blind Husbands*, *The Devil's Passkey*, and *Foolish Wives*.

THE HOLLYWOOD ERA

After 1910, film companies began moving to a small town outside of Los Angeles, California, known as Hollywood. Some film historians feel that the independent companies moved west to avoid the wrath of the MPPC. In addition, filming in Hollywood had many advantages—the climate permitted year-round shooting, and California provided a great number of locations, from mountains to ocean to desert. By the 1920s, large studios were being built.

The Academy of Motion Picture Arts and Sciences (AMPAS) was founded in 1927 by Louis B. Mayer and other film industry innovators, including Cecil B. DeMille, Douglas Fairbanks, and Mary Pickford. The purpose of the AMPAS was to raise the educational, cultural, and technical standards of American movies. The Academy of Motion Picture Arts and Sciences was pioneered by writers, actors, producers, and directors.

INTRODUCTION OF SOUND IN FILM

Sound was introduced in 1926 with the release of *Don Juan*, a film with an orchestral accompaniment, sound effects, and a series of vaudeville shorts. Warner Brothers, in an attempt to promote the concept of films with sound, released *The Jazz Singer* (1927), a part sound/part silent film that was a huge success. In the same year, Warner Brothers decided that all of its silent films would include musical accompaniment and announced plans to purchase one major theater in every large American city. In 1928, Walt Disney produced *Steamboat Willie*, his first musical cartoon, contributing to the sound film genre and introducing to the world the beloved character, Mickey Mouse. By 1930, most American theaters were wired for sound. Silent films became part of film history by the late 1930s.

INTRODUCTION OF COLOR

During the 1930s, color film became widely used for the first time. Although photographic color had been used in various forms since 1908, only a few films in the 1920s had **Technicolor** sequences, because the process was too expensive to use on a large-scale basis. However, by the mid-1930s, three-strip Technicolor proved to be economically feasible. After the release of the all-color feature-length film, *Becky Sharp,* in 1935, and the release of *The Trail of the Lonesome Pine* in 1936, film studios began using Technicolor extensively.

THE ACADEMY AWARDS

The main function of the AMPAS is the annual presentation of the Academy Awards, or "Oscars," for distinguished film achievement in the previous year. The first film to win an academy award was *Wings* in 1928. *Gone with the Wind* won the most academy awards in a single year in 1939, and featured Oscar winners Vivien Leigh (Best Actress) and Hattie McDaniel (Best Supporting Actress). *Gone with the Wind* also marked the first time a black actor or actress (McDaniel) won an academy award. Other Best Picture winners of the 1930s and 1940s included *Grand Hotel* (1932), *It Happened One Night* (1934), *You Can't Take It with You* (1938), *Mrs. Miniver* (1942), *Casablanca* (1943), *The Lost Weekend* (1945), and *All the King's Men* (1949). Best Actor winners of the 1930s and 1940s included Clark Gable, Spencer Tracy, James Stewart, Bing Crosby, Ray Milland, and Laurence Olivier. Best Actress winners of the 1930s and 1940s included Bette Davis, Katharine Hepburn, Ginger Rogers, Ingrid Bergman, Joan Crawford, and Olivia de Havilland.

TELEVISION, COLOR, AND FILM

Television affected box-office sales. Americans who owned television sets stayed home rather than go to the cinema and spend money. As a result, profits were not being generated. Hollywood fought back by exploiting the technological advantages which film possessed—the vast size of the images and the capacity to produce the images in color. As a result of the competition between television and films, Hollywood made a rapid conversion from black-and-white to color production between 1952 and 1955. In 1947, only 12 percent of American feature films were made in color. By 1954, the figure rose to over 50 percent.

The transition was made possible largely through a 1950 anti-trust decree which disassembled the Technicolor Corporation's monopoly on color cinematography and ordered it to release its basic patents to all producers. When this occurred, new color systems were developed quickly, aided by the war-time development of a new type of color film stock called "integral tripak." By 1952, the Eastman Kodak Corporation had developed the Eastmancolor system. Although the system has since come to be known by the trade names of the studios who pay to use it or the laboratories that process it, it was Kodak Eastmancolor that initiated and maintained the full-color age with dye-coupler printing. By 1975, even the Technicolor Corporation had changed to an Eastman-based process. Ninety-six percent of all American feature films by 1979 were being made in color.

FILMS IN THE 1950s AND 1960s

Hollywood's mania for producing films on a large scale in the 1950s damaged the conventional dramatic film. First, the standard length of a feature film rose from 90 minutes to an average of three hours before settling at a more manageable two hours in the mid-1960s. Second, there was a tendency on behalf of the studios to package every A-class film as a dazzling, big-budget spectacle, whether or not this format suited the material of the film. From 1955 to 1965, most traditional American genres experienced an inflation of production values that destroyed their original forms and caused them to be recreated into new ones. These genres included **musicals**, **comedies**, **Westerns**, **science fiction**, **gangster** and **anti-communist** films.

The musical genre underwent a period of great change in the 1950s and 1960s. Hollywood abandoned original scripts in favor of successful stage plays. This tendency peaked with the release in 1965 of *The Sound of Music*, which grossed more money than any other film had before. Comedy suffered in the early 1950s due to a focus on production values rather than verbal or visual humor. By the 1960s, the genre shifted to big-budget sex comedies concerned with strategies of seduction (*Sex and the Single Girl*, 1965, *A Guide for the Married Man*, 1967), which reflected the sexual revolution of the decade, and to corporate comedies, which dealt with business fraud and government deceit in a humorous light. American comedy became increasingly sophisticated in the 1950s and 1960s.

The Western experienced major changes in attitude and theme in correspondence to changes in American society. The heroic, idealized epic westerns of John Ford and his imitators remained popular in the 1950s but were gradually replaced by the adult Western which concentrated on the psychological and moral conflicts of the hero in society. Furthermore, by the 1960s, the portrayal of the Native American changed from one of hostile savages to one of intelligent, gentle people who were murdered by the U.S. military.

Science fiction emerged as a distinct genre in the 1950s. The common theme in the science fiction films of the 1950s was some form of a world-threatening crisis, usually produced by nuclear war or alien invasion. Another popular theme was the arrival of a dangerous creature from another planet, as in *The Thing* (1951).

In the 1960s, low-budget monster films were replaced by medium-to-high budget science fiction films, including *The Time Machine* (1960) and *Planet of the Apes* (1967). Serious filmmakers, including Stanley Kubrick (*2001: A Space Odyssey*, 1968), became interested in science fiction.

The gangster film re-emerged in the late 1940s after being replaced by domestic espionage films during the war. Two types of gangster films appeared in the 1950s—the caper film and the anti-communist film. The caper film concentrated on a plan to pull off a big heist, which could be either serious or humorous. The first caper film was John Huston's *The Asphalt Jungle* in 1950. The anti-communist film was a centered, original form that appeared only in the early 1950s. In these films, the criminal figure was a Communist spy and the syndicate was the international Communist conspiracy. However, the traditional concept of the gangster film was preserved. Although the anti-communist films appeared only in the 1950s, the theme of these movies can be seen in the James Bond espionage thrillers and imitations in the 1960s. These films replaced the gangster genre in the early 1960s by presenting criminal conspiracy on a world-wide scale and offering violence on the part of both the conspirators and the hero.

Academy Award-winning films in the 1950s and 1960s included *All About Eve* (1950), *From Here to Eternity* (1953), *The Bridge on the River Kwai*

(1957), *Ben-Hur* (1959), *West Side Story* (1961), *My Fair Lady* (1965), *The Sound of Music* (1965), and *Midnight Cowboy* (1969). Best Actor winners in the 1950s and 1960s included Gary Cooper, William Holden, Yul Brynner, Charlton Heston, Rod Steiger, and John Wayne. Best Actress winners included Audrey Hepburn, Grace Kelly, Joanne Woodward, Susan Hayward, Anne Bancroft, Elizabeth Taylor, and Sophia Loren. In 1963, Sidney Poitier won an academy award for Best Actor for his performance in *Lilies of the Field*. Nineteen sixty-eight marked the occurrence of the first tie in the Best Actress category. Both Katharine Hepburn, for her performance in *The Lion in Winter*, and Barbra Streisand, for her performance in *Funny Girl*, shared the Oscar.

FILMS IN THE 1970s AND 1980s

The enormous success in 1970 of two conventional films, *Love Story* and *Airport*, restored Hollywood's faith in the big-budget feature. Production costs of American films were the largest in the industry's history. Between 1972 and 1977, the average production budget for a film increased by 178 percent. By the end of 1979, average production costs had nearly doubled the 1977 figure to reach the sum of $7.5 million per feature film. Profits were based on the film's success, so the financial risks of production multiplied. Consequently, fewer and fewer films were made every year, and there was a steady increase in the amount spent on advertising campaigns to ensure the success of the film. Often, the price for advertising would cost twice as much as the production cost of the film itself.

With fewer than 70 major films being produced each year, compared to 538 in 1937, there were serious questions about the creative spirit of the American cinema. However, the 1970s could be considered a renaissance of creative talent, as a result of many young directors who studied at American film schools, compared to the directors of the 1960s who were trained in television. Some of the directors of this renaissance were Francis Ford Coppola, George Lucas, Martin Scorsese, Steven Spielberg, and Brian DePalma. Coppola's epic of organized crime in the United States, *The Godfather Parts I, II*, and *III*, is one of the most significant American cinematic achievements of the 1970s. Lucas's *Star Wars* and Spielberg's *Jaws* (1975) and *Close Encounters of the Third Kind* (1977) were historically important for their use of dazzling special effects. DePalma directed some of the most stylish horror films of the 1970s, including *Carrie* (1976), while Scorsese directed *Taxi Driver* (1976). Not only were these films critically acclaimed, but they were financially successful. *Star Wars* grossed over $200 million, *Jaws* over $130 million, and *Close Encounters of the Third Kind*, over $83 million.

Some of the academy award winners for Best Picture in the 1970s were *The Godfather* (1972), *The Godfather II* (1974), *One Flew over the Cuckoo's Nest* (1975), *The Deer Hunter* (1978), and *Kramer vs. Kramer* (1979). Some of the Best Actress winners were Jane Fonda, Ellen Burstyn, Faye Dunaway, Diane Keaton, and Sally Field. Some of the Best Actor winners were Gene Hackman, Jack Lemmon, Jack Nicholson, Richard Dreyfuss, and Jon Voight. Two Best Actor winners, George C. Scott for his role in *Patton* in 1970, and Marlon Brando for his role in *The Godfather* in 1972, made history by refusing their awards.

FILM IN THE PRESENT

As in the 1950s with the invention of television, in the 1980s Hollywood was again faced with technological advances that would affect box office sales. **Cable television** services and **video cassette recorders** (VCRs) brought theatrical movies into the home for a monthly subscription or rental fee, transforming the entire system of film distribution. However, the speculation that movie theaters would become obsolete and that all films would one day be distributed through some form of home video technology remains a theory in the 1990s. People are still going to the movies in theaters and paying rising prices for tickets to experience the spectacle of the big screen. Directors like Allison Anders, Spike Lee, and Jim Jarmusch have produced innovative work and introduced new film techniques in the 1980s and 1990s.

Some of the Best Picture winners for the 1980s and 1990s were *Ordinary People* (1980), *Gandhi* (1982), *Amadeus* (1984), *Platoon* (1986), *Rainman* (1988), *Schindler's List* (1993), *Forrest Gump* (1994), and *Braveheart* (1995). Some of the Best Actor winners included Robert DeNiro, William Hurt, Michael Douglas, Paul Newman, Dustin Hoffman, Sir Anthony Hopkins, Tom Hanks, and Nicholas Cage. Some of the Best Actress winners included Sissy Spacek, Meryl Streep, Shirley MacLaine, Cher, Jodie Foster, Jessica Tandy, Emma Thompson, Jessica Lange, and Susan Sarandon.

Drill: Performing Arts

1. American choreographer Martha Graham often used sets designed by which of the following sculptors?

   (A) Henry Moore
   (B) Isamu Noguchi
   (C) David Smith
   (D) Louise Nevelson

2. Which of the following contemporary filmmakers sees a connection between Marxist politics and gender relations?

   (A) Werner Herzog
   (B) Woody Allen
   (C) John Ford
   (D) Lina Wertmüller

3. Igor Stravinsky's ballet *Petrouchka* drew heavily on which of the following influences?

   (A) Renaissance dance music
   (B) Russian folklore and tradition
   (C) Medieval mystery plays
   (D) Eighteenth-century Italian opera

4. Which of the following films was the work of the visionary German director Werner Herzog?

   (A) *Love and Anarchy*
   (B) *Reds*
   (C) *Aguirre, The Wrath of God*
   (D) *Love and Death*

5. Which film tells the story of a totalitarian society in which books are banned and burned?

   (A) *A Clockwork Orange*
   (B) *1984*
   (C) *Fahrenheit-451*
   (D) *Brazil*

6. Which of the following individuals would be out of place in the musical and theatrical circles of 1920s Paris?

   (A) Stravinsky
   (B) Satie
   (C) Nijinsky
   (D) Shostakovich

7. John Ford's 1939 epic Western *Stagecoach* featured which actor as the classic American male?

   (A) Humphrey Bogart
   (B) Gary Cooper
   (C) John Wayne
   (D) David Wayne

8. Which of the following directors is not associated with the French "New Wave" cinema?

   (A) Abel Gance
   (B) Louis Malle
   (C) Alain Resnais
   (D) Jean-Luc Godard

9. Composer Stephen Sondheim scored all of the following musicals EXCEPT

   (A) *Company.*
   (B) *A Little Night Music.*
   (C) *Sunday in the Park with George.*
   (D) *Pippin.*

10. Which Wagner opera tells the story of a legendary, doomed love affair?

   (A) *Parsifal*
   (B) *Tristan and Isolde*
   (C) *Siegfried*
   (D) *Die Meistersinger*

11. Which of the following operas tells the tragic story of a young Japanese bride?

    (A) *La Bohème*
    (B) *Tosca*
    (C) *Aida*
    (D) *Madama Butterfly*

12. Which of the following best describes *opera buffa*?

    (A) Tragedy
    (B) Serial
    (C) Melodrama
    (D) Comedy

13. Which film established James Dean as an icon of American youth?

    (A) *East of Eden*
    (B) *Rebel Without a Cause*
    (C) *The Wild One*
    (D) *Giant*

14. The popular Broadway show *West Side Story* was loosely based on the play

    (A) *Measure for Measure.*
    (B) *The Taming of the Shrew.*
    (C) *A Midsummer Night's Dream.*
    (D) *Romeo and Juliet.*

15. The controversial practice developed during the 1960s in which artists confronted or interacted with spectators, or used their own bodies as an artistic medium is called

    (A) Pop art.
    (B) minimalism.
    (C) video sculpture.
    (D) performance art.

16. Which modern choreographer, based in New York City and featuring a company of young black, white, and Asian dancers, used dance as a means to explore and interpret the American black experience?

   (A) Paul Taylor
   (B) Alwin Nikolais
   (C) Merce Cunningham
   (D) Alvin Ailey

Performing Arts Review

Answer Key

1.	(B)	5.	(C)	9.	(D)	13.	(B)
2.	(D)	6.	(D)	10.	(B)	14.	(D)
3.	(B)	7.	(C)	11.	(D)	15.	(D)
4.	(C)	8.	(A)	12.	(D)	16.	(D)

Detailed Explanations of Answers

Drill: Performing Arts

1. **(B)** Japanese-American sculptor Isamu Noguchi (1904–1988) collaborated with Martha Graham on such abstract ballet sets as *Frointeir* in 1935. Neither Henry Moore (A), David Smith (C), nor Louise Nevelson (D) are known for their theater designs.

2. **(D)** Italian director Lina Wertmüller, a student of Federico Fellini, often analyzes sex in terms of Marxist politics in works such as *Love and Anarchy* (1973) and *Swept Away* (1974). Werner Herzog (A) is the proponent of German visionary cinema, while Woody Allen (B) directs modern urban comedies and dramas. John Ford (C) was an American director who often made westerns and adventure films.

3. **(B)** Stravinsky's *Petrouchka*, produced by Diaghilev's Ballet Russe in 1911 in Paris, draws its narrative from the story of a Russian country fair at which Petrouchka is one of the three dolls brought to life by a magician. Although Stravinsky was an eclectic composer with a strong religious strain, he drew neither from Renaissance dance (A), medieval mystery (C), nor Italian opera (D).

4. **(C)** Herzog's *Aguirre, The Wrath of God* (1972) tells the heavily symbolic tale of an obsessive Spanish conquistador's journey into the Amazonian jungle to find the mystical city El Dorado. *Love and Anarchy* (A) is a political film by the Italian Lina Wertmüller, while *Love and Death* (D) is a Woody Allen spoof of Tolstoy's novels. *Reds* (B) is Warren Beatty's film about the Russian Revolution.

5. **(C)** Francois Truffaut's 1966 film *Fahrenheit-451* was adapted from the Ray Bradbury novel, in which a repressive future world employs firemen not to stop fires, but to burn books. *A Clockwork Orange* (A) is Stanley Kubrick's version of Anthony Burgess's book set in an anarchistic future England, while *1984* (B) was based on George Orwell's prophetic novel of the same name. *Brazil* (D), by director Terry Gilliam, is a futuristic fantasy with a heavy debt to Orwell.

6. **(D)** Dmitri Shostakovich (1906–1975) was the Russian composer whose mature career coincided with the Stalinist regime in the Soviet Union, and whose works were often circumscribed by the Soviet party line. He was never a member of the musical/theatrical avant garde in 1920s Paris, where composer Igor Stravinsky (A) and dancer Vaslav Nijinsky (C) were all associated with the *Ballet Russe*. Eric Satie (B) was the irreverent leader of the *Les Six*.

7. **(C)** John Wayne starred as the Ringo Kid in John Ford's *Stagecoach*, the 1939 film shot in Monument Valley which featured spectacular scenery as a major element in the action, and which set the tone for decades of Westerns to come. Humphrey Bogart (A) created an image of the cynical, laconic American male in such films as *The Treasure of the Sierra Madre*, while Gary Cooper (B) developed a similar persona in *High Noon*. David Wayne (D) portrayed more intellectualized heroes.

8. **(A)** Abel Gance (1889–1981) was the French film director of the 1920s, whose masterpiece was *Napoleon* (1927), a grand, sweeping epic which used such devices as a triple screen and early color to mythologize the French dictator. All of the other directors listed were members of the generation which reached maturity in post World War II France, and whose films explored new levels of social, political, and psychological complexity.

9. **(D)** *Pippin*, the fictionalized story of the youngest son of Charlemagne, was composed by the young American Stephen Schwarz. All of the other musicals were hits written by Stephen Sondheim.

10. **(B)** Wagner's 1865 opera *Tristan and Isolde*, his most fully developed treatment of romantic love and passion, is drawn from a medieval legend of Celtic origin, and tells the story of two people fated to die because of their love. *Parsifal* (A) is Wagner's version of the Holy Grail legend, *Siegfried* (C) is a section of Wagner's enormous Ring cycle, and *Die Meistersinger* (D) tells of a medieval German guild of singers.

11. **(D)** Giacomo Puccini (1858–1924) wrote *Madama Butterfly* in 1904; in it he dramatized the tale of a young Japanese bride first wooed and then abandoned by an American naval lieutenant. *La Bohème* (A) is Puccini's opera about a colony of poor artists, and *Tosca* (B), also by Puccini, is about a nineteenth-century singer in Rome. *Aida* (C) is Verdi's lavish opera about an African princess in Egypt.

12. **(D)** *Opera buffa* was the Italian comic opera of the early eighteenth century which, with its emphasis on humor, farcical plots, frivolity, and catch musical numbers, closely parallels modern musical comedy. "Tragedy" (A) and "melodrama" (C) would best describe Wagner's Romantic works, while "serial" (B) would define a work such as Alban Berg's 12-tone *Wozzeck*.

13. **(B)** Nicholas Ray's 1955 film *Rebel Without a Cause* cast the young James Dean as a searching, alienated youth who rejects both the hypocritical values of his middle-class parents and the competitive violence of his peers. *East of Eden* (A) and *Giant* (D) were films which reinforced Dean's star status, while *The Wild One* (C) featured Marlon Brando as a cynical, rebellious youth.

14. **(D)** *Romeo and Juliet* provided the source for *West Side Story*, which was written by Jerome Robbins, Arthur Laurents, Leonard Bernstein, and Stephen Sondheim, and which opened on Broadway in 1957. Shakespeare's story of the doomed young lovers from feuding families was updated as the tale of New York City teenagers Tony and Maria.

15. **(D)** Performance art is a broad ranging term which includes environments and happenings, staged by such artists as Jim Dine, Claes Oldenberg, and Yves Klein in order to bombard the spectator with sensations and experiences which were extreme, bewildering, and often, subversive, of the social status quo. Pop art (A) was a predecessor of performance; minimalism (B) is a non-objective style; and video sculpture (C) exploits the kinetic imagery of television sets.

16. **(D)** Black choreographer Alvin Ailey (1931–1989) formed his own dance company in 1958, and drew a whole new kind of audience to modern dance with works such as *Revelations*, which used Negro spiritual music or blues and jazz to express the experience of the American black. Each of the other figures listed is also a prominent contemporary choreographer.

PRACTICE TEST 1

CLEP Humanities

Also available at the REA Study Center (*www.rea.com/studycenter*)

This practice test is also offered online at the REA Study Center. All CLEP exams are computer-based, and our test is formatted to simulate test-day conditions. We recommend that you take the online version of the test to receive these added benefits:

- **Timed testing conditions** – helps you gauge how much time you can spend on each question
- **Automatic scoring** – find out how you did on the test, instantly
- **On-screen detailed explanations of answers** – gives you the correct answer and explains why the other answer choices are wrong
- **Diagnostic score reports** – pinpoint where you're strongest and where you need to focus your study

PRACTICE TEST 1

CLEP Humanities

(Answer sheets appear in the back of the book.)

TIME: 90 Minutes
140 Questions

DIRECTIONS: Each of the questions or incomplete statements below is followed by five possible answers or completions. Select the BEST choice in each case and fill in the corresponding oval on the answer sheet.

1. In ancient Egyptian architecture, the large, sloping walls which flank the entrance to a temple complex are called

    (A) pyramids
    (B) mastabas
    (C) tombs
    (D) pylons
    (E) obelisks

2. An improvised performance, usually held in churchyards or city squares, that was performed in a circle and involved playing the role of redeemers, by the act of scourging and whipping themselves, which made them move and gesture, was performed by

    (A) fools
    (B) flagellants
    (C) minnesingers
    (D) mimes
    (E) joculators

3. An *a priori* truth is known to be true

    (A) independently of experience.
    (B) after careful experimentation or observation.
    (C) as a result of mathematical calculation.
    (D) only by God.
    (E) because its denial is a contradiction.

4. The fourth degree of a major scale is given what name?

(A) Tonic
(B) Dominant
(C) Leading tone
(D) Subdominant
(E) Mediant

5. A natural minor scale contains five whole steps and two half steps. Between which scale degrees do the half steps occur?

(A) 2-3, 5-6
(B) 3-4, 7-8
(C) 1-2, 7-8
(D) 2-3, 7-8
(E) 3-4

6. An example of the use of primitivism can be found in which musical selection?

(A) "Prélude á l'après-midi d'un faune"
(B) "Le Sacre du Printemps"
(C) "Salome"
(D) "Wozzeck"
(E) "The Liberty Bell"

7. Which of the following is the earliest and clearest demonstration of the principles of romanticism?

(A) Pope's "The Rape of the Lock"
(B) Rousseau's *The Social Contract*
(C) Blake's *Songs of Innocence and Experience*
(D) James's *Daisy Miller*
(E) Shakespeare's *Romeo and Juliet*

8. Which of the following works is known for defining the parameters of existentialism?

(A) *L'Étranger*
(B) *Le Morte D'Arthur*
(C) *Candide*
(D) *Saint Joan*
(E) *Le Misanthrope*

9. Which American classic is known for its comprehensive description of frontier families' lives in the Midwest during the nineteenth century?

   (A) *The Last of the Mohicans*
   (B) *The History of the Dividing Line*
   (C) *On Plymouth Plantation*
   (D) *My Antonia*
   (E) *Huckleberry Finn*

10. Which of the following is a "coming of age" novel that utilizes the concept of the anti-hero?

   (A) *Tom Sawyer*
   (B) *Martin Chuzzlewit*
   (C) *Catcher in the Rye*
   (D) *The Great Gatsby*
   (E) *Sister Carrie*

11. Of the following poems, which is known as one of the most poignant elegies to President Abraham Lincoln?

   (A) "Elegy Written in a Country Churchyard"
   (B) "When Lilacs Last in the Dooryard Bloomed"
   (C) "After Death"
   (D) "Howl"
   (E) "Elegiac Stanzas"

QUESTION 12 refers to the following.

12. Which of the following is an important feature of the building pictured above?

   (A) A dependence on rectilinear lines and angles
   (B) An emphasis on the structural framework of the building
   (C) An interplay of large and small geometric shapes
   (D) The use of curvilinear forms to suggest organic growth or motion
   (E) An orderly, classically inspired floor plan

QUESTIONS 13–15 refer to the following illustrations (A) through (E).

(A)

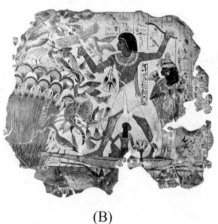

(B)

(C)

(D)

(E)

13. Which example is intent on a naturalistic rendering of an animal's anatomy?

14. Which example uses animals as a metaphor for human behavior?

15. In which example are animals seen in a magic or ritual context?

QUESTION 16 refers to the following.

16. The example pictured above most likely presents which of the following?

(A) A passage from a classical epic
(B) A scene from a Wagnerian opera
(C) An eighteenth-century satire on human foibles
(D) An episode from a Shakespearean drama
(E) An incident from the French Revolution

17. Which of the following lines is an example of iambic pentameter?

      ⏑ / ⏑ /   ⏑ / ⏑ /
(A) Her deck / once red / with he/roes' blood /

      / ⏑ / ⏑ / ⏑ /   ⏑
(B) Here goes / the try / I've al/ways know /

      / ⏑ /   ⏑⏑ / ⏑ ⏑
(C) She loves the / way I hold / her hand/

      / / ⏑ / / ⏑ / /
(D) Although I/ knew the road / led home/

      ⏑ / ⏑ / / ⏑ /   /
(E) As I lay / wait ing / for the / morn

QUESTIONS 18 and 19 refer to the following verses.

> O God, do you hear it, this persecution,
> These my sufferings from this hateful
> Woman, this monster, murderess of children?
> Still what I can do that I will do:
> I will lament and cry upon heaven,
> Calling the gods to bear me witness
> How you have killed my boys to prevent me from
> Touching their bodies or giving them burial.
> I wish I never begot them to see them
> Afterward slaughtered by you.

18. These lines are spoken by

    (A) the murderer.
    (B) the father of the dead children.
    (C) one of the gods.
    (D) a bystander.
    (E) a judge.

19. It can be inferred from this passage that

    (A) the woman had a right to kill her children.
    (B) the man deserved to lose his children.
    (C) the rites and ceremonies of burial are extremely important.
    (D) the gods decreed the death of the children.
    (E) the woman will get away with the murders.

QUESTIONS 20–22 refer to the following verses (A) through (E).

    (A) For shade to shade will come too drowsily,
        And drown the wakeful anguish of the soul.
    (B) Rocks, caves, lakes, fens, bogs, dens, and shades of death.
    (C) 'Twas brillig, and the slithy toves
        Did gyre and gimble in the wabe
    (D) Because I could not stop for Death—
        He kindly stopped for me—
    (E) ... yet from these flames
        No light, but rather darkness visible

20. Which passage contains an oxymoron?

21. Which passage uses assonance?

22. Which passage is written in iambic pentameter?

23. Which of the following are African-American playwrights who won awards and critical recognition for their plays in the 1920s?

    (A) August Wilson and Lorraine Hansberry
    (B) Charles Gordone and Imamu Amiri Baraka
    (C) Ed Bullins and Sonia Sanchez
    (D) Zora Neale Hurston and Marita Bonner
    (E) Eugene O'Neill and Clifford Odets

24. A well-made play may have all of the following EXCEPT

    (A) a tight and logical construction.
    (B) a plot based on a withheld secret.
    (C) a misplaced letter and documents.
    (D) an obligatory scene.
    (E) an episodic structure.

25. Frank Lloyd Wright was the original architect/designer of which of the following twentieth-century museums?

    (A) Solomon R. Guggenheim Museum, New York
    (B) East Wing, National Gallery of Art, Washington, D.C.
    (C) Museum of Architecture, Frankfurt-am-Main
    (D) The High Museum of Art, Atlanta
    (E) None of the above.

QUESTIONS 26–28 refer to the following ballet definitions.

(A) Quick springing movement that resembles a cat walk by alternating feet.

(B) Placing and applying body weight to one foot that is against the floor while sliding the other foot into fifth position.

(C) Positioning one foot in front of the other while the feet remain one step apart.

(D) Weight proportioned incorrectly, creating the body to shift and lean in that direction.

(E) One left leg lifted at a 45-degree angle rotating from front to outer side, from back to inner side.

26. Which description describes glissade?

27. Which description describes improper balance?

28. Which description is fourth position crossed?

29. The predecessor of the modern-day piano is the _____

    (A) lute.
    (B) harpsichord.
    (C) synthesizer.
    (D) harp.
    (E) xylophone.

30. A poem set to music is a(n) _____

    (A) madrigal.
    (B) art song.
    (C) opera.
    (D) aria.
    (E) symphony.

31. A high male voice is classified as a(n)

    (A) soprano.
    (B) tenor.
    (C) bass.
    (D) baritone.
    (E) alto.

32. Which of the following well-known writers is famous for his verses about the struggle for Irish independence?

    (A) James Joyce
    (B) J. P. Donleavy
    (C) W. B. Yeats
    (D) G. B. Shaw
    (E) John O'Hara

33. The idea of evolution is propounded by which of the following English writers?

    (A) Alfred Lord Tennyson
    (B) Dr. Samuel Johnson
    (C) Charles Darwin
    (D) Robert Browning
    (E) Thomas Henry Huxley

34. Which of the following early American novels deals with the author's personal attempt to exorcise many of the negative aspects of his Puritan heritage?

    (A) Irving's *The History of New York*
    (B) Melville's *Moby Dick*
    (C) Brown's *Wieland*
    (D) Cooper's *The Pathfinder*
    (E) Hawthorne's *The Scarlet Letter*

35. Though once condemned as indecent and controversial, this modern English autobiographical novel is now acclaimed for its originality.

    (A) *The Metamorphosis*
    (B) *Sons and Lovers*
    (C) *Time and Again*
    (D) *Heart of Darkness*
    (E) *Ethan Frome*

36. Known for its transcendentalist underpinnings, this early American work also emphasizes the importance of self-reliance.

    (A) *The Scarlet Letter*
    (B) *The Open Boat*
    (C) *Walden*
    (D) *The Last of the Mohicans*
    (E) *The Red Badge of Courage*

QUESTIONS 37–39 refer to illustrations (A) through (E).

(A)

(B)

(C)

(D)

(E)

37. Which example characterizes a culture which values logic and order?

38. In which example are architectural forms and materials used for a whimsical effect?

39. Which example best characterizes a culture which values technological precision and efficiency?

QUESTION 40 refers to the following.

40. In the building pictured above, the cantilevered horizontal forms do all of the following EXCEPT

   (A) echo the natural waterfall's rock ledge.
   (B) emphasize the structural framework of the building.
   (C) deny the mass and weight of the materials.
   (D) integrate the building with the natural setting.
   (E) rely on industrial construction materials.

QUESTION 41 refers to the following.

41. The architect of the building pictured above probably relied primarily on which of the following?

    (A) Steel
    (B) Concrete
    (C) Wood
    (D) Stone masonry and mortar
    (E) Sheet glass

QUESTIONS 42 and 43 refer to the following poem.

> **The Sick Rose**
> O Rose, thou art sick.
> The invisible worm
> That flies in the night
> In the howling storm
>
> Has found out thy bed
> Of crimson joy,
> And his dárk sécret love
> Does thy life destroy.
>   — *William Blake*

42. The imagery in this poem is mainly

   (A) religious.
   (B) sexual.
   (C) animal.
   (D) light.
   (E) darkness.

43. The word "life" in line 8 means

   (A) passion.
   (B) spirit.
   (C) love.
   (D) beauty.
   (E) memory.

QUESTIONS 44–46 refer to the following poem.

> Apparently with no surprise
> To any happy flower
> The Frost beheads it at its play
> In accidental power.
> The blonde Assassin passes on,
> The Sun proceeds unmoved
> To measure off another Day
> For an Approving God.

44. Line 3 demonstrates

   (A) alliteration.
   (B) personification.
   (C) onomatopoeia.
   (D) assonance.
   (E) conceit.

45. "The blonde Assassin" line 5 refers to

   (A) fate.
   (B) disease.
   (C) the frost.
   (D) the sun.
   (E) an approving god.

46. Which of the following best describes the meaning of the poem?

    (A) The cruelty of God
    (B) The inevitability of death
    (C) The indifference of God
    (D) The happiness of flowers
    (E) The inevitability of winter

47. Poetic drama is best described as

    (A) poetry in dialogue.
    (B) a poem in dialogue written for performance.
    (C) ancillary to action.
    (D) a one-act play.
    (E) a play with no well-defined scenes.

48. *The Threepenny Opera* is best described as

    (A) an adaptation of John Gay's *The Beggar's Opera.*
    (B) a melodrama.
    (C) a comedy.
    (D) an epic drama.
    (E) historification.

49. The belief that a human being has an absolute power to choose his or her own destiny is a hallmark of

    (A) existentialism.
    (B) essentialism.
    (C) pragmatism.
    (D) Marxism.
    (E) Platonism.

50. "Cyclopean" is a term which is often used to refer to the masonry building of which of the following civilizations?

    (A) Ancient Egyptian
    (B) Mesopotamian
    (C) Aztec
    (D) Roman
    (E) Mycenean

51. Descartes used his *cogito* argument ("I think; therefore, I am") to establish

    (A) an indubitable foundation for knowledge.
    (B) the basis of personal identity.
    (C) metaphysics on a firm footing.
    (D) the existence of God.
    (E) the foundation of mathematics.

52. Which analysis represents a through-composed form?

    (A) AB
    (B) ABA
    (C) ABCDE
    (D) ABACA
    (E) A

53. Which of the following can be a synonym for Gregorian chant?

    (A) plainchant
    (B) motet
    (C) canon
    (D) aria
    (E) fugue

54. Which composer is best known for his technique of weaving favorite melodies, often patriotic, into his compositions?

    (A) Sousa
    (B) Ives
    (C) Bernstein
    (D) Stravinsky
    (E) Haydn

55. Which of the following is perhaps the most curious – even hilarious – novel written in the eighteenth century?

    (A) *Tristram Shandy*
    (B) *Don Quixote*
    (C) *Candy*
    (D) *Catch-22*
    (E) *Where the Bee Sucks There Suck I*

56. Which Shakespeare play is considered by many critics to be the Bard's finest study of guilt and conscience following a crime?

    (A) *Julius Caesar*
    (B) *Macbeth*
    (C) *Hamlet*
    (D) *A Midsummer Night's Dream*
    (E) *Love's Labor Lost*

57. In which of the following tales is a house presented as a personification of a family?

    (A) *Anne of Green Gables*
    (B) *The House of Morgan*
    (C) *The Young Housewife*
    (D) *The House of the Seven Gables*
    (E) *An Angel on the Porch*

58. Which of the following is a twentieth-century novel about the Wild West written in the tradition of realistic movement?

    (A) *Huckleberry Finn*
    (B) *The Bird Comes to Yellow Sky*
    (C) *The Oxbow Incident*
    (D) *The Occurrence at Owl Creek Bridge*
    (E) *The Red Badge of Courage*

59. Which of the following poets is known as an American original who experimented with extensive works of detailed images and free verse?

    (A) Alexander Pope
    (B) Samuel Langhorne Clemens
    (C) Walt Whitman
    (D) Emily Dickinson
    (E) Anne Bradstreet

QUESTION 60 refers to the following.

60. The pose of the horse in the sculpture pictured above serves to express

    (A) physical aging and decay.
    (B) stability.
    (C) strength.
    (D) lightness and motion.
    (E) moral fortitude.

QUESTION 61 refers to the following.

61. Which of the following best describes the example pictured above?

    (A) Monumental architecture dominates the scene.
    (B) The scene is viewed from the window of a passing train.
    (C) Human drama is the artist's main concern.
    (D) The composition has a dramatic central focus.
    (E) The scene is viewed as though from a second-story window.

QUESTION 62 refers to the following.

62. Which of the following is probably true of the sculpture pictured above?

    (A) The artist modelled it with his hands.
    (B) The artist poured it into a mold.
    (C) The artist shaped his materials with a blowtorch and welding tools.
    (D) The artist shaped natural materials with a chisel.
    (E) The artist used industrial forms as he found them.

QUESTION 63 refers to the following.

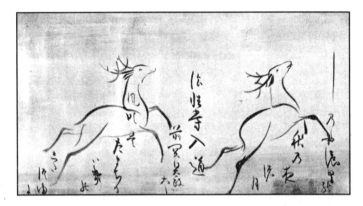

63. Which of the following is the most important artistic device in the example shown above?

(A) Line
(B) Tone
(C) Perspective
(D) Volume
(E) Hue

QUESTION 64 refers to the following.

64. Which of the following does NOT contribute to order and regularity in the example pictured on the previous page?

   (A) The repeated second-story window design
   (B) A facade which lacks deep recesses and voids
   (C) The use of columns at the center and corners of the building
   (D) A subtle use of the arch
   (E) The balustrade running across the roof line

QUESTIONS 65 and 66 refer to the following stanza.

> When my mother died I was very young
> And my father sold me while yet my tongue
> Could scarcely cry "'weep! 'weep! 'weep! 'weep!"
> So your chimneys I sweep, and in soot I sleep.

65. The above stanza was taken from a longer poem written by which of the following?

   (A) Shakespeare
   (B) Milton
   (C) Chaucer
   (D) Blake
   (E) Hardy

66. Which of the following best explains the use of the word "'weep!" in line 3 of the stanza?

   (A) The child is so young he cannot yet pronounce the word.
   (B) The child has a speech impediment because of neglect.
   (C) The child is weeping because he was sold as a chimney sweep.
   (D) The child wants to make you feel guilty about sweeping your chimneys.
   (E) The child is so young he is upset at having to sweep chimneys.

QUESTIONS 67–71 refer to the following epic poem.

> A whole day's journey high but wide remote
> From this Assyrian garden, where the Fiend
> Saw undelighted all delight, all kind
> Of living creatures new to sight and strange:
> Two of far nobler shape erect and tall,
> God-like erect, with native honor clad

In naked majesty seemed lords of all,
And worthy seemed, for in their looks divine
The image of their Maker shone,

...

For contemplation he and valor formed,
For softness she and sweet attractive grace,
He for God only, she for God in him:

67. The term "epic" refers to

   (A) a long poem written in rhyming couplets about a hero.
   (B) a long poem translated from Latin.
   (C) a long poem written about heroic actions.
   (D) a long poem written by Virgil.
   (E) a long poem about death.

68. The above lines are from

   (A) Dante's *Inferno.*
   (B) Virgil's *Aeneid.*
   (C) *The Iliad.*
   (D) *Arabian Nights.*
   (E) *Paradise Lost.*

69. The viewpoint of the lines is

   (A) Faust's.
   (B) God's.
   (C) Scheherazade's.
   (D) Satan's.
   (E) Dante's.

70. Which best describes the couple in lines 4-6?

   (A) Beowulf and Grendel's mother before the crucial fight.
   (B) Grendel and Grendel's mother after the crucial fight.
   (C) Adam and Eve before "The Fall."
   (D) Hector and his wife before the crucial battle.
   (E) Adam and Eve after "The Fall."

71. Which best describes the poet's views on the roles of men and women?

    (A) Men and women are equal.
    (B) Men are made for thoughtful action and women for beauty.
    (C) Women must be submissive to the god in men.
    (D) Men must be powerful and women soft.
    (E) Men are reasonable and strong and women soft and graceful.

72. Which of the following plays focuses on a marriage built on a lie and problems with eyesight?

    (A) *The Wild Duck*
    (B) *Oedipus*
    (C) *Electra*
    (D) *Antigone*
    (E) *Andromache*

73. *Tartuffe* is best described as a play about

    (A) the downfall of a noble king.
    (B) the problems of a marriage.
    (C) a man of considerable stature duped by a hypocrite.
    (D) individuals who wait and do not act.
    (E) children who are ingrates.

74. An *insula* refers to a(n)

    (A) Greek public meeting square.
    (B) multi-storied Roman apartment block.
    (C) western portion of a Carolingian church.
    (D) Greek cross plan.
    (E) vertical groove on the surface of a column.

75. Berkeley's famous dictum, "Esse est percipi" ("To be is to be perceived"), is associated most strongly with the outlook known as

    (A) idealism.
    (B) pragmatism.
    (C) empiricism.
    (D) rationalism.
    (E) phenomenology.

76. Which jazz saxophonist was named "Bird"?

    (A) Charlie Parker
    (B) John Coltrane
    (C) Dizzy Gillespie
    (D) Paul Desmond
    (E) Stan Getz

77. Which jazz tenor saxophonist is famous for his "Giant Steps"?

    (A) Charlie Parker
    (B) Stan Getz
    (C) John Coltrane
    (D) Coleman Hawkins
    (E) Ornette Coleman

78. A collaboration between Aaron Copland and the dance-choreographer Agnes de Mille resulted in the creation of which ballet suite?

    (A) "West Side Story"
    (B) "Rodeo"
    (C) "Porgy and Bess"
    (D) "Phantom of the Opera"
    (E) "Salome"

79. Which of the following novels of adventure presents the most detailed picture of eighteenth-century English manorial and city life?

    (A) *Great Expectations*
    (B) *Moby Dick*
    (C) *Jane Eyre*
    (D) *Tom Jones*
    (E) *Silas Marner*

80. Which of the following is among the most famous of English works by the group of writers called the "Decadents"?

    (A) Coleridge's "Rime of the Ancient Mariner"
    (B) Lawrence's *Sons and Lovers*
    (C) Fielding's *Joseph Andrews*
    (D) Wilde's *The Picture of Dorian Gray*
    (E) Joyce's *The Dubliners*

81. The important literary concept of the "pathetic fallacy" was first set forth in

    (A) Ruskin's *Modern Painters.*
    (B) Emerson's *Nature.*
    (C) Shakespeare's *As You Like It.*
    (D) Thomas Lodge's *Rosalynde.*
    (E) Samuel Johnson's *Dictionary.*

82. A reaction against utilitarianism – the theory of ethics formulated in England in the eighteenth century – can be seen in nineteenth-century literature, such as

    (A) Eliot's *Middlemarch.*
    (B) Dreiser's *Sister Carrie.*
    (C) Melville's *Billy Budd.*
    (D) James's *Washington Square.*
    (E) Dickens' *David Copperfield.*

83. Which of the following writers participated energetically in the Celtic Revival of the eighteenth century?

    (A) James Joyce
    (B) John O'Hara
    (C) J. P. Donleavy
    (D) James Macpherson
    (E) W. B. Yeats

QUESTION 84 refers to the following.

84. In the painting illustrated above, all of the following are important compositional devices EXCEPT

   (A) the perspective grid of the checkerboard floor.
   (B) the strong highlighting of the foreground figures.
   (C) the arcade of arches in the background.
   (D) the vigorous movement of the main figure group.
   (E) the intersecting lines of the arms and the swords.

QUESTION 85 refers to the following.

85. The building pictured above was produced in which of the following countries?

   (A) Japan
   (B) Indonesia
   (C) Easter Island
   (D) Greece
   (E) Nigeria

QUESTIONS 86–88 refer to the following illustrations (A) through (E) below.

(A)

(B)

(C)

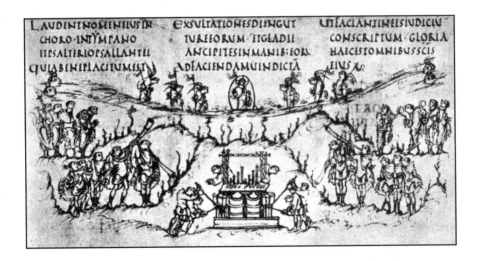

(D)

(E)

86. Which example seeks to give a schematic representation of a ceremonial event?

87. In which example is the human figure most stylized and repeated in order to fit its container?

88. In which example do the figures show the greatest tendency toward rhythmic calligraphy?

QUESTIONS 89–91 refer to the following lines.

> As when in the sky the stars about the moon's shining
> are seen in all their glory, when the air has fallen to stillness.
> and all the high places of the hills are clear, and the shoulders
> out-jutting,
> and the deep ravines, as endless bright air spills from the heavens
> and all the stars are seen, to make glad the heart of the shepherd:
> such in their numbers blazed the watchfires the Trojans were burning
> between the waters of Xanthos and the ships, before Ilion.

89. The lines above are an example of

    (A) a Homeric simile.
    (B) an extended metaphor.
    (C) Augustan couplets.
    (D) English heroic verse.
    (E) Miltonic free verse.

90. What is being described as what?

    (A) The stars are like hills.
    (B) The stars are like shepherds.
    (C) The stars are like rivers.
    (D) The Trojan fires are like the stars.
    (E) The Trojan ships are like the stars.

91. The shepherd is introduced in line 5 in order to

    (A) humanize the description.
    (B) give some humor to the description.
    (C) give some depth to the description.
    (D) give some gladness to the description.
    (E) glamorize the description.

QUESTIONS 92–95 refer to lines (A) through (E) below.

(A) As soon as April pierces to the root
    The drought of March, and bathes each bud and shoot
    …

(B) Of man's first disobedience, and the fruit
    Of that forbidden fruit whose mortal taste
    …

(C) My heart leaps up when I behold
    A rainbow in the sky;
    …

(D) I placed a jar in Tennessee,
    And round it was, upon a hill.

(E) Because I could not stop for Death—
    He kindly stopped for me—

92. Which is written by a woman?

93. Which is by Chaucer?

94. Which represents the Romantic period?

95. Which represents the epic?

96. As Gregor Samsa awoke one morning from an uneasy dream he found him-
    self transformed into a gigantic insect.

    This opening line is

    (A) Genet's
    (B) Sartre's
    (C) Ionesco's
    (D) Kafka's
    (E) Tolstoy's

97. The best definition for the original use of scapegoat is

    (A) a table ornament used when royalty was unable to appear.
    (B) a fur-bearing animal that was used to provide milk.
    (C) an animal tethered to lure animals terrorizing the village.
    (D) a victim sacrificed for the redemption of the tribe being driven into
        the wilderness.
    (E) a royal personage like Oedipus who went into exile.

98. Which of the following types of ancient Roman architecture most directly influenced the development of early Christian church planning?

    (A) Temple
    (B) Basilica
    (C) Bath
    (D) Forum
    (E) Villa

99. Dance was originated by

    (A) religious groups.
    (B) Egyptians.
    (C) Greeks.
    (D) Romans.
    (E) savage hunters.

100. The logical fallacy involved in concluding that the universe itself must have a cause because every event in the universe has cause is
    (A) the fallacy of composition.
    (B) the fallacy of division.
    (C) the slippery slope fallacy.
    (D) the *ad hominem* fallacy.
    (E) the fallacy of ignorance.

101. The themes of many musical compositions are often that of folk music. Which composer is most famous for his folk music settings for wind ensemble?

    (A) Sousa
    (B) Grainger
    (C) Beethoven
    (D) Strauss
    (E) Haydn

QUESTIONS 102-105 refer to the following musical notation.

102. What is the key of this excerpt?

    (A) B flat
    (B) F
    (C) C
    (D) D
    (E) A

103. The time signature for the above excerpt is not noted. What should it be?

    (A) $\frac{4}{4}$

    (B) $\frac{2}{4}$

    (C) $\frac{6}{8}$

    (D) $\frac{3}{4}$

    (E) $\frac{12}{8}$

104. How many measures are present?

    (A) 1
    (B) 2
    (C) 3
    (D) 0
    (E) 5

105. What is the arrow pointing towards?

    (A) Key signature
    (B) Clef sign
    (C) Double bar
    (D) Repeat sign
    (E) Time signature

106. Which of the following is considered among the "American Ethnic" body of literature?

(A) James's *Daisy Miller*
(B) Poe's *Cask of Amontillado*
(C) Roth's *Goodbye Columbus*
(D) Updike's *Rabbit Redux*
(E) Hawthorne's *Scarlet Letter*

107. One of the most famous and prophetic descriptions of settlements in the young American nation was

(A) *The Journals of Lewis and Clark.*
(B) *Main Street.*
(C) *Letters From an American Farmer.*
(D) *The Last of the Mohicans.*
(E) *The Diary of Captain John Smith.*

108. Which of the following modern novels describes the difficulties faced by African-Americans in twentieth-century America?

(A) *As I Lay Dying*
(B) *Ethan Frome*
(C) *Heart of Darkness*
(D) *The Metamorphosis*
(E) *The Invisible Man*

109. Which of the following nineteenth-century novels was used as an accurate travel guide well into this century?

(A) *Journey to the Center of the Earth*
(B) *The Mysterious Island*
(C) *Robinson Crusoe*
(D) *20,000 Leagues Under the Sea*
(E) *Gulliver's Travels*

110. Which of the following novels recalls a time of medieval chivalry?

(A) Eliot's *Middlemarch*
(B) Scott's *Ivanhoe*
(C) Poe's *The Fall of the House of Usher*
(D) King's *The Shining*
(E) West's *The Dreamlife of Balso Snell*

111. It has been said that Victorian poetry is essentially a continuation of the poetry of the romantic movement. This can be seen in

   (A) Hemingway's veneration for Eliot.
   (B) Tennyson's veneration for Browning.
   (C) Arnold's veneration for Wordsworth.
   (D) Rossetti's veneration for Browning.
   (E) Wordsworth's veneration for Scott.

112. Which of the following is one of the most hilarious stories in *Huckleberry Finn* – one which demonstrates both the accepting nature and eventual canniness of the heartland Americans?

   (A) *The Duke and the Dauphin*
   (B) Tom Sawyer and his painted fence
   (C) Huck's escape from Pap
   (D) Jim's escape to freedom
   (E) Huck "lighting out for the territories"

QUESTION 113 refers to the following.

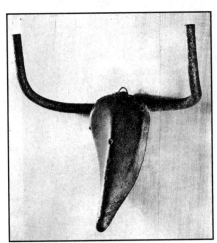

113. In combining found objects to make the sculpture shown above, the artist sought to create

   (A) a contrast of line and tone.
   (B) a religious symbol.
   (C) a visual analogy to a living creature.
   (D) a metaphor for human experience.
   (E) a functional device.

QUESTIONS 114–116 refer to the following illustrations (A) through (E)

(A)

(C)

(B)

(D)

(E)

114. In which example do carefully rendered decorative details in the painting help to visually relate the main subject to the background?

115. In which example is an off-center subject cropped to produce the effect of a casual photograph?

116. In which example does the subject's off-center position lead the viewer's eye out of the picture?

QUESTION 117 refers to the following.

117. The staircase in the Hotel van Eetvelde, designed by Victor Horta in 1895, illustrates which one of the following art historical styles?

(A) Surrealism
(B) Post-Modernism
(C) Neo-Classicism
(D) Post-Impressionsim
(E) Art Nouveau

QUESTIONS 118 and 119 refer to the following illustrations (A) through (D) below.

(A)

(B)

(C)

(D)

118. Which is Gothic?

    (A) Building (A)
    (B) Building (B)
    (C) Building (C)
    (D) Building (D)
    (E) None of the above.

119. Which was NOT constructed as a place of religious worship?

    (A) Building (A)
    (B) Building (B)
    (C) Building (C)
    (D) Building (D)
    (E) None of the above.

QUESTIONS 120 and 121 refer to the following verse.

> On the one-ton temple bell
> a moonmoth, folded into sleep,
> sits still.

120. The above is an example of

(A) hyperbole.
(B) an ode.
(C) haiku.
(D) an epigram.
(E) doggerel.

121. The original work above was written in

(A) French.
(B) Japanese.
(C) Chinese.
(D) British English.
(E) Persian.

122. Which of the following best defines the term *bathos*?

(A) A gross exaggeration
(B) A build to a climax
(C) An abrupt fall from climax
(D) An abrupt fall from the beautiful to the funny
(E) An abrupt build to a climax

123. Which poet gave us the term "negative capability"?

(A) William Carlos Williams
(B) T. S. Eliot
(C) William Wordsworth
(D) e. e. cummings
(E) John Keats

124. If all tragedies are finished by death, and all comedies by a marriage, then which of the following is the best example of tragedy?

(A) *A Death of a Salesman*
(B) *A Midsummer Night's Dream*
(C) *Oedipus*
(D) *The Tempest*
(E) *The Bad-Tempered Man*

QUESTIONS 125–127 refer to what happens when:

    (A) misunderstandings are cleared up.
    (B) action not intended by the main character takes place.
    (C) the public is aided in its discovery of the villain.
    (D) the main character whispers an "aside" to the audience.
    (E) the hero's understanding of the true nature of the situation and the self changes.

125. Which of the choices best defines *anagnorisis*, the Greek word for "recognition" or "discovery"?

126. Which choice best describes Mark Antony's intent in the public oration that he makes regarding Julius Caesar's death?

127. Which choice is best used to characterize Othello's description of himself as "one that loved not wisely, but too well"?

128.   "So the whole ear of Denmark
    Is by a forged process of my death
    Rankly abused."

    The speaker is

    (A) the Royal Dane.
    (B) King Lear.
    (C) Puck.
    (D) Falstaff.
    (E) Caliban.

129. The unglazed opening in the center of the dome of the Pantheon in Rome is called a(n)

    (A) window.
    (B) oculus.
    (C) splayed window.
    (D) stained-glass window.
    (E) clerestory.

130. Parallel feet, flat-footed steps, undulating torso, body isolation, and syn-copated rhythms refer to

    (A) beledi dance (abdominal dance).
    (B) jazz dance.
    (C) danse mora (Flamenco dance).
    (D) tap dance.
    (E) country dance.

131. Suppose two theories are equally powerful in explaining certain phenom-ena, but one of them (**X**) postulates a larger number of unobservable entities than the other (**Y**). Which is preferable and why?

    (A) **Y**, because of Occam's Razor
    (B) **Y**, because of the Principle of Plenitude
    (C) **X**, because of the Open Question Argument
    (D) **X**, because of Underdetermination
    (E) **Y**, because of Scientific Realism

132. The hero of what nineteenth century novel states that "...vanity is a weak-ness indeed. But pride– where there is a real superiority of mind, pride will be always under good regulation."

    (A) *Silas Marner*
    (B) *Emma*
    (C) *Gone with the Wind*
    (D) *Pride and Prejudice*
    (E) *Gulliver's Travels*

133. A trumpet can play different notes by adjusting the lip or by doing what?

    (A) Pressing down a valve
    (B) Striking a string
    (C) Covering a hole
    (D) Using an octave key
    (E) Using a slide

QUESTIONS 134 and 135 refer to the following musical notation.

134. The diagram is an example of

    (A) hemiola.
    (B) paradiddle.
    (C) fermata.
    (D) crescendo.
    (E) glissando.

135. The C in measure 1 is a C sharp. Therefore, the C in measure 2 is a

    (A) C natural.
    (B) C sharp.
    (C) C flat.
    (D) B.
    (E) D.

136. What is another name for the bass clef?

    (A) F clef
    (B) G clef
    (C) Tenor clef
    (D) Treble clef
    (E) Alto clef

137. One of the greatest modern chronicles of a famous incident during the Civil War is

    (A) Hoover's *None Dare Call It Treason.*
    (B) Wouk's *Caine Mutiny.*
    (C) Mailer's *The Naked and the Dead.*
    (D) Catton's *A Stillness at Appomatox.*
    (E) Crane's *Red Badge of Courage.*

138. Which of the following is Edward Albee's memorable drama of the trials and tribulations of a university professor and his wife?

    (A) *Troilus and Cressida*
    (B) *Who's Afraid of Virginia Woolf*
    (C) *The American Dream*
    (D) *Brighton Beach Memoirs*
    (E) *A View from the Bridge*

139. One of the greatest diarists of the Restoration was

    (A) Sir Laurence Olivier.
    (B) Laurence Sterne.
    (C) O. E. Rolvaag.
    (D) Samuel Pepys.
    (E) Jonathan Swift.

140. In the early 1800s, which American minister and writer promoted the philosophical and literary movement called transcendentalism?

    (A) Jonathan Edwards
    (B) Sir William Pitt
    (C) Ralph Waldo Emerson
    (D) Henry David Thoreau
    (E) Dr. Samuel Fuller

PRACTICE TEST 1

Answer Key

1.	(D)	33.	(C)	65.	(D)
2.	(B)	34.	(E)	66.	(A)
3.	(A)	35.	(B)	67.	(C)
4.	(D)	36.	(C)	68.	(E)
5.	(A)	37.	(A)	69.	(D)
6.	(B)	38.	(D)	70.	(C)
7.	(C)	39.	(B)	71.	(E)
8.	(A)	40.	(B)	72.	(A)
9.	(D)	41.	(D)	73.	(C)
10.	(C)	42.	(B)	74.	(B)
11.	(B)	43.	(D)	75.	(A)
12.	(D)	44.	(B)	76.	(A)
13.	(D)	45.	(C)	77.	(C)
14.	(A)	46.	(B)	78.	(B)
15.	(E)	47.	(B)	79.	(D)
16.	(C)	48.	(D)	80.	(D)
17.	(A)	49.	(A)	81.	(A)
18.	(B)	50.	(E)	82.	(E)
19.	(C)	51.	(A)	83.	(D)
20.	(E)	52.	(C)	84.	(D)
21.	(B)	53.	(A)	85.	(A)
22.	(A)	54.	(B)	86.	(A)
23.	(D)	55.	(A)	87.	(C)
24.	(E)	56.	(B)	88.	(D)
25.	(A)	57.	(D)	89.	(A)
26.	(B)	58.	(C)	90.	(D)
27.	(D)	59.	(C)	91.	(A)
28.	(C)	60.	(C)	92.	(E)
29.	(B)	61.	(E)	93.	(A)
30.	(B)	62.	(C)	94.	(C)
31.	(B)	63.	(A)	95.	(B)
32.	(C)	64.	(D)	96.	(D)

97.	(D)	112.	(A)	127.	(E)
98.	(B)	113.	(C)	128.	(A)
99.	(E)	114.	(B)	129.	(B)
100.	(A)	115.	(C)	130.	(B)
101.	(B)	116.	(D)	131.	(A)
102.	(B)	117.	(E)	132.	(D)
103.	(D)	118.	(C)	133.	(A)
104.	(C)	119.	(A)	134.	(A)
105.	(D)	120.	(C)	135.	(A)
106.	(C)	121.	(B)	136.	(A)
107.	(C)	122.	(D)	137.	(D)
108.	(E)	123.	(E)	138.	(B)
109.	(A)	124.	(A)	139.	(D)
110.	(B)	125.	(E)	140.	(C)
111.	(C)	126.	(C)		

PRACTICE TEST 1

Detailed Explanations of Answers

1. **(D)** Pylons serve as large "gates" to ancient Egyptian temple complexes. Pyramids (A), mastabas (B), and tombs (C) were burial sites and were not as a rule located near the entrances of temples. (E) Obelisks, while positioned near the entrance to many Egyptian temple complexes, are tall, narrow, vertical shafts, which are physically quite unlike wide, massive pylon walls.

2. **(B)** The group of performers who used such techniques for the purpose of displaying power were called flagellants. Fools used crude jokes and quick wit in their technique (A). Minnesingers were a group of entertainers who sang about war, political issues, and love (C). The mimes mimicked and acted out a situation without speech (D). Joculators were seen as actors and jesters, dancing mimes, acrobats, poets, and musicians (E).

3. **(A)** Although the definition of an *a priori* truth is not altogether clear, it is usually said that such truths are known independently of experience or "from the first." Thus, (B) cannot be correct. Mathematical calculation can count as a kind of experience, so (C) is incorrect. Human beings are believed to know truth "from the first" by many philosophers; thus, (D) is incorrect. A truth whose denial is a contradiction (E) is called an "analytic" truth.

4. **(D)** The fourth degree of a major scale is called the subdominant. Each degree is given a name to show its relation within the scale. Choice (D) is correct. The tonic is the first step of a scale; choice (A) is incorrect. The dominant is the fifth degree of the scale; choice (B) is incorrect. The leading tone is the seventh degree of the scale; choice (C) is incorrect. The mediant is the third degree of a scale; choice (E) is incorrect.

5. **(A)** A minor scale ascends from the tonic in the following pattern: $w \frac{1}{2} w w \frac{1}{2} w w$. Therefore, the half steps occur between the 2-3 and 5-6 scale degree, so choice (A) is correct. Half steps between steps 3-4 and 7-8 are found in a major scale, $w w 2 w w w 2$. Choice (B) is incorrect. Half steps between steps 1-2 and 7-8 and 2-3 and 7-8 are not defined scales; choices

(C) and (D) are incorrect. A half step between the third and fourth degrees of a scale is found in the blues scale; choice (E) is incorrect.

6. **(B)** Stravinsky's "Le Sacre du Printemps" is an example of the use of primitivism – employing rhythms that are explosive and powerful; choice (B) is correct. Debussy employs impressionism for "Prélude á l'après-midi d'un faune"; choice (A) is incorrect. "Salome" is a tone poem by Richard Strauss which experiments with atonality. Choice (C) is incorrect. "Wozzeck" is a 12-tone opera by Alban Berg; choice (D) is incorrect. "The Liberty Bell" is a march composed by John Phillip Sousa; choice (E) is incorrect.

7. **(C)** William Blake (1757-1827) has been described as "the first clear voice of romanticism" and perhaps his greatest work was *Songs of Innocence and Experience* (C), in which many of the characteristics of romantic poetry can be seen: the poetry expresses the poet's personal feelings, not the actions of other men; spontaneity and freedom; natural scenes and pictures of flora and fauna. Pope's (A) "hero-comical" poem from the seventeenth century demonstrates none of the above. *The Social Contract* (B) is a sociological and philosophical essay. *Romeo and Juliet* (E), while commonly understood to be a romance between two teenagers, is not "romantic," and, in fact, predates romanticism by 200 years. James's novel (D) belongs to the American realist period.

8. **(A)** The titles presented here, of course, are mostly in French (except for (D) which is about a French historical figure) – the language of Albert Camus, the father of existentialism. Camus' *L'Étranger (The Stranger)* – the story of an expatriate Frenchman in Algeria – presents many of the precepts of existentialism: an emphasis on existence rather than essence, and the inadequacy of human reason to explain the enigma of the universe. *Le Morte D'Arthur* (B) was written in English by Tennyson; *Candide* (C) was by Voltaire and *Le Misanthrope* (E) was a comedy of the 1700s by Molière. While the latter title might indicate existential estrangement, the work appears 200 years before the literary movement. *Saint Joan* (D), a dramatic tragedy by G. B. Shaw, is biographical.

9. **(D)** All of the writings listed here describe life on an American frontier – but only *My Antonia* deals with frontier life in the Midwest during the nineteenth century – the rough weather, the difficulties of farm life, and the blossoming of romance in harsh conditions. Cooper's famous work (A), while written during that century, refers to upstate New York during the eighteenth century.

William Byrd's work (B) deals with defining the border between Virginia and North Carolina during the late eighteenth century. Bradford's diary (C) is a Pilgrim document written in colonial Massachusetts, and Twain's classic (E), while it tangentially involves Illinois and the shores of Iowa on the Mississippi River, does not deal with the Midwest per se.

10. **(C)** Salinger's work is recognized as a coming of age novel in which his main character, Holden Caulfield, is an "antihero" – a character whose appeal is that his flaws are dominant. *Tom Sawyer* (A) has always been viewed by critics as a children's novel, because Tom can be seen as the "All-American Boy," unlike Huck Finn, Twain's later, more complicated creation. Dickens' work (B) does not deal with coming of age. Dreiser's *Sister Carrie* (E), on the other hand, does concern itself with changes in the protagonist through time, but Carrie is more a classic heroine in her rigid self-reliance and conquest over adversity. Fitzgerald (D) creates a number of interesting figures – some, like Gatsby, who have anti-heroic qualities – but all have basically "come of age" before the summer in which the story takes place.

11. **(B)** Whitman's poem is one of four elegies, entitled "Memories of President Lincoln," which were made part of *Drum-Taps* after Lincoln's death in 1864. Whitman, who volunteered as a male nurse in Washington during the Civil War – like so many Americans – mourned greatly for the president. The Englishman Gray's "Elegy" (A) is of a much earlier vintage (late 1700s). Christina Rossetti's "After Death" (C) is not an elegy, nor is Allen Ginsburg's "Howl" (D). Wordsworth's work (E) deals with the death of Sir George Beaumont, the poet's patron.

12. **(D)** The architect of the building illustrated was intent on avoiding traditional building forms in the search for a new, expressive use of space. The design pictured, therefore, carefully avoids all reminders of the symmetrical, balanced floor plans of classical and Renaissance architecture. It also dispenses with a conventional structural framework and with the geometric forms and angles of traditional buildings. Instead, it exploits fully the potential of a new material – in this case, poured concrete – to create dynamic, curving forms whose arcs and spirals echo both the shape of growing organisms and the motion of wind and water.

13. **(D)** Answer choices (A), (B), and (E) each contain images of animals which are based to some degree on naturalistic observation. In each case, however, the animals are presented either as black-and-white line drawings

or as schematic, two-dimensional renderings, with no attempt to model the forms of the animals; and in each case, the imagery functions in either a narrative or magical context and does not intend to explore anatomy. Answer choice (C) presents a basically realistic, well-modelled animal, based on naturalistic observation and with close attention to detail, but the addition of the wings adds a fantastic touch and the animal as a whole is elegantly designed and positioned to act as the functional handle of a jar. Only answer choice (D) explores the expressive forms of the animal's musculature, here conveying a sense of untamed emotion and animal energy through the tensed, swelling muscles of the crouched jaguar.

14. **(A)**   Answer choices (B) and (E) each present somewhat schematic representations of animals, the first in order to document the character and activities of an Egyptian noble, and the second to fulfill a magical, ritual function. The animal in answer choice (C) exists solely as a decorative detail on a purely functional object. Answer choice (D) shows animal behavior which might be called analogous to human behavior – i.e., the violence of the strong over the weak – but the image itself does not intend to comment directly on human life. Only answer choice (A) uses animal imagery to directly caricature human behavior. In this case, the Japanese scroll employs monkeys, frogs, hares, and foxes to mimic Buddhist religious practices.

15. **(E)**   Answer choice (E) presents animal images with a high degree of naturalism in a sophisticated, abstract, almost "modern" style. The artist, however, despite his naturalism, was not concerned with perspective or with conventional pictorial space, and concentrated solely on the overlapping images of the animals, which have no narrative function. He has included a view of the animals ascending, possibly to indicate a magical essence of these animals. These paintings were executed on the walls of a cave in what appears to be a sacred precinct, and seem to function as magical images to ensure success in the hunt.

16. **(C)**   The example pictured, by the English painter William Hogarth, satirizes eighteenth-century English life in a comic way. In telling the story of the human characters illustrated in the work, the picture uses a wealth of carefully chosen detail which the viewer is to "read" in a novelistic manner. The period details, therefore (as of dress, architecture, furnishings, etc.), and the attitudes and actions of the figures (the exasperated look, for instance, of the servant on the left) tell us that this is a human comedy set in the eighteenth century. Of the other answer choices, (A), (B), and (D)

would be both historically anachronistic and weightier in subject matter. Answer choice (E) would fall roughly within the correct period, but it, too, would likely present a more dramatic context.

17. **(A)** Choice (A) is the only correctly scanned line. It contains five iambic feet and is an example of iambic pentameter. The other examples have incorrectly marked accents and feet.

18. **(B)** This passage comes from the Greek play *Medea* by Euripides. Medea, a woman who is being cast aside so her husband, Jason, can marry a princess, kills their two sons in retaliation. This passage shows Jason lamenting over the boys' deaths and invoking the gods to punish his ex-wife.

19. **(C)** In the passage, Jason mourns that Medea killed the boys "to prevent me from/Touching their bodies or giving them burial." In Greek society, the dead were honored by elaborate burial rites and ceremonies. To be buried without ceremony was considered to be dishonorable to the dead, especially when they were related to great warriors, such as Jason.

20. **(E)** An oxymoron is an apparent contradiction in terms, such as "jumbo shrimp," "cruel kindness," or "peace force." Passage (E) contains an oxymoron because it mentions flames give "No light, but rather darkness." Choice (E) is the correct answer.

21. **(B)** Assonance is the repetition of vowel sounds in a single line of poetry. Passage (B) contains three examples of assonance: the words "Rocks" and "bogs," the words "caves," "lakes," and "shades," and the words "fens" and "dens." Thus, passage (B) is the correct answer.

22. **(A)** Iambic pentameter refers to the meter, or rhythm, of a line of poetry composed of five feet, each of which is an iamb, having one unstressed syllable followed by a stressed syllable. A line of poetry written in iambic pentameter is ten syllables long. Passage (A) contains two lines of poetry written in iambic pentameter. When read aloud, the unstressed-stressed pattern emerges: "For SHADE to SHADE will COME too DROWsiLY, / And DROWN the WAKEful ANGuish OF the SOUL." Thus, choice (A) is the correct answer.

23. **(D)** is the correct answer. Zora Neale Hurston and Marita Bonner won awards and recognition for their plays in the 1920s. (A) Wilson and Hansberry are of different generations; Wilson is a contemporary playwright and Hansberry wrote her plays between 1961 and 1964. (B) Gordone and Baraka were best known in the 1970s. Ed Bullins was a novelist/poet who

came to prominence in the late 1960s, too late for this question. Sonia Sanchez is a contemporary poet and is also too late to be considered as a correct answer for this question. O'Neill and Odets (E) are not African-American playwrights.

24. **(E)** is the correct answer. A well-made play is characterized by (A) tight and logical construction, (B) a plot based on a withheld secret, (C) misplaced letters or documents, and (D) an obligatory scene. (E) Episodic structure is antithetical and characterized by little more than a series of incidents and has little logical arrangement; therefore, (E) is the exception to the well-made play and is the best answer.

25. **(A)** Solomon R. Guggenheim Museum, New York. The (B) East Wing of the National Gallery of Art in Washington, D.C., was designed by I. M. Pei. O. M. Ungers designed the (C) Museum of Architecture in Frankfurt-am-Main. Richard Meier was the architect of the (D) High Museum of Art in Atlanta.

26. **(B)** To brush one foot against the floor is to glissade. Pas de chat is a quick "cat-like" step (A), feet positioned in front of one another with a step separating them and legs turned out is fourth position crossed (C), body weight shifted incorrectly is improper balance (D), and a pointed foot and extended leg moving in a circular motion is a demi-rond de jambe (E).

27. **(D)** Weight and body shifted incorrectly is improper balance. Choices pas de chat (A), glissade (B), fourth position crossed (C), and demi-rond de jambe (E) are specific ballet movements.

28. **(C)** One foot in front of the other with a step separating them describes fourth position crossed. Pas de chat (A) and glissade (B) are steps in motion, improper balance is incorrect body alignment caused by uneven weight distribution (D), and demi-rond de jambe is a circular foot motion (E).

29. **(B)** The harpsichord is the predecessor of the piano, also called a spinet. The strings of the harpsichord were plucked with quills; this limited dynamics and tone colors. The piano was called the piano forte because it could play dynamics based on the performer's force. The harpsichord was widely used during the baroque period; choice (B) is correct. The lute is similar to the guitar; choice (A) is incorrect. The synthesizer is an electronic keyboard using analog and/or digital technology to produce sound; choice (C) is incorrect. The harp is a stringed instrument that is plucked with the

fingers; choice (D) is incorrect. The xylophone is a percussion instrument which is struck with a mallet; choice (E) is incorrect.

30. **(B)** An art song, or "lieder," is a poem set to music, for solo voice and piano; choice (B) is correct. A madrigal is verse set to music for two or more voices, which often follows a prescribed form; choice (A) is incorrect. An opera is a theatrical drama which is sung, often with instrumental accompaniment; choice (C) is incorrect. An aria is a solo for voice with accompaniment, occurring during a longer form such as an opera; choice (D) is incorrect. A symphony is a three or four movement work for orchestra; choice (E) is incorrect.

31. **(B)** A tenor is a high male voice; choice (B) is correct. The range of voices is classified from high to low; that is, soprano, alto, tenor, baritone, bass. A soprano is a high female voice; choice (A) is incorrect. A bass is the lowest male voice; choice (C) is incorrect. A baritone has a range between the tenor and the bass; choice (D) is incorrect. An alto is a medium female voice; choice (E) is incorrect.

32. **(C)** W. B. Yeats is the correct answer. The famous Irish poet and essayist of the early twentieth century is always remembered for his devotion to Irish nationalism – most specifically in his volumes of collected poems such as "In the Seven Woods" and "The Green Helmet and Other Poems." James Joyce (A) is known for his depiction of Irish life, and dramatist George B. Shaw (D) is generally regarded more in a strictly literary and not political tradition. The other two choices – Donleavy (B) and O'Hara (E) – are modern American writers, whose literary interests tend more to romance and mystery than Irish nationalism and unification.

33. **(C)** Charles Darwin's *On the Origin of Species* helped shape Victorian English thought as well as considerations of natural history throughout the world. Tracing the origin of man from mammals, and species before them, was a monumental scientific effort and a shock so great to the religious community that many still attempt to deny Darwin's Theory of Evolution. Tennyson (A) referred to Darwin's theory of evolution in some of his major poems. English scientist and essayist Huxley (E) was a proponent of Darwin's theories. Dr. Johnson's (B) degree was not in science; his work as an essayist, commentator, and lexicographer remains an enormous contribution to arts and letters. Browning's (D) wonderful poetic monologues, while written during the Victorian Age, in no way represent a suitable answer to the question.

34. **(E)** *The Scarlet Letter.* While much writing is autobiographical, some works are known more than others for serving particular personal purposes. Hawthorne's work is among them. Hawthorne, a descendant of Judge John Hathorne (no *w*), one of the three judges who presided over the Salem Witch Trial, believed that a curse on male members of his family was still a matter of personal concern during his life in the early 1800s. He changed the spelling of his name and wrote *The Scarlet Letter,* in which Puritan justice is seen as harsh, overreactive, and heartless. In this and other ways, he hoped to atone for the cruelty of his ancestors. Irving (A) was an entertaining historian with no such worries. Melville (B) and Cooper (D) were great tale tellers, and Charles Brockden Brown's (C) main claim to fame is as the first American novelist.

35. **(B)** Lawrence's *Sons and Lovers* shocked an entire generation of critics when it was published in the early 1900s. Its passionate prose and erotic evocations will still shock the more innocent contemporary reader. Kafka's story (A) about a man who changes into an insect is dense with philosophy. Conrad's great work (D) is vivid in its natural descriptions, but hardly a novel to be "banned in Boston." Jack Finney's (C) modern novel of dimensional travel is also tame by any comparison, as most certainly is Edith Wharton's (E).

36. **(C)** Thoreau's *Walden* most clearly engages his friend Emerson's precepts of rugged individualism which the minister set down in his essay "Self Reliance." Thoreau writes about his month-long sojourn living off the land in a cabin near Walden Pond in Massachusetts. Hawthorne's work (A), while written at about the same time, demonstrates few of these concerns. Crane's works (B) and (E) are brilliant descriptions of an accident and warfare, and great stories – as is Cooper's (D) – but none is based in transcendentalist theory – a reliance on individual and conscience – and expressed powerfully through prose.

37. **(A)** Answer choices (C), (D), and (E) illustrate buildings which employ arching, curving, cylindrical, and circular forms, often in elaborate, complex combinations, and suggest the play of emotion, fantasy, or romance, but do not seem founded on any general cultural need for logic and order. Choice (B) shows a modern building whose design certainly proceeds from logical precepts, but, of the principles offered in the answer choices, technological precision seems to best characterize this example. Example (A), however, the famous fifth century B.C.E. Parthenon in Athens, presents a building whose design reflects perfectly the logical philosophies which

defined Classical Greek culture. The Parthenon's architects were careful to construct a building of simple, refined forms, methodically repeated according to calculated ratios of size and space. The result is an effect of perfect balance and order which would be undermined by altering any one of the building's essential components.

38. **(D)**   Choices (A) and (B) illustrate structures whose severe, regularized forms seem to deny the possibility of humor and whimsy. Choice (C), a Gothic cathedral interior, uses soaring arches and strong vertical thrust to express spirituality and religious fervor, while choice (E), an Italian baroque church exterior, conveys a sense of intellectual, nervous agitation through a contrast of convex and concave curves and the use of an overabundance of ornamental detail. Only choice (D), a nineteenth-century English pleasure pavilion, combines a fanciful assortment of playful, whimsical shapes – as in the "Islamic" domes and minarets – to create an effect of exotic fantasy and underscore its function as a place of recreation.

39. **(B)**   Alone among the five answer choices, example (B) pares its structural forms to an absolute minimum, stressing the industrial materials – the steel of its framework and its extensive window glass – to achieve an effect of absolute structural logic and clarity. This "international style" architecture typifies the skyscrapers in large cities throughout the industrial world and reflects the high cultural value placed on industrial and commercial efficiency in the modern urbanized society.

40. **(B)**   In the example, the 1939 "Fallingwater" house by the American architect Frank Lloyd Wright, the horizontal forms which project dramatically over the small waterfall do not emphasize the building's structural framework but, rather, deny the presence of a structural support altogether and seem almost to defy gravity. All of the other observations offered in the answer choices are valid. Consistent with Wright's conception of an "organic" architecture, the cantilevered forms echo the horizontal axis of the waterfall's rock shelf, and, even though they are rigidly cubic in form, help to merge the house with its setting. This bold construction was only possible to the architect through the use of such modern, industrial-strength building materials as poured, pre-stressed concrete, whose great strength and flexibility made possible the long projecting forms supported at one end only.

41. **(D)**   The building pictured in the example is the *Abbaye-aux Hommes at Caen*. It was built and dedicated to Saint Stephen by William the Conqueror and is a good example of the Norman Romanesque style. Though

the church was founded in the eleventh century, the vaults are a reconstruction from the first half of the twelfth century. The original building was wooden-roofed, but stone masonry is the most important element. All of the other materials listed in the answer choices are industrial-age materials which were unavailable to the medieval architect.

42. **(B)** The rose has, for centuries, been a symbol of virginal love and beauty. By calling the rose "sick," the poet is implying that somehow this virginal beauty has been lost. This is due to, as the poet states, an "invisible worm," that has found the rose's "bed/Of crimson joy." The loss of virginity has been equated with "sickness," and the sex act causing the loss is alluded to in terms of "worms" and "beds of crimson joy."

43. **(D)** Because of the "worm," the "rose" is "sick"; choice (D) is the best answer because it addresses the archetypical symbol of the rose as virginal love and beauty. Since the rose is "sick," this beauty is gone. Some of the other choices may adequately answer the question, but not as well as (D).

44. **(B)** Personification means an object or emotion has been made into a person with human attributes – here the frost is seen beheading as if in battle as a show of power. Easily detected, the personified word is frequently capitalized. Alliteration (A) is a device that repeats the initial consonants (or vowels) as in "crowing cocks" or "weeping widows." Onomatopoeia (C) uses verbs that sound like the action, as in "ooze" or "hiss" or "swish." Assonance repeats the vowel sounds in a line or sentence. In fact, lines 6-8 demonstrate assonance in the words "unmoved," "another," and "approving," but for the technique in line 3 (D) is incorrect. Conceit (E) is a term connected with the metaphysical poets like John Donne where outrageous comparisons are made between unlike objects – the most famous is Donne's use of a drawing compass to link two people saying good-bye. Here frost is referred to as a killer of flowers, not compared to a weed-whacker. Study hint: find a glossary in the back of a poetry anthology and learn these figures of speech.

45. **(C)** The frost has already been described as a killer beheading the flowers in line 3; it is a clear connection to see frost as blonde or icy white and the whole point of the poem is the killing power as of an assassin. Go through each of the possible suggestions and analyze the closest meaning of the line: fate (A) is part of the poem's *interpretation* but not the meaning of this particular line; disease (B) is not mentioned, rather, random acts of violence; the sun (D) follows the act of frost and is not involved in the killing;

it is "unmoved." An approving god (E) watches but is not the assassin here. (C) is the best possible answer.

46. **(B)** Although the other choices have something to do with the meaning of the poem, the "best," meaning the central or core description of what the poem is about, is that death comes to everyone; it cannot be planned for nor avoided. Certainly a cruelty is indicated in the frost's action but that is not (A) God's cruelty. God is shown not to be indifferent, but in fact approving, so (C) is incorrect. The flowers being happy (D) suggests that we put human experience into plants, but this is not the poem's central theme, nor is the fact that we know winter comes each year, so (E) is likewise an idea that is in the poem but is not the central point.

47. **(B)** Note that what is required here is both a knowledge of drama as well as an awareness of qualifying terms in both the question stem and answer. You are asked what poetic drama is "best" described as, while (A) asks for a value judgment; (B) is a full description incorporating both the fact that poetic drama is comprised of poetry and performance. (C) demonstrates value judgment; (D) is too limiting; so, too, is (E).

48. **(D)** Bertolt Brecht described his work as (D) epic drama, not (B) melodrama. It was based on (A) John Gay's *The Beggar's Opera*, but this is not the most important fact. The major characteristic of *The Threepenny Opera* is that Brecht's adaptation of it corresponds with his view of what drama should be. Brecht was concerned about defamiliarizing his audience with what they felt they knew. He thought that theaters should make things strange through (E) historification, the use of material drawn from other times and places, which allowed the audience to view the performance in a detached manner. This method of alienating the audience was the most important criterion for the development of an "epic" (meaning narrative, or non-dramatic) work. Since drama is antithetical to comedy, (C) should be eliminated immediately.

49. **(A)** Existentialism is a philosophy that arose in France and Germany in the late nineteenth century, which claims that "existence precedes essence" or that what one becomes is a matter of choice and not something usually called "human nature" or "essence." Essentialism (B) is thus incorrect because it is the opposite of existentialism. Pragmatism (C) is a distinctively American philosophy that the worth of an idea is its "cash value" or power to solve a problem. Marxism (D) depends on the supposition that

humans have an essence or nature, as does Platonism (E). Platonists are clear examples of essentialism.

50. **(E)** The ancient Greeks, upon viewing the massive masonry blocks used in much Mycenean construction, believed that they could only have been placed by giants; thus they are referred to as "cyclopean" after the giant Cyclops of Greek mythology. Although (A) ancient Egyptian, (B) Mesopotamian, (C) Aztec, and (D) Roman methods of construction often included the use of very large, heavy stone blocks, the term "cyclopean" is never used to identify them.

51. **(A)** The *cogito* resolves Descartes' methodological doubt and establishes a firm foundation for knowledge. He does not question the basis of personal identity (B) in the way that, say, Locke does. Descartes uses a separate argument to establish the existence of God (D). He then uses his proof of God's existence to put metaphysics (C) and mathematics (E) on firm foundations. The *cogito* is the foundation for his epistemology.

52. **(C)** Through-composed form is represented by ABCDE. This is because new music is created for each verse; choice (C) is correct. AB is binary form that starts in the tonic key and may modulate before the end. This is considered an open structure; choice (A) is incorrect. ABA is ternary form in which both A sections are in the tonic and the B section modulates and contains new material; choice (B) is incorrect. ABACA is a rondo form that contains multisections. These utilize modulations with new material and return to the tonic; choice (D) is incorrect. A form of A would only contain one musical idea; choice (E) is incorrect.

53. **(A)** Gregorian chant is often referred to as plainchant. Plainchant is monophonic vocal music, which was primarily used in church; choice (A) is correct. A motet is a polyphonic vocal composition used in church music for two or more voices; choice (B) is incorrect. A canon is imitated polyphonic vocal composition consisting of two or more voices; choice (C) is incorrect. An aria is a vocal solo with accompaniment found in a larger composition; choice (D) is incorrect. A fugue is imitative polyphony with variations; choice (E) is incorrect.

54. **(B)** Charles Ives mastered the technique of weaving bits of patriotic melodies within his compositions; choice (B) is correct. Sousa popularized patriotic marches; choice (A) is incorrect. Bernstein worked in many genres using classical and jazz elements; choice (C) is incorrect. Stravinsky

explored primitivism and tonalities; choice (D) is incorrect. Franz Joseph Haydn was a composer of the classical period; choice (E) is incorrect.

55. **(A)** *Tristram Shandy* was written by Laurence Sterne, a parish clergyman and small landowner. His sometimes bawdy, often hilarious novel demonstrated an extraordinary playfulness with the language, and with concepts of space and time in storytelling. Cervantes' (B) work was amusing, but the gentleman author was Spanish. *Candy* (C) is an American bawdy novel of the 1960s not to be confused with the French novel *Candide*. *Catch-22* (D) is at least as funny as the others, but is of the same vintage as the previous novel; and (E), though possessed of an amusing title, is a Shakespearean song.

56. **(B)** Shakespeare's *Macbeth* deals with the powerful influence of guilt and conscience after the fact of an illicit deed. Lady Macbeth sleepwalks and tries to wash the imagined blood of King Duncan off of her hands, and Macbeth himself sees the ghost of the bloodied Banquo during a public celebration, thereby providing one more clue to the populace that he and his wife were responsible of the death of the rightful king. *Julius Caesar* (A) deals with many political themes including ambition – but conscience does not seem prominent. *Hamlet* (C) demonstrates the restraining power of conscience – even in the face of seeking revenge for a vile act. The fantasy (D) and the comedy (E) are artful treatments of happier themes.

57. **(D)** Hawthorne's famous work is well known for its personification of the fading fortunes of the Pyncheon family in the famous seven gabled structure still to be visited in Salem, Massachusetts. The imploding and collapse of the structure at the end of the novel represents the end of the family that had been cursed during the witchcraft trials 150 years before. (A) of course, is a delightful children's book. (B), by Dos Passos, is a twentieth century description of the banking family. William Carlos Williams wrote the brief poem (C); and (E) was the first piece of fiction published by Thomas Wolfe, but does not deal with the subject in question.

58. **(C)** The 1940 book deals with a hanging in the fictional Western town of Bridger's Wells. While Realism was a nineteenth-century movement, Clark employs Realistic techniques – accurate usage of concrete details to raise interest or create an effect – in relating his compelling story. Twain's famous story (A) had realistic elements in it, but was written during the nineteenth century – though only in one section can he be said to deal with the Wild West. Crane's work (B) was realistic and was about the Wild

West, but was a short story also written in the nineteenth century. Bierce's tale (D) – though again in a similar tradition, and while it also deals with a hanging – also takes place during the Civil War.

59. **(C)** Walt Whitman's poetry, including "Song of Myself" and "The Sleepers," presented American critics with a new American voice: one not bounded by the constraints of rhyme schemes and meter. His long listing of examples of American characters and prototypes are so detailed that they provide us with an accurate picture of the mid-nineteenth century nation of Whitman's day. The Englishman Pope (A) does not qualify for reason of nationality alone. Clemens (B) is the novelist Mark Twain's real name. Emily Dickinson (D) is known for short, rhyming verse, and Anne Bradstreet (E) – perhaps our first American poet – wrote in traditional rhyme schemes and meter.

60. **(C)** This is an example from Donatello, one of the most representative sculptors of the early Renaissance. This piece, the equestrian statue of Gattamelta, is his first from Padua. It expresses strength, not lightness and motion, stability, and completely denies any suggestion of physical decay. Additionally, this sculpture does not allude in any specific way to moral fortitude.

61. **(E)** This city view by the French Impressionist Camille Pissarro is one of many in which the artist painted the scenes he saw beneath his second- or third-story Paris hotel windows; the correct answer is (E). The tilted perspective, with diagonal street axes and no horizon line, may owe a debt to photography, to Japanese prints, or to the example of his Impressionist peers. The resulting composition lacks not only a central focal point, but any single focal point at all; likewise, the only architecture visible does not dominate the scene, but, rather, acts as incidental local detail. The anonymous figures in the crowds below the artist's window share this lack of focus: they are busy in normal daily activity, without the least suggestion of drama. Finally, the idea that this scene was recorded from the window of a train lacks evidence: the scene is distinctly urban, not rural, and it is unlikely that a train would either pass through the crowded centers of a city or that it would be elevated to this height.

62. **(C)** In the work pictured, the American sculptor David Smith used power tools to cut, weld, and polish industrial-strength steel to create an ensemble in which the heavy, cubic forms balance in arrested motion. The sculptor obviously neither modelled the materials with his hands nor poured them

into a mold: these forms have a rigid, machinelike, technological perfection to them and lack any such irregularities as those resulting from the molding action of human fingers. This same cubic perfection, and the gleaming, reflective surfaces, refute the idea of chisel work as well. And, finally, the erroneous suggestion that the artist merely joined ready-made industrial forms as he found them stems from this same sense of rigid, cubic perfection in the work's individual components.

63. **(A)**   The seventeenth-century Japanese ink-on-paper scroll painting shown in the example relies almost exclusively on the qualities of line to convey the graceful forms of two leaping deer. In this painting, called *Deer and Calligraphy,* both the animals and the scripted characters share the same quality of fluid, rhythmic, spontaneous "writing." Gradations of tone are unimportant here, since the images are defined by black line on white, and volume, too, is absent, since these forms show no shading or modulation of tone. Perspective is not an issue here since this drawing does not attempt to reproduce a third dimension.

64. **(D)**   The arch, whether rounded or pointed, is completely absent from the building pictured in the example, even though the alternating use of windows with rounded pediments in the lower story seems to suggest the presence of arches. Otherwise, all of the other features listed in the answer choices do help regularize the design of this seventeenth-century English Renaissance structure. The uniform second-story windows assert a regularity over the alternating window designs below them; they also emphasize a strong horizontal thrust across the building's facade, which is repeated in the balustrade at roof-level. The nearly flush front surface of the building is broken only by the window openings and by the engaged columns at the building's center and the pilasters at the outer corners. Both of these features project just enough to establish a vertical contrast to the horizontal facade, but not enough to create a system of alternating solids and voids.

65. **(D)**   You may not have come across this poem by William Blake so you need to look at the language and the topic. Blake often writes about the ugliness and horror of the Industrial Revolution – you may know "The Tiger." The topic of child labor gives you an immediate clue. Shakespeare (A), Milton (B), and Chaucer (C) may be familiar, so you can see the difference in their rhyme schemes and language. This rhyme and meter suggest a more modern style than the older writers. Hardy (E) often uses a similar simple rhyme and rhythm but his topics are more of fate and destiny, war

and lost loves. By such a process of elimination, you should come to (D) as the correct answer.

66. **(A)**   The word is cleverly used because it does suggest the child's weeping but the meaning of the line carries on from the opening line when he was sold before he could clearly say the chimney sweeper's cry for business: "Sweep! Sweep!" – not because of neglect (B), but because he is so young he still lisps on the "s" sound. The other suggestions all deal with emotions conjured up by the child's plight – of course he is upset at being sold (C); "the your" pronoun does make for guilt (D) but you are looking for the reason the poet chose this word, not the "message" of the poem. Of course he hates cleaning chimneys (E), but analyze the word's usage in the line itself and the best answer is (A).

67. **(C)**   The epic is long and tells of heroes engaged in battles and actions involving valor. Look at the rhyme scheme and analyze. There are no rhyming couplets (A), epics are not all written in Latin (B), nor by Virgil (D), and although death (E) is usually featured, epics are not just about death.

68. **(E)**   If you do not know *Paradise Lost,* a look at the context reveals a great deal – the garden idea, the noble couple made in God's image. Dante would be describing Hell so (A) is incorrect. Virgil (B) deals with family and honor in Latinate verse; *The Iliad* (C) deals with battles and the Greek gods; and *The Arabian Nights* (D) tells fantastic stories, so none of these apply.

69. **(D)**   The key word here is "viewpoint" – but from which not the poem or story is told. Even if you do not know *Paradise Lost,* you will no doubt have heard of the fiend – place that fiend in a garden and the answer is Satan; not Faust (A), which is another story; not God (B) – the fiend is watching God's creation; not Scheherazade (C), who tells of magical things not people in a garden; and not Dante (E), who watches fiends in hell – he is not a fiend himself.

70. **(C)**   The situation in the Garden is idyllic; the couple is naked – all such signs point to before the Fall. The references to God and "the image of their maker" eliminate both (A) and (B); the fiend is not a Homeric character, so (D) is incorrect; as stated, the idyllic setting indicates that this is before the Fall, so (E) is also incorrect.

71. **(E)**   The last three lines need to be carefully equated with each of the options: equality is not possible if she sees God in the man (A); women are

not just made for beauty but softness and grace (B); and (C) and (D) tell only half the meaning of the lines.

72. **(A)**   is the correct answer. (B) *Oedipus* is also a play about a man who kills his father and blinds himself. In *The Wild Duck* Gregers returns home to find that Gina, who was once a maid in his family, is now married to Hjalmar. Gregers believes that Gina was impregnated by his father, Old Werle, who is slowly losing his eyesight. Gregers believes that Gina and Hjalmar's marriage is based on a lie. Old Werle's diminished eyesight may be read symbolically, but it does not hold the same significance as Oedipus' blinding. The eyesight motif joins *The Wild Duck* and *Oedipus* and makes it easier to eliminate the other three answer choices. Both Sophocles and Euripides wrote plays they titled *Electra;* Sophocles also wrote *Antigone* and Euripides, *Andromache.* Basically, these answers are meant to confuse; therefore, (C), (D), and (E) should be eliminated immediately.

73. **(C)**   is the correct answer. It is much more specific. Orgon is rich, middle class, and middle-aged. He is duped by Tartuffe, who assumes a mask of religious piety. This question is testing your ability to recognize the situation of each play. For example, (A) is too vague, as the downfall of a king is a frequent theme in plays. (B) is also vague, as are (D) and (E).

74. **(B)**   A multi-storied Roman apartment block, the type which existed in large numbers in urban areas of the Roman Empire. A Greek public meeting square (A) is called an *agora;* the western portion of a Carolingian church (C) is referred to as a *westwerk.* A Greek cross-plan (D) is that of a centrally planned church whose four arms are all of equal length. A vertical groove on the surface of a column (E) is called a *flute.*

75. **(A)**   Berkeley held, in his famous dictum, that "to be is to be perceived," or that only ideas are real. Hence, the view expressed is known as (A) idealism. Pragmatism (B) is the view that ideas which work should be believed true. Empiricism (C) and rationalism (D) are broad tendencies to answer a question about the source of knowledge either as in experience or in the mind itself. Phenomenology (E) is a position in metaphysics that takes a special view of experience. Berkeley is perhaps the clearest advocate of idealism in the history of philosophy.

76. **(A)**   Charlie Parker was nicknamed "Bird" due to his rapid alto saxophone Bebop figures. Choice (A) is correct. John Coltrane was a master of the tenor and soprano saxophone; choice (B) is incorrect. Dizzy Gillespie was a master of the trumpet; choice (C) is incorrect. Paul Desmond was the

alto saxophonist in the Dave Brubeck Quartet, which played classical jazz styles; choice (D) is incorrect. Stan Getz was a tenor saxophonist of the "cool" jazz style; choice (E) is incorrect.

77. **(C)** John Coltrane made a lasting impact on the jazz scene with his album "Giant Steps." Choice (C) is correct. Charlie Parker played alto, not tenor saxophone, and performed such works as "Ko-ko" and "YardBird Suite"; choice (A) is incorrect. Stan Getz is the tenor saxophone player famous for his work on "The Girl from Ipanema"; choice (B) is incorrect. Coleman Hawkins is considered the father of jazz tenor saxophone; choice (D) is incorrect. Ornette Coleman experimented with "free jazz" on the alto saxophone; choice (E) is incorrect.

78. **(B)** "Rodeo" is the result of a collaboration between Aaron Copland and Agnes de Mille. It incorporated music with dance; choice (B) is correct. "West Side Story" is a musical by Leonard Bernstein. It is a modern-day version of "Romeo and Juliet"; choice (A) is incorrect. "Porgy and Bess" is an opera with music by George Gershwin, portraying the struggles of black Americans in the South; choice (C) is incorrect. "The Phantom of the Opera" is a novel by Gaston LeRoux that has been adapted for film, stage, and most recently, a Broadway musical. Choice (D) is incorrect. "Salome" was a composition of Strauss; choice (E) is incorrect.

79. **(D)** *Tom Jones,* Henry Fielding's (1707-1754) wonderful and raucous novel, is the only one here both written in and about the eighteenth century. Tom's travels take him from the seat of manorial propriety to the very bawdiest of tumbletown inns. Known for its wanton characterization and surprising turns of plot, it is considered by many to be one of the most picturesque of the picaresque novels (defined as the "life story of a rascal of low degree… consisting of a series of thrilling incidents"). Dickens' work (A) is about England in the following century, as are Brontë's *Jane Eyre* (C) and George Eliot's *Silas Marner* (E). *Moby Dick* (B) is an American work by Melville.

80. **(D)** Oscar Wilde's famous work is in the well-known tradition of the Decadents – a group of writers in the late nineteenth and early twentieth century in France, England, and America. One of their major precepts was that the finest beauty was that of dying or deteriorating things. Thus, Dorian – a character of low virtues – ages grotesquely and supernaturally on a canvas, while the actual person seems to be forever young. The Mariner (A) may be aging, but the lengthy romantic poem is not in the Decadent tradition,

nor written at that time. Fielding's work (C) may be about decadence, but was written 100 years earlier than the movement. The same might be said about Lawrence's mid-twentieth century work (B), and Joyce's *Dubliners* (E), which is even less a possibility.

81. **(A)** Ruskin in *Modern Painters* actually introduced the phrase "pathetic fallacy" to denote a tendency of some poets and writers to credit nature with the emotions of human beings – as in the phrase "the cruel, crawling foam." Nowadays it has come to mean writing that is false in its emotionalism – even if the topic considered is not nature. Emerson's work (B) is about the importance and reality of the natural world. Shakespeare's comedy (C) has nothing whatsoever to do with the topic, except that its plot does involve deception and falseness. Lodge's 1590 work (D) is considered a pastoral romance – in that it sets forth a romance in a beautiful natural setting. Johnson's *Dictionary* (E) could not have listed the term, as it was published over 50 years before Ruskin invented it.

82. **(E)** Dickens' *David Copperfield* is one of his many works that present an opposing argument to utilitarianism – the powerful argument from the former century that defined utility in government and society as "the greatest happiness for the greatest number." The theory was proposed in the eighteenth century by Jeremy Bentham, and was modified and promoted in the nineteenth by James Mill and his son John Stuart Mill. Dickens' England is a place where misery counts – even for a statistical minority of orphans, waifs, and honest, if impoverished, men and women of the working class. Elliot's *Middlemarch* world (A) is the antithesis – as is James's *Washington Square* (D). Dreiser (B) does write about the seedier side of nineteenth century American life, but does not seem to "take sides" as far as the economic system itself is concerned. *Billy Budd* (C), of course, is an adventure novel by Melville.

83. **(D)** While all of the writers suggested might claim Celtic origins, James Macpherson, the eighteenth-century composer of the poems "Fingal" (1762) and "Temora" (1763) is the most likely candidate. Macpherson invented, recorded, and reinterpreted Gaelic pieces preserved in the Scottish Highlands and published translations of the great early Celtic poet Ossian. His works, along with those of Thomas Gray, influenced many minor poets of the late eighteenth century. Joyce (A) and Yeats (E) were Irishmen of the twentieth century. O'Hara (B) and Donleavy (C) are contemporary American writers.

84. **(D)**   The late eighteenth-century neoclassical painting shown in the example illustrates an episode from ancient Roman legend and attempts to simulate the static, balanced, monumental character of much classical relief sculpture. The men in the main figure group, therefore, are represented in statuesque, absolutely motionless poses, and the correct answer choice here is (D). The compositional devices listed in all of the other answer choices are important to the painting. The figures stand within a shallow pictorial space, which is marked off by the arches in the background; these arches also serve to place the focus on the man in the center. This shallow space, however, is modified somewhat by the checkerboard floor, which creates a slight perspective recession into the background and makes the figures' space seem logical and convincing. The strong highlighting on the foreground figures accentuates their static, sculptural quality, even as it pulls them to the absolute front of the picture. The intersecting lines of arms and swords establish the central focal point of the composition.

85. **(A)**   This question asks you to consider both geographical proximity and some general characteristics of Eastern architecture in order to logically determine who would have the most direct influence on Japanese style. Of the answer choices, Greece and Nigeria fall well outside the Asian sphere both in distance and in building styles, while Easter Island, a Pacific site, is not known for a distinctive native architecture. Indonesian temple buildings may share something of the exotic, heavily ornamented character of the structure pictured but the most representative Indonesian buildings are both much larger and are constructed of stone. The seventh-century building pictured, in fact, illustrates the strong dependence of Japan on the arts of China. The Chinese character of the structure is visible in the distinctive silhouette of the roof, with its long sweeping pitch and upturned corners in the heavy tiled roof, and in the wealth of elaborate brackets which support the dramatically projecting eaves.

86. **(A)**   Three of the answer choices – (B), (C), and (D) – show groups of figures engaged in activities which might be interpreted as ceremonial. Choice (C) illustrates a column of soldiers marching across the midsection of a ceramic vessel; while they could be marching in a ceremonial function such as a parade or assembly, they are most likely intended to be shown advancing into battle, and, in any case, their primary function on this vase is decorative. Choice (D) shows figures engaged in music-making activities in formally arranged groups, but here, too, the illustrations serve the secondary purpose of amplifying the accompanying text. Only answer choice

(A), an ancient Persian relief sculpture, uses a rigidly schematized, formal composition and style to record an actual ceremonial event. Here, the clear-cut, well-defined figures are strictly arranged in three horizontal tiers, and each carries an accessory or attribute which identifies his role within this state occasion.

87. **(C)**   Only answer choices (A) and (C) repeat the simplified forms of the human figure within a sculptural or ceramic context. Choice (A) appears to continually repeat a series of nearly identical figures arranged on three horizontal levels, but close inspection reveals several types of figures here, each marked by a variety of detail in posture, costume, accessories, etc. Further, the figures are sculpted in a softly rounded, convincing style. The figures in choice (C), in contrast, are grouped in a horizontal sequence which appears to show variety and movement; close examination, however, shows that the artist here has simply repeated figures whose clothing, weapons, postures, positions, and facial features are identical. While this serves to illustrate an anonymous mass of marching soldiers, it is even more important in helping the group of figures fit neatly, conveniently, and decoratively into its allotted space on the round "belly" of the vase.

88. **(D)**   Calligraphy, or "fine writing," implies a two-dimensional or graphic format. Three of the possible answer choices, (A), (B) and (E), are forms of sculpture or sculptural relief, and therefore contain no drawn, calligraphic elements. Choice (C) presents a flat, two-dimensional illustration painted in black and white and minimal color. However, the images here are rigidly formalized and static, and display none of the rhythmic curves or flourishes of artistic penmanship. Only choice (D), a ninth-century manuscript illustration, links calligraphy with figure drawing in the same rhythmic, linear style. In this illustration of the Bible's Psalm 150, the text written in ink above accompanies the figures below. Each is drawn in the same bold, agitated black-and-white line, with a sketchy spontaneity that creates an animated, nervous tension.

89. **(A)**   If you familiarize yourself with *The Iliad* and *Odysseus*, you will see how Homer uses the simile with the long-extended idea clinched at the end – look out for the words "such" or "so" which signal the last clause of the simile. An extended metaphor (B) is close except that the metaphor never has the signal words *as when, as if, like*; (C) is not an option as the verse is "free form" rather than rhymed couplets; the other options mix terms. Be on the lookout for terms that sound reasonable but, upon analysis, are gibberish.

90. **(D)** This is a case of working your way through the simile until you come to the signal word "such," which cues the image of the watchfires. The stars are not compared to hills (A), shepherds (B), rivers (C), or ships (E), so these are all incorrect choices.

91. **(A)** Again, the more familiar you become with Homer, the more you will see touches like this to humanize the lofty, godlike themes and characters, so the answer is (A). If this had been a medieval English piece, humor of a coarse, ribald kind, especially in the drama, might have been the answer, but there is no humor here (B). Depth in Homer comes from the poetry itself rather than the people who figure in the poetry (C). Gladness (D) takes a back seat to the power of the simile and in any poetry shepherds never glamorize (E)!

92. **(E)** Questions such as these rely on identification of famous lines; read through anthologies and see the often repeated poems. If you do not recognize Emily Dickinson (the use of the long dash often gives her away – it is one of her "trademarks"), work your way through and eliminate each choice in its turn. Obviously this is not Chaucerian since the language is stark and modern (A); nor is the passage epic in its voice or theme: think of lofty topics and rhythm and rhyme – this is conversational and choppy in its rhythm (B). However, (B) does fit all the criteria of epic so save that for the last answer. Wordsworth is taught in most high-school poetry classes and this opening line is much quoted – even if you do not recall the poem itself, you might recall that Wordsworth was not a woman (the Romantic males dominated the field of poetry), so the answer cannot be (C). The jar and Tennessee is unique and should immediately make you think of one of the most famous modern male American poets, Wallace Stevens, so (D) is incorrect.

93. **(A)** This is the famous opening line of *The Canterbury Tales*; it would be worth looking over the poem (this is in translation from the middle English language), as Chaucer is said to be the "father of English poetry." If you do not recognize the lines, look again at each of the answers and, as for the previous explanation, eliminate: (B) sounds too modern and conversational, as does (C) and (E), so eliminate both those on voice alone. (D) Tennessee did not exist in Chaucer's time and is definitely not the answer.

94. **(C)** Even if you do not recognize Wordsworth, the idea of a love of nature would clue you to the Romantics, who looked upon nature as a rejuvenating force for the human spirit. You are working your way through the

process of elimination, narrowing down your field through language and topic, so none of the other possibilities apply.

95. **(B)** If you recognize the opening of *Paradise Lost*, this is straightforward; if not, think of epics that you have read with the lofty, heroic subjects – none of the others fit this category.

96. **(D)** is the correct answer. In your reading, be very aware of opening and closing lines in whatever genre. Kafka's famous opener from *Metamorphosis* sets symbol and theme for the entire work. All the other possibilities involve striking writers, but Genet and Ionesco are primarily playwrights, and Sartre and Tolstoy have less dramatic starting points. Even if you don't remember the first line of the *Metamorphosis*, recall that the story was about a man who awoke one morning as a bug.

97. **(D)** is the correct answer. (A) refers to the coat of arms representing royal presence; (B) should be eliminated immediately because it is too vague; the same is true of (C). While (E) Oedipus did go into exile, he was not sacrificed for the redemption of the tribe.

98. **(B)** The basilica, a large, hall-like building with a minimum of internal supporting members, served a variety of public functions in the Roman era and was designed to accommodate large crowds. The basilican plan was thus an appropriate building type to contain large numbers of Christian worshippers. Roman temples (A) were not designed to regulate crowds, and, with their overt pagan associations, were not favored for use within a Christian context. Roman baths (C) consisted of several bathing rooms and facilities, and did not adhere to a specific type of plan. A Roman forum (D) is an open air, public city square, not a building type. A Roman villa (E) is a private domestic dwelling, composed of multiple rooms and courtyards, the design of which is inappropriate for the containment and regulation of communal worship.

99. **(E)** Dance began with the savage hunters. Religious groups (A), Egyptians (B), Greeks (C), and Romans (D) succeeded the savage hunters and created their own style of dance for self-expression, religious and political rituals, and entertainment.

100. **(A)** The fallacy of composition (A), as the name suggests, consists in thinking that what is true of the parts of something must be true of the whole composed by those parts. For instance, it would be fallacious to think that because every member of a team is outstanding, the team must

be outstanding, since teamwork is involved in the performance of the team in a way that it isn't with respect to its members individually. The fallacy of division (B) is just the opposite: what is true of the whole is incorrectly reasoned to be true of the parts. The slippery-slope fallacy (C) is committed when one thinks small differences never add up to a significant difference, while the *ad hominem* fallacy (D) involves personal attacks. The fallacy of ignorance (E) is committed when one reasons that because something has not been proven false, it is true.

101. **(B)** Percy Grainger wrote extensively for wind ensemble. Most of his compositions were based on folk songs such as "Country Gardens" and "Ye Banks and Braes o' Bonnie Doon"; choice (B) is correct. Sousa composed primarily for military band; choice (A) is incorrect. Beethoven composed many works, including symphonies for orchestra and piano concertos. Choice (C) is incorrect. Strauss is famous for his tone poems; choice (D) is incorrect. Franz Joseph Haydn composed for the orchestra; choice (E) is incorrect.

102. **(B)** The key signature of this excerpt is F major. The key signature of F major contains a B flat, which can be determined by using the Circle of Fifths and proceeding counterclockwise from C to the scale with one flat, F. Choice (B) is correct. The B flat scale contains B flat and E flat; choice (A) is incorrect. The key of C contains no flats or sharps; choice (C) is incorrect. The key of D contains an F sharp and a C sharp; choice (D) is incorrect. The key signature of A major contains an F#, C#, and G#. Choice (E) is incorrect.

103. **(D)** The time signature of this excerpt should be $\frac{3}{4}$. The total number of beats in each measure is three, and a quarter note would equal one beat. Choice (D) is correct. A time signature of $\frac{4}{4}$ would require four beats in each measure; choice (A) is incorrect. A time signature of $\frac{2}{4}$ would require two beats in each measure; choice (B) is incorrect. A time signature of $\frac{6}{8}$ would have six beats in each measure; choice (C) is not correct. A time signature of $\frac{12}{8}$ would have 12 beats in each measure. Choice (E) is incorrect.

104. **(C)** The excerpt is divided into three measures. The measures are divided by the number of beats found in each and marked by a vertical line through the staff; choice (C) is correct. The following choices, one measure, two measures, and zero measures (choices (A), (B), and (D)) are incorrect. Five measures cannot be calculated from the material presented; choice (E) is incorrect.

105. **(D)** The arrow is pointing at the repeat sign. This directs the musician to repeat the selection; choice (D) is correct. The key signature is the B flat symbol; choice (A) is incorrect. The clef sign is the G clef; choice (B) is incorrect. The double bar is a symbol which denotes the end of the music; choice (C) is incorrect. The time signature is not in the figure. The time signature would be $\frac{4}{4}$. Choice (E) is incorrect.

106. **(C)** Philip Roth's *Goodbye Columbus* was a big literary hit in the late 1950s ushering in the age of the American Ethnic novelist. Roth's novel deals with the rocky road of young romance within a suburban New York Jewish-American context. It is both an American success story, and a recollection of transformation for generations between immigrant and native born. James's (A) novel concerns a pre-"recent" immigrant America of 100 years ago. Hawthorne's work (E) concerns the earliest Pilgrim immigrants, but ethnic Pilgrim has long been recognized as "ruling class standard." Updike's novels (D) of midwest suburbia do not involve "ethnics" so much as the descendants of Hawthorne's folk – and Poe's famous short story (B) takes place in Italy, not America.

107. **(C)** Alexis de Tocqueville's *Letters From an American Farmer* is considered one of the most perceptive and accurate portraits of the newly independent American nation. The Frenchman, who later became a citizen of the U.S. and a property owner, traveled widely and recorded his observations and perceptions. Lewis and Clark (A), the famed adventurers, explored the uninhabited West under orders from President Thomas Jefferson. Sinclair Lewis's novel (B) deals with the early decades of this century. Cooper's *Mohicans* (D) describes the frontier of New York State 200 years ago. Smith's *Diary* (E) predates the establishment of the United States by almost 200 years.

108. **(E)** Ralph Ellison's powerful novel defined for America of the 1950s the second-class status of African-Americans and is still referred to as a great work of literature that galvanized a nation at the height of the battle for civil rights. Faulkner's work (A), while it may have a seemingly appropriate title, does not deal with this subject – neither does Wharton's (B), about a white man in New England. Conrad's (C) powerful novel deals with Africa, and Kafka's (D) strange story superficially deals with a man's transformation into a bug.

109. **(A)** *Journey to the Center of the Earth* by Jules Verne has a remarkable history. Though its subject deals with a phenomenon – a hollow earth – that

apparently does not exist, the description it gives of Iceland is so accurate that travelers there were urged to take the book with them well into the 1950s. Ironically, Verne rarely left Paris, never traveled to Iceland, and did all his research for the book in the libraries of the French capital. Stevenson's island (B) is invented, as is Defoe's (C). Verne's other work here (D) is not focused in its description of a single spot. Swift's "travel" novel (E) is not one at all, but rather a well-known political satire.

110. **(B)** Sir Walter Scott's famous nineteenth century romance *Ivanhoe* deals with the thirteenth century – now recognized by many scholars such as Barbara Tuchman as a dreadful period in history – but until recently it was thought of as the flower of the Middle Ages, replete with knights in shining armor and damsels in distress. Eliot's work (A) is a picture of manorial England in the nineteenth century and Poe's (C) of a formerly wealthy family in America at approximately the same time. King's terrifying book (D) is modern and also American, as is West's hilarious short novel (E).

111. **(C)** Like many Victorian poets, Matthew Arnold venerated the works of Wordsworth. In Arnold's preface to the "Poems" of 1853, he pleads for poets to turn to the epic or drama – as epitomized, perhaps, by Wordsworth in lyrical ballads such as "The Ruined Cottage." The major problems with the other possible answers here is one of time sequence. Hemingway and Eliot (A) are modern, not Victorian. Tennyson and Browning (B) are Victorian contemporaries, as are Rossetti and Browning (D). Wordsworth and Scott (E) are Romantic contemporaries.

112. **(A)** In the *Duke and the Dauphin,* Twain relates the story of a bogus pretender to the French throne and his accompli who perform what they hope will pass as Shakespeare to frontier audiences. Initially taken by the idea, the settlers get wise to their scam and chase them out of town. The famous fence-painting scene (B) took place in *Tom Sawyer.* Huck's escape from Pap (C) does not prove the quote; neither does Jim seeking freedom (D). At the end of the famous novel, Huck "lights out for the territories" (E). The West certainly represented a future of promise to Huck and Twain, but again, clearly does not prove the point.

113. **(C)** In the example shown, the *Bull's Head* of 1943, the Spanish artist Pablo Picasso joined a bicycle seat and a set of handlebars in a clever, unexpected combination to produce a sculptural analogy to an actual bull. Thus, the artist was concerned here with form and substance, not with a contrast of line and tone and, even though the resulting artwork resembles a

hat- or coat-rack the sculptor's first purpose was not to produce a functional device. Likewise, even though the bull has mythological connotations and figures prominently in many ancient religions, the artist was intent not on creating a religious symbol, but in exploring the visual unity of common objects brought together in new ways. The result is a strictly visual, sculptural effect, and in no way provides a metaphor for human experience.

114. **(B)** Three of the answer choices, (A), (C) and (E), illustrate Impressionist paintings, which tend to suppress or eliminate secondary or decorative detail in the search for a quick, spontaneous, and optically "true" impression of the subject. None can be said to concentrate on details pointedly. Choice (D) shows a work of exhaustive detail, in which each tree branch, leaf, and grass stem, and the details and textures of clothing, stand out with stark realism. The main figure subject, however, far from merging into the background detail, is dramatically set off against it, especially in the face, neck, and arms. Only choice (B), by the American James MacNeill Whistler, accentuates decorative detail at the expense of the subject. In this case, the details of tiny flowers running up the back of the woman's dress connect visually to the delicate floral details in the wallpaper to the left, while the pale form of the woman's figure shades and merges into the background and almost reduces her to a flat pattern.

115. **(C)** Two of the answer choices crop, or cut off, the main subject, much as the arbitrary framing of a photograph might do. Choice (E), a study of two women and a child by the American Impressionist Mary Cassatt, pulls the figures to the very front of the picture plane, and cuts them off abruptly at the bottom edge and right side of the picture. The result seems to be an unposed, accidental image produced by a moment's glance. These figures, however, are firmly centered within the picture's borders, with a definite focal point in the image of the child with the book at center. Choice (C), by contrast, presents an extremely random composition in which the human subject is so far off-center and so dramatically cropped that she barely retains pictorial "presence" in the composition. This picture by the French Impressionist Edgar Degas produces an effect of seemingly unplanned, immediate realism which resembles a casually aimed photographic snapshot.

116. **(D)** Only two of the answer choices, (C) and (D), create their desired effect by positioning the primary subject noticeably off-center, thereby undermining the pictures formal visual balance. Choice (C), by the French painter Degas, shows a woman seated at a table on which rests an enormous bouquet of flowers. Even though the woman, apparently the main subject

or sitter, glances out of the picture to the right and invites the viewer's gaze to follow, the huge bunch of flowers dominates the picture and calls the viewer's eye continually back to the painting's focal center. Answer choice (D), however, by the French Realist Bastien-Lepage, clearly positions the primary subject off-center, as she stares and steps to the right with her arm outstretched. The figure seems to have just left the empty center of the picture and is about to exit the painting at the right. Her glance, her pose, and her position create a strongly directional thrust which draws the viewer's eye out of the picture as the figure moves.

117. **(E)** Art Nouveau is the correct answer. Art Nouveau is distinguished by the extensive use of such curvilinear, decorative details of interior design. Post-Modernism (B) is a later period in the history of architecture, and is not defined by such decorative elements. Neo-Classicism (C), a nineteenth-century era of architecture, is chracterized by the use of classical Greek and Roman architectural details, which are more austere in nature. Post-Impressionism (D) and surrealism (A) are movements in painting that have no equivalents in the history of architectural design.

118. **(C)** Reims Cathedral (ca. 1211-60) is an example of the High Gothic style. The sheer verticality of the twin towers, the overall upward movement, and the multitude of pinnacles are identifying characteristics of the Gothic style and would most clearly set Reims apart from the most closely related structure in this group, St. Peter's (D), a work of the late Renaissance in Rome. (A) The Taj Mahal, Agra, India, (1630-48) is incorrect because it is the finest example of Mughal architecture, a mix of Indian, Persian, and Islamic styles. (B) The Parthenon, Acropolis, Athens (448-432 B.C.E.), is incorrect because it represents the classical phase of Greek architecture. (D) St. Peter's, Rome (1546-64), by Michelangelo is incorrect because it is an example of the colossal order in Renaissance architecture. It has a symmetrical plan crowned by a central dome, very different from the longitudinal emphasis of the Gothic cathedral. St. Peter's basilica lacks the exterior ornamentation of Reims, but its monumental dome creates a dramatic exterior profile.

119. **(A)** The Taj Mahal was built by Shah Jahan, one of the Moslem rulers of India, as a home for his wife. She died before it was finished and so in its completion the Taj Mahal became a memorial to her. (B) is incorrect because the Parthenon has served as a place of worship for four different faiths. It was originally built by the Greeks to honor the Goddess Athena. In Christian times it became the first Byzantine church, then a Catholic cathedral, and, finally, under Turkish rule, a mosque. (C) is incorrect because the

Reims Cathedral is a Catholic church. (D) is incorrect because St. Peter's is a Roman Catholic church. (E) is incorrect because (A) was not constructed as a place of worship.

120. **(C)** Become aware of different types of poems: this is the short 17-syllable form that is highly evocative. Hyperbole (A) is characterized by exaggeration, which is not present. Odes (B) honor or exalt a specific person or subject, also not present. An epigram (D) is usually a witty expression of a particular idea. Doggerel (E) describes loose, inferior verse.

121. **(B)** If you are not aware of the original language of the form, start discounting the others – French and Chinese would be more symbolic; British English would not be so succinct and evocative; Persian would be on topics of love or religion.

122. **(D)** If you are not aware of the term, it is a useful one to learn – Pope uses it frequently to attain humor. Eliminate the other terms by what you know: (A) is hyperbole; (B) is crescendo; (C) is anticlimax; and (E) is not related to the question. Analyze that a climax suggests a building toward or upward.

123. **(E)** As well as learning meter, rhyme, and rhythm, look into what poets themselves say about poetry. Keats had a lot to say, especially about the ways to read and the use of the imagination, as did Wordsworth and Coleridge, but they frequently spoke of poetry being of and for the common man: this phrase often bemuses the "average" man so (C) is incorrect. T. S. Eliot wrote copiously on the art of writing poetry but his comments are not so easily captured in a phrase, except perhaps "objective correlative," but this phrase can only be fit into a long explanation – definitely not (B). If you are not aware of the term, think of the sorts of poetry the others wrote: Keats is the only one here who wants the mystery (of something like the "Grecian Urn" for example); neither William Carlos Williams nor e.e. cummings wanted mystery, preferring to have cryptic to-the-point statements about their art, so clearly neither (A) nor (D) are correct.

124. **(A)** is the correct answer. Though you may disagree with the quotation, you must make your selection based on the quotation. (B) *A Midsummer Night's Dream* is a comedy. *Oedipus* (C) is indeed a tragedy, but it does not fit the requirements for tragedy as established in the quotation. *Oedipus the King* is not completed by a death. Jocasta commits suicide, but Oedipus, the central character, remains within the walls of the city for many years before he is exiled. *Oedipus the King* is thus eliminated on the basis of this

argument. (D) Shakespeare's *The Tempest* and (E) Menander's *The Bad-Tempered Man* should also be eliminated because both are comedies.

125. **(E)** is the correct answer. *Anagnorisis* means recognition or discovery. Therefore, when the hero's understanding of the true nature of the situation and the self is evident in drama or fiction, then this is an example of *anagnorisis*. As a complete definition, this differs from (A), which is vague.

126. **(C)** is the correct answer. After the idealistic Brutus tells the people that he participated in Caesar's murder because he loved Rome more, he and the other conspirators make the mistake of allowing the wily Mark Antony to speak. Antony must aid the public, or rabble, in understanding the villainy of the murder of Caesar, no matter the motivation. Thus, the statement he makes is ironic as what he wishes to do is arouse the people to act against Caesar's murderers.

127. **(E)** is the correct answer. Othello's great weakness is his inability to recognize Iago's villainy and Desdemona's innocence. Iago is able to convince Othello that Desdemona is not the "chaste and heavenly true" wife she appears to be. Not until after he kills Desdemona does Othello understand the true nature of the situation and his own weakness.

128. **(A)** is the correct answer. Though all of the characters listed are from plays by Shakespeare, "Dane" and "Denmark" are the contextual clues here. One who comes from or resides in Denmark is a Dane.

129. **(B)** Oculus, meaning "eye," refers to the round opening in the dome, which is without glass and thus open to the sky. The terms (A) "window," (C) "splayed window," and (D) "stained-glass window" are all defined as wall openings that are glazed in some form, which is not applicable here. A clerestory (E) refers to the upper portion of a building whose walls are pierced with windows and which emits light to the remainder of the building below; this type of construction refers to fenestrated walls only.

130. **(B)** The basic rules to jazz dance are parallel feet, flat-foot steps, undulating torso, body isolation, and syncopated rhythms. Beledi dance (abdominal dance) (A), danse mora (Flamenco dance) (C), tap dance (D), and country dance (E) each have their own different specific rules.

131. **(A)** Occam's Razor contends that one should not multiply entities beyond necessity: since both theories are equally powerful, choose the simpler one. The Plenitude Principle (B) says that the universe contains as many types of things as possible. The Open Question Argument (C) applies to claims

about the nature of goodness, not theories in general. The Underdetermination Principle (D) involves the notion that a given set of facts is compatible with many theories. Scientific Realism (E) is the view that the entities postulated by science actually exist.

132. **(D)**   Jane Austen's *Pride and Prejudice* is the source of this quote. The word *pride*, found in both the quote and the title, should give you a clue to the correct answer, even if you have not read these books. (B) Austen's *Emma* and (C) Margaret Mitchell's *Gone with the Wind* also deal with the issues of pride and vanity, although to a lesser extent than does *Pride and Prejudice*. However, neither of these is the source of the quote. In addition, Mitchell's novel, although set in the nineteenth century, was written in 1936. (A) George Eliot's *Silas Marner*, written in 1861, is a story of an old linen-weaver and his adopted daughter. (E) Jonathan Swift's *Gulliver's Travels* describes the four voyages of Lemuel Gulliver; it was written in the 1720's.

133. **(A)**   A trumpet can play different notes by pressing a valve down. A trumpet has three valves that, when combined in different prescribed combinations, help produce various notes; choice (A) is correct. Violins and pianos use strings to produce sound; choice (B) is incorrect. By covering and uncovering holes, the clarinet can change notes; choice (C) is incorrect. Saxophones use octave keys to change octaves; choice (D) is incorrect. Trombones use a slide to change pitches; choice (E) is incorrect.

134. **(A)**   The diagram is an example of a hemiola. The hemiola is a rhythmic term that is used to define three notes of a given value occupying the space of two notes of the same value. It is also referred to as three against two; choice (A) is correct. A paradiddle is a percussion roll that follows a pattern such as RLRR LRLL; choice (B) is incorrect. A fermata, ⌢, directs a musician to hold the note until the conductor cuts it off; choice (C) is incorrect. A crescendo, < , indicates to increase in volume; choice (D) is incorrect. A glissando is sliding through the pitches quickly; choice (E) is incorrect.

135. **(A)**   The C in measure one is sharp because the accidental makes it sharp. This accidental affects all C's in the given measure. As a result, the C in measure two is C natural because there are no accidentals before the note; choice (A) is correct. Consequently, the C is not sharp, flat, or a B. Choices (B), (C), and (D) are incorrect. A D would be located on the fourth line, choice (E) is incorrect.

136. **(A)** The bass clef is also referred to as the F clef. The symbol locates F below middle C, which is the fourth line; choice (A) is correct. The G clef and treble clef locate the G above middle C; choice (B) and (D) are incorrect. The tenor clef is used for cello, bassoon, and trombone to locate middle C; choice (C) is incorrect. The alto clef is used primarily by the viola; choice (E) is incorrect.

137. **(D)** Catton's work about the surrender of Lee at Appomatox stands as one of the great Civil War accounts, though it was written almost 100 years after the incident. The temptation here is to respond with (E) Crane's work, but *Red Badge* was written during the last century. Mailer's war novel (C) concerned Word War II in the Pacific, as did Wouk's novel (B). That leaves Hoover's anti-Communist screed (A) written during the 1950s.

138. **(B)** Albee's 1960 popular play was made into a movie starring Richard Burton and Elizabeth Taylor as the university professor and his wife, who display their troubled marriage to a young faculty couple who they had invited to their home for a visit. Albee's *American Dream* (C) does not concern itself with this subject matter. Miller's work (E) concerns long-shoremen and immigrants in Red Hook, Brooklyn. Neil Simon's reflective comedy (D) also relates the experience of growing up in a distinctly blue-collar immigrant world. (A) is a medieval play.

139. **(D)** Pepys' diary, written during the restoration of the Stuarts and Charles II in 1660, is still compelling material, especially his account of the Great Fire of London. Many critics consider that Pepys pioneered the form as literature, though he was not the first by any means to keep a diary. The time factor alone eliminates from consideration the satirists Swift (E) and Sterne (B), who wrote in the 1700s. O. E. Rolvaag (C) is a twentieth-century Swedish novelist. Sir Laurence (A), of course, is the recent star of stage and screen whose work included iconic Shakespearean performances.

140. **(C)** Ralph Waldo Emerson, Unitarian Minister, writer, and philosopher, is generally considered the chief promoter of transcendentalism. His influence was widely felt – on no less a personage than Henry David Thoreau (D) – with whom, eventually, Emerson had a falling out due to the inappropriate attentions Thoreau was said to have paid to Emerson's wife. Jonathan Edwards (A) was a New England minister of the early 1700s. Pitt (B) was a British parliamentarian of the American Revolutionary period. Dr. Samuel Fuller (E) was the only doctor to accompany the pilgrims to Massachusetts in 1620.

PRACTICE TEST 2
CLEP Humanities

Also available at the REA Study Center (*www.rea.com/studycenter*)

This practice test is also offered online at the REA Study Center. All CLEP exams are computer-based, and our test is formatted to simulate test-day conditions. We recommend that you take the online version of the test to receive these added benefits:

- **Timed testing conditions** – helps you gauge how much time you can spend on each question
- **Automatic scoring** – find out how you did on the test, instantly
- **On-screen detailed explanations of answers** – gives you the correct answer and explains why the other answer choices are wrong
- **Diagnostic score reports** – pinpoint where you're strongest and where you need to focus your study

PRACTICE TEST 2

CLEP Humanities

(Answer sheets appear in the back of the book.)

TIME: 90 Minutes
140 Questions

DIRECTIONS: Each of the questions or incomplete statements below is followed by five possible answers or completions. Select the BEST choice in each case and fill in the corresponding oval on the answer sheet.

Question 1 refers to the following.

1. The "bridges" on the exterior of the church above function as

   (A) arches.
   (B) cantilevers.
   (C) ribbed vaults.
   (D) flying buttresses.
   (E) windows.

2. Which of the following dance techniques has no established steps or patterns, and requires the dancer to create his or her own, emanating from movements of the body?

   (A) ballet
   (B) jazz
   (C) modern dance
   (D) danse mora (Flamenco dancing)
   (E) tap dancing

3. Who believed that a life of virtue or excellence is a matter of knowledge?

   (A) Socrates
   (B) Aristotle
   (C) Kant
   (D) John Stuart Mill
   (E) Rousseau

4. The following instruments are all members of the brass family EXCEPT

   (A) the trumpet.
   (B) the tuba.
   (C) the alto saxophone.
   (D) the French horn.
   (E) the trombone.

5. When a piece of music has a time signature of $\frac{4}{4}$, a quarter note receives _____ beats.

   (A) 4
   (B) 2
   (C) 1
   (D) 3
   (E) $1\frac{1}{2}$

6. Which musical style is characterized by a swing feel, a strong rhythmic beat, and improvisation?

   (A) Fugues
   (B) Jazz
   (C) Rock
   (D) Symphonies
   (E) Opera

Question 7 refers to the following passage.

> 'Twas on a lofty vase's side,
> Where China's gayest art had dyed
> The azure flowers, that blow;
> Demurest of the tabby kind,
> The pensive Selima reclined,
> Gazed on the lake below.
>
> Her conscious tail her joy declared;
>
> The fair round face, the snowy beard,
> The velvet of her paws,
> Her coat that with the tortoise vies,
> Her eyes of jet, and emerald eyes,
> She saw; and purred applause.

7. What is the subject of the stanzas?

   (A) A snake
   (B) A turtle swimming in a lake
   (C) A vase
   (D) A dog watching a cat
   (E) A cat

Question 8 refers to the following passage.

The shore was fledged with palm trees. These stood or leaned or reclined against the light and their green feathers were a hundred feet up in the air. The ground beneath them was a bank covered with coarse grass, torn everywhere by the upheavals of fallen trees, scattered with decaying coconuts and palm saplings. Behind this was the darkness of the forest proper...

8. The above passage can best be described as

   (A) surrealistic
   (B) expressionistic
   (C) realistic
   (D) romantic
   (E) Gothic

Questions 9 and 10 refer to the following passage.

Can we expect to glean information about places and times from a novel? Can anybody be so naive as to think he or she can learn anything about the past from those buxom best-sellers that are hawked around by book clubs under the heading of historical novels? But what about the masterpieces? Can we rely on Jane Austen's picture of landowning England with baronets and landscaped grounds when all she knew was a clergyman's parlor? And *Bleak House,* that **fantastic** romance within a **fantastic** London, can we call it a study of London a hundred years ago? Certainly not. And the same holds for other such novels in this series. The truth is that great novels are great fairy tales – and the novels in this series are supreme fairy tales.

9. The word "fantastic" in bold means

   (A) loaded with adventure.
   (B) unreal.
   (C) ridiculous.
   (D) historical.
   (E) nonsensical.

10. The author's attitude toward such writers as Jane Austen and Charles Dickens is one of

    (A) respect.
    (B) defiance.
    (C) mockery.
    (D) disdain.
    (E) condescension.

11. The Director of Companies was our captain and our host. We four affec-
tionately watched his back as he stood in the bows looking to seaward.
On the whole river there was nothing that looked half so nautical. He
resembled a pilot, which to a seaman is trustworthiness personified.

The above is an example of

(A) prose.
(B) unrhymed iambic pentameter.
(C) an elegy.
(D) a non sequitur.
(E) free verse.

12. A group of townspeople stood on the station siding of a little Kansas town,
awaiting the coming of the night train, which was already 20 minutes over-
due. The snow had fallen thick over everything; in the pale starlight the
line of bluffs across the wide, white meadows south of the town made soft,
smoke-colored curves against the sky.

This passage is most likely taken from which of the following?

(A) The conclusion of a short story
(B) The beginning of a short story
(C) The climax of a short story
(D) The dénouement of a short story
(E) None of the above.

Question 13 refers to the following diagram.

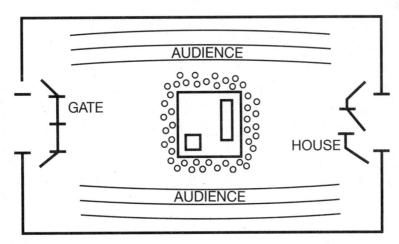

13. The picture shown on the previous page is an example of which of the following types of staging?

    (A) Thrust
    (B) Proscenium
    (C) Theater-in-the-round
    (D) Central
    (E) Open

Question 14 refers to the following.

14. From which of the following structures is the above picture taken?

    (A) Notre Dame Cathedral
    (B) The Parthenon
    (C) The Sistine Chapel
    (D) Versailles Palace
    (E) The Taj Mahal

Question 15 refers to the following.

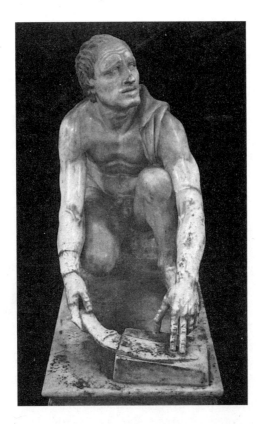

15. The figure pictured above was most likely which of the following?

    (A) A slave or menial servant
    (B) A knight's page
    (C) A religious novice
    (D) A farmer
    (E) A carpenter's apprentice

Question 16 refers to the following.

16. All of the following can be construed from the print above EXCEPT

(A) the three figures portrayed are musicians.

(B) the artwork conveys a strong sense of depth.

(C) the drawing is representative of Egyptian tomb paintings.

(D) the artist was not concerned with modeling the figures in three dimensions.

(E) the artist employed a standardized figure type.

Question 17 refers to the following.

17. Which of the following best describes the statue pictured above?

    (A) Comic
    (B) Tragic
    (C) Ornate
    (D) Imposing
    (E) Introspective

Question 18 refers to the following.

18. From this picture, one can assume that the music being played and sung is

    (A) an opera.
    (B) a sad, serious melody.
    (C) a dirge.
    (D) a light, boisterous tune.
    (E) a hymn.

Questions 19-21 refer to the following poem.

> My mistress' eyes are nothing like the sun;
> Coral is far more red than her lips' red;
> If snow be white, why then her breasts are dun;
> If hairs be wires, black wires grow on her head.
> I have seen roses damasked, red and white,
> But no such roses see I in her cheeks;
> And in some perfumes is there more delight
> Than in the breath that from my mistress reeks.
> I love to hear her speak, yet well I know
> That music hath a far more pleasing sound;
> I grant I never saw a goddess go;
> My mistress, when she walks treads on the ground.
> And yet, by heaven, I think my love as rare
> As any she belied with false compare.

19. This poem is different from other sonnets in that

    (A) it is Shakespearean.
    (B) it is Italian.
    (C) it describes the appearance of a beloved woman.
    (D) it does not describe the woman as beautiful.
    (E) it does not follow the proper sonnet conventions.

20. The last two lines of the poem

    (A) reaffirm the argument held throughout the poem.
    (B) start a new topic.
    (C) refute the argument held throughout the poem.
    (D) are a continuation of the ideas introduced in the poem.
    (E) use extensive metaphors.

21. The poem can best be described as

    (A) witty and satirical.
    (B) intense.
    (C) sarcastic.
    (D) brooding.
    (E) sentimental.

22. King: Take thy fair hour, Laertes; time be thine,

        And thy best graces spend it at thy will!

        But now, my cousin Hamlet, and my son, –

    Hamlet: *(Aside)* A little more than kin, and less than kind.

    In the above lines, what does the stage direction "*(Aside)*" mean?

    (A) The actor steps aside to make room for other action on stage.
    (B) The actor directly addresses only one particular actor on stage.
    (C) The actor directly addresses the audience, while out of hearing of the other actors.
    (D) The previous speaker steps aside to make room for this actor.
    (E) The actor speaks to someone off stage.

Question 23 refers to the following.

23. The mask above represents which of the following cultural traditions?

    (A) African
    (B) Greek
    (C) Roman
    (D) Dutch
    (E) Persian

Question 24 refers to the following.

24. Hagia Sophia, shown above, in Constantinople (present-day Istanbul) was originally built as a

   (A) Turkish mosque.
   (B) Gothic cathedral.
   (C) Byzantine palace church.
   (D) Roman temple.
   (E) monastic church.

25. The art of using movement instead of words to create a story refers to

   (A) pantomime.
   (B) mimetic imitation.
   (C) mime.
   (D) improvisation.
   (E) commedia dell'arte.

26. Every event has a cause, and so either there is some uncaused, primary cause or else the chain of causes goes backwards infinitely.

This sentence expresses part of an argument. What is the argument called and what is it meant to prove?

(A) The Cosmological Argument for the existence of God
(B) A Slippery Slope argument for a first cause
(C) The Ontological argument for the existence of God
(D) A Physical Argument for the "Big Bang" theory
(E) The Argument from Design for God

27. John Phillip Sousa, an American composer and band leader, popularized which style of music?

(A) Opera
(B) Marches
(C) Symphonies
(D) Fugues
(E) Nocturnes

28. Which of the following composers was to music as Claude Monet was to art?

(A) Stravinsky
(B) Debussy
(C) Gillespie
(D) Bach
(E) Mozart

29. All of the following educators/musicians/composers developed teaching methods. Of the group, whose method emphasizes the use of rote learning?

(A) Gordon
(B) Orff
(C) Suzuki
(D) Jaques-Dalcroze
(E) Carabo-Cone

30. It pleased God that I was still spared, and very hearty and sound in health, but very impatient of being pent up within doors without air, as I had been for 14 days or thereabouts, and I could not restrain myself, but I would go to carry a letter for my brother to the post-house.

    The above is most likely an excerpt from which of the following?

    (A) Poem
    (B) Play
    (C) Journal
    (D) Myth
    (E) Song

31. In his "Speech in the Virginia Convention," Patrick Henry says, "Suffer not yourselves to be betrayed with a kiss." Which of the following best describes this quote?

    (A) An example of personification
    (B) A mixed metaphor
    (C) A Shakespearean illusion
    (D) Hyperbole
    (E) A biblical allusion

Question 32 refers to the following passage.

From the mountains on every side rivulets descended that filled all the valley with verdure and fertility and formed a lake in the middle, inhabited by fish of every species and frequented by every fowl whom nature has taught to dip the wing in water. This lake discharged its superfluities by a stream, which entered a dark cleft of the mountain on the northern side, and fell with dreadful noise from precipice to precipice till it was heard no more.

32. The narrative technique in this passage can be described as

    (A) painstakingly descriptive.
    (B) full of comparisons and contrasts.
    (C) vague in its descriptions of landscape.
    (D) negative in connotation.
    (E) surrealistic.

Question 33 refers to the following passage.

There was a time when I went every day into a church, since a girl I was in love with knelt there in prayer for half an hour in the evening and I was able to look at her in peace.

Once when she had not come and I was reluctantly eyeing the other supplicants I noticed a young fellow who had thrown his whole lean length along the floor. Every now and then he clutched his head as hard as he could and sighing loudly beat it in his upturned palms on the stone flags.

33. By using the term "supplicants," the author implies that

(A) everyone in the church is there to celebrate a mass.
(B) everyone in the church is devout.
(C) everyone in the church is guilty of something.
(D) everyone in the church is a hypocrite.
(E) everyone in the church is damned.

Questions 34–36 refer to the following passage.

It was the best of times, it was the worst of times, it was the age of wisdom, it was the age of foolishness, it was the epoch of belief, it was the epoch of incredulity, it was the season of Light, it was the season of Darkness, it was the spring of hope, it was the winter of despair, we had everything before us, we had nothing before us, we were all going direct to Heaven, we were all going direct the other way – in short, the period was so far like the present period, that some of its noisiest authorities insisted on its being received, for good or for evil, in the superlative degree of comparison only.

There were a king with a large jaw, and a queen with a plain face, on the throne of England; there were a king with a large jaw, and a queen with a fair face, on the throne of France. In both countries it was clearer than crystal to the lords of the State preserves of loaves and fishes, that things in general were settled for ever.

34. The vast comparisons in the above passage indicate that the speaker is describing

    (A) a placid historical time period.
    (B) a time of extreme political upheaval.
    (C) a public event.
    (D) a time when anything was possible.
    (E) the attitudes of people at war.

35. The last sentence of the passage

    (A) mocks the self-assuredness of the governments of England and France.
    (B) comments on the horrible poverty of the two nations.
    (C) most likely foreshadows an upcoming famine or drought.
    (D) attacks the two governments for neglecting the poor, hungry masses.
    (E) alludes to the Bible to hint at the magnitude of the upcoming events.

36. The phrase, "some of its noisiest authorities insisted on its being received, for good or for evil, in the superlative degree of comparison only"

    (A) mocks the arrogance of the governments.
    (B) mocks the arrogance of the people.
    (C) compares the attitude of the people to the attitude of the governments.
    (D) Both (A) and (B).
    (E) Both (B) and (C).

Question 37 refers to the following.

Unité d'Habitation, Marseilles.

37. The designer of the building pictured seems to have been concerned with which of the following?

 (A) The amount of light available to the building's inhabitants
 (B) Building a modern skyscraper
 (C) Cylindrical shapes
 (D) Hidden staircases
 (E) Blending the building into its setting

Question 38 refers to the following.

38. The building pictured above suggests which of the following?

 (A) Undulating waves of water
 (B) A congested city street
 (C) A chambered nautilus
 (D) A massive mountain
 (E) A tree with spreading branches

Questions 39–41 refer to the illustrations (A) through (E).

(A)

(B)

(C)

(D)

(E)

39. Which of the examples pictured does not share cultural heritage with the others?

40. In which example does the composition set up a circular motion within the picture's borders?

41. Which example tends most strongly to represent human features as a composite of stylized, abstracted forms?

Question 42 refers to the following poem.

> Whilom ther was dwellynge at Oxenford
> A riche gnof, that gestes heeld to bord,
> And of his craft he was a carpenter.
> With hym ther was dwellynge a povre scoler.

42. What can we assume about this passage?

   (A) It is probably a translation of some other language into English.
   (B) It is written in Middle English.
   (C) It is romantic in style.
   (D) It is written in Elizabethan English.
   (E) The speaker is a foreigner.

Questions 43-45 refer to the following passages.

   (A) That's my last duchess painted on the wall,
   Looking as if she were alive. I call
   That piece a wonder, now: Fra Pandolf's hands
   Worked busily a day, and there she stands.
   (B) Nov. 24. A rainy morning. We were all well except that my head ached
   a little and I took my breakfast in bed. I read a little of Chaucer, prepared the goose for dinner, and then we all walked out. I was obliged
   to return for my fur tippet and Spenser it was so cold.
   (C) There were times in early autumn – in September – when the
   greater circuses would come to town – the Ringling Brothers, Robinson's, and Barnum & Baily shows, and when I was a route-boy
   on the morning paper, on those mornings when the circus would
   be coming in, I would rush madly through my route in the cool and

thrilling darkness that comes before the break of day, and then I would go back home and get my brother out of bed.

(D) This American government – what is it but a tradition, though a recent one, endeavoring to transmit itself unimpaired to posterity, but each instant losing some of its integrity? It has not the vitality and force of a single living man; for a single man can bend it to his will. It is a sort of wooden gun to the people themselves; and, if ever they should use it in earnest as a real one against each other, it will surely split.

(E) Miniver Cheevy, born too late,
    Scratched his head and kept on thinking;
Miniver coughed, and called it fate,
    And kept on drinking.

43. Which of the above passages creates a mood of strange excitement?

44. Which of the passages is most likely taken from a dramatic monologue?

45. Which of the passages uses a metaphor to make a point?

Question 46 refers to the following.

1   2   3   5   6

46. Which of the figures pictured above would be most appropriate for a medieval cycle play?

(A) 1
(B) 2
(C) 3
(D) 4
(E) 5

Question 47 refers to the following passage.

(The veranda of the Voynitzevs' country house. It looks out onto a sun-lit garden, with the tall trees of the forest beyond, bisected by a grassy walk.

The whoosh of a rocket taking off. The lights come up to reveal YAKOV in the garden with a large box of assorted fireworks in his arms. Beside him stands DR. TRILETZKY, a match in his hand. They are gazing up into the sky – DR. TRILETZKY with delight, YAKOV with apprehension. There is a smell of sulfur in the air. The rocket bursts, off.)

47. The above passage is most likely taken from

(A) a Victorian novel.
(B) the stage directions of a play.
(C) the critical notes to a literary work.
(D) the rough draft of a literary work.
(E) an epistolary novel.

48. The "skyscraper," as first pioneered by architects such as Henry Hobson Richardson and Louis Sullivan, saw its earliest development in which of the following cities?

(A) Paris
(B) London
(C) New York
(D) St. Louis
(E) Chicago

49. The term "carole" or Reigen is a choral dance involving skipping and/or leaping to ring-shaped form, and probably falling. Which group in the early Middle Ages took joy in practicing this type of dance?

(A) Royalty
(B) Mime
(C) Franciscan monks
(D) Fools
(E) Pantalone

50. The question whether "knowledge is justified true belief" is a question in what branch of philosophy; and is most closely associated with what famous philosopher?

    (A) Epistemology / Plato
    (B) Metaphysics / Aristotle
    (C) Epistemology / Descartes
    (D) Metaphysics / Plato
    (E) Epistemology / Spinoza

51. The following musicians/educators/composers developed teaching methods. Of these selected, who also researched and employed folk songs with his method?

    (A) Kodaly
    (B) Orff
    (C) Gordon
    (D) Carabo-Cone
    (E) Jaques-Dalcroze

52. Edwin E. Gordon used the music learning theory to develop an appreciation for music. Which musical concept is essential in the music learning theory process?

    (A) Rhythm
    (B) Folk music
    (C) Eurythmics
    (D) Audiation
    (E) Rote learning

53. When a conductor reads a score with a time signature of $\frac{4}{4}$, which of the following conducting patterns should be executed?

(A)

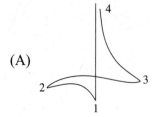

(B)

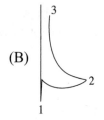

(C)

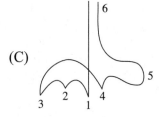

(D)

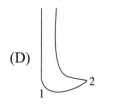

(E)

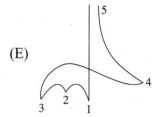

Question 54 refers to the following passage.

> Merry days were these at Thornfield Hall; and busy days too: how different from the first three months of stillness, monotony and solitude I had passed beneath its roof! All sad feelings seemed now driven from the house... there was life everywhere, movement all day long.

54. In the above passage, what is the significance of the three consecutive periods?

(A) They indicate a lapse in thought on the author's part.
(B) They indicate that the speaker is unable or unwilling to finish his/her sentence.
(C) They indicate that part of the quote has been omitted.
(D) They indicate that part of the original manuscript has been lost.
(E) They eliminate the need for further punctuation in the sentence.

Questions 55–57 refer to the following passages:

(A) Once upon a time and a very good time it was there was a moocow coming down along the road and this moocow that was coming down along the met a nicens little boy named baby tuckoo...

(B) And thus have these naked Nantucketers, these sea hermits, issuing from their ant-hill in the sea, overrun and conquered the watery world like so many Alexanders...

(C) A large rose tree stood near the entrance of the garden: the roses growing on it were white, but there were three gardeners at it, busily painting them red. Alice thought this a very curious thing, and she went nearer to watch them, and, just as she came up to them, she heard one of them say "Look out now, Five!"

(D) Emma was not required, by any subsequent discovery to retract her ill opinion of Mrs. Elton. Her observation had been pretty correct. Such as Mrs. Elton appeared to her on the second interview, such she appeared whenever they met again – self-important, presuming, familiar, ignorant, and ill-bred. She had a little beauty and a little accomplishment, but so little judgment that she thought herself coming with superior knowledge of the world, to enliven and improve a country neighborhood...

(E) TRUE! – nervous – very, very dreadfully nervous had I been and am; but why *will* you say that I am mad? The disease had sharpened my senses – not destroyed – not dulled them. Above all was in the sense of hearing acute. I heard all things in heaven and in the earth. I heard many things in hell.

55. Which passage makes use of allusion?

56. Which passage employs a discreet voice to imitate the speech of a character?

57. Which passage is most likely taken from a nineteenth-century novel of manners?

58. As he walked through the office, Raskolnikov noticed that many people were looking at him. Among them he saw the two porters from *the* house whom he has invited that night to the police-station. They stood there waiting. But he was no sooner on the stairs than he heard the voice of Porfiry Petrovitch behind him. Turning round, he saw the latter running after him, out of breath.

The preceding paragraph is most probably an excerpt from which of the following?

(A) British spy novel
(B) Nineteenth-century Russian novel
(C) A modern romance
(D) An existentialist short story
(E) A nineteenth-century Victorian novel

Question 59 refers to the following.

59. Which of the following best identifies the medium of the work above?

    (A) Oil painting on canvas
    (B) Stained-glass window
    (C) Marble sculpture
    (D) Mosaic tile inlay
    (E) Woven wool tapestry

Questions 60–62 refer to the illustrations (A) through (E).

(A)

(B)

(C)

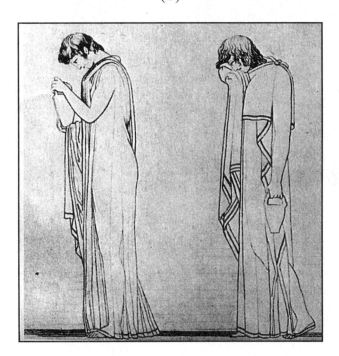

(D)

(E)

60. Which example depends most heavily on the decorative contrasts of black and white?

61. Which example seems to use coarse texture to emphasize an expressive effect?

62. In which example do the contents seem most like unrelated, documentary notations?

Questions 63–65 refer to the following passages.

(A) Fair is foul and foul is fair.
   Hover through the fog and filthy air.
(B) Weary of myself, and sick of asking
   What I am, and what I ought to be,
   At this vessel's prow I stand, which bears me

Forward, forward o'er the starlit sea
And a look of passionate desire
O'er the sea and to the stars I send:
"Ye who from my childhood up have calmed me,
Calm me, ah, compose me to the end!

(C) There were a king with a large jaw and a queen with a plain face,
on the throne of England; there were a king with a large jaw and a
queen with a fair face on the throne of France. In both countries it was
clearer than crystal to the lords of the state preserves of loaves and
fishes, that things were in general settled for ever.

(D) no thats no way for him he has no manners nor no refinement nor no
nothing in his nature slapping us behind like that on my bottom because I didnt call him Hugh the ignoramus doesnt know poetry from
a cabbage thats what you get for not keeping them in their proper
place

(E) The worthy woman bustled off, and I crouched nearer the fire; my
head felt hot, and the rest of me chill; moreover I was excited,
almost to a pitch of foolishness, through my nerves and brain. This
caused me to feel, not uncomfortable, but rather fearful (as I am
still) of serious effects from the incidents of today and yesterday.

63. Which passage describes a person seeking personal insight and solace?

64. Which passage uses the "stream of consciousness" technique to mimic the
workings of the human mind?

65. Which passage contains examples of alliteration?

Question 66 refers to the following verse.

The curfew tolls the knell of parting day,
The lowing herd wind slowly o'er the lea,
The plowman homeward plods his weary way,
And leaves the world to darkness and to me.

66. Which of the following sounds is NOT referred to in the above lines?

    (A) Bells
    (B) Wind through the trees
    (C) Footsteps
    (D) Cows
    (E) A man walking

Question 67 refers to the following verse.

    We think our fathers fools, so wise we grow;
    Our wiser sons, no doubt, will think us so.

67. Which is the best paraphrase of the above lines?

    (A) As we grow older, we think our fathers wiser.
    (B) As we grow older, we think our fathers are fools, and our sons will probably think the same of us.
    (C) Sons always believe their fathers are fools, but fathers always think their sons are wise.
    (D) Fathers always think they are smarter than their sons.
    (E) Fathers and sons are always trying to prove that they are wiser than each other.

Question 68 refers to the following.

68. The costumes pictured above would be most appropriate for which of the following?

(A) Ancient Greek drama
(B) A medieval cycle play
(C) A mid-nineteenth century play
(D) A passion play
(E) A Shakespearean play

Question 69 refers to the following.

69. The setting pictured above is an example of which of the following?

(A) Expressionism
(B) Symbolism
(C) Impressionism
(D) Realism
(E) None of the above.

Question 70 refers to the following.

70. The church of St. Peter in the Vatican, Rome, was built according to which of the following architect's designs?

(A) Michelangelo
(B) Bramante
(C) Borromini
(D) Bernini
(E) Leonardo da Vinci

Questions 71 and 72 refer to the following description of stage formats in theaters.

(A) Typical in American theaters, this is a "picture frame" stage with a large space separating the audience from the stage.
(B) A stage completely surrounded by the audience. This can also be described as theater-in-the-round.
(C) An intimate theater space in which the audience typically is seated around three-quarters of the stage.
(D) A space without a specific format that can be adjusted to any desired arrangement.
(E) An area designed to accommodate 500-600 dancers and several thousand spectators. This dance area is circular in shape, resembling a large doughnut. The middle of the donut is the area where the dancer performs; the outer rim provides protection for the audience.

71. Which best describes a thrust stage?

72. Which is a proscenium stage?

73. A philosopher who speaks of true ideas as those which "work" or lead to satisfaction or success is best described as

    (A) a pragmatist.
    (B) an empiricist.
    (C) a rationalist.
    (D) a Correspondence theorist.
    (E) a Coherentist.

74. Many directions are given on a music score. When a dot is over a note, this indicates to play the note

    (A) tenuto.
    (B) staccato.
    (C) fortissimo.
    (D) piano.
    (E) loud.

75. Count Basie, a jazz pianist/band leader, employed which style of playing in his accompaniment?

    (A) Comping
    (B) Scat singing
    (C) Riffs
    (D) Figured bass
    (E) Ghost note

76. Which one of the following scales contains three flats in the key signature?

    (A) B flat major
    (B) E flat major
    (C) F major
    (D) G major
    (E) D major

Questions 77-79 refer to the following passage.

It is very seldom that mere ordinary people like John and myself secure ancestral halls for the summer.

A colonial mansion, a hereditary estate, I would say a haunted house and reach the height of romantic felicity – but that would be asking too much of fate!

Still I will proudly declare that there is something queer about it.

Else, why should it be let so cheaply? And why have stood so long untenanted?

John laughs at me, of course, but one expects that.

John is practical in the extreme. He has no patience with faith, an intense horror of superstition, and he scoffs openly at any talk of things not to be felt and seen and put down in figures.

John is a physician, and *perhaps* (I would not say it to a living soul, of course, but this is dead paper and a great relief to my mind) – *perhaps* that is one reason I do not get well faster.

You see, he does not believe I am sick! And what can one do?

If a physician of high standing, and one's own husband, assures friends and relatives that there is really nothing the matter with one but temporary nervous depression – a slight hysterical tendency – what is one to do?

My brother is also a physician, and also of high standing, and he says the same thing.

So I take phosphates or phosphites – whichever it is – and tonics, and air and exercise, and journeys, and am absolutely forbidden to "work" until I am well again.

Personally, I disagree with their ideas.

77. John is characterized by the speaker as

  (A) arrogant.
  (B) trustworthy.
  (C) cunning.
  (D) realistic.
  (E) possessive.

78. The speaker views writing as

    (A) annoying.
    (B) therapeutic.
    (C) laborious.
    (D) painful.
    (E) whimsical.

79. We can infer from the passage that the speaker

    (A) is insane.
    (B) is of solid mental health.
    (C) has no real occupation.
    (D) strongly dislikes her husband.
    (E) is planning to murder her husband.

Questions 80 and 81 refer to the following passage.

> Come, now, there may as well be an end of this! Every time I meet your eyes squarely I detect the question just slipping out of them. If you had spoken it, or even boldly looked it; if you had shown in your motions the least sign of a fussy or fidgety concern on my account; if this were not the evening of my birthday and you the only friend who remembered it; if confession were not good for the soul, though harder than sin to some people, of whom I am one, – well, if all reasons were not at this instant converged into a focus, and burning me rather violently in that region where the seat of emotion is supposed to lie, I should keep my trouble to myself.

Bayaro Taylor, *Beauty and the Beast, Tales from Home* (1872)

80. The speaker of the above passage feels

    (A) guilty.
    (B) anxious.
    (C) ashamed.
    (D) sorrowful.
    (E) relieved.

81. The speaker feels that confession is

    (A) unnecessary.
    (B) nonsensical.
    (C) healthy.
    (D) impossible.
    (E) comical.

Question 82 refers to the following verse.

> Gallants, attend, and hear a friend
> Trill forth harmonious ditty:
> Strange things I'll tell, which late befell
> In Philadelphia city.

82. Judging from the first stanza of this poem, which of the following is true?

    (A) The poem has a serious tone.
    (B) The poem has no predictable rhyme scheme.
    (C) The poem may be satirical or humorous.
    (D) The rhyme scheme will be a-b-a-b.
    (E) The rhyme scheme will be a-a-b-b.

Question 83 refers to the following.

83. Which of the following is most evident about the building pictured above?

    (A) It relies on broad areas of unbroken surfaces.

    (B) It uses industrial forms and materials to suggest a living organism.

    (C) It is conceived and designed on a human scale.

    (D) It owes a debt to the Classical past.

    (E) It achieves an effect of poetic calm, balance, and remove.

Question 84 refers to the following.

84. Which of the following best describes the sculpture on the building pictured above?

    (A) It tells a detailed story with a definite sequence.

    (B) It dominates the facade of the building.

    (C) It draws heavily on classical mythology.

    (D) It is contained by the architectural forms of the doorways.

    (E) It was probably applied as an afterthought.

Question 85 refers to the following.

85. The sculpture pictured above suggests which of the following?

    (A) The rolling motion of a wheel
    (B) The balanced action of a lever
    (C) The twisting spiral of a screw
    (D) The flowing motion of liquid
    (E) The interlocking action of gears

Question 86 refers to the following.

86. In the example shown above, which of the following contributes most to the effect of a photographic snapshot?

    (A) The inclusion of the horse and the dog
    (B) The middle-class character of the subjects
    (C) The perspective grid behind the figures
    (D) The off-center composition and the random cropping of the figures
    (E) The strong dependence on outline

Question 87 refers to the following.

87. The building pictured on the previous page depends for its effect on

    (A) the interplay of diagonal and vertical lines.
    (B) the broad expanse of window glass.
    (C) a subtle arrangement of curving, rhythmic forms.
    (D) the viewer's point of view from ground level.
    (E) the bold massing of simple cubic forms.

Questions 88 and 89 refer to the following verse.

> Now thou art dead no eye shall ever see,
> For shape and service, spaniel like to thee.
> This shall my love do, give thy sad death one
> Tear, that deserves of me a million.

88. The above poem is an example of a(n)

(A) allegory.
(B) elegy.
(C) ballad.
(D) kenning.
(E) refrain.

89. Lines 3-4 contain an example of

(A) enjambment.
(B) personification.
(C) onomatopoeia.
(D) Homeric simile.
(E) epigram.

Questions 90–93 refer to the following verse.

> Study is like the heaven's glorious sun,
> That will not be deep-searched with saucy looks.
> Small have continual plodders won
> Save base authority from others' books.
> These earthly godfathers of heaven's lights,
> That give a name to every fixed star
> Have no more profit of their shining nights
> Than those who walk and wot* not what they are.
> (*know)

90. The speaker of these lines is most likely a

(A) student.
(B) professor.
(C) clergyman.
(D) thief.
(E) villain.

91. The lines "Small have continual plodders won / Save base authority from others' books" mean

    (A) books are key in the acquisition of knowledge.
    (B) only one's opinions are important – not facts found in books.
    (C) study is long and tedious, but ultimately rewarding.
    (D) knowledge and authority are eventually given to those who pursue them.
    (E) all that is gained by study are the simple and worthless opinions of others.

92. The last four lines of the passage suggest that

    (A) study is a pursuit for the old and tired.
    (B) anyone, whether he be a genius or simpleton, can name things and recite facts.
    (C) many geniuses are simpletons, and vice versa.
    (D) study ruins intuitive wonder, such as that caused by the stars.
    (E) All of the above.

93. "These earthly godfathers" are most likely

    (A) professors.
    (B) astronomers.
    (C) artists.
    (D) lovers.
    (E) poets.

94. This ruler has decided to retire and distribute his wealth and his responsibilities among his children, but he requires loyalty oaths from them. The action described above takes place in which of the following plays?

    (A) *Tartuffe*
    (B) *Measure for Measure*
    (C) *King Lear*
    (D) *Hamlet*
    (E) *Waiting for Godot*

95. *Everyman* is one among a number of **morality** plays. Abstractions such as beauty, strength, discretion, and five wits are personified as Everyman's companions. Within the context of the preceding sentences, which is the most precise meaning of morality?

    (A) Ethics
    (B) Pride
    (C) Mischief
    (D) Diffidence
    (E) Sloth

96. The use of concrete as a construction material was first widely exploited during which of the following periods?

    (A) Ancient Greek
    (B) Ancient Rome
    (C) The Middle Ages
    (D) The eighteenth century
    (E) The twentieth century

97. Which of the following choreographers was the first contributor to modern dance?

    (A) Agnes de Mille
    (B) Martha Graham
    (C) Ruth St. Denis
    (D) Isadora Duncan
    (E) Ted Shawn

98. If a philosopher believes in reincarnation, that philosopher's general view in the philosophy of mind will be known as

    (A) dualism.
    (B) eliminative materialism.
    (C) epiphenomenalism.
    (D) functionalism.
    (E) behaviorism.

99. What scale contains B flat, E flat, A flat, and D flat?

   (A) C major
   (B) F major
   (C) A minor
   (D) A flat major
   (E) C minor

100. A scale composed of half steps is a _____ scale.

   (A) major
   (B) chromatic
   (C) minor
   (D) whole tone scale
   (E) blues scale

101. How many sixteenth notes are equal to one quarter note?

   (A) 1
   (B) 3
   (C) 2
   (D) 4
   (E) 6

Question 102 refers to the following passage.

Nothing else was said; a new danger was being carried towards them by the river. Some wooden machinery had just given way on one of the wharves, and huge fragments were being floated along. The sun was rising now, and the wide area of watery desolation was spread out in dreadful clearness around them – in dreadful clearness floated onwards the hurrying, threatening masses. A large company in a boat that was working its way along under the Tofton houses, observed their danger, and shouted, "Get out of the current!"

But that could not be done at once, and Tom, looking before him, saw Death rushing on them. Huge fragments, clinging together in fatal fellowship, made one wide mass across the stream.

"It is coming, Maggie!" Tom said, in a deep hoarse voice, loosing the oars, and clasping her.

102. The above passage contains which of the following conflicts?

   I.   Man vs. Man
   II. Man vs. Society
   III. Man vs. God
   IV. Man vs. Nature
   V.   Man vs. Self

   (A) III only.
   (B) IV only.
   (C) I and II only.
   (D) I, II, and III only.
   (E) I, II, IV, and V only.

Questions 103 and 104 refer to the following passage.

Morning clatters with the first L train down Allen Street. Daylight rattles through the windows, shaking the old brick houses, splatters the girders of the L structure with bright confetti.

The cats are leaving the garbage cans, the chinches are going back into the walls, leaving sweaty limbs, leaving the grimetender necks of little children asleep. Men and women stir under blankets and bedquilts on mattresses in the corners of rooms, clots of kids begin to untangle to scream and kick.

At the corner of Riverton the old man with the hempen beard who sleeps where nobody knows is putting out his picklestand. Tubs of gherkins, pimentos, melonrind, piccalilli give out twining vines and cold tendrils of dank peppery fragrance that grow like a marsh garden out of the musky bedsmells and the rancid clangor of the cobbled awakening street.

The old man with the hempen beard who sleeps where nobody knows sits in the midst of it like Jonah under his gourd.

103. The language of this passage is reminiscent of

   (A) the Bible.
   (B) Shakespeare.
   (C) stage directions.
   (D) a literature textbook.
   (E) a rough draft.

104. The man's namelessness lends him an air of

    (A) anxiety.
    (B) insignificance.
    (C) fear.
    (D) heroism.
    (E) humor.

105. Often recalled as a medieval horror story of giants and demons, this magnificent epic was intended to outline the importance of leading a spiritual life.

    The passage above discusses

    (A) "The Pilgrim's Progress."
    (B) "The Canterbury Tales."
    (C) "The Song of Roland."
    (D) "Beowulf."
    (E) "The Divine Comedy."

106. Which of the following deals with a 20-year search for home?

    (A) *Rip Van Winkle*
    (B) *The Wizard of Oz*
    (C) *Exodus*
    (D) "The Odyssey"
    (E) *Don Quixote*

Question 107 refers to the following.

107. Which of the following is fundamental to the design of the building pictured above?

(A) A combination of intersecting diagonal lines
(B) A simple repetition of vertical and horizontal forms
(C) A continuous expanse of unbroken wall surface
(D) A combination of columns and arches
(E) A complex interplay of many varied shapes

Questions 108-110 refer to the following illustrations (A) through (E).

(A)

(B)

(C)

(D)   (E)

108. Which of the examples pictured above makes the most direct contact with the viewer?

109. In which example does the pose and expression of the sitter convey aristocratic disdain?

110. Which example breaks down the forms of the subject and merges them with the background?

Question 111 refers to the following.

111. Which of the following seems most true of the example pictured above?

(A) The artist attempted a realistic depiction of three-dimensional space.
(B) The picture probably illustrates an episode in a narrative.
(C) The execution was slow, painstaking, and deliberate.
(D) Both the script and the leaves share a quality of quick, fluid calligraphy.
(E) The painting depends on a wide range of contrasting tones.

Questions 112–114 refer to the following passages.

(A) There was a knight who was a lusty liver.
One day as he came riding from the river
He saw a maiden walking all forlorn
Ahead of him, alone as she was born.
And of that maiden, spite of all she said,
By very force he took her maidenhead.

(B) That time of year thou mayst in me behold
When yellow leaves, or none, or few, do hang
Upon those boughs which shake against the cold,
Bare, ruined choirs where late the sweet bird sang.

(C) My love is like to ice, and I to fire.

(D) With how sad steps, O moon, thou climb'st the skies!
   How silently, and with how wan a face.

(E) Hail to thee, blithe Spirit!
   Bird thou never wert –
   That from Heaven, or near it,
   Pourest thy full heart
   In profuse strains of unpremeditated art.

112. Which passage uses the literary device of simile?

113. Which passage employs personification?

114. Which passage uses the device of apostrophe?

Questions 115–117 refer to the following passages.

(A) Of man's first disobedience, and the fruit
   Of that forbidden tree whose mortal taste
   Brought death into the world, and all our woe,
   With loss of Eden, till one great Man
   Restore us, and regain the blissful seat,
   Sing, Heavenly Muse…

(B) My poem's epic, and is meant to be
   Divided in twelve books; each book containing,
   With love, and war, a heavy gale at sea,
   A list of ships, and captains, and kings reigning,
   New characters; the episodes are three;
   A panoramic view of Hell's in training,
   After the style of Virgil and of Homer,
   So that my name of Epic's no misnomer.

(C) Yet once more, O ye Laurels, and once more
   Ye Myrtles brown, with Ivy never-sear,
   I come to pluck your Berries harsh and crude,
   And with forc'd fingers rude,
   Shatter your leaves before the mellowing year.
   Bitter constraint, and sad occasion dear,
   Compels me to disturb your season due:
   For Lycidas is dead, dead ere his prime…

(D) But at my back I always hear
     Time's winged chariot hurrying near;
     And yonder all before us lie
     Deserts of vast eternity.
     Thy beauty shall no more be found,
     Nor, in thy marble vault, shall sound
     My echoing song; then worms shall try
     That long-preserved virginity,
     And your quaint honor turn to dust,
     And into ashes all my lust:
     The grave's a fine and private place,
     But none, I think, do there embrace.

(E) Lo! 'tis a gala night
     Within the lonesome latter years!
     An angel throng, bewinged, bedight
     In veils, and drowned in tears,
     Sit in a theater, to see
     A play of hopes and fears,
     While the orchestra breathes fitfully
     The music of the spheres.

115. Which passage comes from a mock epic?

116. Which passage employs the theme of *carpe diem?*

117. Which passage is from a pastoral elegy?

118. She depended for her well-being upon the kindness of strangers; he relied upon being well-liked for his security.

   This statement describes which pairing of characters and plays?

   (A) Jocasta in *Oedipus;* Ekdal in *The Wild Duck*
   (B) The Caretaker in *The New Tenant;* Walter in *A Raisin in the Sun*
   (C) Blanche Dubois in *A Streetcar Named Desire;* Willy Loman in *Death of a Salesman*
   (D) Nora in *A Doll's House;* Euelpides in *Aristophanes*
   (E) Hedda in *Hedda Gabler;* Algernon in *The Importance of Being Earnest*

Question 119 refers to an excerpt from Shakespeare's *Hamlet.*

119. Why, what should be the fear?
    I do not set my life at a pin's fee,
    And for my soul, what can it do to that,
    Being a thing immortal as itself?
    It waves me forth again: I'll follow it.

Which of the following terms are best used to describe the "it" referred to in the passage?

(A) An animal
(B) An opponent
(C) A path
(D) A rule
(E) A ghost

Question 120 refers to the following.

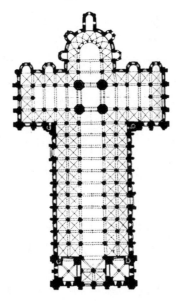

120. The plan illustrated above is an example of a type of medieval church that is commonly referred to as a(n)

(A) early Christian monastic church.
(B) Romanesque pilgrimage church.
(C) subterranean crypt.
(D) Gothic cathedral.

121. In ballet, the term *port de bras* refers to

    (A) movement of the head, shoulders, and upper torso.
    (B) all body parts in correct relative position with one another.
    (C) exercises that help develop coordination, control, and balance. This is practiced by alternating feet.
    (D) a pose standing on one leg while the other leg is raised up, turned out, and bent with the foot open in the opposite direction of the body.
    (E) A group of exercises for the arms.

122. If a consequentialist in ethics is someone who believes that only the consequences of actions make them good or bad, then which of the following ethical theories is consequentialistic?

    (A) Utilitarianism
    (B) Kantianism
    (C) Intuitionism
    (D) Virtue ethics
    (E) Aristotelian ethics

123. A chord (three or more pitches sounding simultaneously) in root position contains which order of notes?

    (A) root, 3rd, 5th
    (B) root, 2nd, 5th
    (C) 3rd, 5th, root
    (D) 5th, root, 3rd
    (E) root, 2nd, 3rd

124. Which of the following dynamic markings, when written below the staff, tells the musician to play softly?

    (A) ff.
    (B) cres.
    (C) p.
    (D) decres.
    (E) rit.

125. How many beats are in each measure if the time signature is $\frac{6}{8}$?

    (A) 4
    (B) 6
    (C) 3
    (D) 2
    (E) 8

126. Which of the following seventeenth century works uses the satiric device of irony to superb effect?

    (A) "Paradise Lost"
    (B) *A Modest Proposal*
    (C) *Everyman*
    (D) *The Way of the World*
    (E) *The Lives of the Poets*

127. Which of the following is a great romantic epic considered by scholars to express the highest ideals of the Renaissance?

    (A) "The Faerie Queen"
    (B) "The Wife of Bath's Tale"
    (C) *Gulliver's Travels*
    (D) "The Rape of the Lock"
    (E) "Beowulf"

128. Which of the following deals with the dreadful working conditions in Chicago meat packing houses at the turn of the twentieth century?

    (A) *Martin Chuzzlewit*
    (B) *The Jungle*
    (C) *Sister Carrie*
    (D) *My Antonia*
    (E) *Main Street*

129. Often remembered as the play in which the main character killed his father and married his mother, which work is often cited as elucidating the Greek concept of "Hubris"?

    (A) *Oedipus Rex*
    (B) *Tiger at the Gates*
    (C) *Zorba the Greek*
    (D) "The Aeneid"
    (E) "Il Purgatorio"

130. Which of the following Elizabethan works is often remembered as the play in which a son murders his uncle and stepfather for the murder of his father, and deals with the question: "Is justice delayed, justice denied?"

    (A) *Twelve Angry Men*
    (B) *Inherit the Wind*
    (C) *Macbeth*
    (D) *Hamlet*
    (E) *Rosencrantz and Guildenstern Are Dead*

Questions 131-133 refer to illustrations (A) through (C) below.

(A)

(B)

(C)

131. Which is NOT an abstract expressionist painting?

    (A) Painting (A)
    (B) Painting (B)
    (C) Painting (C)
    (D) All of the above.
    (E) None of the above.

132. Which is a *mixed media* piece?

    (A) Painting (A)
    (B) Painting (B)
    (C) Painting (C)
    (D) All of the above.
    (E) None of the above.

133. Which is by Jasper Johns?

    (A) Painting (A)
    (B) Painting (B)
    (C) Painting (C)
    (D) All of the above.
    (E) None of the above.

Question 134 refers to the following.

134. Which of the following work of art is depicted in the photograph shown on the previous page?

    (A) Donatello's *St. George*
    (B) Lorenzo Ghiberti's *St. John the Baptist*
    (C) Nanni di Banco's *Quattro Santi Coronati*
    (D) Auguste Rodin's *The Thinker*
    (E) Jacques Lipchitz's *Figure*

Question 135 refers to the following.

135. In the example pictured above, which of the following contributes most to an effect of stability and changeless grandeur?

    (A) The strong horizontal thrust of the architecture
    (B) The wealth of elaborate ornamental detail
    (C) The vast open courtyard with its surrounding columns
    (D) The simplified geometry of the massive forms and the sloping diagonal walls
    (E) The enormous relief carvings of the pharaohs and the gods

Questions 136 and 137 refer to the following verse.

> Careful observers may foretell the hour
> (By sure prognostics) when to dread a shower:
> While rain depends, the pensive cat gives o'er
> Her frolics, and pursues her tail no more.
> Returning home at night, you'll find the sink*
> Strike your offended sense with double stink.
> If you be wise, then go not far to dine;
> You spend more in coach hire than save in wine.
> A coming shower your shooting corns presage,
> Old aches throb, your hollow tooth will rage.
>
> (* sewer)

136. Which genre of poetry does this passage exemplify?

    (A) Epic
    (B) Satiric
    (C) Parodic
    (D) Ode
    (E) Lyric

137. The phrase "(By sure prognostics)" is _____ in tone.

    (A) sarcastic
    (B) playful
    (C) angry
    (D) Both (A) and (B).
    (E) Both (A) and (C).

Questions 138 and 139 refer to the following poem.

WHEN BRITAIN REALLY RULED THE WAVES

> When Britain really ruled the waves
>   (In good Queen Bess's time)—
> The House of Peers made no pretense
> To intellectual eminence,
>   Or scholarship sublime;
> Yet Britain won her proudest bays*
> In good Queen Bess's glorious days!

When Wellington thrashed Bonaparte,
      As every child can tell,
The House of Peers, throughout the war,
Did nothing in particular,
      And did it very well:
Yet Britain set the world ablaze
In good King George's glorious days!

And while the House of Peers withholds
      Its legislative hand,
And noble statesman do not itch
To interfere with matters which
      They do not understand,
As bright will shine Great Britain's rays
As in good King George's glorious days!

(* honors)

138. In this poem, the ruling body of Britain is described as

    (A) a very successful legislative institution.
    (B) a body which makes wise decisions.
    (C) a body which is supported by the British.
    (D) a group of disinterested and unintelligent noblemen.
    (E) a group of highly talented diplomats and legislators.

139. The tone of this poem can be described as

    (A) lauding.
    (B) parodic.
    (C) satiric.
    (D) satisfied.
    (E) patriotic.

140. "Let Sleeping Dogs Lie" is a warning delivered in which of the following plays?

    (A) *The Cherry Orchard*
    (B) *Death of a Salesman*
    (C) *Pygmalion*
    (D) *Aristophanes*
    (E) *Oedipus the King*

PRACTICE TEST 2

Answer Key

1.	(D)		32.	(C)		63.	(B)
2.	(C)		33.	(C)		64.	(D)
3.	(A)		34.	(D)		65.	(A)
4.	(C)		35.	(A)		66.	(B)
5.	(C)		36.	(A)		67.	(B)
6.	(B)		37.	(A)		68.	(E)
7.	(E)		38.	(D)		69.	(D)
8.	(C)		39.	(B)		70.	(A)
9.	(B)		40.	(D)		71.	(C)
10.	(A)		41.	(B)		72.	(A)
11.	(A)		42.	(B)		73.	(A)
12.	(B)		43.	(C)		74.	(B)
13.	(D)		44.	(A)		75.	(A)
14.	(B)		45.	(D)		76.	(B)
15.	(A)		46.	(B)		77.	(D)
16.	(B)		47.	(B)		78.	(B)
17.	(D)		48.	(E)		79.	(C)
18.	(D)		49.	(C)		80.	(B)
19.	(D)		50.	(A)		81.	(C)
20.	(C)		51.	(A)		82.	(C)
21.	(A)		52.	(D)		83.	(B)
22.	(C)		53.	(A)		84.	(D)
23.	(A)		54.	(C)		85.	(B)
24.	(C)		55.	(B)		86.	(D)
25.	(C)		56.	(A)		87.	(E)
26.	(A)		57.	(D)		88.	(B)
27.	(B)		58.	(B)		89.	(A)
28.	(B)		59.	(B)		90.	(A)
29.	(C)		60.	(E)		91.	(E)
30.	(C)		61.	(B)		92.	(D)
31.	(E)		62.	(A)		93.	(B)

94.	(C)	110.	(A)	126.	(B)
95.	(A)	111.	(D)	127.	(A)
96.	(B)	112.	(C)	128.	(B)
97.	(D)	113.	(D)	129.	(A)
98.	(A)	114.	(E)	130.	(D)
99.	(D)	115.	(B)	131.	(A)
100.	(B)	116.	(D)	132.	(A)
101.	(D)	117.	(C)	133.	(A)
102.	(B)	118.	(C)	134.	(D)
103.	(C)	119.	(E)	135.	(D)
104.	(B)	120.	(B)	136.	(B)
105.	(E)	121.	(E)	137.	(D)
106.	(D)	122.	(A)	138.	(D)
107.	(B)	123.	(A)	139.	(C)
108.	(C)	124.	(C)	140.	(E)
109.	(B)	125.	(B)		

PRACTICE TEST 2

Detailed Explanations of Answers

1. **(D)** These are flying buttresses, a feature of church construction used frequently during the Gothic period. They support, on the exterior of the building, key points of stress in the wall, where the lateral thrust of the roof vaults is greatest. While these members are in the approximate form of (A) arches, they do not *function*, in a supporting sense, as arches. (B) Cantilevers are supporting members which project independently from a wall or beam. This is a twentieth century invention, used in the context of modern building. (C) Ribbed vaults are also a feature of Gothic church construction, but are used *within* a church, not on the exterior. (E) Windows is not a correct choice because these structural members are obviously perpendicular to the wall, rather than parallel to it as windows are.

2. **(C)** Of the choices given, a dance technique drawing its material from natural human movement allowing the artist to be free and create and build his or her own unique movements is modern dance. Ballet (A), jazz (B), danse mora (Flamenco dancing) (D), and tap dance (E) all require complete control of the body and are specific in the movements of each dance technique.

3. **(A)** Although Socrates claimed not to know anything himself, he seems convinced that the unexamined life is not worth living because virtue and happiness come only with the search for knowledge. Aristotle (B) thought such a view placed too much emphasis on knowledge, for virtuous activity is largely a matter of habit and training. Kant (C) claimed that the only good thing is a good will, and that one can know what is right without willing it. Mill's utilitarianism (D), based on the idea that one should do what creates the most pleasure for the greatest number, is a radical departure from virtue ethics altogether. Rousseau (E) believed that human beings are good by nature but are corrupted by their social environment.

4. **(C)** Although it resembles a brass instrument, the alto saxophone is a member of the woodwind family. In order to produce a sound, air blown through the mouthpiece causes the reed to vibrate; choice (C) is correct. The trumpet, tuba, and French horn are all members of the brass family.

These instruments are made of brass and produce sound by the vibration of the airstream from the lips through the mouthpiece. Choices (A), (B), and (D) are not correct. The trombone is a brass instrument. It changes notes by moving a slide. Choice (E) is incorrect.

5. **(C)** The top number of a time signature is equal to the number of beats in a measure. The bottom number denotes which note is equal to one beat. For example, in $\frac{4}{4}$ there are four beats in each measure and a quarter note receives one beat. Therefore, choice (C) is correct. In $\frac{4}{4}$ a whole note would receive four beats, a half note would receive two beats, and a half quarter note would receive three beats. Therefore, choices (A), (B), and (D) are incorrect. A dotted quarter note receives one-and-a-half beats in $\frac{4}{4}$. Choice (E) is incorrect.

6. **(B)** Jazz is a musical style that incorporates a swing feel, a strong rhythmic beat, and improvisation. Choice (B) is correct. Fugues employ one melodic fragment in variations; therefore, choice (A) is incorrect. Rock 'n' Roll combines elements of country, rhythm and blues, and other black idioms, such as gospel and the blues; therefore, choice (C) is not correct. A symphony is an orchestral work with three or four movements; therefore, choice (D) is incorrect. Opera is a vocal dramatic work; choice (E) is incorrect.

7. **(E)** These two stanzas are taken from Robert Gray's "Ode on the Death of a Favorite Cat." There is no mention of a snake, so (A) is wrong. The passage does mention a "tortoise," but only because Gray is comparing the cat's coat with a tortoise's stripes; therefore, (B) is wrong. A vase is mentioned, but only because the cat "reclined" on it; (C) is also wrong. There is no mention at all of a dog, so (D) is wrong. The word "tabby" and such characteristics as "snowy beard" (whiskers) and "velvet paws" describe a cat, so (E) is correct.

8. **(C)** This question asks you to read the excerpt from William Golding's *Lord of the Flies* and determine the literary movement to which Golding ascribes. Surrealism (A) goes beyond the real into the realm of the "superreal" and often includes the world of the unconscious or dreams. Since there is nothing to suggest that this passage is anything but a true-to-life description, this choice is incorrect. Expressionistic writers (B) present life as they feel it to be, not as it appears. Again, this passage does not incorporate this style. Romantic writing (D) presents life as the writer wishes it could be and usually describes strange lands and adventures; this "normal"

beach scene contains no romantic elements, so (D) is incorrect. Gothicism (E) is a style used by novelists of the eighteenth and nineteenth centuries which relies on greater-than-life heroes, villains, and a grandiose sense of the macabre. Since the passage features none of this, (E) is wrong. The correct answer is (C), because realistic writing concerns detailed de-scriptions of everyday life; "fledged with palm trees," "their green feathers were a hundred feet up in the air," "scattered with decaying coconuts," etc., are all realistic descriptions of the scene.

9. **(B)** The author's point here is that the so-called "historical novels" which exist in our canon of literature are, in fact, anything but "historical." "Fantastic" usually refers to something unreal, as it does here, making choice (B) the correct answer.

10. **(A)** If you selected anything but choice (A), you were too hasty in making your decision. The author is not mocking the famous *writers*, but those readers which read their works as historical treatises. The author refers to their novels as "fairy tales," but not in a condescending way; he is simply categorizing the novels as works of fiction ("supreme," in fact) which should be read as such.

11. **(A)** Prose is non-metrical language, the opposite of verse. Since this passage is not written in verse, (A) is the correct answer. Iambic pentameter is five units (or "feet") of an unstressed syllable followed by a stressed syllable, so (B) is incorrect. An elegy is a poem of lamentation for the dead, so (C) is wrong. A non sequitur is a type of reasoning pattern in which the conclusion does not follow the line of reasoning used to reach it, so (D) is incorrect.

12. **(B)** Since the selection seems to be creating a setting by describing the townspeople and weather in the "little Kansas town," choice (B) is correct. It seems highly unlikely that it is taken from the climax of a short story (C) (the point of highest tension where the elements of the plot are brought together), the dénouement (D) (the unwinding of the plot following the climax), or the conclusion (A) (the final images or actions described by an author).

13. **(D)** The first four choices given are types of staging. Choice (E) is not; therefore, it is an invalid choice. Thrust staging has the stage projecting into the audience and the audience surrounding the stage on three sides. The audience in the picture is on only two sides of the stage, which is known as central staging (D). Proscenium (B) is traditional staging in a theatre with

a proscenium arch. Theater-in-the-round has the audience completely surrounding the playing area. Choice (D) is the correct answer.

14. **(B)** You are asked to determine which of the buildings named is pictured. Each edifice listed is built in a different style, which should be easily recognizable. Notre Dame Cathedral (A) is French, characterized by its flying buttresses. This is a picture of the frieze of the west cella of the Parthenon, which is characterized by Doric columns (as pictured) and the high-relief metopes of the Doric frieze. The Sistine Chapel (C), Michelangelo's masterpiece, is known for its frescoes and barrel-vaulted ceilings. Versailles (D) is the palace of Louis XIV, outside of Paris, and is an example of the ornate style of baroque grandeur. One distinguishing factor is that all the choices other than the Parthenon are structures which are in much better repair, since they are more recent than the pictured ruins of the Parthenon.

15. **(A)** The squatting position of the figure is indicative of a low position, like that of a slave (A). Since he is wearing only a cloak thrown back over one shoulder, this, too, indicates the clothing of a commoner or a person of low status. The action, that of sharpening a knife, is a job which would be designated to a slave. The muscle structure of the figure would not really indicate social level, making (B), (C), (D), and (E) unlikely choices.

16. **(B)** This question asks you to look at the print and come to some conclusions. Since each figure is holding or playing a musical instrument (double aulos, lute, and harp), it can be surmised that they are musicians (A). Choice (B) states that the artwork creates the illusion of depth. Since there is not a strong sense of depth, and you are looking for the exceptional choice, this is the correct answer. The lack of a three-dimensional aspect (D) and the absence of a background against which the figures are placed, all add to the conclusion that this is an Egyptian tomb painting (C).

17. **(D)** The pictured statue is a portrait of Augustus that was found near Rome. The effect of this figure, with the serious expression and gesture, is not comic (A). There is nothing in the stance, expression, or dress to suggest levity. Conversely, although the face is not smiling, it is also not a tragic figure (B). Although the breastplate or cuirass has scenes in low relief carved on it, the figure itself is not ornate or excessively decorated (C). Finally, the large gesture and stance of an imperator, or commander-in-chief, makes for an imposing figure (D). The carved armor, careful draping of the cloak and the rod the figure holds, all add to this impression. Thus, (D) is the correct answer.

18. **(D)** This question requires that you study the mood of the people in the picture and make a connection between the instruments pictured, the actions of those pictured, and the type of music being played. Since an opera (A) is usually a formal, upper-class form of music and the picture is of a coarse tavern scene, the music would not be operatic. The individuals appear festive and seem to be enjoying taking part in the merry-making, not singing a sad, serious melody (B), or a funeral hymn (C) dirge. Therefore, the correct answer is (D). The music is a light, boisterous tune.

19. **(D)** While the sonnet "My mistress' eyes are nothing like the sun" is Shakespearean, this does not make it different from other sonnets. A majority of sonnets are written in this form, so (A) is incorrect. The poem does describe the appearance of a beloved woman; this choice is incorrect, however, because many other sonnets do the same. Beautiful women were traditional subject matter for Elizabethan sonneteers. The sonnet does follow the proper conventions necessary to label it as one, so (E) is also wrong. (D) is the correct answer because Shakespeare undermines the traditional beauty of the women who are normally written about and states that his mistress is far more beautiful than the other "goddesses," even though she is realistically ordinary.

20. **(C)** The last two lines of a Shakespearean sonnet generally provide an ironic twist to the rest of the poem. In this sonnet, the lines refute the argument of the rest of the poem because the speaker states that even though his mistress is ordinary he still finds her beautiful. Thus, choice (C) is the correct answer.

21. **(A)** Choice (A) is correct because the poem is witty in the way it takes standard sonnet conventions (a woman's eyes, lips, hair, etc.) and twists them to make a point. By doing this, Shakespeare is also satirizing standard sonnet conventions of his time (which he himself never hesitated to employ). The poem is not intense (B), sarcastic (C), brooding (D), or sentimental (E). "Sentimental" denotes "looking fondly back on," which the speaker is not doing; the woman is his mistress, not his past mistress.

22. **(C)** This question tests your knowledge of the use of the dramatic term "aside." An aside is a comment spoken directly to the audience that the other actors on stage are supposedly unable to hear. Thus, the correct answer is choice (C).

23. **(A)** You are asked to decide which culture this mask represents. The mask reproduced in the picture was designed to be worn by African tribesmen as

they danced by firelight to the accompaniment of drums. The nonrealistic features are intended to conjure up the presence of an invisible spirit. The African tradition is noted due to the large features. The correct answer is (A). The mask is not representative of the Greek culture (B), whose sculpture is clean-lined and realistic, as is the Roman (C). The Dutch culture (D) is characterized by extremely domestic-related arts with a reality of simple truths. Thus, a mask showing elongated and distorted features would not characterize the Dutch culture. Persian art (E) also would not be distorted in the manner of this mask.

24. **(C)** The church of Hagia Sophia was built as part of the palace complex of the Byzantine Emperor Justinian in the first half of the sixth century. The building has the *appearance* of a (A) Turkish mosque; this is due to the four minarets which were added after the Moslem conquest of the Byzantine Empire, when the building was in fact converted (for a time) into a mosque. The building reveals no characteristics whatsoever that may be identified with (B) a Gothic cathedral, although the centralized plan and large central dome are somewhat reminiscent of certain (D) Roman temples. Hagia Sophia was originally built as a *cathedral*, not as a (E) monastic church.

25. **(C)** Mime is the art of imaging the world together with an audience. The best choice is mime. Pantomime is a composition of mime (A), mimetic imitation is the ability to adapt the body to the properties of things (B); improvisation is a technique in which a performer creates circumstances and applies it to games (D); and commedia dell'arte is a group of masked characters presenting plays in an improvisational form (E).

26. **(A)** This sentence expresses part of the Cosmological Argument for God's existence, in which God is thought of as an Unmoved Mover. A Slippery Slope argument (B) is a logical fallacy that minimizes the differences between similar things or events and does not prove anything. The Ontological argument (C) is based not on causation but on the conception of God as the most perfect being. The "Big Bang" theory (D) does not answer the question, Why was there a Big Bang?, and so does not presuppose a first cause of all things. The Design Argument (E) takes God to be responsible not for the chain of causes but for the order of the universe: just as a watch presupposes a watchmaker, so an ordered universe presupposes a Cosmic Designer.

27. **(B)** John Phillip Sousa composed and popularized marches, such as "The Washington Post March" and "The Liberty Bell." He was known

as the "March King," so choice (B) is correct. Giuseppe Verdi is known for his operas, so choice (A) is incorrect. Symphonies were a specialty of Ludwig van Beethoven; therefore, choice (C) is not correct. Fugues are associated largely with Johann Sebastian Bach; therefore, choice (D) is incorrect. Frederic Chopin composed lyrical nocturnes for piano; choice (E) is incorrect.

28. **(B)**   Claude Debussy experimented with musical impressionism. His music painted a picture with sounds; choice (B) is correct. Stravinsky composed with a number of twentieth century styles, so choice (A) is not correct. Dizzy Gillespie was a composer and performer of jazz music; choice (C) is incorrect. Bach composed fugues, suites, concertos, and choral works during the Baroque period, so (D) is not correct. W.A. Mozart composed symphonies during the classical period. Choice (E) is incorrect.

29. **(C)**   Dr. Shinichi Suzuki developed a teaching philosophy called "Talent Education," which employed the "mother-tongue" method. Music is taught in a similar fashion to children learning their native language, by rote. The use of imitation, repetition, and observation are emphasized. Choice (C) is the correct answer. Edwin Gordon emphasized audiation, the use of inner hearing; choice (A) is incorrect. Carl Orff's approach employed the use of rhythm; choice (B) is not correct. Emile Jaques-Dalcroze is primarily recognized for the use of eurythmics and improvisation; choice (D) is incorrect. The Carabo-Cone method believed the students learn by using the body; choice (E) is incorrect.

30. **(C)**   You are asked to decide the literary form of the quote. Since it seems to have no poetic form, the first choice is easily negated, as is choice (E), for songs are similar in form to poems. Although a long speech in a play could be similar to this, there is no dialogue, which would normally indicate a play (B). A journal, or diary, is written in first person, as the excerpt is. Also, it puts forth everyday events and feelings, the purpose we normally associate with a journal. A myth (D) is a traditional story, usually connected with the religion of people, and attempts to account for something in nature. This quote gives no indication of mythological allusions. The correct answer is (C).

31. **(E)**   This quote from Patrick Henry's speech is a reference to Judas Iscariot, who betrayed Jesus with a kiss, giving him up to the soldiers to be crucified. This is a biblical allusion from Luke 22: 47-48 (E). Since there is no personification in the line, nor is there a metaphorical comparison, (A) and

(B) are incorrect. Choice (C) is incorrect because an "illusion" is a false idea or conception. Choice (D), hyperbole is also an incorrect choice, since there is no overstatement in the quote.

32. **(C)** is the correct response because the author of this passage does little to give the reader a sense of what the landscape looks like in detail. Phrases such as "filled all the valley with verdure and fertility" do nothing to describe the details of the scene, such as the flora and fauna "Fish of every species" and "every fowl whom nature has taught to dip the wing in water" are extremely vague, giving no description of what the fish and birds look like. The passage involves no comparisons or contrasts (B), and it does not have a negative connotation. Although the description is vague, it is still realistic, not surrealistic (E).

33. **(C)** A supplicant is one who seeks forgiveness in a religious sense. Therefore, by labeling the parishioners as such, the author is implying that they are all guilty of various crimes against their religion and have come to the church seeking forgiveness.

34. **(D)** The passage, which opens Charles Dickens's *A Tale of Two Cities*, contains numerous and vast comparisons. By making these com-parisons and descriptions of the time period ("we had everything before us, we had nothing before us, we were all going direct to Heaven, we were all going direct the other way," etc.), Dickens is illustrating how during this period (just before the French Revolution) anything was possible: "wisdom," "foolishness," "Light," or "Darkness." This "anything is possible" tone also foreshadows the French Revolution, which the aristocracy never expected. Dickens will, later in the novel, describe extreme political upheaval, but does not here, so (B) is wrong. (A) is wrong because "placid" implies settled and calm; if "anything is possible," then the times are the exact opposite. There is no mention of a public event or the attitudes of people at war, so (C) and (E) are also incorrect.

35. **(A)** The Bible tells of how Christ was able to feed hundreds of hungry people with only seven loaves of bread and fish until all were satiated. By jokingly suggesting that the two governments contain the positions "lords of the state preserves of loaves and fishes," Dickens mocks their self-assuredness and unflinching certainty that the "preserves" will never be depleted and that "things in general [are] settled for ever." The phrase "clearer than crystal" helps, through its sarcasm, to give this attack more

sting. All of the other choices are not alluded to or discussed in the passage, and are thus incorrect.

36. **(A)** The "superlative degree" refers to the utmost degree of something being compared (the *hottest* day, the *fastest* runner, the *most beautiful* object, etc.). The phrase indicates that some of the time periods "noisiest authorities" (a sarcastic euphemism for members of the governments) wanted time to be remembered as the "most" or "best" of something – regardless of whether it was "the most evil" or "the most productive." All that mattered to these "authorities" was to be at the top of every comparison, regardless of its implications. Thus, (A) is correct. The people are not mentioned here, so (B) and (C) are both incorrect, as are (D) and (E).

37. **(A)** Le Corbusier's Unité d'Habitation (Union for Living) is an apartment house in Marseilles. Corbusier set out to build apartments vibrating with light. This is obvious from the many windows almost covering the side of the building. Thus, choice (A) is correct. The building is obviously not a skyscraper (B), since there are no more than eight floors. The building is structured around rectangular and linear shapes, rather than cylindrical (C). And, the staircase at left is not hidden, but in full view (D).

38. **(D)** You are asked to look at the structure of a building and relate to it in terms of natural forms. Since this contemporary building stacks and masses cubes or facets from a broad base to an increasingly narrow peak, much like a mountain, the correct answer is (D). It does not have wave-like lines which would connote undulating water, nor does it display any branch-like elements projecting from a trunk as on a tree. Likewise, it does not reveal the concentric spirals of a snail or nautilus shell, while answer choice (B), a city street, offers an example of a man-made, not a natural object, and is therefore not relevant to the question.

39. **(B)** Answer choices (A), (C), (D), and (E) all share in some way the forms and ideals of the Western Classical tradition as it was established in the arts of Greece and Rome. This tradition emphasizes the value of the human individual and expresses its humanistic convictions, in part, through an idealized representation of the human figure. Answer choice (A), a Hellenistic marble relief of the second century B.C.E., shows this figure style in one of its earliest contexts. Examples (D) and (E), paintings from the Renaissance and Baroque periods in Europe, directly echo the ideal figure forms found in the Greek work. Choice (C), a modern work, abstracts and stylizes the human form somewhat more severely, but remains focused on

the complete, nude human figure as a humanistic ideal. Only choice (B), a sixteenth-century African bronze head, falls outside of the long continuous stream of Western European culture.

40. **(D)** Answer choices (B) and (C) show static, isolated forms which display no motion at all. Choice (E) presents subjects arranged around a central focal point in a somewhat circular format, but the painting aspires to an effect of balanced calm and stillness and cannot be said to be at all animated. Choices (A) and (D) both exhibit vigorous movement, but the motion in (A), the Greek relief, depends on the counteracting thrust of intersecting diagonal lines and repeated V-forms. Only choice (D), the Galatea by the Renaissance painter Raphael, establishes a truly circular motion, in which the arched form of the cupid at the bottom of the picture leads the viewer's eye upwards to the right, through the cupids in the sky, all of whom circle around the main subject in the center of the picture.

41. **(B)** Answer choices (A), (D), and (E) all follow the Classical tradition of idealized figures presented in an illusionistic, well-modelled, three-dimensional mode. Only choices (B) and (C) begin to abstract the figure to any significant degree, although choice (C), a twentieth-century sculpted image of female nude, retains the sense of a rounded, softly-modelled, corporeal mass. Choice (B), however, an African bronze head, begins to facet the facial features into a series of angular planes and lines (evident in the sharp line from cheekbone to jaw) and overemphasizes the size and shape of the eyes.

42. **(B)** This question tests your knowledge of the development of the English language. This passage is taken from one of Chaucer's *Canterbury Tales*, written in the late fourteenth century. This is evident from the highly "irregular" spelling of words such as "dwellynge" ("dwelling") and "povre" ("poor"). (A) is incorrect because a translation would be translated into standard, modern English. Choice (C) is wrong, because while the poem may be romantic, it is impossible to tell from this passage. Elizabethan English is completely different from Middle English, so (D) is incorrect, and (E) is wrong because it is impossible to tell from the passage whether or not the speaker is a foreigner. (B) is the correct answer.

43. **(C)** This question asks you to read and determine the mood created by an author in a short selection. Passage (C), taken from Thomas Wolfe's "Circuses at Dawn," uses such words and phrases as "thrilling darkness" and

"rush madly" to let the reader share the narrator's strange excitement as he anticipates the circus. Therefore, (C) is the correct answer.

44. **(A)**   A dramatic monologue is a poem in the form of an extended speech by an identifiable character. Passage (A), the beginning of Robert Browning's "My Last Duchess," is unquestionably spoken by one character to another; therefore, (A) is the correct answer.

45. **(D)**   A metaphor is a literary device whereby an author compares two seemingly unlike things to achieve an effect. Passage (D), taken from Henry David Thoreau's essay "Civil Disobedience," compares two seemingly unlike things – the American government and a wooden gun – to make a point; therefore, (D) is the correct answer.

46. **(B)**   Figure 1 is an Elizabethan nobleman, appropriate for a play set in the 1600s. Figure 2 is a medieval old man and would be appropriate for a medieval cycle play. This is the style appropriate during the medieval period. Figure 3 is a Royalist trooper. Figure 4 is a Chinese Mandarin. Figure 5 is a late nineteenth-century "Dandy." Choice (B) is the correct answer.

47. **(B)**   You can tell that this passage is taken from the stage directions of a play because of the visual and auditory descriptions you are given. Also, you are told that "lights come up" and a "rocket bursts, off," here meaning "offstage." (B) is the correct answer.

48. **(E)**   These architects are known for their contributions to the development of urban architecture in Chicago, which, because of financial and land constraints, ultimately led to "skyscrapers." This is an American invention in architecture, so (A) Paris and (B) London are incorrect. (C) New York is a seemingly logical answer due to the number of skyscrapers built there over the course of the past century and a half; however, while close behind Chicago in their development, key design features were first employed by architects working in Chicago. (D) St. Louis did not play an important role in the early building of skyscrapers.

49. **(C)**   The Franciscan monks expressed their joy by singing, skipping, leaping, and falling. Royalty (A) would not be seen in public acting in an uncontrolled manner; mime (B) could mimic part of this dance solely through movement and no words; a fool (D) would cruelly mimic this type of expression; and (E) a commedia dell'arte character like Pantalone would improvise the movement and voice.

50. **(A)** The question arises in the theory of knowledge, or epistemology (from the Greek word *episteme*), and Plato argues that knowledge is justified true belief: mere true belief is necessary but not sufficient for knowledge, because a true belief might be the product of a lucky guess. A person who knows has a good reason for the true belief. Metaphysics is the branch of philosophy that explores very general questions about what exists, so (B) and (D) are incorrect. (C) is incorrect because Descartes held that knowledge is a matter of clarity and distinctness, the resolution of doubt, and (E) is incorrect because Spinoza held that when we know, we know that we know and need no justification.

51. **(A)** Zoltan Kodaly researched the folk music of Hungary. He believed using folk songs for study would strengthen a musical culture. Choice (A) is correct. Carl Orff used rhythm and participation; choice (B) is not correct. Gordon used audiation, inner hearing, as the foundation of his learning theory; choice (C) is incorrect. The Carabo-Cone method incorporated sensory-motor skills for students to use their bodies to learn music; choice (D) is incorrect. Emile Jaques-Dalcroze primarily used eurythmics and improvisation; choice (E) is incorrect.

52. **(D)** Audiation, to hear music in the mind, is essential to Edwin E. Gordon Learning Theory. Musical context and technique are built upon the foundation of audiating skills. Choice (D) is the correct answer. Rhythm, the duration of tone or the pulse, is often incorporated in most learning methods; choice (A) is incorrect. Folk music is employed in the method of Zoltan Kodaly; choice (B) is incorrect. Eurythmics is a term used by Jaques-Dalcroze describing the physical response to music; choice (C) is not correct. The core of Dr. Suzuki's method includes imitation, repetition; and rote learning; choice (E) is incorrect.

53. **(A)** In $\frac{4}{4}$ the top number of the time signature indicates four beats per measure. Therefore, a conductor would follow a four beat pattern because each point or movement represents one beat; choice (A) is correct. Choice (B) is incorrect because it contains a three beat pattern that would be utilized in $\frac{3}{4}$. Choice (C) contains a six beat pattern that would be used with six beats in a measure of $\frac{6}{8}$; choice (C) is incorrect. Choice (D) has a two beat pattern that would be used for two beats in each measure of $\frac{2}{4}$; choice (D) is incorrect. A pattern with five points would be used in a measure which contains five beats. Choice (E) is incorrect.

54. **(C)** This question asks you to demonstrate knowledge and awareness of a widely used symbol, the ellipsis. Within a sentence, three periods with a space after each period indicate that material has been purposefully omitted while quoting from the original. Thus, choice (C) is the correct answer.

55. **(B)** This passage from Melville's *Moby Dick* contains an allusion in the phrase, "like so many Alexanders." Melville is illustrating the strength and power of whalers ("naked Nantucketers") by alluding and comparing them to Alexander the Great, the famous conqueror who died in 323 B.C.E.

56. **(A)** This passage, which opens James Joyce's *A Portrait of the Artist as a Young Man*, is written in "baby talk" ("moocow," "nicens," "baby tukoo") to convey to readers the age, speech, and mental set of the narrator. While choice (E) does imitate the speech of a character, the voice used is not nearly as discreet as choice (A).

57. **(D)** Nineteenth-century novels of manners employed such themes as the importance (or unimportance) of "good breeding," the elation (and suffocation) caused by society, and the interaction of individuals within the confines of a closed country community (to name just a few). This passage, taken from Jane Austen's *Emma*, mentions "opinions" of other characters, the importance of "beauty" and "accomplishment" (note how Emma sees them as almost saving graces for Mrs. Elton), and the "improvement" of a "country neighborhood."

58. **(B)** This question asks you to judge, from the paragraph given, the type of literature from which the excerpt was taken. The only choice for which any support is given is choice (B), because the names given are Russian. The other choices can be ruled out, because there is nothing in the paragraph to support them as choices. We see no evidence of British terminology or dialect (A), nor are there specific elements of a modern romance (C). Likewise, there is not enough information to determine whether or not this is a short story with existentialist qualities (D). Therefore, you must choose the answer you *can* support, which is choice (B).

59. **(B)** This question asks that you view the picture and decide what type of artwork is pictured. This is a detail of a stained-glass window at Chartres Cathedral (B). The design is two-dimensional, a characteristic which artists of stained glass preferred. Stained glass is also characterized by the fine strips of lead that hold the small pieces of glass in place. These can be seen between the glass pieces in the picture. A mosaic design would have smaller pieces of tile making up the design (D). An oil painting (A)

is characterized by dramatic use of high intensities to spotlight principal figures and deeper shadow for subordinate ones, subtle modeling of figures, and softness of contours. Even in a black-and-white photograph, it is easy to tell that there is little blending or softness in the figures and colors portrayed. Finally, a marble sculpture (C) would be three-dimensional and free standing. Thus, the correct answer is (B).

60. **(E)** Of the five possible answer choices, (A) and (D) use predominantly a black outline on a white background, with (C) being a different medium as a sculpture. Choices (B) and (E) share similar densities of pure black against a white ground. Answer choice (B), however, uses the pale white faces of the figures against the heavy black for an expressive effect; in this case, the technique serves the emotional content of the picture and avoids a purely decorative effect. Only choice (E) contrasts broad areas of pure black with a large field of pure white to establish a flowing linear rhythm and produce a sophisticated decorative result.

61. **(B)** Choices (A), (D), and (E) employ either pure black line on a white background or pure black line with broad areas of flat black. All avoid the use of contrasting textures almost completely, and only choice (B) develop textural effects to any noticeable degree. In choice (C), the sculpture does not employ the use of black and white as do the other works. The predominant effect is that of black line against white, and there is no expressive human content in evidence. Choice (B), a woodblock print, uses the rough gouging to model and texture the grieving human faces, setting them off against the dense black and reinforcing the emotional content of the image.

62. **(A)** Choices (B) and (E) all merge and join the forms on the page into integrated compositions, although in different ways and with differing effects. Only choices (A) and (D) present a number of unconnected images, drawn in fine black line on a white page. The images in choice (D), however, although they are separate and discrete, are arranged in a planned, composed manner which implies a motion to the left and suggests a narrative action of some sort. In contrast, choice (A), a page of sketches from a medieval architect's notebook, presents a random assortment of unrelated subjects and motifs which are composed in no special order and suggest no specific meaning.

63. **(B)** The first two lines tell us that the speaker has been doing some inner questioning and searching. The last two lines are almost a prayer to the sea, a prayer that asks the sea to calm the speaker and "compose (him) to

the end." The line that reads, "Ye who from my childhood up have calmed me" suggests that the sea has been able to calm the speaker before; it is this same calming which the speaker now "passionately desire(s)."

64. **(D)** The "stream of consciousness" technique is a modern invention used by writers to mimic, and, if possible, duplicate, the quick workings of the human mind. This passage from James Joyce's *Ulysses* describes Molly Bloom's thoughts of the character Hugh as she thinks of him: how he slapped her "on my bottom," and how he is an "ignoramus" who "doesn't know poetry from a cabbage." The passage lacks punctuation because (as the technique ascribes) people do not think in properly punctuated sentences. The passage is meant to display how thoughts lead to other thoughts by association.

65. **(A)** Alliteration is a poetic device where writers repeat consonant sounds at the beginning of successive (or almost successive) words. "Fair is foul and foul is fair" is an example of alliteration because of the repeated "f" sound; the same is true for "fog and filthy."

66. **(B)** This question asks you to interpret the passage and look for specific sounds hinted at in the lines. Line 1 refers to the tolling of a bell (A). Line 2 refers to the "lowing herd" or sound of cows (D). Line 3 hints at the footsteps of the plowman as he "plods his weary way" (C); this is the same sound as a man walking (E). There is no mention of the wind, however, so (B) is the correct answer.

67. **(B)** This question asks you to choose the best paraphrase or restatement of the quotation. The correct answer is (B). "We think our fathers fools, so wise we grow," means that as we grow older, we think our fathers are fools and we are wise. "Our wiser sons, no doubt, will think us so," means that our sons will do the same, and thus think of us in the same way. The other choices are misinterpretations of the lines.

68. **(E)** The costuming shown is Elizabethan dress and would be appropriate for most Shakespearean plays (E). The puffing and slashing sleeves, the farthingale skirt and the male's gartered hose are all indicative of this period. Choice (E) is correct.

69. **(D)** You are asked to view the setting of a play and determine which style of scene design has been used. Symbolism (B) is the visualization of a play's idea through special scenic treatment. Expressionism is exaggerated symbolism. It usually distorts the scenic elements (A). Impressionism (C)

attempts to enable the audience to see through the character's eyes. It is usually expressed through exaggeration and contrasts. Since the setting pictured does not use distortion or exaggeration, but is a actual presentation from the Victorian era, we realize it is a realistic setting. Choice (D) is correct.

70. **(A)** The design was by Michelangelo. Although (B) Bramante drew up plans for a new church of St. Peter prior to Michelangelo, his designs were never carried out. (C) Borromini is an architect of the Baroque period and therefore was working after the Renaissance church of St. Peter was constructed. (D) Bernini, also a Baroque-period architect, designed the large elliptical colonnade built in the piazza of St. Peter. (E) Leonardo da Vinci, although living at the time of the early planning of the church, was not involved in the design process.

71. **(C)** A thrust stage provides an intimate space for the audience, whereas a proscenium stage (A) is the "formal" stage most common in American theater. Choice (B) describes an arena stage, the type of stage where Greek dramas were first performed. In this arrangement, the audience encircles the stage. A black box theater (D) has no format and is commonly used for experimental theater performances. A dance arbor (E) is an outdoor theater space using the earth as the stage floor and the sky as the rooftop.

72. **(A)** A proscenium stage has a space separating the audience from the stage; whereas the arena stage (B), thrust stage (C), dance arbor (E), and black box theater (D) all do not have an open space and are less "formal."

73. **(A)** A pragmatist, such as Dewey or James, thinks that truth is a matter of the utility of an idea, its "cash value," as it is sometimes metaphorically put. An Empiricist (B) would stress the origin of true ideas in sensory experience, while a rationalist (C) is someone who sees the origin of true ideas in the mind itself, independently of experience. Thus, (B) and (C) are incorrect. The Correspondence and Coherence theories of truth (D) and (E) are competitors of pragmatism, locating truth not in the success of an idea but in its correspondence with reality or coherence (its "fit") with other ideas.

74. **(B)** Staccato, to play the note detached or separated, is indicated by a dot over or under the note. Choice (B) is correct. Tenuto instructs to play the note for its full value; choice (A) is incorrect. Fortissimo is a dynamic marking to play very loud; choice (C) is not correct. Piano is a dynamic marking, which means to play soft; choice (D) is also incorrect. An "F" would be the dynamic marking for a loud volume; choice (E) is incorrect.

75. **(A)** Comping, which is short for accompaniment, is the style of playing that Count Basie mastered. Often used in jazz, comping had a bounce, syncopation, and flexibility that allowed soloists the freedom to improvise. Choice (A) is correct. Scat singing is also used in jazz. It is a vocal technique that does not use words. This was popularized by Louis Armstrong among others; choice (B) is incorrect. Riffs are short phrases often used as accompaniment; choice (C) is not correct. Figured bass is a notation below the bass line and tells the performer which chords to follow. This technique was incorporated into the composing of Johann Sebastian Bach; choice (D) is incorrect. A ghost note is a jazz technique often used by horn players in which a note is fingered but does not sound; choice (E) is incorrect.

76. **(B)** E flat major has three flats. When building a scale upon E flat, the major pattern is w w $\frac{1}{2}$ w w w $\frac{1}{2}$. This pattern on E flat would result in B flat, E flat, and A flat. This can also be determined by using the Circle of Fifths. Choice (B) is correct. A scale built upon B flat would result in a key signature of B flat and E flat; choice (A) is incorrect. A major scale on F would result in a B flat in the key signature; choice (C) in incorrect. A major scale upon G would result in an F sharp in the very signature; choice (D) is incorrect. The D major scale contains an F sharp and a C sharp; choice (E) is incorrect.

77. **(D)** John is described by the speaker as "practical in the extreme." We are also told that he has "no patience with faith, an intense horror of superstition, and scoffs openly at any talk of things not to be felt and seen and put down in figures." John is concerned with concrete reality, not "romantic felicity" as is the speaker. Choice (D) is the correct answer.

78. **(B)** The speaker says of her story that she "would not say it to a living soul, of course, but this is dead paper and a great relief to my mind." Writing is, for her, an outlet, a way for her to address her problems. Choice (B) is the correct answer.

79. **(C)** When not used to signal direct discourse, quotation marks indicate that the speaker or writer is being sarcastic and that the word being used has a different meaning than its dictionary definition. The fact that "work" (line 26) is in quotation marks tells us that the speaker is being sarcastic about her "occupation." Choice (C) is the correct answer.

80. **(B)** The passage serves to introduce an upcoming story to be told by the narrator. He begins by exclaiming, "there may as well be an end of this!" and then gives a list of reasons why he has finally decided not to "keep my

trouble to myself." He is about to relate an event, or series of events, to his friend, because keeping silent has been "burning [him] rather violently." He is very excited about what he has to say; choice (B) is correct. There is no evidence that the speaker feels guilty, ashamed, sorrowful, or relieved, so (A), (C), (D), and (E) are all incorrect.

81. **(C)** The speaker gives, as one of the reasons for telling his story, "if confession were not good for the soul, though harder than sin to some people, of which I am one," showing that he regards confession as a healthy, although difficult activity. (C) is the correct answer. He never speaks of confession as being unnecessary, nonsensical, impossible, or comical, so (A), (B), (D), and (E) are all incorrect.

82. **(C)** This first stanza sets the tone for the rest of the poem. The poet tells us that this will be a "harmonious ditty," which clues us that the poem will not have a serious tone; therefore, (A) is wrong and (C) is correct. The rhyme scheme for this stanza is a-b-c-b, familiar, and will probably be repeated throughout the poem, so (B) is also incorrect. Choices (D) and (E) feature incorrect rhyme schemes for the stanza, and are, therefore, incorrect as well.

83. **(B)** The building pictured in the example – the contemporary "Beaubourg" art museum and cultural center in Paris – dispenses entirely with the ideas and philosophies of the classical past and with the styles and forms of traditional architecture. It is conceived instead on a huge industrial scale and, rather than projecting an atmosphere of quiet balance and poetic calm, it seeks to involve itself and its visitors in the dynamic life and culture of the modern city. Therefore, rather than concealing its structural and mechanical components behind a finished, exterior wall, the Beaubourg intentionally exposes its "anatomy," using pipes, ducts, tubes, and funnels of a modern industrial plant to reveal both its structure and its functions to the people in attendance. The visitor's ability to perceive the building's processes at work creates the sense that both building and people are part of a huge living organism.

84. **(D)** The jamb statues on the Early Gothic cathedral at Chartres, France (c. 1145-1170 c.e.) draw their subject matter and thematic content not from classical mythology but from Christian ideology and belief. The figure groupings in the three main portals illustrate scenes from the Life and Passion of Christ, such as His birth, the Presentation in the Temple, and, in the center, the Second Coming. However, these scenes are not specifically

arranged in a continuous narrative sequence and do not "tell a story." The sculpture itself, though it covers much of the building's facade, cannot be said to dominate, since it is strictly controlled and contained within the space allotted to it. The static, motionless figures conform closely to their architectural framework and are therefore subordinate to the structural forms of the doorways.

85. **(B)**   The Renaissance sculptor who created the small figure group shown in the example was intent on conveying the physical stresses and strains of two wrestlers in violent conflict. To express the ferocity of the fight, he has exaggerated the tautness of the muscles and the rigid tension in the bodies; to illustrate the climatic moment at which one fighter lifts the other from the ground to break his back, he has shown the brief instant during which the raised figure is balanced against his opponent's stomach. In the viewpoint shown, there is no suggestion of either the rolling motion of a wheel or the flowing of liquid, and there is apparently none of the spiral torsion of a screw. The figures do seem to interlock somewhat like a set of gears, but the simple machine they most resemble is the lever, with the fulcrum located at the balance point between the two men's abdomens.

86. **(D)**   Edgar Degas (1834-1917), the French Impressionist artist who painted the picture shown in the example, was strongly influenced by the ability of the camera to capture a subject in a fleeting moment and in a spontaneous, seemingly unposed manner. In *Viscount Lepic and His Daughters*, 1873, the artist has constructed an off-center composition in which the main subject moves to the right and seems about to exit the picture. Both the viscount and his two young daughters are abruptly cut off at or near the waist, the dog is half-hidden behind one of the children, and the man standing to the left barely enters the picture. This random cropping of objects is reminiscent of a photographic snapshot. Further, the focal center of the picture is located in the empty plaza behind the figures. The painting therefore owes little either to Greek sculpture, which usually represented the full human figure in idealized form, or to Renaissance perspective, which carefully balanced its figures within an illusionistic space. It also shows no apparent debt to the numerous styles of children's book illustration or to the severe abstractions of much primitive art.

87. **(E)**   The example shows the church of St. Michael's at Hildesheim, Germany (c. 1001-1031 C.E.). It is typical of Early Romanesque architecture in its dependence on thick blank walls with little or no ornamental decoration, and in its massing of simple cubic and cylindrical forms. The effect of

this building is less that of a structural framework supporting walls, roofs, and windows, than of a combination of building blocks which have been sectioned and then glued together. Except for the arched shape of the windows, with their tiny glassed areas, the building completely avoids curving forms, while the only diagonals are those of the roof lines, which are functionally necessary but not fundamental to the building's cubic character. Finally, a spectator's ground-level point of view might make this building seem larger and more dramatic, but it, too, is not essential to the architects' conception.

88. **(B)** An elegy is a serious poem lamenting the death of an individual or group of individuals. Passage (B) is Robert Herrick's "Upon His Spaniel Tracy," an elegy which mourns the death of his favorite dog. Thus, passage (B) is the correct answer.

89. **(A)** Enjambment occurs when a line of poetry "runs on" to the next line, causing a slight pause in mid-sentence or thought. Line 3 reads, "This shall my love do, give thy sad death one." The reader is left wondering, "One what?" It is not until line 4 that the poet explains that he will give one "Tear." Thus, choice (A) is the correct answer.

90. **(A)** The speaker of these lines is Berowne, a reluctant student in Shakespeare's *Love's Labor's Lost*. You can discern that the lines are spoken by a student because they are a reaction against study and those who pursue it ("Small have continual plodders won..."). It would be highly unusual for a professor to say such things, and the other three choices are, of course, possible, but not within the limited context of the passage.

91. **(E)** Restated, the lines mean, "Little (small) have those who constantly (continually) plod through their studies gained (won), except (save) for some common, throwaway knowledge (base authority) from others' books." Choice (E) comes closest to this and is thus the correct answer.

92. **(D)** These lines suggest that the astronomers who name "every fixed star" get no more out of their studies than simpletons "that walk and wot not what they are." Choice (D) comes closest to this meaning and is thus the correct answer.

93. **(B)** The meaning of this phrase can be found in the words which follow it: "That give a name to every fixed star." Astronomers are usually responsible for the naming of stars, so choice (B) is correct.

94. **(C)** *King Lear* is the correct answer. This question focuses on the main character in a drama as well as on the dramatic developments caused by his actions. Thus, the focus is on a single character of significant import. This should lead the reader to conclude that the answer focuses on a dramatic figure powerful enough to have a play named after him. Hamlet is a memorable character whose actions are central to the play of the same name. However, three plays in which the name of the play is the same as that of the main character requires a shift to the second level of reasoning: making distinctions among the three. (A) Tartuffe is unveiled as a hypocrite near the end of the play, while Lear's autocratic actions take place near the opening of the play. The same reasoning must be used to eliminate (E) *Waiting for Godot,* as this is a play in which the character of the same name is the person for whom the two characters are waiting. (B) *Measure for Measure* does not focus on a main character but on a group of characters.

95. **(A)** Ethics is the correct answer. Given the limitations of both possible answers and the parameters of the passage, this is the best possible answer. Though both evil and good exist within morality plays, the focus is on the choice one must make between the two. With the exception of (D) diffidence, which is an obvious variance from the other three choices, all other choices, (B) pride, (C) mischief, and (E) sloth, suggest characteristics that are either positive or negative. Only ethics encompasses both aspects; hence, morality concerns ethics.

96. **(B)** Concrete was one of the most significant contributions the ancient Romans made to the history of architecture. Mortar, but not concrete, was used by the (A) ancient Greeks; and the knowledge of concrete as a building material had somehow become lost by (C) the Middle Ages. Concrete was "rediscovered" and widely used once again by (D) the eighteenth century, and of course used almost exclusively in various forms in (E) the twentieth century.

97. **(D)** Isadora Duncan was the first choreographer to rebel against formality and to practice the expression of oneself through free bodily movement. Agnes de Mille (A), Martha Graham (B), Ruth St. Denis (C), and Ted Shawn (E) were choreographers who followed Isadora Duncan's ideas and concepts.

98. **(A)** Reincarnation, as the name implies, presupposes that a soul united with one body can become united with another. This belief in turn assumes that souls and bodies are not only distinct but separable. The view that a person consists of a body and a separable soul is dualism. An eliminative

materialist (B) believes that the soul can be eliminated, that a person is nothing more than a complex material object. Since, on this view, souls do not exist, there can be no "incarnation" of the soul in a body and, hence, no reincarnation. An epiphenomenalist believes that the soul and body are distinct but inseparable, much as the bubbling of a brook is distinct but not separable from the brook. So (C) cannot be correct. Functionalism and behaviorism hold that the soul is really just a kind of state or condition of a body – a functional state or the condition of its behaving in a certain way. Hence, choices (D) and (E) cannot be correct.

99. **(D)** A flat major contains B flat, E flat, A flat, and D flat. This major scale has four flats. This is determined by following the major scale pattern, which is w w $\frac{1}{2}$ w w w $\frac{1}{2}$. Choice (D) is correct. C major contains no sharps or flats; choice (A) is incorrect. F major is found one scale below C major on the Circle of Fifths counterclockwise from C, so as a result it contains one flat, B flat. Choice (B) is incorrect. A minor is parallel to C major, so it also contains no flats or sharps; choice (C) is incorrect. C minor is the relative minor of E flat major which contains three flats; choice (E) is incorrect.

100. **(B)** A chromatic scale is a scale of half steps. Within each octave a scale is divided into 12 notes. For example, between middle C and its octave, a chromatic scale would be all of the white and black keys. Choice (B) is correct. A major scale is a diatonic scale composed of two tetrachords. It follows the pattern w w $\frac{1}{2}$ w w w $\frac{1}{2}$. Choice (A) is not correct. A relative minor scale is composed of the pattern w $\frac{1}{2}$ w w $\frac{1}{2}$ w w. Choice (C) is incorrect. A whole tone scale is composed of all whole steps; choice (D) is incorrect. A blues scale is built on the tonic to a minor third, whole step, half step, minor third, and a whole step. Choice (E) is incorrect.

101. **(D)** Four sixteenth notes are equal to one quarter note. For example, $\frac{1}{4} = \frac{4}{16}$. The quarter note equals one beat: a down beat and an upbeat. This can be simplified into one eighth note on each part of the beat, therefore, two sixteenth notes need to be on the down beat and two on the upbeat in order to equal one full beat. Choice (D) is correct. One sixteenth note, three sixteenth notes, or two sixteenth notes would each only equal a fraction of the quarter note. Choices (A), (B), and (C) are incorrect. Six sixteenth notes would equal one-and-a-half beats; choice (E) is incorrect.

102. **(B)** The passage describes large pieces of machinery coming toward two characters in a boat. The pieces of machinery are propelled by the water, a force of nature, making (B) the correct answer. None of the other conflicts are present in this passage.

103. **(C)** The way in which the passage describes, in detail, the setting, as well as the way in which the focus narrows as the passage proceeds (it moves from an entire neighborhood to a single man) marks it similar in tone and style to the opening stage directions of a play. Choice (C) is correct.

104. **(B)** The fact that this character is known only as "the old man with the hempen beard who sleeps where nobody knows" lends him an air of insignificance – he is a type, not an individual, and is thus unworthy of a specific name. Choice (B) is correct.

105. **(E)** Dante Alighieri's (1265-1321) "The Divine Comedy" is the famous medieval epic of a journey through hell, purgatory, and paradise – replete with unforgettable references to frightening Satanic beasts (including Satan himself) and horrific landscapes. It is also viewed by scholars as Dante's spiritual autobiography – a story with a happy ending in which every person might attain redemption and the vision of God through Christianity. "The Pilgrim's Progress" (A), written 400 years after "The Divine Comedy," is perhaps the closest to Dante's famous epic, in that it also presents an allegory of the life of a Christian in this world. (B) and (C) are roughly of the same time period but of vastly different concerns, and (D), while it deals with giants, is an Anglo-Saxon work which predates Dante by at least five centuries.

106. **(D)** Homer's "Iliad" deals with events leading up to and including the Battle of Troy. His "Odyssey" concerns the hero Odysseus' attempt to return home after having helped win that battle. The voyage – which was delayed by storm, bad luck, and imprisonment – took 20 years. *Rip Van Winkle* (A) does deal with a return to home after approximately the same period of time, but Rip never left his hideaway in the Catskills and, in fact, never knew he was "gone" until he woke up two decades later. *The Wizard of Oz* (B) deals with an almost "instantaneous" departure and return, as Dorothy comes back to Kansas only a few moments after being knocked unconscious as a result of the tornado. *Exodus* (C) deals with the Hebrews coming out of Egypt and their 40 years of subsequent wandering, and (E) *Don Quixote* involves neither a return or a long period of absence.

107. **(B)** The Greek Doric temple pictured in the example illustrates a type of architecture known as post-and-lintel (or *trabeated*) construction, in which long horizontal beams rest atop a series of vertical supports. In the Greek temple, the cylindrical columns act as supports for the large marble "beam" (or the *architrave*), which, in turn, supports the roof. The Doric temple thus achieves an appearance of Classical balance and perfection through the

calculated repetition of a minimum variety of forms. The temple avoids unbroken wall surfaces, instead playing off the solids and voids of the columns and the spaces between, while the only diagonals are those of the triangular front gable (the *pediment*). The building is completely devoid of arches, which were known to the Greeks but were rarely used and gained prominence only in Roman architecture.

108. **(C)**   Two of the examples shown, choices (D) and (E) are profile portraits, in which the sitters do not turn their gazes out of the picture space, thus eliminating any possibility of eye contact with the viewer. Two other examples, choices (A) and (B), show the subjects in nearly full face, but the sitter in choice (A) glances introspectively down to his left, while the subject in choice (B) looks toward us but, with aristocratic remove, keeps his own gaze just out of the line of our view. Only choice (C) presents a subject in full face who looks directly at the viewer with his large, warm eyes. This sarcophagus portrait from Roman Egypt, c. C.E. 160, intent on expressing the warmth and humanity of the deceased subject, not only effected full eye contact with the viewer, but also portrayed the subject's eyes as abnormally large and deep.

109. **(B)**   Neither the clothing, the sitters, the expressions, nor the styles of choices (A) and (C) convey in any specific way that the subjects are aristocrats. Choice (E) appears to be a royal person and is therefore probably an aristocrat, but the painting is highly stylized and abstracted and projects little of the sitter's personality. Only choices (B) and (D) show subjects who are clearly wealthy, well-born, and wellbred. Choice (D), however, is a profile portrait which is so formalized as to be neutral and devoid of expression. Choice (B), by contrast, presents a subject whose rich clothing, haughty posture, elegantly cocked wrists, and, especially, distant expression mark him as a wealthy young man whose circumstances make him superior to most.

110. **(A)**   The two Renaissance portraits, choices (B) and (D), show the forms and features of their subjects as clearly defined, well-modelled, and set within a basically naturalistic space. The portrait in choice (C), too, though painted in a sketchier style, models the forms of the face in a lucid, convincing, realistic manner in order to project the sitter's personality. Only choices (A) and (E) begin to abstract the figure and undermine the conventional sense of form in the search for new pictorial styles. Choice (E), however, stresses the flatness of the design and encloses all of its forms in a bold black outline. Only in choice (A), the *Boy in a Red Vest* by the French

painter Paul Cézanne, is the specific subject less important than the way the artist treats it. Here, the painter breaks the outlines of the figure and disintegrates its forms, linking them with the background space in a new kind of picture construction.

111. **(D)** In the Chinese ink painting shown in the example, the artist exploited the fluid, calligraphic character of the ink-and-brush technique. In rendering the graceful bamboo leaves, he did not attempt to suggest illusionistic three-dimensional space, as a Western artist might, but let his forms lie firmly on the two-dimensional picture plane. Further, he restricted his range of tones to a dense black and one grey, and, even though written script is included in the picture, this isolated image of the bamboo plant does not relate an episode in a story. Instead, the artist has drawn upon years of technical training and practice to create a picture in which both the script and the plant forms act as kind of spontaneous, rhythmic "writing."

112. **(C)** A simile is a literary device which uses the word "like" to compare two often unlike things. "My love is like to ice, and I to fire" suggests that the speaker's love interest is cold to him, while he or she is very much in love with the other.

113. **(D)** Personification is a literary device which gives human characteristics to inanimate objects or animals. In the phrase in choice (D), the moon is given a face which has a "wan" expression, and it is given legs, with which it "climb'st the skies." Thus, the moon has attained human aspects and is therefore personified.

114. **(E)** Apostrophe is the act of addressing someone or something directly in a poem. Choice (E) begins with "Hail to thee, blithe Spirit!" which is the first line of Percy Bysshe Shelley's "To a Skylark." The poet addresses the bird directly at the very start of the poem.

115. **(B)** This passage from Byron's "Don Juan" is an example of mock epic: a poem written in epic style designed to parody and satirize this literary tradition. The playful spirit of the passage ("So that my name of Epic's no misnomer") as well as its larger implications (epics are formulamatic and predictable) mark it, like Chaucer's *The Nun's Priest's Tale*, as a true mock epic.

116. **(D)** The theme of *carpe diem*, Latin for "seize the day," urges people to enjoy their present pleasures and lives, because the future is so uncertain. In Andrew Marvell's "To His Coy Mistress," the speaker is attempting to

seduce his mistress by reasoning with her along these lines. He states that "time's winged chariot" is always near and that, once dead, she will no longer hear his "echoing song."

117. **(C)** A pastoral elegy is, by definition, a poem dealing with rural life which mourns the death of someone. Choice (C), taken from John Milton's "Lycidas," fits this description. It begins with the speaker plucking berries "harsh and crude" because "Lycidas is dead, dead ere his prime." The speaker is comparing the berry, whose leaves are "shattered before the mellowing year," to Lycidas, who also died "ere his prime." (Actually, the poem is about a friend of Milton's, Edward King, who was drowned in the Irish Sea.) The combination of nature and death mark "Lycidas" as a pastoral elegy.

118. **(C)** Blanche DuBois in Tennessee Williams' *A Streetcar Named Desire* and Willy Loman in Arthur Miller's *Death of a Salesman*. Both these characters have become part of American folklore. Therefore, the reader who does not recognize both should be able to make a choice based on recognition of one of the pair.

119. **(E)** A ghost is the correct answer. Though based on a particular passage from a specific play, this question also depends upon the reader's ability to analyze prose. Hamlet, the speaker, is referring to the ghost of his father, the murdered King of Denmark. In these five lines, the speaker establishes clearly that the answer cannot be either (C) or (D), for these are inanimate objects. "Soul" and "it" are key words in line three; "immortal" and the verbs "being," "waves," and "follow" in lines four and five all combine to suggest that the "it" is a ghost. Because "it" is usually not used to refer to human, (B) an opponent, must also be eliminated.

120. **(B)** This is a Romanesque pilgrimage church, characterized most notably by the nave and side aisles, the transept, the ambulatory encircling the apse, and the chapels which radiate from the apse. Pilgrimage churches housed important relics and, in the Middle Ages in Western Europe, faithful Christians made pilgrimages to these churches to view the relics. Churches planned in this manner were designed to accommodate large crowds of people. (A) Early Christian monastic churches were often basilican in plan, but varied widely from one monastery to the next, and did not incorporate such elements as an ambulatory or radiating chapels. A (C) subterranean crypt is a burial chamber located *below* the main body of a church. (D) Gothic cathedrals were often similar in plan to pilgrimage churches, but the strict compartmentalization of the various elements of pilgrimage churches was abandoned in the Gothic period. (E) Centrally planned churches are

those whose components radiate from a central point, unlike the church illustrated in this example, which is designed along a longitudinal axis.

121. **(E)** A group of arm exercises is *port de bras*. Epaulements is (A), alignment is (B), exercises au milieu is (C), and attitude is (D).

122. **(A)** Utilitarianism is the view that the goodness or badness of an action depends on whether it brings about the greatest amount of pleasure or happiness for the most people, compared to its alternatives. Hence, it is consequentialistic. Kant (B) argues that the only good thing is a good will, or that what makes an action right or wrong is the intention behind it, no matter what its consequences. Intuitionism (C) holds that an ethical principle is true if it appears to be true to a person with the necessary insight, independently of its consequences. Both virtue ethics (D) in general and Aristotelian ethics (E), a type of virtue ethics, assert that moral excellence is largely a matter of character and training, not the consequences of action.

123. **(A)** A chord in root position is built upon the root or tonic. From the root, the chord increases by thirds. Therefore, root, 3rd, 5th would be in root position. Choice (A) is correct. A chord built root, 2nd, 5th does not follow the pattern of increasing by thirds; choice (B) is incorrect. A chord built 3rd, 5th, root is considered to be in the first inversion; choice (C) is incorrect. A chord built 5th, root, 3rd is in second inversion; choice (D) is incorrect. A combination of a root, 2nd, 3rd would not produce a chord; choice (E) is incorrect.

124. **(C)** When a *p* is written below the staff, it directs the musician to play "piano" softly. Choice (C) is the correct answer. The dynamic marking ff directs the musician to play fortissimo or very loud; choice (A) is incorrect. Crescendo, notated as cres., directs the musician to gradually increase volume; choice (B) is incorrect. Decrescendo, notated as decres, indicates to gradually play softer; choice (D) is not correct. The abbreviation rit. denotes ritard or to slow down. Choice (E) is incorrect.

125. **(B)** When reading a time signature the top number indicates the number of beats in each measure and the bottom indicates which note receives each beat. So, in $\frac{6}{8}$ there would be six beats in each measure. Choice (B) is correct. There would be four beats in each measure if the time signature were $\frac{4}{4}$; choice (A) is incorrect. There would be three beats in a measure of $\frac{3}{4}$; choice (C) is incorrect. A measure of $\frac{2}{4}$ would contain two beats per measure; choice (D) is incorrect. The eight in $\frac{6}{8}$ represents which note receives one beat, an eighth note; choice (E) is incorrect.

126. **(B)** *A Modest Proposal* is Jonathan Swift's famous tongue-in-cheek extended proposal that the Irish consider eating their young as a solution to poverty and starvation. From the use of the word "Modest" in his title, to the last sentence (a profession of sincerity), Swift emphasizes the true horror of the state to which Ireland had been reduced by the absentee English landlords. Each of the other possibilities is serious in tone: *Everyman* (C) is a morality play; and "Paradise Lost" (A) is an epic of serious religious proportions. *The Way of the World* (D) is an example of a comedy of manners aiming at moral insight; and Cowley's *Lives of the Poets* (E) is a serious critical work.

127. **(A)** Spenser's (1552-1599) "The Faerie Queen" is strongly influenced by Renaissance Neoplatonism and in many ways expresses the spirit of experimentalism that characterized the Elizabethan age. Chaucer's "The Wife of Bath's Tale" (B) was written 200 years before, and, while the "Cantebury Tales" themselves might be considered an adventure, the Wife's tale is usually enjoyed as a bawdy revel. *Gulliver's Travels* (C) is a tale of adventure, but more certainly expresses the spirit of the Enlightenment. "The Rape of the Lock" (D) is based upon a trivial incident when Lord Petre cut off a lock of hair from the head of Arabella Fermor and has been called a "hero-comical poem." "Beowulf," the Anglo-Saxon adventure, was written in the first half of the eighth century (E).

128. **(B)** Upton Sinclair's powerful tract about conditions in Chicago led to Congressional passage of laws that were intended to ensure the health of industrial workers. Dreiser's *Sister Carrie* (C) was written about Chicago at the turn of the century, but did not concern itself with reform. *Main Street* (E) was written by Sinclair Lewis – he and Sinclair are sometimes confused – and is a classic in its own right, but deals with life in a small town in the Midwest. Cather's *My Antonia* (D) deals with frontier life in the Midwest; and Dickens' *Martin Chuzzlewit* (A), written 50 years beforehand, is based on his travels through England and America.

129. **(A)** *Oedipus Rex (Oedipus the King)* is the first in the famous trilogy (*Oedipus at Colonnus* and *Antigone* being the others) by Sophocles in which the Greek concept "pride going before a fall" (hubris), is presented through a plot that still shocks and surprises. Oedipus' hubris was not that he unknowingly sinned, but that he never considered that the King of Thebes could have been the "contagion" that was destroying his kingdom. *Tiger at the Gates* (B) and *Zorba the Greek* (C) are minor works with Greek

themes. The "Aeneid" (D) was written by the Roman Virgil, and Dante's work "Il Purgatorio" (E) is of medieval origin.

130. **(D)** Shakespeare's *Hamlet* is both of Elizabethan origin and deals with the plot as described. Hamlet is famous for this speech that ends: "Thus, conscience doth make cowards of us all." The character Hamlet vacillates between inaction and plans to murder his uncle – so much so that the ghost of his father must appear to prod him on to revenge. The ghost's message is that, by delaying revenge, Hamlet is denying his father and Denmark proper justice for the heinous deeds that the king's brother has committed. *Macbeth* (C), while written in the same period, has a markedly different plot. *Twelve Angry Men* (A) and *Inherit the Wind* (B), while they deal with themes of justice, are of contemporary origin. *Rosencrantz* (E) is contemporary, though it purports to be an extension of the plot of Hamlet.

131. **(A)** *Target with Four Faces* (1955) is by Jasper Johns. This piece has none of the gestural mark-making crucial to an abstract expressionist painting. It also uses a recognizable image, a target and four plaster casts of faces. This piece has elements of surrealism and pop but is a post-expressionist painting historically and stylistically. (B) is incorrect because it is a famous abstract expressionist painting, *The Voyage* (1949) by Robert Motherwell. (C) is incorrect, it is a typical abstract expressionist painting by Franz Kline, *New York* (1953). (D) is incorrect because only (A) is not an abstract expressionist painting. (E) is incorrect because (A) is not an abstract expressionist painting.

132. **(A)** Mixed media is a term that describes work that incorporates more materials than just the conventional paint and canvas. In this piece, Johns is mixing the media of wood, plaster, newspaper (underneath the target), and encaustic (oil paint mixed with beeswax). (B) is incorrect because Motherwell has only used oil paint on canvas in this piece. (C) is incorrect because Kline has used only oil paint on canvas in this piece. (D) is incorrect because only (A) is a mixed media piece. (E) is incorrect because (A) is a mixed media piece.

133. **(A)** *Target with Four Faces* (1955) is one of Johns' most famous works and one of the most famous works of the second half of the twentieth century and should be familiar to students. It has Johns' deadpan rendition of a common image but transformed in a way so that its meaning becomes mysterious. (B) is incorrect because it is by Robert Motherwell, one of the most famous of the abstract expressionists. (C) is incorrect because it is by

Franz Kline, one of the most famous of the abstract expressionists. (D) is incorrect because only (A) is by Johns. (E) is incorrect because (A) is by Jasper Johns.

134. **(D)** This question tests your ability to recognize and identify renowned sculptors and their works. Choice (D) is correct, as this shows *The Thinker* by Auguste Rodin, the French sculptor of bronze and marble figures, considered by some critics to be the greatest portraitist in the history of sculpture. Donatello's *St. George* (A), Lorenzo Ghiberti's *St. John the Baptist* (B) and Nanni di Banco's *Quattro Santi Coronati* (C) are examples of renowned sculptures from the Renaissance period. Jacques Lipchitz's *Figure* exemplifies a style based on Cubism.

135. **(D)** The Egyptian Temple of Horus, c. 212 B.C.E., pictured in the example displays elements typical of the monumental architecture which developed during Egypt's Old Kingdom period (c. 2600-2100 B.C.E.) and continued until Egypt became a province of the Roman Empire (c. 31 B.C.E.). This architecture achieved an effect of imposing grandeur and durability through the use of simple, solid geometric forms, constructed on an overwhelming scale and laid out with exacting symmetry. The Temple of Horus avoids any emphasis on horizontal lines, and relies instead on the sloping outer walls to visually "pull" the massive building to the ground and make it seem immovable and eternal. Additionally, although the temple carries minor ornamental detail, displays huge reliefs of figures, and is set within a large open courtyard, all of these elements are secondary to the massive character of the building itself.

136. **(B)** The passage, taken from Jonathan Swift's "Description of a City Shower," is satiric in that it attacks, with humor, a subject or practice which the poet finds ridiculous; in this case, it is the practice of assigning meaning to seemingly "unrelated" occurrences to foretell the weather. Swift is mocking those who feel that such things as a cat which stops chasing its tail, the sewer letting out a "double stink," or even the raging of a "hollow tooth" could "foretell the hour... when to dread a shower."

137. **(D)** The phrase is certainly sarcastic because in this passage Swift is mocking those who feel that such things as sewers and "old aches" can foretell the weather; "By sure prognostics," then, comes to mean exactly the opposite, i.e., these "signs" foretell nothing! This phrase, like the rest of the passage, is also playful in tone, not angry as choice (C) states. Thus, choice (D), which covers both (A) and (B), is correct.

138. **(D)**   This poem, written by William S. Gilbert in 1882, is a satiric look at the ineffectuality of the British Parliament and its inability (in the poet's opinion) to do anything worthwhile. Phrases such as "The House of Peers made no pretense / To intellectual eminence" and "The House of Peers, throughout the war, / Did nothing in particular, / And did it very well" show the author's disdain for the noble men who inherited their Parliament seats and had no real interest in the political goings-on of England. The fact that, as the poet mentions, Britain becomes an empire in spite of the House of Peers adds to the satiric yet humorous tone of the poem.

139. **(C)**   The satire in the poem is evident in the author's depiction of the success of Britain in spite of the ineffectual "House of Peers," and the satire is given a prophetic nature as the author wonders if the same success will continue, as if the Parliament will always be useless. The poem certainly does not laud (praise) the Parliament (A), and the poet is not satisfied (D) with the House's past performances. The poem is not a parody (B), and although the poet seems proud of England's successes, the poem is not patriotic in its tone (E).

140. **(E)**   This often-used expression is from Sophocles' *Oedipus the King*, the Greek tragedy. Concerned that Oedipus is about to learn the terrible truth about his parentage, Jocasta urges him to stop making further inquiries – to "Let Sleeping Dogs Lie."

ANSWER SHEETS

Practice Test 1
Practice Test 2

PRACTICE TEST 1

Answer Sheet

1. Ⓐ Ⓑ Ⓒ Ⓓ Ⓔ	27. Ⓐ Ⓑ Ⓒ Ⓓ Ⓔ	53. Ⓐ Ⓑ Ⓒ Ⓓ Ⓔ
2. Ⓐ Ⓑ Ⓒ Ⓓ Ⓔ	28. Ⓐ Ⓑ Ⓒ Ⓓ Ⓔ	54. Ⓐ Ⓑ Ⓒ Ⓓ Ⓔ
3. Ⓐ Ⓑ Ⓒ Ⓓ Ⓔ	29. Ⓐ Ⓑ Ⓒ Ⓓ Ⓔ	55. Ⓐ Ⓑ Ⓒ Ⓓ Ⓔ
4. Ⓐ Ⓑ Ⓒ Ⓓ Ⓔ	30. Ⓐ Ⓑ Ⓒ Ⓓ Ⓔ	56. Ⓐ Ⓑ Ⓒ Ⓓ Ⓔ
5. Ⓐ Ⓑ Ⓒ Ⓓ Ⓔ	31. Ⓐ Ⓑ Ⓒ Ⓓ Ⓔ	57. Ⓐ Ⓑ Ⓒ Ⓓ Ⓔ
6. Ⓐ Ⓑ Ⓒ Ⓓ Ⓔ	32. Ⓐ Ⓑ Ⓒ Ⓓ Ⓔ	58. Ⓐ Ⓑ Ⓒ Ⓓ Ⓔ
7. Ⓐ Ⓑ Ⓒ Ⓓ Ⓔ	33. Ⓐ Ⓑ Ⓒ Ⓓ Ⓔ	59. Ⓐ Ⓑ Ⓒ Ⓓ Ⓔ
8. Ⓐ Ⓑ Ⓒ Ⓓ Ⓔ	34. Ⓐ Ⓑ Ⓒ Ⓓ Ⓔ	60. Ⓐ Ⓑ Ⓒ Ⓓ Ⓔ
9. Ⓐ Ⓑ Ⓒ Ⓓ Ⓔ	35. Ⓐ Ⓑ Ⓒ Ⓓ Ⓔ	61. Ⓐ Ⓑ Ⓒ Ⓓ Ⓔ
10. Ⓐ Ⓑ Ⓒ Ⓓ Ⓔ	36. Ⓐ Ⓑ Ⓒ Ⓓ Ⓔ	62. Ⓐ Ⓑ Ⓒ Ⓓ Ⓔ
11. Ⓐ Ⓑ Ⓒ Ⓓ Ⓔ	37. Ⓐ Ⓑ Ⓒ Ⓓ Ⓔ	63. Ⓐ Ⓑ Ⓒ Ⓓ Ⓔ
12. Ⓐ Ⓑ Ⓒ Ⓓ Ⓔ	38. Ⓐ Ⓑ Ⓒ Ⓓ Ⓔ	64. Ⓐ Ⓑ Ⓒ Ⓓ Ⓔ
13. Ⓐ Ⓑ Ⓒ Ⓓ Ⓔ	39. Ⓐ Ⓑ Ⓒ Ⓓ Ⓔ	65. Ⓐ Ⓑ Ⓒ Ⓓ Ⓔ
14. Ⓐ Ⓑ Ⓒ Ⓓ Ⓔ	40. Ⓐ Ⓑ Ⓒ Ⓓ Ⓔ	66. Ⓐ Ⓑ Ⓒ Ⓓ Ⓔ
15. Ⓐ Ⓑ Ⓒ Ⓓ Ⓔ	41. Ⓐ Ⓑ Ⓒ Ⓓ Ⓔ	67. Ⓐ Ⓑ Ⓒ Ⓓ Ⓔ
16. Ⓐ Ⓑ Ⓒ Ⓓ Ⓔ	42. Ⓐ Ⓑ Ⓒ Ⓓ Ⓔ	68. Ⓐ Ⓑ Ⓒ Ⓓ Ⓔ
17. Ⓐ Ⓑ Ⓒ Ⓓ Ⓔ	43. Ⓐ Ⓑ Ⓒ Ⓓ Ⓔ	69. Ⓐ Ⓑ Ⓒ Ⓓ Ⓔ
18. Ⓐ Ⓑ Ⓒ Ⓓ Ⓔ	44. Ⓐ Ⓑ Ⓒ Ⓓ Ⓔ	70. Ⓐ Ⓑ Ⓒ Ⓓ Ⓔ
19. Ⓐ Ⓑ Ⓒ Ⓓ Ⓔ	45. Ⓐ Ⓑ Ⓒ Ⓓ Ⓔ	71. Ⓐ Ⓑ Ⓒ Ⓓ Ⓔ
20. Ⓐ Ⓑ Ⓒ Ⓓ Ⓔ	46. Ⓐ Ⓑ Ⓒ Ⓓ Ⓔ	72. Ⓐ Ⓑ Ⓒ Ⓓ Ⓔ
21. Ⓐ Ⓑ Ⓒ Ⓓ Ⓔ	47. Ⓐ Ⓑ Ⓒ Ⓓ Ⓔ	73. Ⓐ Ⓑ Ⓒ Ⓓ Ⓔ
22. Ⓐ Ⓑ Ⓒ Ⓓ Ⓔ	48. Ⓐ Ⓑ Ⓒ Ⓓ Ⓔ	74. Ⓐ Ⓑ Ⓒ Ⓓ Ⓔ
23. Ⓐ Ⓑ Ⓒ Ⓓ Ⓔ	49. Ⓐ Ⓑ Ⓒ Ⓓ Ⓔ	75. Ⓐ Ⓑ Ⓒ Ⓓ Ⓔ
24. Ⓐ Ⓑ Ⓒ Ⓓ Ⓔ	50. Ⓐ Ⓑ Ⓒ Ⓓ Ⓔ	76. Ⓐ Ⓑ Ⓒ Ⓓ Ⓔ
25. Ⓐ Ⓑ Ⓒ Ⓓ Ⓔ	51. Ⓐ Ⓑ Ⓒ Ⓓ Ⓔ	77. Ⓐ Ⓑ Ⓒ Ⓓ Ⓔ
26. Ⓐ Ⓑ Ⓒ Ⓓ Ⓔ	52. Ⓐ Ⓑ Ⓒ Ⓓ Ⓔ	78. Ⓐ Ⓑ Ⓒ Ⓓ Ⓔ

(Continued)

PRACTICE TEST 1

Answer Sheet

79. Ⓐ Ⓑ Ⓒ Ⓓ Ⓔ	100. Ⓐ Ⓑ Ⓒ Ⓓ Ⓔ	121. Ⓐ Ⓑ Ⓒ Ⓓ Ⓔ
80. Ⓐ Ⓑ Ⓒ Ⓓ Ⓔ	101. Ⓐ Ⓑ Ⓒ Ⓓ Ⓔ	122. Ⓐ Ⓑ Ⓒ Ⓓ Ⓔ
81. Ⓐ Ⓑ Ⓒ Ⓓ Ⓔ	102. Ⓐ Ⓑ Ⓒ Ⓓ Ⓔ	123. Ⓐ Ⓑ Ⓒ Ⓓ Ⓔ
82. Ⓐ Ⓑ Ⓒ Ⓓ Ⓔ	103. Ⓐ Ⓑ Ⓒ Ⓓ Ⓔ	124. Ⓐ Ⓑ Ⓒ Ⓓ Ⓔ
83. Ⓐ Ⓑ Ⓒ Ⓓ Ⓔ	104. Ⓐ Ⓑ Ⓒ Ⓓ Ⓔ	125. Ⓐ Ⓑ Ⓒ Ⓓ Ⓔ
84. Ⓐ Ⓑ Ⓒ Ⓓ Ⓔ	105. Ⓐ Ⓑ Ⓒ Ⓓ Ⓔ	126. Ⓐ Ⓑ Ⓒ Ⓓ Ⓔ
85. Ⓐ Ⓑ Ⓒ Ⓓ Ⓔ	106. Ⓐ Ⓑ Ⓒ Ⓓ Ⓔ	127. Ⓐ Ⓑ Ⓒ Ⓓ Ⓔ
86. Ⓐ Ⓑ Ⓒ Ⓓ Ⓔ	107. Ⓐ Ⓑ Ⓒ Ⓓ Ⓔ	128. Ⓐ Ⓑ Ⓒ Ⓓ Ⓔ
87. Ⓐ Ⓑ Ⓒ Ⓓ Ⓔ	108. Ⓐ Ⓑ Ⓒ Ⓓ Ⓔ	129. Ⓐ Ⓑ Ⓒ Ⓓ Ⓔ
88. Ⓐ Ⓑ Ⓒ Ⓓ Ⓔ	109. Ⓐ Ⓑ Ⓒ Ⓓ Ⓔ	130. Ⓐ Ⓑ Ⓒ Ⓓ Ⓔ
89. Ⓐ Ⓑ Ⓒ Ⓓ Ⓔ	110. Ⓐ Ⓑ Ⓒ Ⓓ Ⓔ	131. Ⓐ Ⓑ Ⓒ Ⓓ Ⓔ
90. Ⓐ Ⓑ Ⓒ Ⓓ Ⓔ	111. Ⓐ Ⓑ Ⓒ Ⓓ Ⓔ	132. Ⓐ Ⓑ Ⓒ Ⓓ Ⓔ
91. Ⓐ Ⓑ Ⓒ Ⓓ Ⓔ	112. Ⓐ Ⓑ Ⓒ Ⓓ Ⓔ	133. Ⓐ Ⓑ Ⓒ Ⓓ Ⓔ
92. Ⓐ Ⓑ Ⓒ Ⓓ Ⓔ	113. Ⓐ Ⓑ Ⓒ Ⓓ Ⓔ	134. Ⓐ Ⓑ Ⓒ Ⓓ Ⓔ
93. Ⓐ Ⓑ Ⓒ Ⓓ Ⓔ	114. Ⓐ Ⓑ Ⓒ Ⓓ Ⓔ	135. Ⓐ Ⓑ Ⓒ Ⓓ Ⓔ
94. Ⓐ Ⓑ Ⓒ Ⓓ Ⓔ	115. Ⓐ Ⓑ Ⓒ Ⓓ Ⓔ	136. Ⓐ Ⓑ Ⓒ Ⓓ Ⓔ
95. Ⓐ Ⓑ Ⓒ Ⓓ Ⓔ	116. Ⓐ Ⓑ Ⓒ Ⓓ Ⓔ	137. Ⓐ Ⓑ Ⓒ Ⓓ Ⓔ
96. Ⓐ Ⓑ Ⓒ Ⓓ Ⓔ	117. Ⓐ Ⓑ Ⓒ Ⓓ Ⓔ	138. Ⓐ Ⓑ Ⓒ Ⓓ Ⓔ
97. Ⓐ Ⓑ Ⓒ Ⓓ Ⓔ	118. Ⓐ Ⓑ Ⓒ Ⓓ Ⓔ	139. Ⓐ Ⓑ Ⓒ Ⓓ Ⓔ
98. Ⓐ Ⓑ Ⓒ Ⓓ Ⓔ	119. Ⓐ Ⓑ Ⓒ Ⓓ Ⓔ	140. Ⓐ Ⓑ Ⓒ Ⓓ Ⓔ
99. Ⓐ Ⓑ Ⓒ Ⓓ Ⓔ	120. Ⓐ Ⓑ Ⓒ Ⓓ Ⓔ	

PRACTICE TEST 2

Answer Sheet

1.	Ⓐ Ⓑ Ⓒ Ⓓ Ⓔ	27.	Ⓐ Ⓑ Ⓒ Ⓓ Ⓔ	53.	Ⓐ Ⓑ Ⓒ Ⓓ Ⓔ
2.	Ⓐ Ⓑ Ⓒ Ⓓ Ⓔ	28.	Ⓐ Ⓑ Ⓒ Ⓓ Ⓔ	54.	Ⓐ Ⓑ Ⓒ Ⓓ Ⓔ
3.	Ⓐ Ⓑ Ⓒ Ⓓ Ⓔ	29.	Ⓐ Ⓑ Ⓒ Ⓓ Ⓔ	55.	Ⓐ Ⓑ Ⓒ Ⓓ Ⓔ
4.	Ⓐ Ⓑ Ⓒ Ⓓ Ⓔ	30.	Ⓐ Ⓑ Ⓒ Ⓓ Ⓔ	56.	Ⓐ Ⓑ Ⓒ Ⓓ Ⓔ
5.	Ⓐ Ⓑ Ⓒ Ⓓ Ⓔ	31.	Ⓐ Ⓑ Ⓒ Ⓓ Ⓔ	57.	Ⓐ Ⓑ Ⓒ Ⓓ Ⓔ
6.	Ⓐ Ⓑ Ⓒ Ⓓ Ⓔ	32.	Ⓐ Ⓑ Ⓒ Ⓓ Ⓔ	58.	Ⓐ Ⓑ Ⓒ Ⓓ Ⓔ
7.	Ⓐ Ⓑ Ⓒ Ⓓ Ⓔ	33.	Ⓐ Ⓑ Ⓒ Ⓓ Ⓔ	59.	Ⓐ Ⓑ Ⓒ Ⓓ Ⓔ
8.	Ⓐ Ⓑ Ⓒ Ⓓ Ⓔ	34.	Ⓐ Ⓑ Ⓒ Ⓓ Ⓔ	60.	Ⓐ Ⓑ Ⓒ Ⓓ Ⓔ
9.	Ⓐ Ⓑ Ⓒ Ⓓ Ⓔ	35.	Ⓐ Ⓑ Ⓒ Ⓓ Ⓔ	61.	Ⓐ Ⓑ Ⓒ Ⓓ Ⓔ
10.	Ⓐ Ⓑ Ⓒ Ⓓ Ⓔ	36.	Ⓐ Ⓑ Ⓒ Ⓓ Ⓔ	62.	Ⓐ Ⓑ Ⓒ Ⓓ Ⓔ
11.	Ⓐ Ⓑ Ⓒ Ⓓ Ⓔ	37.	Ⓐ Ⓑ Ⓒ Ⓓ Ⓔ	63.	Ⓐ Ⓑ Ⓒ Ⓓ Ⓔ
12.	Ⓐ Ⓑ Ⓒ Ⓓ Ⓔ	38.	Ⓐ Ⓑ Ⓒ Ⓓ Ⓔ	64.	Ⓐ Ⓑ Ⓒ Ⓓ Ⓔ
13.	Ⓐ Ⓑ Ⓒ Ⓓ Ⓔ	39.	Ⓐ Ⓑ Ⓒ Ⓓ Ⓔ	65.	Ⓐ Ⓑ Ⓒ Ⓓ Ⓔ
14.	Ⓐ Ⓑ Ⓒ Ⓓ Ⓔ	40.	Ⓐ Ⓑ Ⓒ Ⓓ Ⓔ	66.	Ⓐ Ⓑ Ⓒ Ⓓ Ⓔ
15.	Ⓐ Ⓑ Ⓒ Ⓓ Ⓔ	41.	Ⓐ Ⓑ Ⓒ Ⓓ Ⓔ	67.	Ⓐ Ⓑ Ⓒ Ⓓ Ⓔ
16.	Ⓐ Ⓑ Ⓒ Ⓓ Ⓔ	42.	Ⓐ Ⓑ Ⓒ Ⓓ Ⓔ	68.	Ⓐ Ⓑ Ⓒ Ⓓ Ⓔ
17.	Ⓐ Ⓑ Ⓒ Ⓓ Ⓔ	43.	Ⓐ Ⓑ Ⓒ Ⓓ Ⓔ	69.	Ⓐ Ⓑ Ⓒ Ⓓ Ⓔ
18.	Ⓐ Ⓑ Ⓒ Ⓓ Ⓔ	44.	Ⓐ Ⓑ Ⓒ Ⓓ Ⓔ	70.	Ⓐ Ⓑ Ⓒ Ⓓ Ⓔ
19.	Ⓐ Ⓑ Ⓒ Ⓓ Ⓔ	45.	Ⓐ Ⓑ Ⓒ Ⓓ Ⓔ	71.	Ⓐ Ⓑ Ⓒ Ⓓ Ⓔ
20.	Ⓐ Ⓑ Ⓒ Ⓓ Ⓔ	46.	Ⓐ Ⓑ Ⓒ Ⓓ Ⓔ	72.	Ⓐ Ⓑ Ⓒ Ⓓ Ⓔ
21.	Ⓐ Ⓑ Ⓒ Ⓓ Ⓔ	47.	Ⓐ Ⓑ Ⓒ Ⓓ Ⓔ	73.	Ⓐ Ⓑ Ⓒ Ⓓ Ⓔ
22.	Ⓐ Ⓑ Ⓒ Ⓓ Ⓔ	48.	Ⓐ Ⓑ Ⓒ Ⓓ Ⓔ	74.	Ⓐ Ⓑ Ⓒ Ⓓ Ⓔ
23.	Ⓐ Ⓑ Ⓒ Ⓓ Ⓔ	49.	Ⓐ Ⓑ Ⓒ Ⓓ Ⓔ	75.	Ⓐ Ⓑ Ⓒ Ⓓ Ⓔ
24.	Ⓐ Ⓑ Ⓒ Ⓓ Ⓔ	50.	Ⓐ Ⓑ Ⓒ Ⓓ Ⓔ	76.	Ⓐ Ⓑ Ⓒ Ⓓ Ⓔ
25.	Ⓐ Ⓑ Ⓒ Ⓓ Ⓔ	51.	Ⓐ Ⓑ Ⓒ Ⓓ Ⓔ	77.	Ⓐ Ⓑ Ⓒ Ⓓ Ⓔ
26.	Ⓐ Ⓑ Ⓒ Ⓓ Ⓔ	52.	Ⓐ Ⓑ Ⓒ Ⓓ Ⓔ	78.	Ⓐ Ⓑ Ⓒ Ⓓ Ⓔ

(Continued)

PRACTICE TEST 2

Answer Sheet

79. Ⓐ Ⓑ Ⓒ Ⓓ Ⓔ	100. Ⓐ Ⓑ Ⓒ Ⓓ Ⓔ	121. Ⓐ Ⓑ Ⓒ Ⓓ Ⓔ
80. Ⓐ Ⓑ Ⓒ Ⓓ Ⓔ	101. Ⓐ Ⓑ Ⓒ Ⓓ Ⓔ	122. Ⓐ Ⓑ Ⓒ Ⓓ Ⓔ
81. Ⓐ Ⓑ Ⓒ Ⓓ Ⓔ	102. Ⓐ Ⓑ Ⓒ Ⓓ Ⓔ	123. Ⓐ Ⓑ Ⓒ Ⓓ Ⓔ
82. Ⓐ Ⓑ Ⓒ Ⓓ Ⓔ	103. Ⓐ Ⓑ Ⓒ Ⓓ Ⓔ	124. Ⓐ Ⓑ Ⓒ Ⓓ Ⓔ
83. Ⓐ Ⓑ Ⓒ Ⓓ Ⓔ	104. Ⓐ Ⓑ Ⓒ Ⓓ Ⓔ	125. Ⓐ Ⓑ Ⓒ Ⓓ Ⓔ
84. Ⓐ Ⓑ Ⓒ Ⓓ Ⓔ	105. Ⓐ Ⓑ Ⓒ Ⓓ Ⓔ	126. Ⓐ Ⓑ Ⓒ Ⓓ Ⓔ
85. Ⓐ Ⓑ Ⓒ Ⓓ Ⓔ	106. Ⓐ Ⓑ Ⓒ Ⓓ Ⓔ	127. Ⓐ Ⓑ Ⓒ Ⓓ Ⓔ
86. Ⓐ Ⓑ Ⓒ Ⓓ Ⓔ	107. Ⓐ Ⓑ Ⓒ Ⓓ Ⓔ	128. Ⓐ Ⓑ Ⓒ Ⓓ Ⓔ
87. Ⓐ Ⓑ Ⓒ Ⓓ Ⓔ	108. Ⓐ Ⓑ Ⓒ Ⓓ Ⓔ	129. Ⓐ Ⓑ Ⓒ Ⓓ Ⓔ
88. Ⓐ Ⓑ Ⓒ Ⓓ Ⓔ	109. Ⓐ Ⓑ Ⓒ Ⓓ Ⓔ	130. Ⓐ Ⓑ Ⓒ Ⓓ Ⓔ
89. Ⓐ Ⓑ Ⓒ Ⓓ Ⓔ	110. Ⓐ Ⓑ Ⓒ Ⓓ Ⓔ	131. Ⓐ Ⓑ Ⓒ Ⓓ Ⓔ
90. Ⓐ Ⓑ Ⓒ Ⓓ Ⓔ	111. Ⓐ Ⓑ Ⓒ Ⓓ Ⓔ	132. Ⓐ Ⓑ Ⓒ Ⓓ Ⓔ
91. Ⓐ Ⓑ Ⓒ Ⓓ Ⓔ	112. Ⓐ Ⓑ Ⓒ Ⓓ Ⓔ	133. Ⓐ Ⓑ Ⓒ Ⓓ Ⓔ
92. Ⓐ Ⓑ Ⓒ Ⓓ Ⓔ	113. Ⓐ Ⓑ Ⓒ Ⓓ Ⓔ	134. Ⓐ Ⓑ Ⓒ Ⓓ Ⓔ
93. Ⓐ Ⓑ Ⓒ Ⓓ Ⓔ	114. Ⓐ Ⓑ Ⓒ Ⓓ Ⓔ	135. Ⓐ Ⓑ Ⓒ Ⓓ Ⓔ
94. Ⓐ Ⓑ Ⓒ Ⓓ Ⓔ	115. Ⓐ Ⓑ Ⓒ Ⓓ Ⓔ	136. Ⓐ Ⓑ Ⓒ Ⓓ Ⓔ
95. Ⓐ Ⓑ Ⓒ Ⓓ Ⓔ	116. Ⓐ Ⓑ Ⓒ Ⓓ Ⓔ	137. Ⓐ Ⓑ Ⓒ Ⓓ Ⓔ
96. Ⓐ Ⓑ Ⓒ Ⓓ Ⓔ	117. Ⓐ Ⓑ Ⓒ Ⓓ Ⓔ	138. Ⓐ Ⓑ Ⓒ Ⓓ Ⓔ
97. Ⓐ Ⓑ Ⓒ Ⓓ Ⓔ	118. Ⓐ Ⓑ Ⓒ Ⓓ Ⓔ	139. Ⓐ Ⓑ Ⓒ Ⓓ Ⓔ
98. Ⓐ Ⓑ Ⓒ Ⓓ Ⓔ	119. Ⓐ Ⓑ Ⓒ Ⓓ Ⓔ	140. Ⓐ Ⓑ Ⓒ Ⓓ Ⓔ
99. Ⓐ Ⓑ Ⓒ Ⓓ Ⓔ	120. Ⓐ Ⓑ Ⓒ Ⓓ Ⓔ	

Glossary

IMPORTANT LITERARY FIGURES AND THEIR MAJOR WORKS

Ancient Greece and Rome

Homer
(ca. ninth century B.C.E.)
Odyssey, Iliad
—Products of a non-literate culture. First works of Western literature.

Sappho
(ca. 612 B.C.E.—?)
Verse fragments
—Early Greek poetry.

Aeschylus
(525 B.C.E.–456 B.C.E.)
Oresteia (Agamemnon, Choephori, and *Eumenides)*
—Responsible for the origin and development of Greek drama; introduced second speaking character and concept of conflict.

Sophocles
(496 B.C.E.–406 B.C.E.)
Oedipus Tyrannus, Antigone, Electra
—Added third speaking character and moved Greek drama further from religious commentary to more basic human interaction.

Euripides
(485 B.C.E.–405 B.C.E.)
The Trojan Women, Helen, The Bacchae
—Chiefly responsible for introducing the technique of *deus ex machina*.

Aristophanes
(450 B.C.E.–385 B.C.E.)
Lysistrata, The Clouds, The Birds
—Considered the father of Greek comedy.

Plato
(428 B.C.E.–399 B.C.E.)
Republic, Apology, Symposium
—Father of Western philosophy.

Aristotle
(384 B.C.E.–322 B.C.E.)
The Poetics
—Introduced and popularized the concept of literary criticism.

Virgil
(70 B.C.E.–19 B.C.E.)
The Aeneid
—(Publius Vergilius Maro) Popularized the pastoral poem and the concept of civic virtue.

Ovid
(43 B.C.E.–18 C.E.)
Metamorphoses, Love's Remedy
—(Publius Ovidius Naso) Brought erotic verse to popularity.

The Middle Ages and the Renaissance

Dante Alighieri
(1265–1321)
Divine Comedy (The Inferno, Purgatorio, Paridiso)
—Considered to have founded modern European literature; perfected "terza rima" (rhyme in threes).

Giovanni Boccaccio
(1313–1375)
The Decameron
—Introduced the use of the vernacular in classically focused literature.

Francesco Petrarch
(1304–1374)
The Canzoniere
—His works provided the basis for love poetry and popularized the theme of humanism.

Geoffrey Chaucer

(1340–1400)

The Canterbury Tales, Troilus and Criseyde
 —Chiefly responsible for bringing literature to the middle class.

Nicolo Machiavelli

(1469–1527)

The Prince, La Mandragola
 —*The Prince* outlined a governmental structure based on the self-interest of the ruler. Such rule is still called Machiavellian.

François Rabelais

(1494–1553)

Gargantua, Pantagruel
 —Introduced satiric narrative.

Miguel de Cervantes Saavedra

(1547–1616)

Don Quixote
 —Wrote the first modern novel.

Edmund Spenser

(1552–1599)

The Faerie Queen, Amoretti
 —Popularized the use of allegory.

Francis Bacon

(1561–1626)

Essays, *The New Atlantis*
 —Founder of the inductive method of modern science and philosophical writings about science.

Christopher Marlowe

(1564–1593)

The Tragedy of Doctor Faustus, Edward the Second
 —Author of first real historical drama and first English tragedy.

William Shakespeare

(1564–1616)

Hamlet, King Lear, Macbeth, Romeo and Juliet, Twelfth Night, Richard III, Julius Caesar, Much Ado About Nothing, Sonnets
 —Considered the greatest English poet and dramatist.

Ben Jonson

(1573–1637)

Every Man in His Humour
 —English playwright.

John Milton

(1608–1674)

Paradise Lost, Paradise Regained
 —Puritan poet noted for allegorical religious epics.

The Neoclassical Period

Molière (Jean-Baptiste Poquelin)

(1622–1673)

Don Juan, Tartuffe, The Misanthrope
 —Perfected literary conversation and introduced everyday speech to theater.

John Dryden

(1631–1700)

Alexander's Feast, Heroic Stanzas
 —Influential in establishing the heroic couplet.

Jean Racine

(1639–1699)

Andromaque, Bernice & Phaedre
 —Renowned for lyric poetry based on Greek and Roman literature.

The Enlightenment

Jonathan Swift

(1667–1745)

Gulliver's Travels, Tale of a Tub
 —Noted for his direct style, clear, sharp prose, and critical wit.

Joseph Addison

(1672–1719)

The Tattler, The Spectator, Cato
 — Outstanding poet, critic, and playwright whose numerous essays marked political free thinking of his time.

Alexander Pope

(1688–1744)

The Dunciad, The Rape of the Lock
 —Classicist and wit who formulated rules for poetry and satirized British social circles.

Voltaire (François-Marie Arouet)

(1694–1778)

Candide, Zadig
 —Progressive philosopher and free thinker best known for synthesizing French and English critical theory.

Benjamin Franklin

(1706–1790)

Poor Richard's Almanac, Observations on the Increase of Mankind, numerous essays and state papers
  —Scientist, educator, abolitionist, philosopher, economist, political theorist, and statesman who defined the colonial New World in his writings; principal figure of the American Enlightenment.

Jean Jacques Rousseau

(1712–1778)

Social Contract
  —Libertine whose focused prose inspired the French Revolution.

William Blake

(1757–1827)

Songs of Innocence, Songs of Experience
  —Visual artist and poet who defied neoclassical convention.

The Romantics and Transcendentalists

William Wordsworth

(1770–1850)

The Prelude, Lyrical Ballads
  —Romantic poet who broke with neoclassical theory in much of his nature poetry.

Jane Austen

(1775–1817)

Sense and Sensibility, Pride and Prejudice
  —Principally known for novels of manners and middle-class English society.

Samuel Taylor Coleridge

(1772–1834)

Rime of the Ancient Mariner
  —Foremost literary critic of the romantic period.

George Gordon Lord Byron

(1788–1824)

Don Juan
  —Major figure in Romantic movement and inspiration for the Byronic hero.

Percy Bysshe Shelley

(1792–1822)

Adonais
  —Romantic poet who mastered metaphor and metrical form.

John Keats

(1795–1821)

Hyperion, Ode on a Grecian Urn
  —Most versatile of the Romantics.

Mary Shelley

(1797–1851)

Frankenstein, The Last Man
  —Romantic novelist whose liberal social and political views underscore her work.

Nathaniel Hawthorne

(1804–1864)

The Scarlet Letter, House of the Seven Gables
  —American transcendentalist.

Elizabeth Barrett Browning

(1806–1861)

Sonnets from the Portuguese, Aurora Leigh
  —English poet.

Edgar Allan Poe

(1809–1849)

Fall of the House of Usher, Tell Tale Heart, The Raven
  —American transcendentalist who dealt with macabre issues of insanity and horror.

Harriet Beecher Stowe

(1811–1896)

Uncle Tom's Cabin
  —American novelist, wrote the most important novel of the abolitionist movement.

Robert Browning

(1812–1889)

Bells and Pomegranates
  —English poet.

Charles Dickens

(1812–1870)

Great Expectations, Oliver Twist
  —English novelist.

Charlotte Brontë
(1816–1855)
Jane Eyre
  —Victorian novelist.

Emily Brontë
(1816–1848)
Wuthering Heights
  —Victorian novelist.

Henry David Thoreau
(1818–1848)
Walden
  —American Transcendentalist and social
  theorist.

George Eliot (Mary Ann Evans)
(1819–1880)
Mill on the Floss, Middlemarch
  —English author.

Herman Melville
(1819–1891)
Moby-Dick, Billy Budd
  —American transcendentalist.

Walt Whitman
(1819–1892)
Leaves of Grass
  —American poet.

Fyodor Dostoyevsky
(1821–1881)
*Crime and Punishment, Notes from the
Underground*
  —Russian novelist.

Gustave Flaubert
(1821–1880)
Madame Bovary
  —French novelist.

Charles Baudelaire
(1821–1867)
Flowers of Evil (Les Fleurs du Mal)
  —French Symbolist poet.

Henrik Ibsen
(1828–1906)
A Doll's House
  —Norwegian playwright and forerunner of the Expressionist movement.

Leo Nikolayevich Tolstoy
(1828–1910)
War and Peace, Anna Karenina
  —Major Russian novelist.

Emily Dickinson
(1830–1886)
Because I Could Not Stop for Death
  —American poet.

Christina Rossetti
(1830–1894)
Goblin Market
  —English poet.

Mark Twain (Samuel Clemens)
(1835–1910)
Huckleberry Finn, Tom Sawyer
  —American novelist, essayist and
  satirist.

Oscar Wilde
(1854–1900)
*The Importance of Being Earnest, The Picture
of Dorian Gray*
  —English novelist, dramatist, and social critic.

George Bernard Shaw
(1856–1950)
Arms and the Man, Saint Joan
  —Irish-born British author and
  playwright.

Joseph Conrad
(1857–1924)
Heart of Darkness, Lord Jim
  —Ukranian born of Polish parents,
  major English post-colonialist
  novelist.

William Butler Yeats
(1865–1939)
*The Wind Among the Reeds, The Wind-
ing Stair*
  —Irish poet and dramatist.

Robert Frost
(1874–1963)
Birches, The Road Not Taken
  —Major American poet.

Gertrude Stein
(1874–1946)
3 Lives
—American modernist author.

Upton Sinclair
(1878–1968)
The Jungle
—American novelist and social critic, characterized as a "muckraker."

James Joyce
(1882–1941)
Portrait of the Artist as a Young Man, Ulysses
—Premier Modernist novelist of Ireland, pioneered stream of consciousness, and non-linear narratives.

Virginia Woolf
(1882–1941)
A Room of One's Own, To the Lighthouse
—Modernist novelist and early feminist.

Franz Kafka
(1883–1924)
Metamorphosis, The Castle
—Major Existentialist novelist.

Ezra Pound
(1885–1972)
The Cantos
—American poet.

D. H. Lawrence
(1885–1930)
Lady Chatterly's Lover, The Rainbow
—English novelist.

Sinclair Lewis
(1885–1951)
Babbitt, Elmer Gantry
—American novelist and social critic.

Eugene O'Neill
(1888–1953)
Anna Christie, The Hairy Ape
—Major American dramatist.

T. S. Eliot
(1888–1965)
The Waste Land
—Modernist poet and theorist.

Henry Miller
(1891–1980)
The Tropic of Cancer, The Tropic of Capricorn
—Controversial American novelist.

e.e. cummings
(1894–1962)
Tulips and Chimneys
—Known for non-traditional forms of poetry.

William Faulkner
(1897–1962)
The Sound and the Fury, Absalom! Absalom!
—Major author of the American South.

Vladimir Nabokov
(1899–1977)
Lolita, Invitation to a Beheading
—Russian novelist.

Ernest Hemingway
(1899–1961)
The Old Man and the Sea, A Farewell to Arms
—Known for lean prose and ardently masculine themes and characters.

Zora Neale Hurston
(1901–1960)
Their Eyes Were Watching God, Tell My Horse
—American novelist and folklorist.

John Steinbeck
(1902–1968)
Grapes of Wrath, Cannery Row
—American novelist whose major theme was the life of the American worker.

Langston Hughes
(1902–1967)
Collected Works
—Harlem Renaissance poet.

Samuel Beckett
(1906–1989)
Waiting for Godot, Happy Days
—Irish-born French playwright and novelist. Themes include existentialism and absurdity.

Elizabeth Bishop
(1911–1979)
Collected Works
—American poet.

Tennessee Williams
(1911–1983)
A Streetcar Named Desire, The Glass Menagerie
—American playwright.

Arthur Miller
(1915–2005)
Death of a Salesman, The Crucible
—American playwright.

Aleksandr Isayevich Solzhenitsyn
(1918–)
The Gulag Archipelago
—Major Russian novelist and social critic.

Jack Kerouac
(1922–1969)
On the Road, Dharma Bums
—American Beat poet and novelist.

Nadine Gordimer
(1923–)
A Sport of Nature
—South African novelist.

James Baldwin
(1924–1987)
The Fire Next Time
—American poet and novelist.

Allen Ginsberg
(1926–1997)
Howl
—American Beat poet.

Adrienne Rich
(1929–)
Aunt Jennifer's Tigers
—American poet.

Toni Morrison
(1931–)
The Bluest Eye, Song of Solomon, Beloved
—American novelist.

V.S. Naipaul
(1932–)
Enigma of Arrival, House for Mr. Biswas
—Post-colonialist novelist, born in Trinidad of Indian parents, raised in England.

Sylvia Plath
(1932–1963)
Ariel, The Bell Jar
—American poet and novelist.

Thomas Pynchon
(1937–)
Vineland, Gravity's Rainbow, The Crying of Lot 49
—Reclusive American novelist.

Alice Walker
(1944–)
The Color Purple, Possessing the Secrets of Joy
—American novelist.

Salman Rushdie
(1947–)
The Satanic Verses, Shame
—Known for death sentence placed upon him by Ayatollah Khomeini owing to what Khomeini and fellow Islamic fundamentalists viewed as blasphemy in *The Satanic Verses*.

LITERARY TERMS

allegory—Poetry or prose in which abstract ideas are represented by individual characters, events, or objects.

alliteration—Rapid repetition of consonants in a given line of poetry or prose.

allusion—Reference to one literary work in another.

anachronism—A chronological displacement in which a relationship between events or objects is historically impossible.

anapest—A metrical foot with two unstressed syllables followed by a stressed syllable.

antagonist—The character in a literary work that goes against the actions of the hero.

anti-hero—The protagonist of a literary work who does not possess heroic qualities.

apostrophe—Direct address to someone or something not present.

assonance—Rapid repetition of vowels in a given line of poetry or prose.

ballad—A poem, often intended to be sung, that tells a story.

bathos—A sudden shift from the lofty to the commonplace.

bildungsroman—A coming-of-age story, usually autobiographical.

blank verse—Unrhymed poetry usually written in iambic pentameter.

caesura—A deliberate pause in a line of poetry.

canto—Analogous to a chapter in a novel, it is a division in a poem.

climax—The peak of action in a literary work.

conceits—Elaborate comparisons between unlike objects.

consonance—Repetition of consonant sounds with unlike vowels—similar to alliteration.

couplet—A pair or rhyming lines of poetry in the same meter.

dactyl—A metrical foot comprised of one stressed syllable followed by two unstressed syllables.

denouement—The action following the climax in a literary work.

diction—Word choice or syntax.

doggerel—Crudely written poetry, in which words are often mangled to fit a rhyme scheme.

elegy—A poem lamenting the passage of something.

enjambment—In poetry, the continuation of a phrase or sentence onto the following line.

epistolary—Refers to a novel or story told in the form of letters.

fable—A story used to illustrate a moral lesson.

foot—A group of syllables that make up a metered unit of verse.

haiku—A Japanese poetical form, having three lines and 17 syllables, five in the first line, seven in the second, and five in the third.

hubris—In tragic drama, the excessive pride that leads to the fall of a hero.

hyperbole—Exaggeration for effect.

iamb—A foot containing two syllables, a short then a long (in quantitative meter).

irony—A deliberate discrepancy between literal meaning and intended meaning.

malapropism—Often used for humorous effect, it is the substitution of a word for one that sounds similar but has radically different meaning.

metaphor—A form of comparison in which something is said to be something else, often an unlikely pairing.

meter—The combination of stressed and unstressed syllables that creates the rhythm of a poem.

metonymy—A figure of speech in which a term is used to evoke or stand for an associated idea.

motif—The recurrence of a word or theme in a novel or poem.

onomatopoeia—A word whose sound suggests its meaning; for example, "crash."

oxymoron—Two contradictory words used together to create deeper meaning; for example, sweet sorrow.

paradox—A seemingly contradictory phrase, which proves to be true upon comparison.

pathos—An appeal that evokes pity or sympathy.

scansion—The annotation of the meter of a poem.

simile—Means of comparison using either "like" or "as."

sonnet—A verse form consisting of 14 lines arranged in an octet (eight lines) and a sextet (six lines), usually ending in a couplet; in common English form, arranged in three quatrains followed by a couplet.

spondee—A metrical foot comprised of two stressed syllables.

synecdoche—The use of part of a thing to represent the whole; for example, "wheels" for a car.

tone—Attitude of the speaker, setting the mood for a given passage.

trochee—A metrical foot composed of a stressed syllable followed by an unstressed syllable.

villanelle—A verse form consisting of five tercets and a quatrain, the first and third lines of the tercet recur alternately as the last lines of the other tercets and together as the last lines of the quatrain.

Index

Rococo style, 110
Rodin, Auguste, 113
Roman, 15
Roman Catholic Church, 154
Romance, 15
Roman de Fauvel, 153
Romanesque style, 101
Romano, Giulio, 106
Romans, 98–100, 179
Romanticism, 15, 29
Romantic period, in musical history, 158
Rome, founding of, 99
Romeo and Juliet, 197
Root, John W., 114
"A Rose for Emily" (Faulkner), 22
Rousseau, Jean-Jacques, 133
Rubens, Peter Paul, 109–110
Rucellai Madonna (Duccio), 103
Russell, Bertrand, 135
Russia
  ballet, 180
  film, 183
  music, 158, 160
  theater, 177

S

Sacred music, 153
Sainte Chapelle, 102
Santayana, George, 135
Sarcasm, 29, 51
Sartre, Jean-Paul, 136
Satire, 13–14, 28–32, 68
Scales, 146–147
Scat, 161
Schlick, Moritz, 136
Scholasticism, 132
Schonberg, Arnold, 159, 160
The School of Athens (Raphael), 106
Schopenhauer, Arthur, 134
Schubert, Franz, 15
Schumann, Robert, 158
Science fiction, 186
Sculpture. *See* Arts, the
Serialism, 160
Sestet, 53
Setting, 20, 59

Seurat, Georges, 113
Sextus, 140
Sexual content, in films, 186–187, 195
Shakespeare, William
  accentual meter, 42–43
  blank verse, 40–41
  Great Chain of Being, 88
  Hamlet, 61–62, 66
  history play, 74–76
  influence of, 175–176
  irony, use of, 30
  Othello, 71
  sonnets, 53, 90
Sharps, 147
Shaw, George Bernard, 60
Shelley, P. B., 50–51
"Shooting an Elephant" (Orwell), 26
Short stories, 21–25
Shostakovich, Dmitri, 196
Siddhartha, 17
Silent films, 184
Similes, 44–45
Simple meter, 144
Singspiel, 168
Sistine Chapel, 106
Skeptics, 140
Skidmore, Owings, and Merrill, 115
Slant rhyme, 40
"Slice of life," 22
Sluter, Claus, 107
Smith, Adam, 134
The Social Contract (Rousseau), 133
Socrates, 131
Solomon (King), 31
Sonatas, 156, 157
Sonnets, 30, 52–53, 90
Sophocles, 59, 172
Sound, 145, 184–185
The Sound of Music, 186
Spain, art of, 111
Speculative essays, 26
Speech act theory, 137
Spielberg, Steven, 188
Spinoza, Benedict, 133
Sprechstimme, 167
St. Anselm, 132
St. George (Donatello), 104

Notes

Notes

Notes

Notes

Notes